The Political Economy of Bank Regulation in Developing Countries

T0323379

The Political Economy of Bank Regulation in Developing Countries

Risk and Reputation

Edited by
EMILY JONES

OXFORD
UNIVERSITY PRESS

OXFORD

UNIVERSITY PRESS

Great Clarendon Street, Oxford, OX2 6DP,
United Kingdom

Oxford University Press is a department of the University of Oxford.
It furthers the University's objective of excellence in research, scholarship,
and education by publishing worldwide. Oxford is a registered trade mark of
Oxford University Press in the UK and in certain other countries

Published in the United States of America by Oxford University Press
198 Madison Avenue, New York, NY 10016, United States of America

British Library Cataloguing in Publication Data
Data available

Library of Congress Control Number: 2019947029

ISBN 978-0-19-884199-9

DOI: 10.1093/oso/9780198841999.003.0001

Printed and bound in Great Britain by
Clays Ltd, Elcograf S.p.A.

Links to third party websites are provided by Oxford in good faith and
for information only. Oxford disclaims any responsibility for the materials
contained in any third party website referenced in this work.

Acknowledgements

This book is the product of a four-year collaboration between the fourteen contributing authors. Our framework and arguments build from our diverse backgrounds in political science, economics, law, and corporate governance, and our knowledge in countries and regions across Africa, Asia, and Latin America. Dominic Byatt, our commissioning editor at Oxford University Press, advised us to write a book that would read like a monograph, with a central argument that brought our different case studies into a coherent whole. We have done our best to do exactly that. We came together as a project team in March 2016 to generate initial hypotheses, and again in June 2017 to peer-review our findings and develop a common analytical framework. Each of us revised our chapters several times to ensure our contributions spoke to each other. I am thankful to each and every contributing author for taking such a collaborative approach from the start to the very end of this project, and hope that they have found our collaboration as richly rewarding as I have.

On behalf of all our team, we express our sincere thanks to Thorsten Beck and Ngaire Woods, who mentored and guided our research team, and the many practitioners, academics, and administrators who have provided us with their expertise, advice, and support. More than 200 practitioners from regulatory institutions, banks and non-bank financial firms, political parties, international organizations, and think tanks across five continents generously shared their insights and reflections with us. Given the political sensitivity of banking regulation, we agreed to preserve the anonymity of our interviewees and have done our utmost to honour this commitment. While their names do not appear on the pages that follow, we are all too aware that this work would not have been possible without their generosity. We hope we have done justice to the insights they shared.

We presented our work and received helpful feedback from meetings of practitioners. We thank participants of the Oxford African Central Bank Governors Roundtable; meetings of the Alliance for Financial Inclusion in Sochi, Russia, and Siem Reap, Cambodia; the Financial Conduct Authority workshop on the Future of Financial Regulation in London; the Committee of African Bank Supervisors meeting in Cairo; the FSI/IMF global meeting on proportionality in financial regulation in Basel; the PEFM Africa Conference in Oxford; the T20 Taskforce on International Finance Architecture for Stability and Development; and seminars at the Bank of Nigeria, Central Bank of Kenya, DFID Rwanda, Bank of England, the Gateway House India, and the Overseas Development Institute. For sharing their reflections and facilitating this engagement, we are particularly thankful to

Svein Andresen, Mathur Askhay, Denzel Bostander, Andrew Cornford, Juan Carlos Crisanto, Papa Lamine Diop, Charles Enoch, Michael Fuchs, Ricardo Gottschalk, Hugues Kamewe Tsafack, Tim Lyman, Guy Menan, Njuguna Ndung'u, Robin Newnham, Liliana Rojas-Suarez, Lemma Senbet, Rupert Thorne, Judith Tyson, Eryk Walczak, Jonathan Ward, Staci Warden, and Rahan Zamil.

We also received useful feedback from academic conferences, workshops, and seminars. We thank participants at the African Studies Association annual conference in Washington DC; the International Studies Association annual conference in Baltimore; the African Studies Association UK annual conference in Birmingham; the Development Studies Association annual conference in Oxford; the Journal of Financial Regulation workshop in Hong Kong; the workshop of the International Political Economy Society, Philadelphia; the Barcelona workshop on Global Governance; the Politics of Economic Regulation in Africa workshop in Oxford; and seminars hosted by the Cambridge Development Studies Centre, global finance research group at SOAS, and Institute for Development Studies, University of Nairobi. We thank the many people who were kind enough to host us, engage in detailed conversations, read drafts, and provide us with constructive criticism. Our particular thanks to Abdul-Gafaru Abdulai, Chris Adam, Dan Awrey, Catherine Boone, Tim Buthe, Ha-Joon Chang, Stephany Griffith-Jones, Thomas Hale, Peter Lewis, Kate Meagher, Victor Murinde, Stefano Pagliari, Anne Pitcher, John Vickers, Andrew Walter, and Alexandra Zeitz. We are also grateful to three anonymous reviewers who gave us a series of insightful criticisms that helped us to sharpen our chapters.

Along the way we have been provided excellent research assistance by Aakash Desai, Vijay Kumar, Max Lyssewski, Mike Norton, Tila Mainga, Nina Obermeier, Chelsea Tabart, and Katherine Tyson. We received high-quality administrative support from Mark Crofts, Reija Fanous, Kim Fuggle, Ellie Haugh, and Ingrid Locatelli, and superb copyediting from Emma Burnett and Shreya Hewett.

This research was made possible thanks to generous funding from the UK Economic and Social Research Council (Grant ES/L012375/1) under the DFID-ESRC Growth Research Programme. We thank Petya Kangalova and Beverley Leahy at ESRC and Louise Shaxson and her team at ODI for their support. We also thank Sharron Pleydell-Pearce in Oxford for helping pull together our original grant application and providing insightful comments.

At OUP we thank Dominic Byatt, commissioning editor, for seeing potential in this project and mentoring us through the process to publication, and Matthew Williams for editorial assistance. We also thank Kayalvizhi Ganesan and Sally Evans-Darby for support during the production process.

On a personal note we thank our various friends, partners, and families who have provided the backup at home that makes research trips and long writing days possible. My own thanks to my partner Al-hassan Adam and our children Rumi and Maya, who will be relieved to know that this manuscript has been submitted.

A final heartfelt thanks goes to Peter Knaack for being such a brilliant colleague throughout the research and writing of this book. He marshalled us all behind the scenes and reviewed numerous versions of every chapter, with unfailing good humour and a constant stream of Trader Joe's chocolate. We are grateful!

Any errors are of course our own.

Emily Jones

Oxford
September 2019

Contents

PART I. INTRODUCTION, CROSS-COUNTRY VARIATION, AND ANALYTICAL ARGUMENT

PART II. CASE STUDIES

PART III. CONCLUSION

List of Figures

List of Tables

List of Contributors

Pritish Behuria, Hallsworth Research Fellow, Global Development Institute, University of Manchester. Previously an LSE Fellow, Department of International Development, London School of Economics. Pritish completed an MSc in International Politics and a PhD in Development Studies at SOAS, University of London on the political economy of Rwanda. He also holds a BSc in Journalism and International Relations from the Medill School of Journalism at Northwestern University.

Florence Dafe, lecturer and postdoctoral researcher at the TUM School of Governance, Munich. Formerly Fellow in International Political Economy at the Department of International Relations at the London School of Economics and Political Science (LSE) and lecturer at City, University of London. Her research interests revolve around finance and development, especially the domestic and external political constraints that governments in developing countries face in governing their financial sectors. Florence holds a Master's degree in Development Studies from the LSE and a PhD in Development Studies from the Institute of Development Studies (IDS) at the University of Sussex.

Rebecca Engebretsen, postdoctoral researcher with the Development Economics Group at ETH Zurich. Rebecca holds a PhD in Politics from the University of Oxford and a Master's degree in International Political Economy from King's College London. Her research interests centre broadly on the political economy of resource-rich states and on the economic and financial sector policies of these countries in particular. Before starting her PhD, Rebecca worked for the Norwegian Agency for Development Cooperation.

Hazel Gray, Senior Lecturer in African Studies and Development, Centre of African Studies, University of Edinburgh. Hazel holds a PhD and MSc from SOAS, University of London, and a degree in politics, philosophy, and economics from the University of Oxford. Previously, she worked as an economist at the Ministry of Finance in Tanzania She is the author of *Turbulence and Order in Economic Development: Institutions and Economic Transformation in Tanzania and Vietnam* (OUP 2018).

Ousseni Illy, Assistant Professor of Law, University Ouaga 2 Burkina Faso and former Oxford-Princeton Global Leader Fellow (2010–12). Ousseni is the Executive Director of the African Centre of International Trade and Development, an independent non-profit think-tank based in Ouagadougou, Burkina Faso. He has a PhD in International Trade Law from the University of Geneva and a Master's in Public Law from the University of Ouagadougou, Burkina Faso.

Emily Jones, Associate Professor in Public Policy, Blavatnik School of Government, University of Oxford. Emily directs the Global Economic Governance Programme, a research programme dedicated to fostering research and debate into how to make the global economy inclusive and sustainable. She has a DPhil in International Political Economy, University of Oxford, and an MSc in Development Economics, SOAS, University of London. She previously worked as an economist in Ghana's Ministry of Trade and Industry, for Oxfam GB, and for the UK Department for International Development.

Peter Knaack, Senior Research Associate at the Global Economic Governance Programme, University of Oxford. Peter has written and published on transatlantic coordination failure in derivatives regulation, the politics of global banking regulation, and the financial regulatory system in Bolivia. He has a PhD and an MA from the University of Southern California in International Relations and Economics, and has done field research in ten countries across four continents with support from the China Scholarship Council and the John Fell Fund of Oxford University Press, among others.

Natalya Naqvi, Assistant Professor in International Political Economy, London School of Economics. Formerly, Natalya was an Oxford-Princeton Global Leader Fellow (2016–18), Global Economic Governance Programme, University of Oxford and Niehaus Center for Globalisation and Governance, Princeton University. She has a PhD and an MPhil from the Centre of Development Studies, University of Cambridge. Natalya's research interests are in the areas of international political economy and comparative political economy of development, with a focus on the role of the state and the financial sector in economic development, as well as the amount of policy space developing countries have to conduct selective industrial policy.

Seydou Ouedraogo, Assistant Professor of Economics, University Ouaga 2 Burkina Faso. Seydou is the Director of FREE Afrik Institute and was an Oxford-Princeton Global Leader Fellow (2015–17). He is an economist who trained in African (Burkina Faso and Benin) and French (Université d'Auvergne/CERDI) universities. His research focuses on banking and monetary economy, development strategies, and economy of culture.

Ricardo Soares de Oliveira, Professor of the International Politics of Africa, Department of Politics and International Relations, University of Oxford. Ricardo is a Fellow of St Peter's College, Oxford, a Fellow with the Global Public Policy Institute, Berlin, and the co-editor of *African Affairs*. His research interests include the politics of the extractive industries, international political economy, and African–Asian relations. He is the author of *Oil and Politics in the Gulf of Guinea* (2007) and *Magnificent and Beggar Land: Angola since the Civil War* (2015) and the co-editor of *China Returns to Africa* (2008).

Que-Giang Tran-Thi, Senior Lecturer in Finance, Fulbright School of Public Policy and Management, Fulbright University Vietnam. Que-Giang has a PhD in Management Sciences and a Master's in Finance from Paris Dauphine University. Her research interests include banking regulations, corporate governance, corporate finance, and education financing.

Radha Upadhyaya, Research Fellow, Institute for Development Studies, University of Nairobi. Radha has a PhD and MSc in Economics from SOAS, University of London, and a BA in Economics from the University of Cambridge. She is a qualified CFA charterholder. Radha has over fifteen years of teaching experience with a particular focus on heterodox research methods, microeconomics, and finance and development. She has written on the Kenyan banking sector, banking regulation in East Africa, African firms, and African entrepreneurs. She also has significant private and non-profit sector experience. She spent four years as the Director of a Kenyan bank and is currently on the board of the Financial Sector Deeping Trust Kenya.

Tu-Anh Vu-Thanh, Dean, Fulbright School of Public Policy and Management, Fulbright University Vietnam. Tu-Anh is also a Senior Research Fellow at the Harvard Kennedy School and an Oxford-Princeton Global Leaders Fellow (2013–15). His primary research interests include political economy of development, institutional economics, public finance, and industrial policy. He received his PhD in economics from Boston College.

Toni Weis, Africa Senior Program Officer, Center for International Private Enterprise and a visiting researcher at Johns Hopkins University (SAIS) in Washington, DC. Prior to joining CIPE, he worked as an independent consultant for the World Bank, risk analysis firms, and private investors. Toni's research focuses on the political economy of Ethiopia, as well as on state–business relations and regulatory affairs in Africa more generally. His work has been published in *Foreign Affairs*, the *China Economic Review*, *Africa Confidential*, and the *Journal of Southern African Studies*. He has a DPhil in Politics from the University of Oxford, an MSc in African Studies (Oxford, with distinction), and an MA in International Relations from Sciences Po Paris.

PART I

INTRODUCTION, CROSS-COUNTRY VARIATION, AND ANALYTICAL ARGUMENT

1

The Puzzle

Peripheral Developing Countries Implementing International Banking Standards

Emily Jones

On 19 January 2016, three days after economic sanctions were lifted, Iran's central bank governor announced that he would move quickly to implement the latest set of international banking standards. Companies across the world had been lining up to explore opportunities in Iran and the government was keen to attract them, but Iran's banking sector was perceived as a critical weakness. By implementing international regulatory standards, the governor sought to reassure the international community that Iranian banks were soundly (Bozorgmehr, 2016; Financial Tribune, 2017; Saul and Arnold, 2016).

Iran is not alone: many countries around the world are implementing international banking standards. What is puzzling is that in most cases, governments are choosing to regulate a vital part of their economy on the basis of international standards over which they had no influence. International banking standards are designed behind closed doors by a select group of regulators from the world's largest financial centres who belong to the Basel Committee on Banking Supervision (hereafter Basel Committee), which takes its name from the small medieval town in Switzerland where the members meet. The standards are intended for the regulation of large, complex, risk-taking international banks with trillions of dollars in assets and operations across the globe. Yet these standards are being implemented by governments across the world, including in many countries with nascent financial markets and small banks that have yet to venture into international markets. Why is this?

In this book we focus on the responses of regulators in low- and lower-middle-income countries to the most recent, and most complex, iterations of international banking standards. These countries are the least likely to adopt the standards as their banks tend to be small and focused on the domestic market, and it is far from obvious that the standards are the best way to address the financial stability risks and challenges of financial sector development these countries face. Yet regulators in many of these countries are moving to implement the standards. What is going on?

Emily Jones, *The Puzzle: Peripheral Developing Countries Implementing International Banking Standards* In: *The Political Economy of Bank Regulation in Developing Countries: Risk and Reputation*. Edited by: Emily Jones, Oxford University Press (2020). © Oxford University Press. DOI: 10.1093/oso/9780198841999.003.0001

Drawing on a wealth of primary evidence from eleven countries in Africa, Asia, and Latin America, we show how regulators' decisions over whether to adopt international standards are made not only in light of technocratic concerns about what regulation is optimal for the banks they oversee, but also based on political considerations. As in advanced economies, banking regulation in developing countries is very important and intensely political. It is important because bank failures are costly for firms, workers, and taxpayers. It is intensely political because how banks are regulated influences how credit is allocated in the economy, and this in turn affects which groups in society get to derive value from processes of economic growth.

What is striking about the politics of banking regulation in low- and lower-middle-income countries is that international considerations loom large. We show how the impetus to *converge* on international standards stems from large banks and regulators in these countries looking to bolster their reputation in the eyes of international investors and regulators in other jurisdictions; the flow of ideas from international policy circles; and politicians and banks on a quest to attract international capital and integration into global finance. Our first contribution, then, is to show the precise ways in which the decisions of regulators based in Washington, DC, London, Beijing, and the capitals of other major financial centres decisively shape the decisions of regulators based in Accra, Hanoi, Ouagadougou, and other developing countries on the periphery of the global financial system.

Yet recognizing the powerful impact of international factors does not mean we can simply dismiss regulators in peripheral developing countries as standard-takers, compelled by pressures from other governments, international organizations, and incentives generated by markets to implement the standards set by regulators from the world's most powerful countries (Drezner, 2008). Integration into global finance does expose peripheral developing countries to external pressures that constrain regulatory choices, but it also provides new opportunities for some domestic actors.

Our second contribution is to show that there is tremendous variation in the responses of regulators in peripheral developing countries to international standards, and to account for it. Very few regulators in peripheral developing countries have adopted these international standards *tout court*. Instead we see regulators responding in very different ways. Some regulators are ambitious in their adoption of international standards, keeping abreast of developments in the Basel Committee and adopting the major elements of international standards as they are issued. Other regulators are more cautious, taking a slower and highly selective approach, only adopting some elements and tailoring them to their local context. Some eschew the latest standards entirely, sticking with regulations based on the much simpler standards issued by the Basel Committee in the 1980s.

To explain cross-country variation in regulators' responses, we identify the incentives that they face to *diverge* from international standards. High among these are concerns among politicians about a loss of control over the domestic financial system and the ability to direct credit in the economy; concerns on the part of regulators about the viability and desirability of implementing standards that are calibrated for more complex financial systems; and opposition from small domestic banks. As peripheral developing countries are embedded in the international financial system to different extents and in different ways, and their domestic politics and institutions vary, regulators face different mixes of incentives. Building from the existing literature and our case studies, we develop analytical framework that explains why it is that some configurations of domestic politics and forms of integration into global finance generate processes of convergence with international standards, while other configurations create processes of divergence.

While we focus on banking regulation, our findings speak to other scholarship exploring the ways in which decisions made by governments and firms in the core of the global economy powerfully shape, although do not determine, decisions made by their counterparts in the periphery (e.g. Phillips, 2017). More broadly, our work contributes to scholarship that seeks to understand the global economy from the vantage point of actors in the periphery, rather than the centre, which yields fresh insights into how the global economy functions as a system. Scholars of international political economy are increasingly researching the ways in which large emerging economies like China, Brazil, and Mexico interface with the global economy. Yet scant attention is paid to smaller countries, particularly small developing countries, and the ways in which actors in these countries navigate the global economy (Acharya, 2014).

Core–periphery dynamics in global finance

Following a dramatic increase in the globalization of markets for goods, services, capital, and information since the 1980s, national economies are more integrated than ever, generating an unprecedented level of economic interdependence.[1] Within this interdependent system, economic wealth and power is heavily concentrated in relatively few countries. As at 2017, the largest four countries (US, China, Japan, and Germany) accounted for half of the world's total economic output, while the largest twenty countries accounted for more than four-fifths.[2] With the fragmentation of production processes, economic power is increasingly

---

[1] The slow-down in cross-border flows of trade and finance after 2008 led some to speculate that globalization is in retreat, but dramatic increases in cross-border data and information flows suggest that it has simply entered a new digital phase (Lund et al., 2017).

[2] Author's calculations based on World Bank data for 200 countries. GDP and population data averaged over 2015–17. Data available at: https://databank.worldbank.org.

concentrated at the firm level too. The vast majority of international trade occurs in global value chains led by transnational corporations and these production systems generate one in five jobs worldwide (UNCTAD, 2013; ILO, 2015). Unsurprisingly, the world's largest firms are overwhelmingly based in the world's largest economies. As at 2013, there were 8,000 companies worldwide with a revenue of more than US$1 billion and half were headquartered in the US, China, Japan, and Germany (Dobbs et al., 2013, p. 22). The global economy then is a hierarchical, interdependent system, with a distinct core and periphery, in which economic power is concentrated among relatively few countries and firms.

With attention in academic and policy circles focused on dynamics in countries in the core of the global economy, it is easy to overlook how many governments, firms, and citizens are located in countries on the periphery. It is conceptually and empirically challenging to precisely delineate between the core and periphery, as it is dynamic and evolving, as the recent experiences of East Asian countries like South Korea and China powerfully illustrate. These countries were peripheral to the global economy three decades ago but are now part of the core.

Yet even a cursory glance at the data indicates the magnitude of the periphery: 180 countries, home to 2.9 billion people, account for less than one-fifth of the world's economy.[3] In more than one hundred countries, governments manage economies less than 1 per cent of the size of the US economy.[4] While some of these peripheral countries have small populations and high incomes, like Malta and Iceland, the vast majority are low- and lower-middle-income developing countries, like Nicaragua and Zambia.

Nowhere is this concentration of wealth more pronounced than in international finance. The globalization of finance has taken a quantum leap since the 1980s, spurred on by the deregulation of banks and liberalization of cross-border capital flows. Financial flows reached dizzying heights by 2007, with US$12.4 trillion moving between countries on the eve of the global financial crisis, equivalent to 23 per cent of global GDP (Lund et al., 2017). Although new financial centres are emerging, financial assets remain heavily concentrated in the US, and to a lesser extent the UK (Oatley et al., 2013), and, as in other sectors of the global economy, have seen the emergence of very large firms. Some banks are so large, complex, and interconnected that twenty-nine of them, including Citigroup and JP Morgan Chase, have been classified by regulators as 'systemically important' on a global level (FSB, 2016). In 2017, the world's ten largest banks had combined assets of more than US$28 trillion, and thirty-seven of the world's largest one hundred banks were located in just three countries (the US, China, and Japan) (Mehmood and Chaudhry, 2018).

The flipside of this heavy concentration of global finance is that more than 150 countries account for less than 10 per cent of all liquid financial assets around the

---

[3] Ibid.   [4] Ibid.

world.[5] These peripheral countries are integrated into this hierarchical system of global finance to an ever-greater extent, a trend that is particularly pronounced in developing countries. Following waves of privatization and liberalization in the 1980s and 1990s, foreign bank presence increased and by 2007 accounted for more than half of the market share in sixty-three developing countries (Claessens and van Horen, 2012). In the wake of the global financial crisis, many European and some US banks have retrenched, closing their operations in peripheral countries. However, this has not reduced the amount of foreign bank presence, as the space they left has been filled by banks from China, Canada, and Japan, as well as rapidly expanding regional banks (Enoch et al., 2015; Lund et al., 2017).

As a result of these changes, developing countries now have a higher level of foreign bank presence than industrialized countries, making them particularly vulnerable to financial crises and regulatory changes in other jurisdictions. This heightened interconnectedness was powerfully illustrated during the 2007–8 global financial crisis which, unlike previous crises, affected all types of countries around the world (Claessens, 2017). Although there are exceptions and regional differences, few peripheral countries have been left out of this trend of increasing financial integration.

Concentrations of power and wealth in the financial system generate distinct core–periphery dynamics (Bauerle Danzman et al., 2017; Ghosh, 2007). As financial globalization has intensified, market movements in the financial core have had ever-increasing effects on financial markets on the periphery (e.g. Aizenman et al., 2015; Akyuz, 2010; Reddy, 2010; Rey, 2015). This was illustrated by the 'taper tantrum' in 2013 as moves by the US Federal Reserve to normalize interest rates led to an outflow of capital from emerging economies. In general, a reduction in demand for capital in the core generates capital inflow bonanzas in the periphery, and banking crises when increased demand in the core leads these flows to reverse (Bauerle Danzman et al., 2017; Rey, 2015).

Similarly, as core countries are home to the world's largest banks and other financial market actors, regulatory decisions in the core shape the worldwide behaviour of these actors, affecting financial markets in the periphery. For instance, changes in the regulatory and enforcement landscape in core countries have significantly contributed to a reduction of correspondent banking relations, particularly in Europe and Central Asia, the Caribbean, Africa, and the Pacific (IMF, 2017).

Low-income countries are positioned particularly precariously in global finance. Increased levels of integrated into the global economy have left low-income

---

[5] Author's calculations. Data on liquid liabilities in millions USD (2000 constant) for 178 countries, calculated as a five-year average (2013–17) extracted from the World Bank's Global Financial Development Database: http://www.worldbank.org/en/publication/gfdr/data/global-financial-development-database.

countries more exposed and vulnerable to international shocks. However, as they have resource-constrained governments and many economically vulnerable citizens, they have the least resources to cope with them (IMF, 2011).

While dynamics in the core have major impacts on the periphery, dramatic changes in the periphery rarely impact the core. A banking crisis in a country in the core reverberates throughout the system because countries in the core are intimately connected to many other countries and hold many of their financial assets. Conversely, because peripheral countries are connected to only a few other countries and any one peripheral country holds a relatively small proportion of the assets of core countries, a banking crisis in a peripheral country has a limited impact on other countries (Oatley et al., 2013).

Peripheral countries: excluded from global financial governance

The fortunes of peripheral countries are increasingly shaped by market dynamics and regulatory decisions in the core of the global economy, but peripheral countries are chronically under-represented in many of the international bodies set up to govern the global economy. Again, this is particularly true in global financial governance, and most pronounced for low- and lower-middle-income countries (Griffith-Jones and Persaud, 2008; Jones and Knaack, 2019).

In the 1970s, in response to growing financial interdependence and the heightened risk of cross-border financial contagion, central bank governors from the world's largest financial centres came together to form the Basel Committee. They came together to agree minimum regulatory and supervisory standards for internationally active banks. As financial globalization intensified, other standard-setting bodies were created, including for securities (the International Organization of Securities Commissions), insurance (the International Association of Insurance Supervisors), and accounting (the International Accounting Standards Board). At the end of the 1990s, leaders of the G7 countries created the Financial Stability Forum (the forerunner of the Financial Stability Board) to bring these disparate standard-setting bodies together in a bid to improve cooperation and international financial stability.

By design, peripheral developing countries found themselves at the margins of these standard-setting bodies. The remit of these bodies was to promote financial stability in the core of the global financial system and membership has been restricted to regulators from the world's largest financial centres. Much of the regulation flowing from the Bank of International Settlements, the Financial Stability Board, the Financial Action Task Force, and other standard-setting bodies is designed to regulate the world's largest international banks.

Membership of the Basel Committee was expanded to incorporate ten emerging market economies following the global financial crisis.[6] However, even among Basel members, regulators from emerging and developing countries are less engaged in Basel Committee proceedings than their counterparts from industrialised countries. In global regulatory politics, institutional capacity and regulatory expertise are important sources of power (Slaughter, 2004; Baker, 2009; Posner, 2010; Seabrooke and Tsingou, 2009). In Basel Committee proceedings, an incumbent network of well-resourced regulators from industrialized countries continues to dominate the regulatory debate (Chey, 2016; Walter, 2016).

The vast majority of developing countries are not members of the Basel Committee, and have minimal input in the standard-setting processes. Only two of the world's eighty-four low- and lower-middle income countries have a seat at the standard-setting table: India and Indonesia. Although the Basel Committee has a long-standing Basel Consultative Group that is designed to promote dialogue between members and non-members, it is dominated by developed countries.

Thus, as Pistor (2013) notes, through the prowess of the financial institutions they house and their control over the key decision-making processes, regulators from the world's largest economies determine the rules of the game when it comes to global finance.

International banking standards: 'best practice' for peripheral developing countries?

Perhaps unsurprisingly, the under-representation of peripheral developing countries in standard-setting processes results in standards that are ill-suited for regulating banks in many developing countries, particularly those with nascent financial markets, resource-constrained regulators, and relatively small banks. There is consensus in academic and policy circles that in financial regulation 'one size does not fit all'. International banking standards are the product of technical discussions and political compromises among regulators from countries in the core of the financial system. Even for these countries, there is a divergence between international standards and the *sui generis* regulations that would be most appropriate to each jurisdiction's industry structure, pre-existing financial

---

[6] After the global financial crisis regulators from the world's largest developing countries (those belonging to the G20) were invited to join the Financial Stability Board and related committees. The Basel Committee now covers twenty-eight jurisdictions, including regulators from several large developing countries: Argentina, Brazil, China, India, Indonesia, Mexico, and South Africa. The current membership comprises forty-five members from twenty-eight jurisdictions, including the G20 countries. See: http://www.bis.org/bcbs/membership.htm.

regulation, and political preferences (e.g. Barth, Caprio, and Levine, 2006; The Warwick Commission, 2009). The gap between international standards and the regulations that would be optimal at the national level is greatest for developing countries, particularly low-income developing countries, as the continued domin-ance of developed countries in decision-making results in standards that are poorly calibrated for their financial sectors and regulatory capacities.

Should banking regulators in countries in peripheral developing countries base their regulations on international standards? The answer is not obvious. An effect-ively regulated banking sector is of vital importance for peripheral developing countries, and effective regulation has become even more important as integration into global finance has intensified. Banking crises have high costs in terms of lost economic growth, unemployment, and the fiscal costs of bailouts (Amaglobeli et al., 2015). Opening up the financial sector exacerbates the risks of banking crisis and sharpens the need for sound regulation (Reinhart and Rogoff, 2013).

The general argument in support of modelling national regulations on 'inter-national best practices' is that effective regulations are costly to design. Rather than spend precious resources designing their own *sui generis* regulations, resource-constrained governments can save time and effort by adopting the tried-and-tested practices of regulators in other countries. Yet practices that have been effective in one context will not necessarily be effective when transposed into a different one (Andrews et al., 2013). Financial systems differ greatly even among advanced industrialized countries (e.g. Haber and Calomiris, 2015; Zysman, 1984) and regu-lations need to be carefully calibrated to reflect local economic and institutional contexts if they are to be effective (Barth et al., 2006; Barth and Caprio, 2018).

The mismatch between international standards and the regulatory needs of peripheral developing countries has grown wider with time, as international standards have become increasingly complex and targeted at reducing specific forms of risk-taking that are most prevalent in large international banks. The first set of international banking standards (Basel I) were agreed by the Basel Committee in 1988 and, along with the accompanying Basel Core Principles, they were relatively simple and straightforward to use. They were widely adopted across the world and are still used by many Basel member countries for the regu-lation of smaller domestic banks (Hohl et al., 2018).

As international banks grew in size and developed increasingly sophisticated financial products, the Basel Committee responded with increasingly complex regulatory standards. Basel II (agreed in 2004) and III (agreed in stages between 2010 and 2017) were designed for regulating internationally active banking groups with complex business models that are subject to a variety of risks, including the ones posed by their own operational complexity (Restoy, 2018). Under Basel I, the regulatory capital a bank needed to hold could be calculated 'on the back of a small envelope by a competent clerk', but ascertaining the capital requirements for a large bank under Basel II can easily require over 200 million calculations (Haldane, 2013, pp. 3–4).

Basel standards have been widely criticized for failing to effectively regulate banks in the core of the global economy, so it is unclear that they are 'best practice' even for regulating the world's largest banks. Critics point out that Basel II espoused a regulatory approach that ceded too much discretion to banks and ultimately contributed to the global financial crisis (e.g. Admati, 2016; Bayoumi, 2017; Haldane, 2013; Lall, 2012; Persaud, 2013; Romano, 2014; Tarullo, 2008; Underhill and Zhang, 2008). Substantial reforms were made following the global financial crisis, embodied in the Basel III standards. While experts agree that Basel III is an improvement on Basel II, the overall level of capital that banks are required to hold remains far too low to ensure stability and banks are still allowed to use complex, potentially flawed, and gameable internal models (e.g. Admati, 2016; Admati and Hellwig, 2014; Haldane, 2013; Hoenig, 2013; Lall, 2012; Romano, 2014).

In addition to these broad criticisms of the Basel approach, regulators in developing countries face particular challenges when they look to implement the standards. These are not a consequence of the regulatory stringency demanded by Basel II and III standards, as pre-existing capital and liquidity requirements in developing countries are often higher than the minimums stipulated. Instead implementation challenges arise from the excessive complexity of the standards, and the fact they are not designed with less developed financial markets in mind. Although the Basel standards do offer a menu of options to regulators, the full range of options proposed by the Basel Committee is not properly thought through for low-income countries, resulting in their adoption of overly complex regulations for the level of economic development and complexity of their financial system (World Bank, 2012).

Overall, the available evidence, which we review in detail in Chapter 2, suggests that while there are strong arguments for strengthening the regulation and supervision of banks in peripheral developing countries, it is far from clear that the Basel standards and accompanying Basel Core Principles are the most effective approach (Barth and Caprio, 2018). The Basel Core Principles and the simplest set of international standards (Basel I) are widely regarded as useful for low- and lower-middle-income countries, but many experts question the appropriateness of the more complex Basel II and III standards, arguing that financial stability may be achieved through simpler regulatory approaches. Indeed, many question the appropriateness of Basel II and III for smaller banks even in the core of the financial system (Buckley, 2016). It is striking that, while regulators in many developing countries are moving to implement Basel II and III standards across their commercial banks, many regulators from Basel Committee countries only subject their largest banks, typically those with balance sheets of US$20–30 billion, to the full suite of international banking standards (Castro Carvalho et al., 2017).

The puzzling response of peripheral developing countries to Basel standards

Given the concerns outlined above, the international policy advice to regulators in developing countries, particularly in smaller, low-income developing countries, is to proceed cautiously with Basel II and III. The World Bank, IMF, and Financial Stability Board advise developing countries with less internationally integrated financial systems and/or with substantial supervisory capacity constraints to 'first focus on reforms to ensure compliance with the Basel Core Principles and *only move to the more advanced capital standards at a pace tailored to their circumstances*' [emphasis added] (FSB, IMF, WB, 2011, p. 14). Yet, peripheral developing countries are moving ahead to implement Basel II and III to a greater extent and at a faster pace than this policy advice appears to warrant.

Data on the implementation of international standards in countries outside of the Basel Committee is patchy, but the evidence we have suggests that Basel standards are being widely implemented, including in many developing countries (Hohl et al., 2018).

Data on implementation of Basel standards in forty-five low- and lower-income countries reveals substantial variation (Figure 1.1). In practice Basel standards are compendia of different regulations, and regulators can choose how many of the different components to implement. As at 2015, out of a possible total of twenty-two components of the latest and more complex international standards (Basel II, II.5, and III), regulators in nineteen of the forty-five countries were not implementing any, preferring to stay with simpler Basel I or *sui generis* standards. Regulators in a further twenty-one countries had implemented between one and nine components, while regulators in five countries had implemented between ten and thirteen. Thus, while many regulators in low- and lower-middle-income countries on the periphery are engaging with the latest international standards, they are doing so in very different ways.

Strikingly, there is substantial variation even among countries in the same geographic region. For instance, among countries in Eastern Africa, regulators in Kenya were implementing nine components in 2015, including aspects of the very latest Basel III standards, while neighbouring Tanzania, Rwanda, and Ethiopia were implementing the much simpler Basel I standard. Similarly, in West Africa, Nigeria, Liberia, and Guinea had adopted components of Basel II and/or III, but Ghana, Gambia, and the eight francophone countries in the West African Economic and Monetary Union (WAEMU) had not.

What explains these patterns of convergence and divergence? Why is it that governments in some peripheral developing countries opt to converge on international standards, while governments in other countries opt to maintain divergent standards? This is the question at the heart of this book.

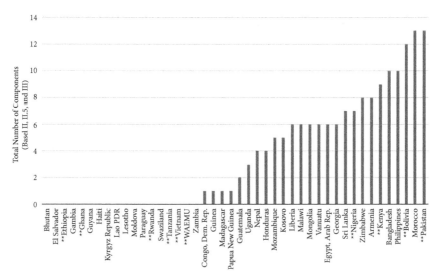

Figure 1.1 Implementation of international banking standards in low- and lower-middle-income countries.

Note: ** denotes a country that is studied in this volume

Source: Data from FSI Survey 2015 covering one hundred jurisdictions outside of the Basel Committee, supplemented with data from case studies in this volume. Income categories are according to World Bank classifications for the same year

Our argument in a nutshell

We examine the political economy of banking regulation in eleven peripheral developing countries and regions, four of which are classified as low income (Ethiopia, Rwanda, Tanzania, and WAEMU) and seven as lower-middle income (Angola, Bolivia, Ghana, Kenya, Nigeria, Pakistan, and Vietnam).[7] Low- and lower-middle-income countries are in many ways the least likely to adopt the latest and most complex international standards (Basel II and III). They have nascent and relatively small financial sectors and their regulatory institutions are particularly resource-constrained.

Drawing on a wealth of primary evidence, including interviews with more than 200 regulators, bank employees, and experts, we trace the responses of each of these countries and regions to international banking standards since the late 1990s. We find that regulators in our case study countries and regions have

---

[7] The eight countries belonging to the WAEMU follow harmonized banking regulations and we study them as a single case. Seven of the eight countries are low income. As at 2019, the World Bank defines low-income economies as those with a GNI per capita, calculated using the World Bank Atlas method, of $995 or less in 2017; lower-middle-income economies are those with a GNI per capita between $996 and $3,895.

responded in very different ways to international banking standards, with their level of engagement increasing over time. At the start of our research project in 2015, only three of the eleven jurisdictions had implemented any components of Basel II and III (Pakistan, Kenya, and Nigeria). By January 2019, Ethiopia was the only country that had not implemented at least one component (Figure 1.2).

Of course, implementation on paper may not lead to substantive compliance in practice. Regulatory authorities may issue regulations that are in line with international standards, but they may be intentionally lax in their enforcement, exercising regulatory forbearance. Scholars have labelled such situations as forms of 'cosmetic' or 'mock compliance' (Chey, 2016, 2006; Walter, 2008). Alternatively, regulatory authorities may be diligent in their supervision but lack the resources to properly monitor and enforce regulations. For their part, banks may comply with the regulations and bring their behaviour into line with regulatory requirements, they may endeavour to comply but fail because the regulations are too complex or cumbersome, or they may intentionally act to circumvent the regulations. Such practices have been documented among Basel Committee members, prompting scholars to question whether the standards change regulatory behaviour in meaningful ways.[8]

In this book we are careful to distinguish between the implementation of international standards and substantive compliance with them. We use the terms 'adoption' and 'implementation' interchangeably, to refer to the incorporation of international standards into domestic regulations through enabling domestic legislation, the issuance of domestic regulations, and guidance. We use the term 'compliance' to refer to the enforcement of these regulations by the relevant authorities and behavioural changes by banks. Empirically it is relatively straightforward to identify the extent to which a country is implementing international standards, as domestic regulations can be compared to international standards. It is much harder to gauge the level of substantive compliance. We focus on the former, seeking to understand why regulators in peripheral developing countries are adopting international standards, but also draw on a range of qualitative evidence to gauge levels of enforcement and substantive compliance.

Drawing on the rich empirical material from our case studies, we develop an analytical framework which sets out the political economy conditions under

Figure 1.2 Implementation of international banking standards in case study countries (January 2019).

---

[8] On Basel I implementation by Basel Committee members see (Chey, 2014; Quillin, 2008). On the failure of the US and EU to implement Basel II and III, respectively, see (Quaglia, 2019).

which we expect to see trajectories of convergence, divergence, or subversion in countries on the financial periphery. These are briefly set out below, and fully elaborated in Chapter 3.

Incentives to converge

We identify four factors that provide strong incentives for regulators in peripheral developing countries to *converge* on international banking standards, above and beyond concerns about mitigating financial risk. Indeed, we find that concern about mitigating financial risk is rarely the main driver of convergence.

The first originates from politicians pursuing a development strategy that identifies integrating into global finance as a major aspect of their country's economic development strategy. In much the same way as politicians in the past sought to emulate East Asia's tiger economies by creating national champions in the manufacturing sector to reap gains from international trade, a new generation of politicians is looking to position their countries as international financial centres like Singapore and Mauritius in order to reap gains from global finance. Politicians promote the implementation of the latest international banking standards in a bid to signal to potential international investors that their country's financial services sector is world-class.

The second stems from large, internationally oriented domestic banks that are seeking to expand into new international markets. As newcomers to international markets, banks from peripheral developing countries face a reputational deficit, and international third parties do not have sufficient information to readily ascertain whether they are soundly regulated. The adoption of international standards is a mechanism for banks to signal to regulators in host countries that they are soundly regulated. Regulators face strong incentives to adopt international standards in order to facilitate the international expansion of large domestic banks.

The third incentive stems from the engagement of regulators with their peers from other countries that are implementing international standards. The expansion of cross-border banking has been accompanied by the creation of transnational professional networks, through which bank regulators come together to exchange experiences and ideas about how best to regulate banks. Regulatory authorities also engage with each other through home–host supervisory relationships, as they work together to supervise international banks. We explain why regular interactions with peers who are implementing international standards generate strong incentives for regulators to follow suit.

Finally, regular interactions with international financial institutions like the IMF and World Bank can provide strong incentives for regulators to implement international standards. The IMF and World Bank provide extensive technical assistance and training, including in the area of bank regulation and supervision.

While regulators often face strong incentives to follow the advice of these institutions, particularly when their country has an ongoing assistance programme, we find that the advice from these institutions is not consistent with regards to international standards, sometimes encouraging extensive adoption and sometimes advising against it.

Incentives to diverge

Working in opposition to these incentives are four factors that generate incentives for regulators to *diverge* from international standards. The first of these originates from politicians pursuing interventionist financial policies, where the state plays an important role in allocating credit. The Basel framework is premised on market-based allocation of credit, with the government only stepping in to address market failures. Policy-directed lending and the general use of financial intermediaries as instruments of government policy are identified under the Basel framework as distorting market signals and impeding effective supervision. Thus, in countries where the government relies extensively on policy-directed lending, the Basel framework is unlikely to be an attractive basis for regulation.

Second, where politicians used their control over banks to allocate credit to political allies, or when powerful economic elites use banks to allocate credit to their own businesses and curry favour with politicians, these groups are likely to oppose the implementation and enforcement of international banking standards.

Third, regulators may be sceptical about the applicability of Basel standards for their local context, particularly the more complex elements of Basel II and III. Fourth, banks with business models focused exclusively on the domestic market in peripheral developing countries are likely to oppose the implementation of complex regulations because of the additional compliance costs this generates. Opposition is likely to be strongest from small, weak banks, for whom the costs of compliance are highest.

Dynamics of convergence and divergence

As the political, economic, and institutional environment differs across peripheral developing countries, regulators experience incentives to converge and diverge through different channels and with varying levels of intensity, prompting them to respond differently to international standards. We explain why the dynamics of convergence and divergence are likely to differ depending on which actors champion implementation and their relative power in domestic regulatory politics. We distinguish between different pathways to convergence, divergence, and mock compliance, and identify the salient features of these pathways.

Our analytical framework focuses on three main actors: the regulator (usually situated within the central bank), large banks, and incumbent politicians. Regulatory outcomes are the product of the relative power position of these three actors and are shaped by the wider domestic and international context in which they are embedded. A striking feature of our empirical findings is that convergence and divergence dynamics in peripheral developing countries are driven mainly by politicians and regulators. In stark contrast to their counterparts in industrialised countries, banks are rarely the most dominant actor in regulatory politics, particularly in the low- and lower-middle-income countries we focus on. While there are some exceptions, the underdeveloped nature of the formal economy and relatively small size of the banking sector leave individual banks, and the banking sector as a whole, with much less power to shape regulatory outcomes than in many advanced economies. Yet this does not mean that financial market players have little purchase on regulators' decisions. Far from it. Operating in a context of capital scarcity, regulators and politicians in peripheral developing countries are particularly attuned to the ways in which international regulators, banks, and investors will react to their decisions. As we explain below, international finance has an outsized impact on regulatory outcomes (see also Mosley (2003a)).

It is this dynamic that sets regulatory harmonization between the core and periphery apart from regularity harmonization among core countries. In explanations of regulatory harmonization among core countries, the interests of large domestic banks loom large. For instance, in his seminal work, Singer (2007) argues that regulators face a dilemma of increasing regulatory requirements in order to mitigate the risk of financial crisis, or easing those requirements and enhancing the international competitiveness of the domestic financial sector (Singer, 2007, p. 19). In this chapter we show how regulators in the periphery face a different dilemma, namely that of implementing overly complex and costly international standards in a bid to attract international finance and help their banks expand abroad, or eschewing those standards to focus on regulations better attuned to supporting their financial sector development.

Strikingly, and in contrast to our initial expectations, we find that the presence of foreign banks does not provide regulators in peripheral developing countries with strong incentives to converge on international standards. Rather than lobby for the adoption of complex and costly global standards to gain a competitive edge over domestic banks, we explain why foreign banks typically adapt their business models to the local context, adopting a similar stance to domestic banks when it comes to regulation in their host jurisdiction.

Contribution to scholarship

Our primary contribution is to develop a new framework that specifies the channels of regulatory interdependence between countries in the core and on the periphery of the global financial system, and to probe its explanatory power through in-depth analysis in eleven countries in Africa, Asia, and Latin America.

We draw on, and contribute to, the literature on the diffusion of global norms. Our comparative country case studies that reveal how international regulatory norms interact with the domestic politics of regulation in a variety of developing country contexts. We parse out the specific ways that cross-border relationships between regulators, politicians, and banks in peripheral developing countries and a variety of international actors generate incentives to converge on international standards. In complementary work, we draw on these insights and use spatial econometrics to reveal how these cross-border relationships help explain patterns of regulatory convergence in the global economy (Jones and Zeitz 2019).

Scholars have previously drawn attention to the ways in which international organizations like the IMF and World Bank have promulgated international standards and the development of financial markets (Lavelle, 2004; Mosley, 2010, 2003b; Wilf, 2017); highlighted the incentives that markets generate to converge on international standards (Simmons, 2001); revealed the ways in which other states harness the reputational dynamics in global markets to pressure convergence (Sharman, 2009, 2008); and the ways in which transnational networks generate processes of learning and emulation that drive convergence (Dobbin et al., 2007; Porter, 2005).

This literature is important in identifying the mechanisms through which international standards spread from the core to the periphery, but tells us little about how actors in peripheral countries engage with these processes and why these mechanisms generate convergence in some peripheral countries but not others. In Jones and Zeitz (2017) we show that there is a correlation between level of financial sector development and the extent of Basel adoption, which suggests that regulators' decisions are strongly influenced by the suitability of the Basel standards to their country's level of financial sector development, but this doesn't explain why countries with similar levels of development respond differently to international standards.

We also contribute to a substantial literature on the politics of financial regulation in developing countries and emerging economies. This literature helped us identify the ways in which domestic politics and institutions are likely to shape responses to international standards. A few scholars have looked specifically at how individual developing countries respond to international financial standards and shown how reformist coalitions can drive the adoption of international standards, often in the face of entrenched vested interests (Walter 2008 and Chey 2007, 2014). Haggard and Maxfield (1996) and Martinez-Diaz (2009) examine the politics surrounding capital account liberalization and bank ownership, respectively, and highlight the role that financial crises have in reconfiguring domestic politics and generating reforms. Others show how varying distribution of power among firms, banks, and governments shapes regulatory outcomes (Haggard and Lee, 1995) and how political economy dynamics help account for variation in the strength of regulatory institutions (Hamilton-Hart, 2002). We contribute to this literature in showing the ways in which integration of sub-national actors into global finance and international policy networks influences the politics of financial regulation within developing countries.

Our approach is inspired by the new interdependence approach in international political economy, which draws attention to the global economy as a hierarchy of interdependent networks (Farrell and Newman, 2016, 2014; Oatley, 2016; Oatley et al., 2013; Quaglia and Spendzharova, 2017). This literature seeks to capture relations of interdependence in ways that have not been possible in the open economy approach that has dominated international political economy in recent years. We contribute to a strand of this literature that is starting to grapple with core–periphery dynamics in global finance (Bauerle Danzman et al., 2017).

Our second contribution is to draw attention to the politics of financial regulation in peripheral developing countries and, in doing so, link debates in international political economy to a set of countries that scholars rarely engage with, and shed light on a topic that is rarely examined by scholars in area studies.

There is a vast, and growing, literature on the politics of financial regulation within and among countries in the core of the global financial system (see for instance Botzem, 2014; Büthe and Mattli, 2011; Haber and Calomiris, 2015; Helleiner, 2014; Kapstein, 1989; Lall, 2012; Lavelle, 2013; Oatley and Nabors, 1998; Perry and Nölke, 2006; Porter, 2005; Quaglia, 2019, 2014; Singer, 2007; Tarullo, 2008; Underhill and Zhang, 2008; Young, 2012; Zysman, 1984). Scholarship on the politics of financial regulation in emerging economies and developing countries is equally insightful yet much less extensive and has tended to focus on the largest emerging and developing countries (Chey, 2014; Haggard and Lee, 1995; Hamilton-Hart, 2002; Hutchcroft, 1998; Knaack, 2017; Lavelle, 2004; Martinez-Diaz, 2009; Naqvi, 2019; Walter, 2008). This reflects a tendency among scholars of international political economy, and international relations more broadly, to focus on countries with the largest economies on the grounds that they exert systemic influence over the global economy and the way it is governed (Drezner, 2008). Yet, as Acharya (2014) forcefully argues, the result is that the discipline 'does not reflect the voices, experiences, knowledge claims and contributions of the vast majority of societies and states in the world, and often marginalizes those outside of the core countries of the West'.

A particularly striking gap in the literature is the dearth of attention paid to the politics of financial regulation in African countries, and low- and lower-middle-income countries in other regions. Economists have studied the financial regulation in these countries from various vantage points and sought to identify reforms that will support development, including Beck (2011), Murinde (2012), and Gottschalk and Griffith-Jones (2016). Yet few political scientists have examined the politics of financial regulation, despite the central role played by the financial sector in economic development. Notable exceptions include Boone (2005), who seeks to explain variation in financial sector reforms across African countries and attributes this to differences in the strength, diversity, and autonomy of private capital vis-à-vis the state. Lewis and Stein (1997) study the politics of financial reform in Nigeria and attribute failure to weaknesses in the capacity of state institutions and private banks. More recently, Dafe (2017) examines how sources of capital shape the policy stances of central banks in Nigeria, Kenya, and Uganda, while Soares de Oliveira and Ferreira (2018) analyse the evolution of banking in Angola. For almost all of our case study countries and regions, our chapters are the first attempt to systemically analyse the politics of financial regulation.

Policy implications

Our research has substantial policy implications. There is an emerging consensus among international policymakers that countries outside of the Basel Committee, particularly low-income and lower-middle income countries, should be cautious in their embrace of international standards and adopt a proportional approach (Barth and Caprio, 2018; Hohl et al., 2018; Restoy, 2018). Yet this well-intentioned advice overlooks the powerful reputational, competitive, and functional incentives generated by financial globalization. that, as we show, may lead regulators to adopt international standards even if they are ill suited to their local context. We show how, in today's world of globalized finance, regulators in peripheral developing countries cannot simply ignore international standards even when they are not appropriately designed for their jurisdiction, as this carries significant reputational risks. Financial regulators in peripheral developing countries face the challenge of harnessing the prudential, reputational, and competitive benefits of international banking standards, while avoiding the implementation risks and challenges associated with wholesale adoption.

Our research shows that there is room for manoeuvre at the national level. Regulators can take a selective approach to implementation, only implementing the components of the international standards that serve a useful regulatory purpose in their jurisdiction, and they can fine-tune these elements to suit the peculiarities of their local financial system. For example, the Central Bank of the Philippines has recalibrated the capital requirements associated with lending to small- and medium-sized enterprises to ensure that banks are not unduly dissuaded from lending to them.[9] Given the high costs of retrofitting international

---

[9] Discussion with senior regulator from the Philippines, via Skype, September 2018.

standards and acute resource-constraints that regulators in peripheral developing countries face, there is a strong rationale for greater sharing of information and experiences among peripheral regulators on the various ways to adapt international standards to better suit their needs.

Our research also provides a compelling argument for reforming international standard-setting processes so that international standards better reflect the interests of countries on the financial periphery. So far, the international standard-setting community has adopted a minimalist 'do no harm' approach when it comes to international banking standards, seeking to establish where there have been negative unintended consequences for developing countries and only then looking for remedies (e.g. FSB, 2012, 2014). Much more could and should be done at the design stage to ensure that international standards work for peripheral developing countries. While international experts are increasingly advising developing countries to take a proportional approach to the implementation of international standards (Hohl et al., 2018; Restoy, 2018), regulators in developing countries are left the onerous task of figuring out exactly how to modify international standards to suit their local context. Instead, proportionality could be built much more systematically into international standards at the design stage, so that this resource-intensive task adjusting standards is not left to the regulators with the least resources. Related to this, standard-setting processes could be opened up to more meaningful input from regulators from peripheral developing countries. While consultative mechanisms exist, they fall far short of providing peripheral developing countries with a voice in standard-setting processes (Jones and Knaack, 2019).

Structure of the book

This book is divided into three parts.

Part I: Introduction, cross-country variation, and analytical argument

Following this introduction, **Chapter 2** analyses in more detail the context for banking regulation in peripheral developing countries, the evidence on the merits and demerits of Basel standards for developing countries, and ways in which peripheral countries are, in practice, responding to Basel II and III. **Chapter 3** provides an analytical framework for understanding the political economy of implementing international standards in developing countries. It builds from the existing literature and the case studies in this volume to identify the conditions under which we can expect countries to converge on, diverge from, or subvert international standards.

Part II: Case studies

In **Chapters 4 to 14**, we present our eleven country case studies, using the analytical framework to guide our analysis. Each chapter follows the same format, to facilitate cross-case comparison. Each chapter starts by providing an analysis of the key features of the financial sector and salient political economy dynamics, noting any major shifts over time. It then assesses the extent to which the country has based its national regulations and supervisory practices on international standards, looking specifically at the adoption and implementation of Basel I, II, and III and compliance with the Basel Core Principles. The heart of each case study is a political economy explanation for these regulatory decisions, which engages with the analytical framework. Each case study concludes with a summary of the main insights.

We present our case studies according to the extent to which they have converged on international standards, starting with the highest adopters, and the specific pathway through which convergence and divergence occurred. This sequence is summarized in Table 1.1 and followed by short summaries of each case study.

Policy-driven convergence
In three cases, politicians championed convergence on international standards. In **Chapter 4**, Natalya Naqvi explores the politics of adoption in **Pakistan**, which has the highest level of implementation among our case study countries. The impetus for converging on international standards has come from different actors over time.

Table 1.1 Pathways to convergence and divergence among case study countries

Country	Pathway	Outcome (number of Basel II and Basel III components implemented out of max. 18)
Pakistan	Policy-driven convergence	Ambitious implementation (14)
Rwanda	Policy-driven convergence	Ambitious implementation (10)
Ghana	Policy-driven convergence	Ambitious implementation (8)
WAEMU	IFI-driven convergence	Ambitious implementation (10)
Tanzania	Regulator-driven convergence	Selective implementation (8)
Kenya	Regulator-driven convergence	Selective implementation (7)
Bolivia	Regulator-driven convergence	Selective implementation (5)
Nigeria	Regulator-driven mock compliance	Mock compliance (6)
Angola	Politically driven mock compliance	Mock compliance (5)
Vietnam	Politically driven mock compliance	Mock compliance (3)
Ethiopia	Policy-driven divergence	No implementation (0)

Notes: Ambitious implementation = includes at least one of the more complex components (internal models under Basel II and/or liquidity or macroprudential/liquidity standards under Basel III); Selective implementation = standardized approaches under Basel II and only microprudential capital requirements under Basel III; Mock compliance = on paper, not enforced.

The adoption of Basel I adoption in the 1980s was driven by the World Bank and IMF. In the 1990s and early 2000s, the adoption of Basel II was driven first by politicians promoting the expansion of financial services, and then by banking sector regulators. Most recently, as banks have internationalized, they have championed the implementation of Basel III. Pakistan is one of the few cases where all three major actors—politicians, regulators, and major banks—are now aligned behind the implementation of the standards, leading to a high and ambitious level of implementation.

As Pritish Behuria shows in **Chapter 5**, for many years, the **Rwandan** government showed little interest in moving beyond Basel I. However, in 2015, the government's stance changed and politicians made a formal commitment to the rapid adoption and implementation of Basel II and III. This exuberance for adopting global standards is puzzling given that Rwanda's financial sector remains largely underdeveloped and the government is aiming to become a developmental state. The motivations behind this policy shift are to reduce risk in the financial sector, encourage harmonization of financial sector regulation across the East African Community (EAC), and develop a service-based economy, including by making Kigali a financial hub. The adoption and implementation of the latest international banking standards has become a strategic policy priority for Rwanda's economic leadership.

In **Chapter 6**, Emily Jones explores the stop-start dynamics of Basel implementation in **Ghana**, a pattern that reflects party politics. Moves to implement Basel and other international standards have coincided with periods when the New Patriotic Party (NPP) has been in office. The NPP has a vision for positioning Ghana as a financial services hub for West Africa and strong ideological and material connections to international finance. In 2017 the NPP government embarked on a radical reform of the banking sector, implementing major elements of Basel II and III and catapulting Ghana to among the most ambitious implementers of Basel standards among our case study countries. In contrast, the National Democratic Congress (NDC) focused on directing finance to the productive sectors of the economy and supporting indigenous banks and the implementation of international standards was not a policy priority during their periods in office.

IFI-driven convergence

In **Chapter 7** Ousseni Illy and Seydou Ouedraogo examine the politics of implementation in the West African Economic and Monetary Union (**WAEMU**). As with Ghana and Rwanda, after implementing Basel I for many years, WAEMU moved to adopt Basel II and III standards in 2016 and began implementation in 2018. Given the weak development of the financial sector in the Union and its poor connectedness to the international financial system, this reform was unexpected. The adoption of Basel standards has been championed by the Central Bank of West African States (BCEAO), under the influence of the IMF, which has strongly encouraged implementation. National governments and domestically oriented banks have not played an active role, complicating the implementation and enforcement of the new regulations. The Central Bank is embedded in regulatory peer networks, has close links with the IMF, and is insulated from domestic political pressure because of its supranational position.

Regulator-driven convergence

In Tanzania, Kenya and Bolivia, regulators have championed the implementation of international standards, although they have often been more circumspect and cautious than the politicians and policymakers that championed adoption in the first group of countries. **Tanzania** has been a slow and cautious adopter of Basel standards, as Hazel Gray explains in **Chapter 8**, although recent moves to implement the standards have led to a higher level of adoption. Tanzania only finished implementing risk-based supervision in 2009 and opted for selective implementation of Basel II and III standards beginning in 2017. From 1991 to 2008 Tanzania liberalized its financial sector under the influence of the IMF and World Bank, but a significant gap emerged between the formal commitment to adopting Basel standards and the actual pattern of implementation and enforcement. It was only from 2009 onwards that Basel implementation was prioritized. This was the result of a number of factors including the appointment of a new Governor at the Bank of Tanzania (BoT) with strong connections to the international policy community, and the influence of regional commitments to regulatory harmonization. The central bank adopted a selective and tailored approach to Basel adoption, with different regulatory requirements for development banks. Domestic and foreign banks initially showed little interest in implementation but their preferences have shifted because of pressures from parent banks and anti-money laundering concerns.

In **Chapter 9**, Radha Upadhyaya examines adoption in **Kenya**. The impetus for Basel implementation has come from the regulator, the Central Bank of Kenya (CBK), which is highly independent, has strong links to international policy networks, and is very receptive to international policy ideas. Since 2003, the incumbent politicians have also been keen to adopt the latest international standards in order to attract investment into Kenya's financial sector. Meanwhile, as the banking sector is relatively well capitalized, there has been little opposition from banks, with some international and large local banks being mildly in favour of Basel II and III adoption. In the Kenyan case the regulator has been the driving force for Basel adoption, supported by internationally oriented politicians and banks. Although they were early movers, Kenyan regulators have also taken a selective approach to implementation.

In **Chapter 10**, Peter Knaack explores why **Bolivia** had very ambitious plans to implement Basel standards, but these only partly came to fruition. A novel financial services law promulgated by the regulator in 2013 established the legal framework for a wholesale adoption of Basel II, including all advanced internal-ratings based components, and elements of Basel III. It is puzzling to see such a wholehearted embrace of Basel standards by a domestically oriented left-wing government that follows a heterodox approach to economic policymaking. Basel adoption has been driven by a regulatory agency that is embedded in trans-national technocratic regulators networks and actively seeks to implement inter-national standards. Bolivian regulators wrote a wide range of Basel rules into the draft legislation. But Bolivian politicians, prioritizing the twin goals of financial stability and inclusive growth, grafted onto this legislation significant interven-tionist policies. Thus, Bolivia's Basel adoption is pulling in two directions: adher-ence to Basel Committee-style best practices and, concurrently, financial interventionism to stimulate economic growth and financial inclusion.

Regulator-driven mock compliance

In another three countries, Nigeria, Angola and Vietnam, we find evidence of mock compliance, where the standards are implemented on paper but not enforced in practice. In **Chapter 11**, Florence Dafe examines **Nigeria's** engagement with international standards where regulators have gradually adopted Basel I, II, and III, although implementation and enforcement has been slow. The impetus for Basel adoption has come primarily from regulators, who are embedded in inter-national policy networks. They consider Basel II and III the most appropriate set of regulatory standards to stabilize and manage risk in Nigeria's large, internation-alized banking sector. While Basel adoption was not a salient issue among Nigeria's politicians, Nigeria's large internationally active banks welcomed the implementa-tion of Basel II as an important means to enhance their competitiveness and signal soundness to markets. However, implementation and enforcement has been slow as regulators have conflicting preferences: while promoting Basel II adoption, they are reluctant to move quickly to implement and enforce the new standards because it might trigger regulatory interventions in several fragile domestic banks. These banks play an important role in providing employment and access to finance for the private sector, and their resolution would meet with resistance from politicians and lead to a loss of confidence in Nigeria's banking sector.

Politically driven mock compliance

In **Chapter 12**, Rebecca Engebretsen and Ricardo Soares de Oliveira examine **Angola's** adoption of Basel standards. As in other resource-rich countries, the financial sector in Angola plays a key role in facilitating outgoing financial flows. The banking sector is also highly politicized, as loans are extended, often without collateral, and bank licences issued to political insiders. The political allocation of credit has been an important avenue for securing political support for the regime. The result has been strong opposition to the ratcheting up of bank regulation and supervision. Yet a balance-of-payments crisis in 2009, falling in oil prices from 2014, and changes in the global regulatory environment together meant that divergence from international standards was no longer an option. For Angolan banks to maintain their links to the global financial market, the country needed to signal its readiness to regulate the sector in line with international standards. The result has been an upsurge in regulatory efforts since 2009, and especially since 2014. Yet, because the politicized nature of the banking sector has not changed, standards are either not implemented or are implemented but not enforced, leading to a situation of 'mock compliance'.

In **Vietnam** the implementation of international banking standards has been the subject of contestation between reformist and conservative factions within the governing political party, as Que-Giang Tran-Thi and Tu-Anh Vu-Thanh explain in **Chapter 13**. In any given period, the speed of implementation has been affected by which of these factions dominates regulatory decision-making, as well as the health of the banking sector. The adoption and implementation of Basel standards in Vietnam has gone through three distinctive periods: from 1999–2006, the reformist faction pursued international regulations in order to discipline state-owned banks and improve the functioning of the financial sector. From 2006–13, the central bank (SBV) formally adopted Basel II but a domestic banking crisis effectively halted implementation. More recently there has been a return to pro-Basel preferences. However, interventionist financial policies, high implementation costs, the low internationalization level of the banking sector, and the lack of competent technocrats inside both the SBV and domestic private banks have all contributed to a high level of regulatory forbearance.

Policy-driven divergence

In **Chapter 14**, Toni Weis explains why **Ethiopia** has chosen to diverge from international standards and not to adopt any aspect of Basel II or III. Ethiopia has the least internationalized banking sector among our case countries. Despite significant exposure to the Basel standards through donors and the IMF, banking supervisors at the National Bank of Ethiopia (NBE) have little use for Basel II and III. Ethiopia's decision to diverge from international the Basel framework results from a strong preference for political control over the financial sector. The Ethiopian government seeks to emulate the example of East Asian 'tiger' economies, for whom financial repression was a key tool in the pursuit of rapid industrialization. However, as Ethiopia's domestic banks struggle to sustain transformative growth, pressures for greater financial openness (and, by extension, for increased regulatory convergence) are beginning to mount.

Part III: Conclusion

The book ends with a short **Conclusion** (**Chapter** 15) that distils comparative insights from across the case studies, identifies areas for future research, and offers policy recommendations. It makes the case for reforming the key institutions of global financial governance to increase the voice and influence of actors from countries on the periphery.

References

Acharya, A., 2014. Global international relations (IR) and regional worlds: A new agenda for international studies. *International Studies Quarterly* 58, 647–59. https://doi.org/10.1111/isqu.12171.

Admati, A.R., 2016. The missed opportunity and challenge of capital regulation. *National Institute Economic Review* 235, R4–14. https://doi.org/10.1177/002795011623500110.

Admati, A.R., Hellwig, M., 2014. *The Bankers' New Clothes: What's Wrong with Banking and What to Do about It.* Princeton Univ. Press, Princeton, NJ.

Aizenman, J., Chinn, M.D., Ito, H., 2015. *Monetary policy spillovers and the trilemma in the new normal: Periphery country sensitivity to core country conditions* (Working Paper 21128). NBER.

Akyuz, Y., 2010. The management of capital flows and financial vulnerability in Asia, in: Griffith-Jones, S., Ocampo, J.A., Stiglitz, J.E. (Eds.), *Time for a Visible Hand: Lessons from the 2008 World Financial Crisis.* Oxford University Press, New York, pp. 219–41.

Amaglobeli, D., End, N., Jarmuzek, M., Palomba, G., 2015. *From Systemic Banking Crises to Fiscal Costs: Risk Factors.* International Monetary Fund, Washington, DC.

Andrews, M., Pritchett, L., Woolcock, M., 2013. Escaping capability traps through problem driven iterative adaptation (PDIA). *World Development* 51, 234–44. https://doi.org/10.1016/j.worlddev.2013.05.011.

Baker, A., 2009. Deliberative equality and the transgovernmental politics of the global financial architecture. *Global Governance: A Review of Multilateralism and International Organizations* 15, 195–218.

Barth, J.R., Caprio, G., 2018. Regulation and supervision in financial development, in: Beck, T., Levine, R. (Eds.), *Handbook of Finance and Development.* Edward Elgar Publishing, Cheltenham, pp. 393–418. https://doi.org/10.4337/9781785360510.

Barth, J.R., Caprio, G., Levine, R., 2006. *Rethinking Bank Regulation: Till Angels Govern.* Cambridge University Press, Cambridge; New York.

Bauerle Danzman, S., Winecoff, W.K., Oatley, T., 2017. All crises are global: Capital cycles in an imbalanced international political economy. *International Studies Quarterly* 61, 907–23. https://doi.org/10.1093/isq/sqx054.

Bayoumi, T., 2017. *Unfinished Business: The Unexplored Causes of the Financial Crisis and the Lessons Yet to Be Learned.* Yale University Press, New Haven, CT; London.

Beck, T., 2011. *Financing Africa: Through the Crisis and Beyond.* World Bank, Washington, DC.

Boone, C., 2005. State, capital, and the politics of banking reform in Sub-Saharan Africa. *Comparative Politics* 37, 401–20.

Botzem, S., 2014. *The Politics of Accounting Regulation: Organizing Transnational Standard Setting in Financial Reporting.* Edward Elgar Publishing Ltd, Cheltenham.

Bozorgmehr, N., 2016. Iran's 'outdated' banks hamper efforts to rejoin global economy. *Financial Times.*

Buckley, R.P., 2016. The changing nature of banking and why it matters, in: Buckley, R.P., Avgouleas, E., Arner, D.W. (Eds.), *Reconceptualising Global Finance and Its Regulation.* Cambridge University Press, Cambridge, pp. 9–27. https://doi.org/10.1017/CBO9781316181553.002.

Büthe, T., Mattli, W., 2011. *The New Global Rulers: The Privatization of Regulation in the World Economy.* Princeton University Press, Oxford; Princeton, NJ.

Castro Carvalho, A.P., Hohl, S., Raskopf, R., Ruhnau, S., 2017. *Proportionality in banking regulation: A cross-country comparison* (FSI Insights No. 1). Financial Stability Institute.

Chey, H., 2014. *International Harmonization of Financial Regulation? The Politics of Global Diffusion of the Basel Capital Accord.* Routledge, New York.

Chey, H., 2016. International financial standards and emerging economies since the global financial crisis, in: Henning, C.R., Walter, A. (Eds.), *Global Financial Governance Confronts the Rising Powers.* CIGI, Waterloo, pp. 211–36.

Chey, H.-K., 2006. Explaining cosmetic compliance with international regulatory regimes: The implementation of the Basle Accord in Japan, 1998–2003. *New Political Economy* 11, 271–89. https://doi.org/10.1080/13563460600655664.

Chey, H.-K., 2007. Do markets enhance convergence on international standards? The case of financial regulation. *Regulation & Governance* 1, 295–311.

Claessens, S., 2017. Global banking: Recent developments and insights from research. *Review of Finance* 21, 1513–55.

Claessens, S., van Horen, N., 2012. *Foreign banks: Trends, impact and financial stability* (No. WP/12/10), IMF Working Paper. IMF.

Dafe, F., 2017. The politics of finance: How capital sways African central banks. *The Journal of Development Studies* 1–17. https://doi.org/10.1080/00220388.2017.1380793.

Dobbin, F., Simmons, B., Garrett, G., 2007. The global diffusion of public policies: Social construction, coercion, competition, or learning? *Annual Review of Sociology* 33, 449–72. https://doi.org/10.1146/annurev.soc.33.090106.142507.

Dobbs, R., Remes, J., Smit, S., Manyika, J., Woetzel, J., Agyenim-Boateng, Y., 2013. *Urban World: The Shifting Global Business Landscape.* McKinsey Global Institute, New York.

Drezner, D.W., 2008. *All Politics Is Global: Explaining International Regulatory Regimes.* Princeton Univ. Press, Princeton, NJ.

Enoch, C., Mathieu, P.H., Mecagni, M., Canales Kriljenko, J., 2015. *Pan-African Banks: Opportunities and Challenges for Cross-Border Oversight.* IMF, Washington, DC.

Farrell, H., Newman, A., 2016. The new interdependence approach: Theoretical development and empirical demonstration. *Review of International Political Economy* 23, 713–36. https://doi.org/10.1080/09692290.2016.1247009.

Farrell, H., Newman, A.L., 2010. Making global markets: Historical institutionalism in international political economy. *Review of International Political Economy* 17, 609–38

Farrell, H., Newman, A.L., 2014. Domestic Institutions beyond the nation-state: Charting the new interdependence approach. *World Politics* 66, 331–63. https://doi.org/10.1017/S0043887114000057.

Ferreira, Caio; Nigel Jenkinson; Christopher Wilson 2019. *From Basel I to Basel III: Sequencing Implementation in Developing Economies* IMF Working Paper 19/127 IMF: Washington DC Available here: https://www.imf.org/en/Publications/WP/Issues/2019/06/14/From-Basel-I-to-Basel-III-Sequencing-Implementation-in-Developing-Economies-46895

Financial Tribune, 2017. Banking system moving toward Basel III. *Financial Tribune.*

FSB, 2012. *Identifying the effects of regulatory reforms on emerging markets and developing economies: A review of the potential unintended consequences.* Report to the G20 Finance Ministers and Central Bank Governors. Financial Stability Board.

FSB, 2014. *Monitoring the effects of agreed regulatory reforms on emerging market and developing economies (EMDEs).* Financial Stability Board.

FSB, 2016. *2016 list of global systemically important banks (G-SIBs).*

FSB, IMF, WB, 2011. *Financial stability issues in emerging market and developing economies: Report to the G20 Finance Ministers and Central Bank Governors.* Financial Stability Board, International Monetary Fund, World Bank.

Ghosh, J., 2007. Cental bank 'autonomy' in the age of finance, in: Bagchi, A.K., Dymski, G. (Eds.), *Capture and Exclude: Developing Economies and the Poor in Global Finance.* Tulika Books, New Delhi, pp. 39–51.

Griffith-Jones, S., Gottschalk, R. (Eds.), 2016. *Achieving Financial Stability and Growth in Africa.* Routledge Taylor & Francis Group, London.

Griffith-Jones, S., Persaud, A., 2008. The pro-cyclical impact of Basel II on emerging markets and its political economy, in: Stiglitz, J.E., Ocampo, J.A. (Eds.), *Capital Market Liberalization and Development.* Oxford University Press, Oxford.

Haber, S.H., Calomiris, C.W., 2015. *Fragile by Design: The Political Origins of Banking Crises and Scarce Credit.* Princeton University Press, Princeton, NJ.

Haggard, S., Lee, C.H. (Eds.), 1995. *Financial Systems and Economic Policy in Developing Countries.* Cornell University Press, Ithaca, NY.

Haggard, S., Maxfield, S., 1996. The political economy of financial internationalization in the developing world. *International Organization* 50, 35–68. https://doi.org/10.1017/S0020818300001661.

Haldane, A., 2013. *Constraining discretion in bank regulation.* Speech given at the Federal Reserve Bank of Atlanta Conference on 'Maintaining financial stability: holding a tiger by the tail(s)', Federal Reserve Bank of Atlanta, Atlanta, 9 April 2013. https://www.bis.org/review/r130606e.pdf.

Hamilton-Hart, N., 2002. *Asian States, Asian Bankers: Central Banking in Southeast Asia*. Cornell University Press, Ithaca, NY.

Helleiner, E., 2014. *The Status Quo Crisis: Global Financial Governance After the 2008 Financial Meltdown*. Oxford University Press, New York.

Hoenig, T., 2013. *Basel III capital: A well-intended illusion*. Speech given to International Association of Deposit Insurers 2013 Research Conference, Basel, Switzerland on 9 April 2013. https://www.fdic.gov/news/news/speeches/spapr0913.pdf.

Hohl, S., Sison, M.C., Sastny, T., Zamil, R., 2018. *The Basel framework in 100 jurisdictions: Implementation status and proportionality practices*. Stefan Hohl, Maria Cynthia Sison, Tomas Stastny and Raihan Zamil (No. 11), FSI Insights on policy implementation. Bank for International Settlements.

Hutchcroft, P.D., 1998. *Booty Capitalism: The Politics of Banking in the Philippines*. Cornell University Press, Ithaca, NY.

ILO, 2015. *World Employment Social Outlook: The Changing Nature of Jobs*. Geneva.

IMF, 2011. *Managing Volatility: A Vulnerability Exercise for Low-Income Countries*. IMF, Washington, DC.

IMF, 2017. *Recent Trends in Correspondent Banking Relationships: Further Considerations*. IMF, Washington, DC.

Jones, E., Knaack, P., 2019. Global financial regulation: Shortcomings and reform options. *Global Policy*. https://doi.org/10.1111/1758-5899.12656.

Jones, E. and A. O. Zeitz 2019. Regulatory Convergence in the Financial Periphery: How Interdependence Shapes Regulators' Decisions *International Studies Quarterly*, https://doi.org/10.1093/isq/sqz068

Jones, E., Zeitz, A.O., 2017. The limits of globalizing Basel banking standards. *Journal of Financial Regulation* 3, 89–124.

Kapstein, E.B., 1989. Resolving the regulator's dilemma: International coordination of banking regulations. *International Organization* 43, 323–47.

Knaack, P., 2017. An unlikely champion of global finance: Why is China exceeding global banking standards? *Journal of Current Chinese Affairs* 46, 41–79.

Lall, R., 2012. From failure to failure: The politics of international banking regulation. *Review of International Political Economy* 19, 609–38.

Lavelle, K.C., 2004. *The Politics of Equity Finance in Emerging Markets*. Oxford University Press, Oxford; New York.

Lavelle, K.C., 2013. *Money and Banks in the American Political System*. Cambridge University Press, Cambridge; New York.

Lewis, P., Stein, H., 1997. Shifting fortunes: The political economy of financial liberalization in Nigeria. *World Development* 25, 5–22. https://doi.org/10.1016/S0305-750X(96)00085-X.

Lund, S., Windhagen, E., Manyika, J., Härle, P., Woetzel, J., Goldshtein, D., 2017. *The New Dynamics of Financial Globalization*. McKinsey & Company, London.

Martinez-Diaz, L., 2009. *Globalizing in Hard Times: The Politics of Banking-Sector Opening in the Emerging World, Cornell studies in political economy*. Cornell University Press, Ithaca, NY.

Mehmood, J., Chaudhry, S., 2018. *Data Dispatch: The World's 100 Largest Banks*. S&P Global: Market Intelligence.

Mosley, L., 2003a. *Global Capital and National Governments*. Cambridge University Press, Cambridge, UK.

Mosley, L., 2003b. Attempting global standards: National governments, international finance, and the IMF's data regime. *Review of International Political Economy* 10, 331–62. https://doi.org/10.1080/0969229032000063243.

Mosley, L., 2010. Regulating globally, implementing locally: The financial codes and standards effort. *Review of International Political Economy* 17, 724–61. https://doi.org/10.1080/09692290903529817.

Murinde, V. (Ed.), 2012. *Bank regulatory reforms in Africa*. Palgrave Macmillan, Basingstoke.

Naqvi, N. (2019). Manias, panics and crashes in emerging markets: an empirical investigation of the post-2008 crisis period. *New Political Economy* 24, 759–779.

Oatley, T., 2016. It's a system, not a sample: Interdependence in the global political economy. *International Studies Quarterly Symposium*. URL https://www.isanet.org/Publications/ISQ/Posts/ID/5326/Its-a-System-not-a-Sample-Interdependence-in-the-Global-Political-Economy.

Oatley, T., Nabors, R., 1998. Redistributive cooperation: Market failure, wealth transfers, and the Basel Accord. *International Organization* 52, 35–54.

Oatley, T., Winecoff, W., Pennock, A., Danzman, S.B., 2013. The political economy of global finance: A network model. *Perspectives on Politics* 11, 133–53.

Perry, J., Nölke, A., 2006. The political economy of International Accounting Standards. *Review of International Political Economy* 13, 559–86. https://doi.org/10.1080/09692290600839790.

Persaud, A., 2013. *Reinventing financial regulation: A blueprint for overcoming systemic risk*. Apress, New York.

Phillips, N., 2017. Power and inequality in the global political economy. *International Affairs* 93, 429–44. https://doi.org/10.1093/ia/iix019.

Pistor, K., 2013. A legal theory of finance. *Journal of Comparative Economics* 41, 315–30.

Porter, T., 2005. *Globalization and finance*. Polity, Cambridge; Malden, MA.

Posner, E., 2010. Sequence as explanation: The international politics of accounting standards. *Review of International Political Economy* 17, 639–64.

Quaglia, L., 2014. The European Union, the USA and international standard setting by regulatory fora in finance. *New Political Economy* 19, 427–44. https://doi.org/10.1080/13563467.2013.796449.

Quaglia, L., 2019. The politics of state compliance with international 'soft law' in finance. *Governance* 32, 45–62. https://doi.org/10.1111/gove.12344.

Quaglia, L., Spendzharova, A., 2017. Post-crisis reforms in banking: Regulators at the interface between domestic and international governance: Post-crisis reforms in banking. *Regulation & Governance* 11, 422–37. https://doi.org/10.1111/rego.12157.

Quillin, B., 2008. *International Financial Co-Operation: Political Economics of Compliance with the 1988 Basel Accord*, Routledge International Studies in Money and Banking. Routledge, London; New York.

Reddy, Y.V., 2010. Regulation of the financial sector in developing countries, in: Griffith-Jones, S., Ocampo, J.A., Stiglitz, J.E. (Eds.), *Time for a Visible Hand: Lessons from the 2008 World Financial Crisis*. Oxford University Press, Oxford, UK, pp. 242–52.

Reinhart, C.M., Rogoff, K.S., 2013. Banking crises: An equal opportunity menace. *Journal of Banking & Finance* 37, 4557–73. https://doi.org/10.1016/j.jbankfin.2013.03.005.

Restoy, F., 2018. *Proportionality in banking regulation*. Presented at the Westminster Business Forum Keynote Seminar: Building a resilient UK financial sector—next steps for prudential regulation, structural reform and mitigating risks, London.

Rey, H., 2015. *Dilemma not trilemma: The global financial cycle and monetary policy independence* (No. w21162). National Bureau of Economic Research, Cambridge, MA. https://doi.org/10.3386/w21162.

Romano, R., 2014. For diversity in the international regulation of financial institutions: Critiquing and recalibrating the Basel architecture. *Yale Journal on Regulation* 31.

Saul, J., Arnold, T., 2016. Iran's banks will need to change to thrive after sanctions. *Reuters Business News*.

Seabrooke, L., Tsingou, E., 2009. Power elites and everyday politics in international financial reform. *International Political Sociology* 3, 457–61.

Sharman, J.C., 2008. Power and discourse in policy diffusion: Anti-money laundering in developing states. *International Studies Quarterly* 52, 635–56. https://doi.org/10.2307/29734254.

Sharman, J.C., 2009. The bark is the bite: International organizations and blacklisting. *Review of International Political Economy* 16, 573–96. https://doi.org/10.1080/09692290802403502.

Simmons, B.A., 2001. The international politics of harmonization: The case of capital market regulation. *International Organization* 55, 589–620.

Singer, D.A., 2007. *Regulating Capital: Setting Standards for the International Financial System*. Cornell University Press, Ithaca, NY.

Slaughter, A.-M., 2004. *A New World Order*. Princeton University Press, Princeton, NJ.

Soares de Oliveira, R., Ferreira, M.E., 2018. The political economy of banking in Angola. *African Affairs*. https://doi.org/10.1093/afraf/ady029.

Tarullo, D.K., 2008. *Banking on Basel: The Future of International Financial Regulation*. Peterson Institute for International Economics, Washington, DC.

The Warwick Commission, 2009. In Praise of Unlevel Playing Fields. University of Warwick, Warwick.

UNCTAD, 2013. *Global Value Chains and Development: Investment and Value-Added Trade in the Global Economy*. UNCTAD, Geneva.

Underhill, G.R.D., Zhang, X., 2008. Setting the rules: Private power, political underpinning and legitimacy in global monetary and financial governance. *International Affairs* 84, 535–54.

Walter, A., 2008. *Governing Finance: East Asia's Adoption of International Standards, Cornell Studies in Money*. Cornell University Press, Ithaca, NY.

Walter, A., 2016. Emerging countries and Basel III: Why is engagement still low? in: Henning, C.R., Walter, A. (Eds.), *Global Financial Governance Confronts the Rising Powers*. CIGI, Waterloo, pp. 179–210.

Wilf, M., 2017. *Market forces or international institutions? The under-emphasized role of IFIs in domestic bank regulatory adoption*. Presented at The Political Economy of International Organizations (PEIO) 2017.

World Bank, 2012. *Global Financial Development Report 2013: Rethinking the Role of the State in Finance*. World Bank, Washington, DC.

Young, K.L., 2012. Transnational regulatory capture? An empirical examination of the transnational lobbying of the Basel Committee on Banking Supervision. *Review of International Political Economy* 19, 663–88. https://doi.org/10.1080/09692290.2011.624976.

Zysman, J., 1984. *Governments, Markets, and Growth: Financial Systems and the Politics of Industrial Change*. Cornell University Press, Ithaca, NY.

2

The Challenges International Banking Standards Pose for Peripheral Developing Countries

Emily Jones

Introduction

The effective regulation of banks in peripheral developing countries is vitally important, just as it is in advanced and emerging economies. But regulators are charged with supervising financial sectors that differ in important ways to those of large industrialized economies like the US and EU, and even large emerging economies like China, India, and Brazil. This chapter explains how the regulatory context differs and why these differences pose specific challenges for regulators in low and lower-middle income counties in deciding whether, and how much, of the latest set of international standards to adopt.

This chapter provides an overview of financial sectors in peripheral developing countries, highlighting the ways in which they differ from financial sectors in countries with more industrialised economies. It provides a brief overviews of the genesis and evolution of international banking standards, setting out the criticisms that have been levelled against their use in more advanced economies, before explaining why implementation challenges are acute in many peripheral developing countries, particularly low-income countries. The chapter then analyses patterns of Basel implementation around the world, situating the responses of regulators in our case studies, within these broader trends.

As this chapter shows, although Basel standards are commonly referred to as 'international best practice' or 'the gold standard' there is surprisingly little evidence to support this claim. While it is important to have minimum standards for the regulation of the world's largest internationally active banks to prevent a regulatory race to the bottom and ensure global financial stability, there is very little evidence that the principles and standards that emanate from the Basel Committee are an effective basis for banking regulation in low and lower-middle income countries. As one well-regarded team of experts states 'While many countries have followed the Basel guidelines and strengthened capital regulations

Emily Jones, *The Challenges International Banking Standards Pose for Peripheral Developing Countries* In: *The Political Economy of Bank Regulation in Developing Countries: Risk And Reputation.* Edited by: Emily Jones, Oxford University Press (2020). © Oxford University Press. DOI: 10.1093/oso/9780198841999.003.0002

and empowered supervisory agencies to a greater degree, existing evidence does not suggest that this will improve banking-system stability, enhance the efficiency of intermediation, or reduce corruption in lending' (Barth et al., 2012).

As international banking standards are soft law (Brummer, 2012) and non-member countries are under no formal obligation to adopt them, it is puzzling that regulators in many countries outside of the Basel Committee are adopting them. In Chapter 3 we explain how international and domestic politics help address this puzzle.

Regulating finance in peripheral developing countries

Financial sectors in low- and lower-middle-income countries differ in important ways from financial sectors in more industrialised economies. A striking feature of financial sectors in low- and lower-middle-income countries is that they are typically much smaller relative to the overall economy than in more developed economies. The size of the financial sector in the economy is commonly assessed by looking at the level of domestic credit to the private sector relative to GDP. On this measure, the size of the financial sector in high-income countries is, on average, almost eight times larger than in low-income countries, and three times larger than in lower-middle-income countries (Table 2.1).

Financial sectors in low- and lower-middle-income countries are dominated overwhelmingly by banks. In low- and lower-middle-income countries banks provide almost all of the credit to the private sector, while in high-income countries banks provide just over half of credit, with a variety of non-bank financial institutions providing the rest (Table 2.1). Related to this, stock markets are much less developed. It is only as countries develop and financial sectors deepen that domestic private bond markets and stock markets grow, followed by the expansion of mutual funds and pension funds (Sahay et al., 2015).

Another difference is in the level of access to financial services (Table 2.1). Fewer than one in five households in African countries have access to any formal banking service—savings, payments, or credit (Beck et al., 2009). Of course, inclusion can be a double-edged sword, and financial exploitation is a common feature of life for many low-income households, so expanded access is no guarantee of increased welfare (Dymski, 2007).

The differing nature of financial sectors between countries in the core and peripheral developing countries results in different policy priorities and regulations. This is vitally important to acknowledge as it helps explain why international standards designed by regulators from advanced economies are often poor fit for low- and lower-middle-income countries.

Table 2.1 Cross-country variation in financial sectors (by income category)

Income category	Domestic credit to private sector (% of GDP)	Share of total domestic credit to private sector from banks (% of total)	Market capitalization of listed domestic companies (% of GDP)	Commercial bank branches (per 100,000 adults)	Automated teller machines (ATMs) (per 100,000 adults)
High	143	58	118	20	66
Upper-Middle	108	98	58	15	50
Lower-Middle	42	98	53	8	18
Low	18	100	NA	3	4

Source: Extracted from World Development Indicators database, World Bank (2017), five-year averages (2013–17)

For financial sector regulators in the core of the global financial system, the primary challenge is to reduce excessive risk-taking and high levels of leverage in their largest banks which makes them a source of instability. These banks are highly complex and opaque, and, rather than intermediating funds, their income is largely derived from trading assets and selling complex financial products. This is reflected in the balance sheets of the largest US and UK banks, where derivates account for 30 to 40 per cent of assets (Buckley, 2016). These institutions are radically different in nature to local community banks, whose primary function is to mobilize savings and convert them into loans to firms and households. As we discuss below, Basel standards have become increasingly focused on the important task of regulating risk-taking in the world's largest banks. As a result, the standards have become less relevant for the regulation of the traditional commercial banks that dominate the financial sectors in most, although not all, peripheral developing countries. Many African financial systems are smaller than a mid-sized bank in continental Europe, with total assets often less than US$1 billion (Beck et al., 2009).

Financial stability is also an important policy objective for regulators in peripheral developing countries, but the sources of instability differ. At the level of individual domestic banks with relatively straightforward business models, sources of fragility stem from 'traditional' problems such as the under-reporting of non-performing loans, related-party lending, and obtaining an operating license on a fraudulent basis. These challenges are addressed in the Basel Core Principles rather than the most recent iterations of Basel II and III standards, which is why many international policymakers encourage regulators in peripheral developing countries to focus first and foremost on compliance with these principles.

At the systemic level, interconnectedness with global finance is a major source of financial instability in peripheral developing countries. As recent studies have shown, changing patterns of demand for capital in the core of the global financial system have a dramatic impact on the flows of capital to and from the periphery (Akyuz, 2010; Bauerle Danzman et al., 2017; Rey, 2015). A pressing question for regulators in developing countries is how best to use regulatory instruments, such as capital controls, to reduce these sources of financial instability that come from aboard (see for example Griffith-Jones et al., 2012; Gallagher, 2015; Grabel, 2017). Yet these sources of instability are not fully addressed in the Basel framework.

For policymakers in peripheral developing countries, financial stability is not the only policy priority; they also look to expand credit provision to the real economy, and to expand access to financial services. In many low- and lower-middle-income developing countries, a major problem is not that banks are taking too much risk but rather that they are taking on too little risk, investing in high-yielding, risk-free, government securities rather than lending to the private sector. Analysis in twenty-one countries in Sub-Saharan Africa revealed that government securities averaged 21 per cent of bank balance sheets in 2017 (Bodo, 2019). In some countries, including Angola, Burundi, and Sierra Leone, the levels were well above 30 per cent (IMF, 2018, p. 9). In such places, lending to governments has become central to banks' business strategies, rather than intermediating funds between depositors and private firms. Even where banks do lend to the private sector it doesn't always go to the most productive sectors. In many countries, banks have redirected credit away from production to trade and consumer financing, fuelling credit-financed consumption booms (Chandrasekhar, 2007).

Regulations are an important mechanism for shaping the incentives that banks face, and hence the purposes to which credit is channelled in the economy. Relatively minor changes such as adjusting loan classification and capital requirements so as not to bias against agricultural or loans to small- and medium-sized enterprises can be important (Beck et al., 2009). National development banks and activist financial policies can play a useful active role in directing finance towards productive sectors (Griffith-Jones and Ocampo, 2018). Yet the mandate of the Basel Committee and the standards it designs focus exclusively on financial stability and do not consider other regulatory objectives like improving access to credit for the productive economy or financial inclusion (Jones and Knaack, 2019).

More broadly, while policymakers in many developing countries are looking to find ways to expand and deepen the financial services sector, in many advanced economies there is a consensus that the financial sector is too big, heightening the risks of financial crises and attendant costs, and acting as a drag on economic growth (Arcand et al., 2012; Sahay et al., 2015).

Basel standards: a good 'fit' for peripheral developing countries?

Given the differing priorities between regulators from major industrialised countries and their counterparts in low- and lower-middle income countries, we can start to understand why international standards might be ill-suited for low and lower-middle income countries. We now turn to examine in more detail the mismatch between international banking standards and the regulation that is needed in peripheral developing countries.

The genesis of Basel standards lies in the costly failure of an internationally active bank in 1974, which prompted the central bank governors of the Group of Ten (G10) countries to create the Basel Committee on Banking Supervision. In its forty-plus-year history, the Basel Committee has formulated a series of cross-border prudential rules that are designed to enhance financial stability worldwide. Basel standards are part of a wider suite of international soft law standards and norms, which are not legally binding and do not have formal enforcement mechanisms. While most pronounced in international finance, international soft law standards have proliferated in many issue areas over the past two decades and they increasingly shape national regulations across the world (Brummer, 2010; Newman and Posner, 2018).

In this section we examine the various elements of the Basel framework in turn: the Basel Core Principles and the three iterations of prudential regulatory standards (Basel I, II, and III). For each, we explain what they are designed to do and the main criticisms levelled against them, focusing on those most pertinent to low- and lower-middle-income countries.

Basel Core Principles: rationale and criticisms

The Basel Core Principles for Effective Banking Supervision (hereafter 'Basel Core Principles') were issued by the Basel Committee in 1997 and have been widely adopted. The twenty-nine Basel Core Principles cover central aspects of what the Basel Committee believes to be an effective supervisory system, including supervisory powers, the need for early intervention, and bank compliance (Basel Committee on Banking Supervision, 2012).

The Basel Core Principles are designed to be a flexible, globally applicable standard, with assessment criteria designed to accommodate a diverse range of banking systems. They take a proportional approach, which allows assessments of compliance with the Core Principles that are commensurate with the risk profile and systemic importance of a broad spectrum of banks (from large internationally active banks to small, non-complex deposit-taking institutions) (Basel Committee on Banking Supervision, 2012). The Basel Core Principles focus on the overall quality and approach of supervisors, and while they are quite prescriptive, they still provide national regulators with considerable discretion. For instance, they require that the bank supervisor 'sets prudent and appropriate capital adequacy requirements' but they explicitly state that these do not need to be based on Basel standards, although for internationally active banks, capital requirements must be 'not less than the applicable Basel standards' (Principle 16).

Although compatible with a wide range of regulatory approaches, the Basel Core Principles are only designed to assess the safety and stability of the banking sector. They do not evaluate supervisors or regulations against other policy objectives such as financial sector deepening or financial inclusion. Moreover, state intervention in credit allocation is perceived as problematic: policy-directed lending and the general use of financial intermediaries as instruments of government policy are identified as distorting market signals and impeding effective supervision (Basel Committee on Banking Supervision, 2012). In line with the underlying market-based approach to credit allocation, the Basel Core Principles expect the institutions charged with responsibility for bank supervision to have operational independence, so they are free from political interference, and have the relevant legal powers to ensure compliance (Basel Committee on Banking Supervision, 2012). Thus, while the Basel Core Principles are generally applicable in countries where governments pursue market-based credit allocation, they are much less relevant to countries pursuing policies of policy-directed credit, including the types of financial sector policies used by many of the East Asian tiger economies, which some governments in low- and lower-middle-income countries are looking to emulate.

The Basel Core Principles have become the *de facto* minimum standard for the sound prudential regulation and supervision of banks and banking systems around the world. In the wake of the East Asian financial crisis of 1997, the IMF and World Bank started to include the Basel Core Principles in their regular Financial Sector Assessment Programmes (FSAPs). Yet, despite their widespread acceptance as the international benchmark for evaluating bank supervision, there is surprisingly little evidence that compliance with the Basel Core Principles actually improves the financial stability or the wider performance of the banking system (Ayadi et al., 2015; Das et al., 2005; Demirgüç-Kunt and Detragiache, 2010; Podpiera, 2004; Sundararajan et al., 2001). The paucity of evidence supporting the Basel Core Principles has led several leading experts to question the desirability of the Basel Committee's approach to banking supervision (Ayadi et al., 2015; Barth et al., 2006; Demirgüç-Kunt and Detragiache, 2010).

Basel I: Rationale and criticisms

Alongside the Basel Core Principles, the Basel Committee has issued a series of minimum standards for capital adequacy regulations. The Basel Accord on the International Convergence of Capital Measures and Capital Standards (Basel I) was agreed in 1988 (Basel Committee on Banking Supervision, 1988). While some scholars argue that Basel I standards were designed to provide the public good of financial stability (Kapstein, 1989), others argue that Basel I standards were motivated by a redistributive logic amidst fierce competition between banks in the United States and Japan (Chey, 2014; Drezner, 2007; Oatley and Nabors, 1998; Simmons, 2001).

The key idea behind capital adequacy requirements for banks, including Basel I, is to ensure that each bank finances a minimum portion of its loan portfolio with shareholders' equity (capital) rather than debt. The basic business model of a commercial bank is to take on liabilities by way of short-term debt provided by retail depositors and the wholesale money markets and use them to make medium- and long-term loans to businesses and households. This is an important social function as banks, particularly in developing countries, can help channel credit to productive economy. Yet it also exposes banks to risks. A bank may mis-judge the creditworthiness of its borrowers (credit risk) or an unexpected withdrawal of funds by short-term lenders, which exhausts its liquid assets (Armour et al., 2016, p. 290).

Capital requirements are the standard regulatory mechanisms for addressing these risks: the higher the level of a bank's capital (shareholders' equity), the less the risk of balance sheet insolvency, because any losses the bank incurs on its assets will first fall on its shareholders (Armour et al., 2016, p. 290). Thus 'leverage'—the ratio of the bank's debt funding to its funding through equity or capital—is always a central issue in regulation. The more equity, the safer the bank, but a bank funded entirely by equity would achieve no transformation (Armour et al., 2016, p. 291). Capital requirements place a restriction on a bank's leverage, constraining the extent to which a bank can finance itself through debt, but aim to do so without quashing the bank's incentive to engage in maturity transformation and lending to the productive economy.

Basel I focused on requiring banks to hold capital against *credit risk*, the risk that borrowers will not repay. In recognition that some assets are riskier than others, the Basel Committee agreed that the level of capital that banks were required to hold would be risk-weighted, so that higher amounts of capital would be held against risker assets. Rather than calculate the credit risk associated with each asset on the bank's balance sheet, Basel I simply categorized assets into five groups, and assigned risk weights ranging from 0 to 100 per cent. For instance, cash and gold held in the bank is risk-free and attracted a risk weight of 0 per cent, residential mortgages attracted a risk weight of 50 per cent, and loans to firms attracted risk weights of 100 per cent. Overall, Basel I required banks to finance at least 8 per cent of their total risk-weighted assets with capital.

Within a few years of Basel I being issued, there were calls for its reform. A key criticism was that the standards only focused on credit risk. With the expansion of the investment banking activities of large banks, it became clear that *trading risk* (the risk that securities banks hold, for market making or proprietary trading, suffer a decline in market value) was an important source of fragility. In 1996, the 'market risk amendment' to Basel I was designed to bring trading risks explicitly within the Basel framework (Basel Committee on Banking Supervision, 1996). As large banks became more complex, the risk of employee fraud rose, prompting calls for *operational risk* (the risk of loss resulting from inadequate or failed internal processes, people, and systems, or from external events) to be incorporated too. Critics further argued that the five categories for establishing credit risk were too crude. Basel I did not sufficiently differentiate between assets and it did not cover all types of assets (Blundell-Wignall and Atkinson, 2010). For instance, risk weights did not differentiate between loans made to small, risky firms and large, highly rated multinationals (Barth et al., 2006). The shortcomings of Basel I led to the negotiation of Basel II standards.

Basel II: Rationale and criticisms

Basel II was agreed in 2004, after several years of intense negotiations in the Basel Committee and heavy lobbying by large banks (Lall, 2012; e.g. Tarullo, 2008; Young, 2012). Under Basel II, the Basel Committee kept several basic parameters of Basel I in place, including the definitions of eligible capital and the 8 per cent minimum capital adequacy requirement. But they made several dramatic changes, including to the system for risk-weighting assets. Crucially, under Basel II, responsibility for risk-weighting and risk assessment was moved from regulators to credit ratings agencies and banks. The market risk amendment of 1996 introduced the principle that, subject to supervisory permission, banks could do the risk-weighting on the basis of their own historical data relating to losses and on the basis of their own evaluation models. This permission was extended to the assessment of credit risk and operational risk assessment in Basel II.

Basel II sets out nine different approaches for risk-weighting and risk assessment (Table 2.2). These can be divided into two general types. Under the 'standardized approaches' the key parameters for assessing risk are either given to banks by the supervisor or generated by third parties (private credit rating agencies or export credit agencies) (Powell, 2004). These include the *simplified-standardized approach* for assessing credit risk; the *standardized approach* for assessing credit risk; the *basic indicator approach* and *standardized approach* for assessing operational risk; and the *standardized approach* for assessing market risk.

The remaining four approaches allow banks to use their own internal models for evaluating the riskiness of assets and assigning risk weights. There are two IRB

Table 2.2 Capital adequacy requirements under Basel II

Credit risk				Operational risk			Market risk	
Simplified-standardized approach	Standardized approach	Foundation-internal ratings-based approach	Advanced-internal ratings-based approach	Basic indicator approach	Standardized approach	Advanced measurement approach	Standardized measurement method	Internal models approach

approaches for assessing credit risk. Under the *foundation IRB approach* banks are allowed to estimate probabilities of default for each borrower, while under the *advanced IRB approach* banks also estimate other parameters, such as loss given default and exposure at default. For operational risk there is the *advanced measurement approach* and for market risk there is the *internal models approach*.

In addition to revised capital adequacy requirements (Pillar 1), Basel II introduced a supervisory review process that built on and integrated many of the Basel Core Principles (Pillar 2). It also introduced financial disclosure requirements that require banks to disclose their financial condition and risk-management processes to investors, in order to improve market discipline (Pillar 3).

General criticisms of Basel II

Basel II has been widely criticized for dramatically increasing the complexity of the regulatory framework and exacerbating many of the risks leading up to the global financial crisis.

The most controversial aspect of Basel II was the introduction of internal model-based approaches, which has been likened to 'allowing banks to mark their own examination papers' (Haldane cited in Parliamentary Commission on Banking Standards, 2013, p. 119). These approaches were enthusiastically embraced by large banks, as the costs of compliance were marginal (they already had sophisticated in-house systems for assessing risk) and they enabled the banks to hold lower levels of capital than they would have under the standardized approaches. The system worked poorly in the run-up to the 2008 crisis, especially for the risk-weighting of items on the trading book. The risk weights that banks assigned to their assets, and hence the amount of regulatory capital they needed to hold declined, at the same time as the risk profile of their investments dramatically increased. As many critics argued, the fatal flaw was to shift responsibility for assigning risk weights from regulators to banks, enabling the banks to calibrate the models to their advantage (Admati, 2016; Bayoumi, 2017; Haldane, 2013; Lall, 2012; Persaud, 2013; Tarullo, 2008; Underhill and Zhang, 2008).

The reliance of standardized approaches on external credit ratings agencies (e.g. Moody's, Standard and Poor's) was also criticized for leading to mechanistic reliance on ratings by market participants, resulting in insufficient due diligence and poor risk management on the part of lenders and investors. In addition, under Basel II, loans to highly rated clients attracted lower capital charges, which negatively affected the many small banks and small corporate clients with low or no ratings, even though they were not necessarily riskier, and were certainly less significant in systemic terms (Underhill and Zhang, 2008). The implementation of Basel II can thus reduce the scale of lending to (low or unrated) small- and medium-sized enterprises.

A further problem with Basel II is that its more market-sensitive risk measurements can exacerbate financial cycles (Persaud, 2013; Repullo and Suarez, 2008). While banking regulation should act as a check on the financial cycle, the switch to a 'risk-sensitive' approach amplified the global financial crisis (Persaud, 2013, p. 61).

Specific challenges for developing countries

Beyond these general criticisms, Basel II poses specific challenges for regulators and banks in developing countries. An immediate challenge arises from the sheer complexity of the Basel II standards. Supervisory capacity is a particularly acute constraint in developing countries, and can be a major deterrent to moving from relatively simple compliance-based supervision under Basel I to risk-based supervision under Basel II (Beck, 2011; Fuchs et al., 2013; Gottschalk, 2010; Griffith-Jones and Gottschalk, 2016). To effectively supervise the standardized approach to credit risk for instance, supervisors face the additional tasks of monitoring credit rating agencies and the appropriate use of their ratings by banks. In a survey conducted by the Financial Stability Board, national supervisors from emerging and developing countries cited a shortage of high-quality human resources as the most important constraint to the implementation of Basel II and III (FSB, 2013). Where supervisory resources are particularly constrained, implementing a simpler regulatory framework may lead to more effective banking supervision.

Regulators in some emerging countries seek to implement internal ratings-based approaches, hoping to improve banks' own internal risk management (Powell, 2004). However, supervisors run the risk that banks will use their comparative advantage over supervisors in resources, expertise, and experience to calibrate the models to their advantage, as they have in more developed countries. Full compliance with the internal model-based approaches relies on highly skilled regulators using judgement and discretion, thereby placing an even bigger onus on regulators to be independent, immune from lawsuits, and willing to challenge the well connected (Calice, 2010; Murinde and Mlambo, 2010).

Recognizing that not all banks (or regulators) have the capacity to use internal models, the Basel Committee provides national authorities with a range of different options to consider when implementing the standards. In many Basel member countries only the largest banks are authorized to use internal models (Castro Carvalho et al., 2017). The simplified-standardized approach was specifically introduced for regulators in developing countries in recognition of the additional resource constraints they face. However, as a World Bank report notes, for small and lower-income countries, the full range of options proposed by the Basel Committee is not properly thought through, resulting in the adoption of overly complex regulations for their level of economic and financial development (World Bank, 2012).

Weaknesses in financial sector infrastructure, particularly gaps in the availability of credit ratings and credit information, can also frustrate efforts to implement Basel II. Many countries outside the Basel Committee do not have national ratings agencies and the penetration of global ratings agencies is limited to the largest corporations (Murinde, 2012). The development of a local credit ratings industry is not straightforward—as well as effective reporting and corporate governance frameworks for companies, it requires strong accounting and external auditing rules, credit bureaus, and the efficient and compliant collection and sharing of borrowers' data (Stephanou and Mendoza, 2005). Where credit ratings are not available the standardized approach can still be used for assessing credit risk, but the risk weights applied to bank assets are very similar to Basel I, undermining the incentive for regulators to move from Basel I to Basel II.

The absence of external credit ratings may also impede implementation of the internal model-based approaches to assessing credit risk under Basel II. Although banks use their own internal models to generate credit ratings under these approaches, supervisors need to validate these models, and they commonly benchmark the ratings generated by banks against those generated by external ratings agencies in order to do so. Where the market or external ratings are shallow, validation becomes harder.

Basel II aims to encourage market discipline as a 'counterweight' to the increased discretion accorded to banks in the estimation of their own capital requirements. However, it is only likely to be useful in countries where banks are publicly listed and capital markets are sufficiently deep and liquid for the market to act as a source of discipline (Powell, 2004). As we have seen above, capital markets are in their infancy in many low- and lower-middle-income countries.

Basel III: Rationale and criticisms

The global financial crisis prompted soul-searching among regulators and led many regulators and experts to call for a major overhaul of international banking standards.

Designed in the wake of the crisis, Basel III seeks to correct many of the deficiencies in Basel II, but many argue it doesn't go far enough. While some aspects of Basel III have been welcomed by regulators from developing countries, particularly the greater emphasis on systemic sources of risk, Basel III is even more complex and challenging to implement than Basel II. Basel II revises capital standards and introduces new liquidity standards (Table 2.3). While an improvement on Basel II, the overall level of capital banks are required to hold still falls far below the minimum levels recommended by many experts, as we discuss below.

Table 2.3 Key components of Basel III

Microprudential						Macroprudential	
Capital requirements				**Liquidity requirements**			
Definition of Capital	Capital Conservation Buffer	Risk Coverage for Counterparty Credit Risk	Leverage Ratio	Liquidity Coverage Ratio	Net Stable Funding Ratio	Countercyclical Buffer	Domestic Systemically Important Banks
							Global Systemically Important Banks

Under Basel III, the basic capital requirement remains 8 per cent of risk-weighted assets, but stricter rules are introduced on the eligibility of capital instruments that can be included (*definition of capital*)[1] and new capital buffers are designed to make banks hold higher levels of capital. The *capital conservation buffer* (2.5 per cent of risk-weighted assets) applies to all banks all of the time and is designed to ensure that banks build up capital buffers outside periods of stress.[2]

While the capital conservation buffer is microprudential in nature as it seeks to improve the stability of individual banks, the other buffers are macroprudential as they aim to reduce systemic risk. The *countercyclical buffer* allows regulators to increase capital requirements by a further 2.5 per cent of risk-weighted assets when they judge credit growth to result in an unacceptable build-up of system-wide risk. Finally, the additional buffers apply to *global systemically important banks* (G-SIBs) and *domestic systematically important banks* (D-SIBs). This buffer varies between 1 per cent and 3.5 per cent of risk-weighted assets for G-SIBs while national regulators determine the size of the buffer for D-SIBs (Basel Committee on Banking Supervision, 2013a).[3]

Basel III also introduces measures to strengthen the capital requirements for trading risk, specifically for the counterparty credit exposures arising from banks' derivatives, repurchase, and securities-financing activities (*counterparty credit risk*).[4] A flaw in Basel II had been to assume that the securities held by banks would be traded in deep and liquid markets, so any potential loss the bank faced from holding securities assets on its books was temporary. The global financial crisis showed that this was not the case for many assets on bank trading books, and banks were exposed to the risk of default by the counterparty. While a welcome addition to Basel III, many argue that the methods for assessing counterparty credit risk remain problematic (Armour et al., 2016, p. 298).

Given all the challenges with accurately assigning risk weights, Basel III introduces a simple *leverage ratio* of capital to non-risk-weighted assets to act as a 'back-stop' to the risk-based capital framework (Basel Committee on Banking

---

[1] The Basel minimum capital requirement comprises two main components: shareholders' equity (called 'core equity Tier 1 capital' or CET1 in the Basel nomenclature). Under Basel I and II, only one-quarter of the 8 per cent (i.e. 2 per cent) had to be contributed through CET1. Under Basel III, that increases to 4.5 per cent (Basel Committee on Banking Supervision, 2010). Under Basel II, the remainder of the 8 per cent capital could be shareholders' equity or subordinated debt. The inclusion of subordinated debt has been heavily criticized as it does not improve the ratio of shareholder equity to assets. The use of subordinated debt is not removed in Basel III, although its use is restricted (Armour et al., 2016, p. 305).

[2] While banks can draw on this buffer, they face restrictions on pay-outs to shareholders and employees.

[3] Overall, then, Basel III raises the CET1 requirement from 2 per cent to 7 per cent (4.5 per cent minimum CET1 plus 2.5 per cent capital conservation buffer) for all banks, and up to 13 per cent for G-SIBs, plus an additional 2.5 per cent if an asset bubble is developing (the countercyclical buffer).

[4] These were introduced under Basel 2.5, and modified under Basel III.

Supervision, 2010). However as it is set at only 3 per cent of assets, it has been criticized for being 'dangerously low' (Admati, 2016; Admati and Hellwig, 2014).

Basel III also introduced liquidity standards for the first time. The objective of the *liquidity coverage ratio* (LCR) is to ensure that banks have an adequate stock of assets that can be converted easily into cash to meet their liquidity needs in a thirty-day stress scenario (Basel Committee on Banking Supervision, 2013b). The *net stable funding ratio* (NSFR) is a longer-term measure to reduce the likelihood that disruptions to a bank's regular sources of funding will erode its liquidity position in a way that would increase the risk of its failure (Basel Committee on Banking Supervision, 2014).

General criticisms of Basel III

Basel III is a clear improvement over its predecessors, as it requires banks to hold more, higher-quality capital and introduces macroprudential standards that address systemic risks in the financial sector. Yet many argue that the changes fall far short of what is needed. The vice-chair of the US Federal Deposit Insurance Corporation (FDIC) called Basel III a 'well-intended illusion' (T.M. Hoenig, 2013).

A major flaw is that Basel III continues to allow banks to use complex, potentially flawed, and gameable internal models (Admati, 2016; Haldane, 2013; T. Hoenig, 2013; Kashyap et al., 2008; Romano, 2014; Tarullo, 2008).[5] It also continues to rely on the assessments of credit rating agencies, despite a wealth of evidence that these are often an unreliable assessment of risk. Attempts by the Basel Committee to reduce the reliance on credit rating agencies have been dropped following intense lobbying by banks and credit ratings agencies (Binham, 2015).

A further problem for Basel III, and indeed for its predecessors, is that regulatory capital ratios are based primarily on accounting conventions that can be quite arbitrary and vary by jurisdictions. Balance sheet disclosures tend to obscure significant exposures to risk, allowing much risk to lurk 'off balance sheet', and to manipulate the disclosures, particularly since auditors are subject to their own conflicts of interest and are unlikely to challenge managers (Admati, 2016).

Overall, then, leading financial sector experts agree that while Basel III makes modest improvements on Basel II, it fails to address the sources of financial instability and has done little to avert future crises. Basel III is still based on a system of risk-weighting which arguably distorts bank portfolios away from business lending and towards government lending and other investments (Admati, 2016). Many argue that much simpler metrics, including leverage ratios

---

[5] The Basel Committee has acknowledged that banks' internal models can be deeply flawed and has introduced a common 'output floor' for risk estimates (Basel Committee on Banking Supervision, 2016; Maxwell and Smith-Meyer, 2017). Basel III also tightens some input estimates for modelling, and removes the internal ratings-based approach for operational risk entirely (Coen, 2017).

that require banks to hold higher levels of equity, are more effective forms of regulation (Haldane, 2013).

Specific challenges for developing countries

Over and above these concerns with the efficacy of Basel III standards for regulating the world's largest banks, regulators of low- and lower-middle-income countries face specific challenges in implementing Basel III.

Basel III adds a further layer of complexity and compliance costs, exacerbating the implementation challenges associated with Basel II (as an indication, Basel I was thirty pages long and the full compendium of Basel III standards runs to more than 1800 pages). Some elements of Basel III are relatively straightforward to implement, including the new definitions of capital, the capital conservation buffer, the simple leverage ratio, and the standard for domestic systemically important banks. Others are more challenging, including the macroprudential elements.

The introduction of macroprudential standards is generally welcomed by regulators from developing countries. However, macroprudential standards under Basel III need to be adapted to reflect the main sources of systemic risk in many developing countries, which often stem from external macroeconomic shocks including fluctuations in commodity prices, volatile capital flows, and a high level of interconnectedness among banks (Gottschalk, 2016, p. 61; Kasekende et al., 2012; Repullo and Saurina, 2011). Many developing countries already impose some form of liquidity requirements. However, Basel III liquidity standards are calculated on more sophisticated methodologies than for most other Basel standards and the assumptions underpinning them do not always hold in countries with less-mature financial markets and banking systems, so the standards need to be modified to suit the local contexts (Beck, 2011; Ferreira et al. 2019; Fuchs et al., 2013; Gobat et al., 2014).

The implementation of Basel III is likely to be impeded by a paucity of credit information as macroprudential standards require regulators to obtain a more comprehensive picture of interconnected risks in the financial sector. Credit registry data is important for evaluating the systemic importance of financial institutions, which is vital for establishing which banks should be subject to additional capital buffers (the D-SIB standard). Such data is also important for making decisions about countercyclical buffers (World Bank, 2012). Regulators may not have the powers or resources to implement macroprudential elements of Basel III. In many countries, national authorities lack dedicated units for conducting macroprudential surveillance, and even where they do exist they often face many practical challenges, including gathering data and specifying models to be used in stress-testing (Murinde, 2012; Ferreira et al. 2019). While there are good arguments for strengthening regulatory authorities, moves to do so may generate opposition, as we discuss in Chapter 3.

More generally, there are concerns that Basel III further increases the incentives of banks to direct credit away from productive sectors of the economy that are key for inclusive economic development (Beck, 2018; Bodo, 2019; Gobat et al., 2014; Rojas-Suarez and Muhammad, 2018). Implementation of such complex standards may also take scarce resources away from other priority tasks of the regulatory agency (Griffith-Jones and Gottschalk, 2016; Barth and Caprio, 2018). Implementation of Basel II/III does not necessarily address underlying weaknesses in the regulatory system or the political entrenchment of vested interests and, where regulators are under-resourced, can open up more opportunities for banks to evade regulations. In sum, the global standards embody a complex financial regulatory regime, not necessarily a strong one (Basel Consultative Group, 2014; Powell, 2004).

How peripheral countries are responding to Basel II and III

So how are peripheral developing countries responding to international standards? How much of the Basel framework are they implementing?

Given the deep-seated challenges facing Basel standards, even in countries that are members of the Basel Committee, regulators rarely apply the full suite of Basel standards to all banks. Regulators from countries on the Basel Committee typically adopt a proportional approach, only applying the full suite of Basel standards to large internationally active banks, with balance sheets of more than US$20–30 billion (Castro Carvalho et al., 2017). In the United States, small banks with less than US$500 million in assets are exempt from Basel III and are regulated under standards similar to Basel I (Masera, 2014). In Brazil, the central bank has divided banks into five different categories, and only applies the Basel III framework to the six largest internationally active banks, with more than US$10 billion in assets abroad. Similarly, in Hong Kong, the regulator allows banks with total assets of less than US$10 billion and a simple and straightforward business model to hold capital against credit risk in accordance with a modified version of Basel I, while banks with small trading books are exempted from the Basel market risk capital framework (Castro Carvalho et al., 2017).

For developing countries, Barth and Caprio (2018) argue that the Basel approach is too cumbersome and costly for countries with small financial sectors, particularly countries with banking systems with total assets of less than US$10 billion. Meanwhile, the Financial Stability Board, World Bank, and IMF explicitly advise countries with limited international financial exposure and supervisory capacity constraints to 'first focus on reforms to ensure compliance with the Basel Core Principles and only move to the more advanced capital standards at a pace tailored to their circumstances' (FSB et al., 2011, p. 7).

As we show in this section, the Basel framework is being widely applied and regulators outside of the Basel Committee vary rarely implement regulations that are not based on the Basel framework in some way. However, implementation is highly selective, with regulators implementing some elements and not others, and there is a high level of variation across countries.

Patterns of Basel implementation

Data on the implementation of the Basel framework is patchy for countries outside of the Basel Committee. The available data suggests that compliance with the Basel Core Principles varies tremendously across countries and are generally correlated with levels of economic development. A study based on 137 Financial Sector Assessment Programme reports between 2000 and 2004 showed that compliance rates averaged 89 per cent in high-income countries, 64 per cent in upper-middle-income countries, 54 per cent in lower-middle-income countries, and 52 per cent in low-income countries (IMF, 2008). More recent analysis of compliance across seventeen African countries based on Financial Sector Assessment Programme reports between 2007 and 2012 revealed variation even among countries at similar levels of development. Three of the seventeen African countries had compliance rates with Basel Core Principles of less than 50 per cent; a further eight had compliance rates between 50 and 80 per cent; while six had compliance rates above 80 per cent (Marchettini et al., 2015, p. 28).

With regards to the implementation of Basel I, II, and III, there is also substantial variation. Basel I standards spread rapidly around the world and within ten years were being implemented by more than one hundred countries outside of the Basel Committee (Quillin, 2008; Stephanou and Mendoza, 2005; Tarullo, 2008). A recent survey of regulators in one hundred countries outside of the Basel Committee shows that Basel I is still the basis for national regulations in many countries: of the one hundred countries, sixty had national regulations based on Basel I, while ten had national regulations based on Basel II, and thirty on Basel III (Hohl et al., 2018).

Another survey, conducted by the Financial Stability Institute (FSI) in 2015 provides the most detailed data we have on Basel II and III implementation in countries outside of the Basel Committee.[6] It provides insights into which elements of Basel II and III are being implemented and identifies countries where

---

[6] This survey covers a similar number of countries to Hohl et al. (2018) but is not directly comparable as it covers a different set of countries and uses a different set of criteria for differentiating between countries.

preparations are underway but implementation is yet to happen.[7] Regulators in ninety of the one hundred responding jurisdictions stated that they were either implementing at least one component of Basel II or had taken steps to do so, including drafting new rules. Only ten reported that they had not taken any steps to implement Basel II. Similarly, eighty-one of the one hundred responding jurisdictions reported that they were implementing at least one component of Basel III, or had taken steps to do so, leaving only seventeen that had not begun the implementation process.

The FSI data from 2015 reveals some regional variations. The highest implementation is in Middle Eastern and North African countries, where all twelve of the reporting jurisdictions were implementing at least one element of Basel II, and nine were adopting at least one component of Basel III. Latin America and the Caribbean had the lowest levels of adoption, with only thirteen of twenty-eight responding countries implementing at least one component of Basel II, and only five implementing at least one component of Basel III. These trends broadly correspond to the trends reported in the survey by Hohl et al. (2018, p. 8).

A striking insight from the FSI survey data is that while many countries are converging on international standards, regulators are taking a highly selective approach to implementation. As at 2015, the one hundred countries responding to the FSI survey were implementing an average of four of the ten components of Basel II and one of the eight components of Basel III. As we might expect, the extent of implementation is correlated with income levels (Figure 2.1). On average, regulators in high-income countries outside of the Basel Committee were implementing double the number of components of the Basel II compared to their counterparts in low- and lower-middle-income countries.

Jones and Zeitz (2017) used the FSI data to analyse the adoption of Basel II and found a robust and positive correlation between a country's financial sector development and the extent of Basel II adoption. This suggests that regulators' decisions are strongly influenced by the suitability of the Basel standards to their country's level of financial sector development. Yet, even among high-income countries where implementation levels were highest, regulators were implementing just under half of the components of Basel II, ten years after the standard had been agreed by the Basel Committee.

---

[7] For Basel II the survey examines ten subcomponents: (1) standardized approach to credit risk; (2) foundation-internal ratings-based approach to credit risk; (3) advanced-internal ratings-based approach to credit risk; (4) basic indicator approach to operational risk; (5) standardized approach to operational risk; (6) advanced measurement approach to operational risk; (7) standardized measurement method for market risk; (8) internal models approach to market risk; (9) Pillar 2 (Supervision); (10) Pillar 3 (Market Discipline). For Basel III the survey covers eight subcomponents: (1) liquidity coverage ratio; (2) definition of capital; (3) risk coverage (for counterparty credit risk); (4) capital conservation buffer; (5) counter-cyclical capital buffer; (6) leverage ratio; (7) domestic-systemically important banks; (8) global-systemically important banks.

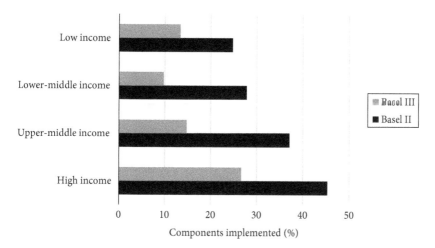

Figure 2.1 Implementation of Basel II and III by income category (countries outside of the Basel Committee).

Source: Data from FSI Survey (2015). Income categories are according to World Bank classifications for the same year

Which components of Basel II and III are being adopted?

Disaggregating the FSI data provides insights into the specific components of Basel II and III that are most and least likely to be adopted by regulators outside of the Basel Committee.

With regards to Basel II, regulators are more likely to adopt standards for credit risk and operational risk than market risk (Figure 2.2). This stands to reason, as many peripheral countries have banks with very small trading books. Relatively few jurisdictions allow banks to use the heavily criticised internal model-based approaches. Regulators in fifty-nine jurisdictions required banks to assess credit risk according to the standardized approach and, of these, only seventeen authorized banks to use internal model-based approaches. Interestingly, the number of countries using internal model-based approaches did not increase between 2010 and 2015, possibly reflecting the criticism attributed to these approaches in the wake of the 2008 financial crisis.

As Basel III was relatively new at the time of the 2015 FSI survey, it is harder to discern trends. However, the data indicates that the more familiar microprudential components of Basel III were being implemented more frequently than the newer macroprudential components (Figure 2.3).

Among the microprudential elements of Basel III, thirty-four of the one hundred jurisdictions responding to the survey had adopted the new definitions of capital and twenty-four had adopted the capital conservation buffer. These components were a modification of Basel II and relatively straightforward to implement. The new Basel III standards for assessing counterparty credit risk had only

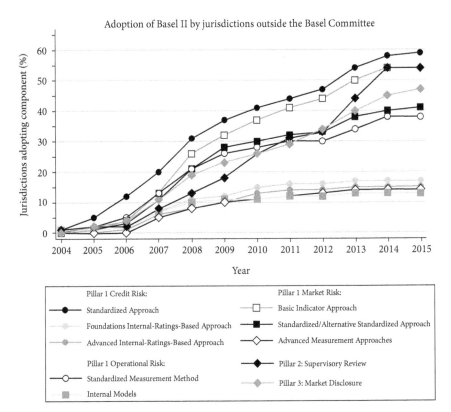

Figure 2.2 Which components of Basel II are being implemented?
Source: Data from FSI Survey (2015)

been implemented by ten jurisdictions, presumably reflecting the small size of trading books in banks in many peripheral countries. The 2015 data shows a relatively rapid take-up of the leverage ratio, the 'back-stop' to risk-weighted capital measures, which had been adopted by thirteen of the forty-one jurisdictions, even though it was only introduced in 2018. Hohl et al. (2018) find similar trends, with regulators in countries outside of the Basel Committee prioritizing the implementation of the Basel III definitions of capital and related capital buffers (Hohl et al., 2018, p. 11).

Although liquidity standards were a new addition to the Basel framework, the 2015 and 2018 data shows that regulators have moved relatively quickly to implement the liquidity coverage ratio (Hohl et al., 2018, p. 12). This may reflect the fact that many countries already had domestic quantitative liquidity rules well before their introduction in the Basel framework, making it relatively straightforward to implement. Regulators proceeding far more slowly in adopting the net stable funding ratio, probably because it is challenging to implement

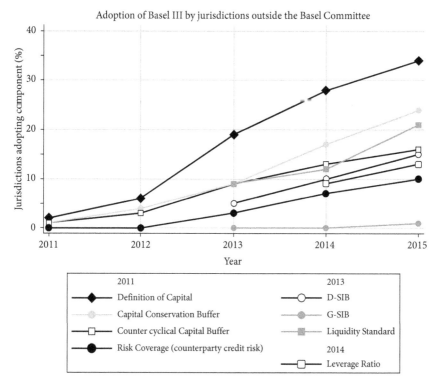

Figure 2.3 Which components of Basel III are being implemented?
Source: Data from FSI Survey (2015)

in countries that do not have well-developed capital markets, leaving fewer options for banks to source the term funding needed to comply with the standard (Hohl et al., 2018, p. 10).

Recent reports show that, in addition to taking a highly selective approach, regulators use other strategies to modify the standards to better fit their local context. Regulators have often made overall capital requirements more stringent than Basel standards. They have also relaxed rules in other areas where, in their view, the adoption of applicable Basel standards may not be warranted based on the risk profile or business model of banks in their jurisdictions. Specific examples of modifications to Basel standards include (Castro Carvalho et al., 2017; Hohl et al., 2018):

- raising minimum risk-weighted capital requirements above 8 per cent
- exempting banks with small trading books from market risk and counter-party credit risk requirements and simplifying risk calculations (e.g. only considering foreign exchange rate risks in market risk calculations)

- exempting small banks from capital charges for operational risk
- regulating large commercial banks according to Basel III risk-based capital requirements, but applying Basel I to small banks and/or specialized banks (e.g. development finance banks)
- exempting some banks from liquidity standards (e.g. development finance institutions)
- imposing leverage requirements that are higher than the Basel III requirement of 3 per cent.

Our case studies

This section provides an overview of the varying responses to Basel standards among our eleven case study countries and regions, and highlights the key attributes of their financial sectors, noting the ways in which they differ. In doing so it provides a context for the analysis of Basel convergence and divergence in subsequent chapters.

Varying responses to Basel standards

There is a striking variation among our case study countries in their responses to the Basel framework. There is limited public data on compliance with Basel Core Principles. A study of Financial Sector Assessment Programme reports between 2007 and 2012 covers seven of our case study countries and reveals substantial variation. Among the seven countries, two had compliance rates with Basel Core Principles of less than 50 per cent (Angola and Ghana); a further three had compliance rates between 50 and 80 per cent (Kenya, Nigeria, and WAEMU); while two had compliance rates above 80 per cent (Rwanda and Tanzania) (Marchettini et al., 2015, p. 28).

While Ethiopia remains on Basel I, regulators in the other case study countries and regions have opted to implement components of the more complex and recent Basel II and III (Table 2.4). Ethiopia aside, all are implementing components of Basel II and, with the further exceptions of Vietnam and Angola, they are also implementing components of Basel III. While no regulator has implemented all eighteen of the key components of Basel II and III, Pakistan comes close, as regulators have implemented fourteen. At the other end of the spectrum, regulators in Vietnam have only implemented three.

Regulators have tended to implement the less complex elements of Basel II and III, in line with the broad trends established above. Among the ten countries and regions implementing Basel II, all regulators have implemented the standardized

Table 2.4 How extensively are case study countries implementing Basel II and III? (January 2019)

| Country | Number of Components Implemented | | |
	Basel II (out of 10)	Basel III (out of 8)	Total
Pakistan	9	5	14
WAEMU	5	5	10
Rwanda	5	4	9
Ghana	3	5	8
Tanzania	5	3	8
Kenya	5	2	7
Nigeria	5	1	6
Bolivia	3	2	5
Angola	5	0	5
Vietnam	3	0	3
Ethiopia	0	0	0

approaches to credit risk, and, with the additional exception of Bolivia, they have also implemented the standardized approaches to operational and market risk. Only Pakistan has authorized the use of internal models. Regulators in all countries except Ghana and Ethiopia have implemented the supervisory review process introduced under Basel II, which built on and integrated many of the Basel Core Principles (Pillar 2). The same group of regulators have also introduced financial disclosure requirements, which require banks to disclose their financial condition and risk-management processes to investors, in order to improve market discipline (Pillar 3).

There is more variation in the implementation of Basel III (Table 2.5). Among the eight countries and regions implementing aspects of Basel III, seven have implemented the revised definitions of capital, six have implemented capital conservation buffers, and five have implemented the leverage ratio. Three countries have implemented requirements for domestic systemically important banks, while two have implemented the countercyclical buffer, and two have implemented liquidity requirements.

Do financial sector differences explain responses?

We might reasonably expect variation across our case studies in their responses to Basel standards to be the result of differing levels of financial sector development. Yet, analysis of the key financial sector attributes across our case study countries suggests this is not the case. There is no obvious correlation between the level of financial sector development and the extent of the Basel framework that is being adopted.

Table 2.5 Which components of Basel III are case study countries implementing? (January 2019)

Microprudential						Macroprudential		
Capital requirements			Liquidity requirements					
Definition of Capital	Capital Conservation Buffer	Risk Coverage for Counterparty Credit Risk	Leverage Ratio	Liquidity Coverage Ratio	Net Stable Funding Ratio	Countercyclical Buffer	Domestic Systemically Important Banks	Global Systemically Important Banks
Bolivia, Ghana, Kenya, Pakistan, Rwanda, Tanzania, WAEMU	Ghana, Kenya, Pakistan, Rwanda, Tanzania, WAEMU	–	Ghana, Pakistan, Rwanda, Tanzania, WAEMU	Pakistan, WAEMU	Pakistan, WAEMU	Bolivia, Ghana	Ghana, Nigeria, Rwanda	–

Our case study countries differ markedly (Table 2.6). A first striking difference is in the level of general economic development and the size of their economies. Per capital incomes range from Angola with a GNI per capita of over US$4,000 per year to Ethiopia and Burkina Faso where it is just over US$400. Our cases include relatively large countries like Nigeria with a total GDP of US$472 billion, and Rwanda with a GDP of just US$8 billion.

The size of the financial sector varies from US$233bn in liquid assets in Vietnam to only US$4bn in Burkina Faso and US$1bn in Rwanda. Relative to the size of the economy, the financial sector is smallest in Tanzania, Ghana, Nigeria, and Pakistan, which all have domestic credit to private sector as a share of GDP below 20 per cent, and largest in Bolivia, Kenya, and Vietnam, where it ranges from 30 per cent to 113 per cent. Vietnam stands out as having a very large financial sector in absolute terms and relative to its economy.

Financial sectors in all our case study countries and regions are overwhelmingly bank dominated, with banks providing almost all of the credit to the private sector. Data on the size of stock markets is patchy, but the available data shows that stock markets remain in their infancy in Tanzania, Ghana, Nigeria, and Bolivia (total stock market capitalization of less than 20 per cent of GDP), although they play more of a role in Pakistan, Kenya, and Vietnam (between 20 per cent and 30 per cent of GDP).

Looking more closely at the nature of the banking sector, there is a striking difference in ownership patterns. While there is no foreign ownership of banks in Ethiopia, all banks in Burkina Faso are foreign owned. Aside from these extremes, Ghana, Angola, Pakistan, and Tanzania have substantial levels of foreign ownership, while levels are lower in Vietnam, Rwanda, Bolivia, Nigeria, and Kenya. While banks provide substantial amounts of credit to government and state-owned enterprises, levels also vary, from a high equivalent to 26 per cent of GDP in Pakistan, to a low of only 1 per cent in Bolivia.

The health of the banking sector soundness also varies markedly. The ratio of capital to assets ranges from a low of just over 7 per cent in Bolivia to a high of more than 14 per cent in Ghana, Kenya, and Rwanda.[8] Levels of non-performing loans also vary, and do not necessarily correlate with levels of capitalization. While banks in Bolivia hold relatively little capital, they also have very few non-performing loans (less than 2 per cent of loans). Conversely, banks in Ghana hold relatively high levels of capital but they also have the highest levels of non-performing loans (over 15 per cent of loans).

Finally, our case study countries and regions vary in terms of citizens' access to formal financial services. The number of bank branches and ATMs per people is highest in Bolivia, where there are more than twelve branches and thirty-seven

---

[8] The bank capital to assets ratio measures total regulatory capital (Tier 1, 2, and 3) against total assets (not risk-weighted).

Table 2.6 Attributes of financial sectors in case study countries

Country	Income category	Per capita GNI (US$, Atlas method)	Total GDP (US$ billions)	Size of financial sector (US$bn of liquid assets)	Domestic credit to private sector (% of GDP)	Share of total domestic credit to private (total)	Stock market capitaliz'n (% of GDP)	Foreign bank ownership (% assets owned by foreign banks)	Credit to government and state-owned enterprises to GDP (%)	Bank capital to assets ratio (%)	Bank non-performing loans to total gross loans (%)	Commercial bank branches (per 100,000 adults)	Automated teller machines (ATMs) (per 100,000 adults)
Angola	LMIC	4,332	124	41	20	100	–	54	16	8.6	9.6	10.3	18
Bolivia	LMIC	2,940	34	21	57	88	16	16	1	7.1	1.6	12.6	37
Nigeria	LMIC	2,632	472	88	14	100	11	19	6	10.0	7.8	5.1	16
Vietnam	LMIC	1,948	196	233	113	100	28	5	16	8.3	2.5	3.7	23
Ghana	LMIC	1,902	56	12	14	100	7	69	11	14.0	15.4	6.9	10
Pakistan	LMIC	1,452	266	99	16	100	25	52	26	8.4	11.0	10.0	9
Kenya	LMIC	1,312	66	24	32	100	25	36	13	15.5	7.1	5.5	10
Tanzania	LIC	896	48	10	14	100	4	47	6	11.4	8.3	2.4	6
Rwanda	LIC	706	8	1	21	95	–	13	4	15.6	6.3	6.0	5
Burkina Faso (WAEMU)	LIC	640	12	4	28	100	–	100	7	–	–	2.8	3
Ethiopia	LIC	604	64	–	–	100	–	0	–	–	–	2.9	0

Notes: Because of missing data, data is averaged over five-year period (2013–17). In the few cases where data is missing for all five years, the last available data point is used (from 2011 or 2012). We use Burkina Faso as an illustration of the financial sectors in the WAEMU region, as it was a focal country for our WAEMU case study.

Source: Extracted from World Development Indicators Database, World Bank (2017)

ATMs per 100,000 people, and lowest in Burkina Faso, where there are only three bank branches and three ATMs per 100,000 people.

What is striking about these trends is that it is hard to argue that the extent of Basel adoption maps onto levels of financial sector development. On many of these measures, Pakistan has a relatively developed financial sector and, as we might expect, a relatively high level of Basel implementation. At the other end of the spectrum, Ethiopia has a low level of financial sector development and is the case study with the lowest level of Basel implementation. Yet WAEMU and Rwanda, which have the smallest, and in many ways the least developed, financial sectors, have relatively high levels of Basel adoption. Conversely, Vietnam, Angola, and Nigeria have financial sectors that are among the most developed in our sample, yet relatively high levels of Basel adoption. As we show in the remainder of this volume, it is only by studying the political economy dynamics within countries that we can explain variation in the implementation of international banking standards.

Conclusion: why do regulators on the periphery differ in their responses to Basel standards?

In this chapter we have argued that the regulatory context in low- and lower-middle-income countries differs in important ways from the context in more advanced countries. For this reason, international banking standards, designed in standard-setting bodies heavily dominated by regulators from advanced economies, are ill suited in many ways to the regulatory needs of low- and lower-middle-income countries. Over time this gap has widened as regulators on the Basel Committee have sought to address the ever-more complex activities of the world's largest banks.

We have shown how, despite the manifold criticisms levelled against Basel standards, particularly Basel II and III, they are still being implemented by regulators across the world. Regulators have not adopted the standards in their entirety: implementation is usually highly selective, with regulators choosing to adopt only some components of the standards and taking steps to modify the standards to suit their local contexts. Yet levels of implementation, including among low- and lower-middle-income countries, are higher than appears warranted on the basis of expert opinion about the merits and demerits of the standards. Moreover, there is substantial variation in responses to Basel standards across low- and lower-middle-income countries, which is difficult to attribute to differences in their financial sectors.

Why is it that regulators in many low- and lower-middle-income countries are opting to converge on international banking standards? And why do some regulators opt to converge on international standards but others opt to diverge? In

Chapter 3 we set out a framework to account for this variation, identifying the specific factors that drive regulatory convergence and divergence among peripheral developing countries.

References

Admati, A.R., 2016. The missed opportunity and challenge of capital regulation. *National Institute Economic Review* 235, R4–14. https://doi.org/10.1177/002795011623500110.

Admati, A.R., Hellwig, M., 2014. *The Bankers' New Clothes: What's Wrong with Banking and What to Do About It.* Princeton Univ. Press, Princeton, NJ.

Akyuz, Y., 2010. The management of capital flows and financial vulnerability in Asia, in: Griffith-Jones, S., Ocampo, J.A., Stiglitz, J.E. (Eds.), *Time for a Visible Hand: Lessons from the 2008 World Financial Crisis.* Oxford University Press, New York, pp. 219–41.

Arcand, J.-L., Berkes, E., Panizza, U., 2012. *Too Much Finance?* International Monetary Fund, Washington, DC.

Armour, J., Awrey, D., Davies, P.L., Enriques, L., Gordon, J.N., Mayer, C.P., Payne, J., 2016. *Principles of Financial Regulation*, First edition. Oxford University Press, Oxford.

Ayadi, R., Naceur, S.B., Casu, B., Quinn, B., 2015. *Does Basel compliance matter for bank performance?* (IMF Working Paper No. WP/15/100). IMF.

Barth, J.R., Caprio, G., 2018. Regulation and supervision in financial development, in: Beck, T., Levine, R. (Eds.), *Handbook of Finance and Development.* Edward Elgar Publishing, Cheltenham, pp. 393–418. https://doi.org/10.4337/9781785360510.

Barth, J.R., Caprio, G., Levine, R., 2006. *Rethinking Bank Regulation: Till Angels Govern.* Cambridge University Press, Cambridge; New York.

Barth, J.R., Gerard Caprio, J., Ross Levine 2012. *The evolution and impact of bank regulations*, Policy Research Working Paper. Washington, DC.

Basel Committee on Banking Supervision, 1988. *International convergence of capital measurement and capital standards.* Bank for International Settlements, Basel, Switzerland.

Basel Committee on Banking Supervision, 1996. *Amendment to the capital accord to incorporate market risks.* Basel, Switzerland.

Basel Committee on Banking Supervision, 2010. *Basel III: A global regulatory framework for more resilient banks and banking systems.* Bank for International Settlements, Basel, Switzerland.

Basel Committee on Banking Supervision, 2012. *Core principles for effective banking supervision.* Bank for International Settlements, Basel, Switzerland.

Basel Committee on Banking Supervision, 2013a. *Global systemically important banks updated assessment methodology and the higher loss absorbency requirement.* Bank for International Settlements, Basel, Switzerland.

Basel Committee on Banking Supervision, 2013b. *Basel III: The liquidity coverage ratio and liquidity risk monitoring tools.* Bank for International Settlements, Basel, Switzerland.

Basel Committee on Banking Supervision, 2014. *Basel III: The net stable funding ratio, Consultative Document.* Bank for International Settlements, Basel, Switzerland.

Basel Committee on Banking Supervision, 2016. *Basel Committee proposes measures to reduce the variation in credit risk-weighted assets.* Basel, Switzerland.

Basel Consultative Group, 2014. *Impact and implementation challenges of the Basel framework for emerging market, developing and small economies* (Working Paper No. 27).

Bauerle Danzman, S., Winecoff, W.K., Oatley, T., 2017. All crises are global: Capital cycles in an imbalanced international political economy. *International Studies Quarterly* 61, 907–23. https://doi.org/10.1093/isq/sqx054.

Bayoumi, T., 2017. *Unfinished Business: The Unexplored Causes of the Financial Crisis and the Lessons Yet to Be Learned.* Yale University Press, New Haven, CT; London.

Beck, T., 2011. *Financing Africa: Through the Crisis and Beyond.* World Bank, Washington, DC.

Beck, T., 2018. *Basel III and emerging markets and developing economies: Challenges on infrastructure and SME lending.* Center For Global Development. URL https://www.cgdev.org/blog/basel-iii-unintended-consequences-emerging-markets-developing-economies-part-iv-challenges (accessed 6.4.18).

Beck, T., Fuchs, M., Uy, M., 2009. *Finance in Africa achievements and challenges, Policy Research Working Paper.* World Bank, Washington, DC.

Binham, C., 2015. Banks score victory on use of ratings in capital calculations. *Financial Times.*

Blundell-Wignall, A., Atkinson, P., 2010. Thinking beyond Basel III. *OECD Journal: Financial Market Trends* 2010, 9–33.

Bodo, G., 2019. SSA banks have become so risk-averse thanks to the actions of their governments. *International Banker.*

Brummer, C., 2010. Why soft law dominates international finance—and not trade. *Journal of International Economic Law* 13, 623–43.

Brummer, C., 2012. *Soft Law and the Global Financial System: Rule Making in the 21st Century.* Cambridge University Press, Cambridge; New York.

Buckley, R.P., 2016. The changing nature of banking and why it matters, in: Buckley, R.P., Avgouleas, E., Arner, D.W. (Eds.), *Reconceptualising Global Finance and Its Regulation.* Cambridge University Press, Cambridge, pp. 9–27. https://doi.org/10.1017/CBO9781316181553.002.

Calice, P., 2010. *A preliminary assessment of the implications of financial regulatory reform for African Countries,* Policy Briefs on the Financial Crisis. African Development Bank.

Castro Carvalho, A.P., Hohl, S., Raskopf, R., Ruhnau, S., 2017. *Proportionality in banking regulation: A cross-country comparison* (FSI Insights on policy implementation No. 1). Bank for International Settlements.

Chandrasekhar, C.P., 2007. Credit risk and bank fragility in the new financial environment, in: Bagchi, A.K., Dymski, G. (Eds.), *Capture and Exclude: Developing Economies and the Poor in Global Finance.* Tulika Books, New Delhi, pp. 195–215.

Chey, H., 2014. *International Harmonization of Financial Regulation? The Politics of Global Diffusion of the Basel Capital Accord.* Routledge, New York.

Coen, W., 2017. *Regulatory equivalence and the global regulatory system.* Keynote address by Mr William Coen, Secretary General of the Basel Committee, at the International Financial Services Forum, London, 25 May 2017. https://www.bis.org/speeches/sp170525.htm.

Das, M.U.S., Yossifov, M.P., Podpiera, R., Rozhkov, D., 2005. *Quality of Financial Policies and Financial System Stress.* International Monetary Fund, Washington, DC.

Demirgüç-Kunt, A., Detragiache, M.E., 2010. *Basel Core Principles and Bank Risk: Does Compliance Matter?* International Monetary Fund, Washington, DC.

Drezner, D.W., 2007. *All Politics Is Global: Explaining International Regulatory Regimes.* Princeton University Press, Princeton, NJ; Oxford.

Dymski, G., 2007. The globalization of financial exploitation, in: Bagchi, A.K., Dymski, G. (Eds.), *Capture and Exclude: Developing Economies and the Poor in Global Finance.* Tulika Books, New Delhi, pp. 172–92.

FSB, 2013. *Monitoring the effects of agreed regulatory reforms on emerging markets and developing economies (EMDEs).* Financial Stability Board.

Ferreira, Caio; Nigel Jenkinson; Christopher Wilson 2019. *From Basel I to Basel III: Sequencing Implementation in Developing Economies* IMF Working Paper 19/127 IMF: Washington DC Available here: https://www.imf.org/en/Publications/WP/Issues/2019/06/14/From-Basel-I-to-Basel-III-Sequencing-Implementation-in-Developing-Economies-46895

FSB, World Bank, IMF, 2011. *Financial stability issues in emerging market and developing economies: Report to the G-20 Finance Ministers and Central Bank Governors.*

FSI, 2015. *FSI Survey—Basel II, 2.5 and III Implementation.* BIS.

Fuchs, M., Losse-Mueller, T., Witte, M., 2013. The reform agenda for financial regulation and supervision in Africa, in: Beck, T., Maimbo, S.M. (Eds.), *Financial Sector Development in Africa: Opportunities and Challenges.* The World Bank, Washington, DC.

Gallagher, K., 2015. *Ruling Capital: Emerging Markets and the Reregulation of Cross-Border Finance.* Cornell University Press, Ithaca, NY.

Gobat, J., Yanase, M., Maloney, J., 2014. *The net stable funding ratio: Impact and issues for consideration.* IMF Working Papers 14, 1. https://doi.org/10.5089/9781498346498.001.

Gottschalk, R. (Ed.), 2010. *The Basel Capital Accords in Developing Countries: Challenges for Development Finance.* Palgrave Macmillan, Basingstoke; New York.

Gottschalk, R., 2016. Assessing capacity constraints for effective financial regulation in Sub-Saharan Africa, in: Griffith-Jones, S., Gottschalk, R. (Eds.), *Achieving Financial Stability and Growth in Africa*. Routledge, London, pp. 61–82.

Grabel, I., 2017. *When Things Don't Fall Apart: Global Financial Governance and Developmental Finance in an Age of Productive Incoherence*. MIT Press, Cambridge, MA.

Griffith-Jones, S., Gottschalk, R. (Eds.), 2016. *Achieving Financial Stability and Growth in Africa*. Routledge Taylor & Francis Group, London.

Griffith-Jones, S., Ocampo, J.A. (Eds.), 2018. *The Future of National Development Banks*, The initiative for policy dialogue series. Oxford University Press, Oxford.

Griffith-Jones, S., Ocampo, J.A., Gallagher, K.P., 2012. *Regulating Global Capital Flows for Long-Run Development*, Task Force Report. Pardee Center.

Haldane, A., 2013. *Constraining discretion in bank regulation*. Speech given at the Federal Reserve Bank of Atlanta Conference on 'Maintaining financial stability: holding a tiger by the tail(s)', Federal Reserve Bank of Atlanta, Atlanta, 9 April 2013. https://www.bis.org/review/r130606e.pdf.

Hoenig, T., 2013. *Basel III capital: A well-intended illusion*. Speech given to International Association of Deposit Insurers 2013 Research Conference, Basel, Switzerland on 9 April 2013. https://www.fdic.gov/news/news/speeches/spapr0913.pdf.

Hohl, S., Sison, M.C., Sastny, T., Zamil, R., 2018. *The Basel framework in 100 jurisdictions: implementation status and proportionality practices* (No. No 11), FSI Insights on policy implementation. Bank for International Settlements.

IMF, 2008. *Implementation of the Basel Core Principles for Effective Banking Supervision Experience with Assessments and Implications for Future Work*. IMF, Washington, DC.

IMF, 2018. *Sub-Saharan Africa: Capital Flows and the Future of Work, Regional Economic Outlook*. IMF, Washington, DC.

Jones, E., Zeitz, A.O., 2017. The limits of globalizing Basel banking standards. *Journal of Financial Regulation* 3, 89–124.

Jones, E., Knaack, P., 2019. Global financial regulation: Shortcomings and reform options. *Global Policy*. https://doi.org/10.1111/1758-5899.12656.

Kapstein, E.B., 1989. Resolving the regulator's dilemma: International coordination of banking regulations. *International Organization* 43, 323–47.

Kasekende, L.A., Bagyenda, J., Brownbridge, M., 2012. *Basel III and the global reform of financial regulation: How should Africa respond? A bank regulator's perspective*. Bank of Uganda mimeo.

Kashyap, A.K., Rajan, R.G., Stein, J.C., 2008. *Rethinking capital regulation*. Presented at Maintaining Stability in a Changing Financial System, Jackson Hole, Wyoming.

Lall, R., 2012. From failure to failure: The politics of international banking regulation. *Review of International Political Economy* 19, 609–38.

Marchettini, D., Mecagni, M., Maino, R., 2015. *Evolving banking trends in Sub-Saharan Africa: Key features and challenges* (No. 15/8). IMF African Departmental Paper.

Masera, R., 2014. US Basel III final rule on banks' capital requirements: A different-size-fits-all approach. *PSL Quarterly Review* 66, 387–402.

Maxwell, F., Smith-Meyer, B., 2017. Basel banking reform talks to prevent future financial crises fail again. *POLITICO*.

Murinde, V. (Ed.), 2012. *Bank Regulatory Reforms in Africa*. Palgrave Macmillan, Basingstoke.

Murinde, V., Mlambo, K., 2010. *Development-Oriented Financial Regulation*. University of Birmingham, African Economic Research Consortium, African Development Bank.

Newman, A.L., Posner, E., 2018. *Voluntary Disruptions: International Soft Law, Finance and Power, Transformations in governance*. Oxford University Press, New York.

Oatley, T., Nabors, R., 1998. Redistributive cooperation: Market failure, wealth transfers, and the Basle Accord. *International Organization* 52, 35–54.

Parliamentary Commission on Banking Standards, 2013. *Changing banking for good (First Report of Session 2013–14, Volume II)*.

Persaud, A., 2013. *Reinventing Financial Regulation: A Blueprint for Overcoming Systemic Risk*. Apress, New York.

Podpiera, R., 2004. *Does compliance with Basel Core Principles bring any measurable benefits?* (SSRN Scholarly Paper No. ID 879029). Social Science Research Network, Rochester, NY.

Powell, A., 2004. *Basel II and developing countries: Sailing through the sea of standards*, Policy Research Working Paper. World Bank.

Quillin, B., 2008. *International Financial Co-Operation: Political Economics of Compliance with the 1988 Basel Accord, Routledge International Studies in Money and Banking*. Routledge, London; New York.

Repullo, R., Suarez, J., 2008. *The procyclical effects of Basel II*. Paper presented at the 9th Jacques Polak Annual Research Conference Hosted by the International Monetary Fund, Washington, DC, 13–14 November 2008. IMF, Washington, DC. https://www.imf.org/external/np/res/seminars/2008/arc/pdf/rs.pdf.

Repullo, R., Saurina, J., 2011. *The countercyclical capital buffer of Basel III: A critical assessment* (No. wp2011_1102), Working Papers. CEMFI.

Rey, H., 2015. *Dilemma not trilemma: The global financial cycle and monetary policy independence* (No. w21162). National Bureau of Economic Research, Cambridge, MA. https://doi.org/10.3386/w21162.

Rojas-Suarez, L., Muhammad, D., 2018. *Basel III and unintended consequences for emerging markets and developing economies—Part 2: Effects on trade finance*. Center For Global Development. URL https://www.cgdev.org/blog/basel-iii-unintended-consequences-emerging-markets-and-developing-economies-part-2-effects (accessed 6.4.18).

Romano, R., 2014. For diversity in the international regulation of financial institutions: Critiquing and recalibrating the Basel architecture. *Yale Journal on Regulation* 31.

Sahay, R., Cihak, M., N'Diaye, P., Barajas, A., Bi, R., Ayala, D., Gao, Y., Kyobe, A., Nguyen, L., Saborowski, C., Svirydzenka, K., Yousefi, S.R., 2015. *Rethinking financial deepening: Stability and growth in emerging markets* (IMF Staff Discussion Note). Washington, DC.

Simmons, B.A., 2001. The international politics of harmonization: The case of capital market regulation. *International Organization* 55, 589–620.

Stephanou, C., Mendoza, J.C., 2005. *Credit risk measurement under Basel II: An overview and implementation issues for developing countries*, World Bank Policy Research Working Paper. World Bank, Washington, DC.

Sundararajan, V., Marston, D., Basu, R., 2001. *Financial system standards and financial stability: The case of the Basel Core Principles* (SSRN Scholarly Paper No. ID 879547). Social Science Research Network, Rochester, NY.

Tarullo, D.K., 2008. *Banking on Basel: The future of international financial regulation.* Peterson Institute for International Economics, Washington, DC.

Underhill, G.R.D., Zhang, X., 2008. Setting the rules: Private power, political underpinning and legitimacy in global monetary and financial governance. *International Affairs* 84, 535–54.

World Bank, 2012. *Global Financial Development Report 2013: Rethinking the Role of the State in Finance.* World Bank, Washington, DC.

World Bank, 2017. *World Development Indicators.* World Bank, Washington, DC.

Young, K.L., 2012. Transnational regulatory capture? An empirical examination of the transnational lobbying of the Basel Committee on Banking Supervision. *Review of International Political Economy* 19, 663–88. https://doi.org/10.1080/09692290.2011.624976.

3

The Politics of Regulatory Convergence and Divergence

Emily Jones

Introduction

Why do regulators in peripheral developing countries, particularly low- and lower-middle-income countries, respond differently to international banking standards? Why do some regulators implement substantial parts of the most recent and complex international standards, while others eschew them? This chapter sets out an analytical framework that explains why regulators in peripheral developing countries respond in different ways to international banking standards. It builds from the existing literature and the case studies in this volume to identify the conditions under which we can expect countries to converge on or diverge from international standards.

We explain how the interplay of international and domestic politics shapes the decisions that regulators make. We identify four factors that generate incentives for regulators to converge on international standards: politicians pursuing a development strategy that prioritizes integration into global finance and expansion of financial services sectors; domestic banks looking to enhance their reputation as they expand into international markets; regulators with strong connections to peer regulators in other countries who are implementing the standards; and sustained engagement with the IMF and World Bank through lending programmes and technical assistance.

Working in opposition to these incentives to converge are four factors that generate incentives for regulators to diverge from international standards: politicians pursuing interventionist financial policies, where the state plays an important role in allocating credit; politicians and business oligarchs using banks to direct credit to political allies; regulators who are sceptical about the applicability of Basel standards for their local context; and banks with business models focused on the domestic market for whom there are high costs and few benefits from implementing the standards, particularly if they are relatively small and weak.

Emily Jones, *The Politics of Regulatory Convergence and Divergence* In: *The Political Economy of Bank Regulation in Developing Countries: Risk and Reputation.* Edited by: Emily Jones, Oxford University Press (2020).
© Oxford University Press. DOI: 10.1093/oso/9780198841999.003.0003

As the political, economic, and institutional context differs across peripheral developing countries, regulators experience these incentives through different channels and with varying levels of intensity, prompting them to respond in different ways to international standards. We distinguish between different pathways to convergence and divergence according to whether they are policy-driven, politically driven, regulator-driven, bank-driven, or IFI-driven, and we identify the salient features of these pathways. We also explain why, when faced with strong and competing incentives to converge and diverge, regulators are likely to respond with 'mock compliance'.

Our analytical framework focuses on three main actors: the regulator (usually situated within the central bank), large banks, and incumbent politicians. Regulatory outcomes are the product of the relative power position of these three actors within society, and are shaped by the wider domestic and international context in which they are embedded. Central to our argument is the observation that banks are rarely the most dominant actor in regulatory politics in peripheral developing countries, particularly the low- and lower-middle-income countries we focus on. While there are some exceptions, the underdeveloped nature of the formal economy and relatively small size of the banking sector leave individual banks, and the banking sector as a whole, with much less power to shape regulatory outcomes than in many advanced economies. Yet this does not mean that financial market players have little purchase on regulators' decisions. Far from it. Operating in a context of capital scarcity, regulators, politicians, and banks in peripheral developing countries are particularly attuned to the ways in which regulators, banks, and investors in other countries will react to their decisions, and, as we explain below, this has an out-sized impact on regulatory outcomes (see also Mosley (2003)).

It is this dynamic that sets regulatory harmonization between the core and periphery apart from regularity harmonization among core countries. In explanations of regulatory harmonization among core countries, the interests of large domestic banks loom large. For instance, in his seminal work, Singer (2007) argues that regulators face a dilemma of increasing regulatory requirements in order to mitigate the risk of financial crisis, or easing those requirements and enhancing the international competitiveness of the domestic financial sector (Singer, 2007, p. 19). It is these trade-offs that shape the nature of regulatory harmonization among core countries. In this chapter we show how the decisions of regulators on the periphery are shaped by power relations between regulators, politicians, and banks, and the extent and nature of the connections of these actors to global finance and networks of global financial governance.

Three key actors: regulators, banks, and politicians

In this section we examine the role and relative power position of regulators, banks, and politicians in regulatory decisions in peripheral developing countries. In the next section we explain how specific factors create incentives for these actors to converge on or diverge from international banking standards.

Regulators

Just as in many advanced and emerging economies, the task of regulating and supervising banks in many peripheral developing countries has been delegated to an independent government body that operates at arm's length from the executive and legislative branches. This is part of a wider trend that accompanied waves of privatization and liberalization in the 1980s and 1990s, often under the guidance of the World Bank. Responsibility for bank regulation and supervision was typically moved to the central bank or a specialized regulatory institution, with substantial operational independence.

The scope of the regulator's powers and the *de jure* and *de facto* independence that it has from the executive branch varies across peripheral developing countries. In general, regulatory authorities have the formal authority to impose and enforce a wide range of regulations on banks, although their actions are circumscribed by the scope of their legal powers, their resources and expertise, and, as we discuss below, political considerations. When it comes to international banking standards, independent regulatory authorities usually have the powers to implement the standards without consulting the legislative or executive branch, by issuing regulatory directives and guidelines which banks are then legally obliged to follow. However, as Basel standards have become more complex, regulatory authorities have needed additional powers to be delegated, and this has required new primary legislation.[1]

In deciding how the banking sector should be regulated, and whether international standards should be implemented, we expect regulators to draw on a

---

[1] For example, the implementation of Pillar 2 of Basel II requires national supervisors to have the powers to ensure prompt corrective action, the legal mandate to impose higher capital requirements, and the ability to conduct supervision at a consolidated level, while Pillar 3 requires the oversight of confidentiality rules (Stephanou and Mendoza, 2005). Under Basel III regulators may require additional legal authority to intervene on the basis of macro-prudential factors rather than institution-specific factors. They may also need quick specific additional powers. Implementation of the new 'definitions of capital' requires that supervisors have sufficient powers to make judgement calls about the point at which a bank is deemed to be unable to continue on its own. Where foreign banks have a systemically important local presence, supervisors may require increased supervisory powers over branches and the ability to require conversion of branches into subsidiaries to implement the requirements on D-SIBs, and prevent banks in host jurisdictions from circumventing the higher loss absorbency requirements (Fuchs et al., 2013).

combination of expert technical knowledge and normative beliefs. Designing banking regulation is intrinsically difficult as regulators face challenges of imperfect information and profound uncertainty (Haldane, 2012). Technical officials navigate uncertainty by drawing on a combination of technical knowledge and normative beliefs to diagnose problems and identify solutions (Chwieroth, 2007). Over time, particular normative frameworks and sets of policy Ideas come to dominate an institution, shaping the manner in which external demands and events are interpreted and the responses that the staff will entertain and, potentially, implement (Chwieroth, 2010, p. 10). In the area of financial regulation, scholars have shown how economic ideology, particularly faith in self-correcting market mechanisms, has deeply influenced regulators' approaches to banking regulation, contributing to the global financial crisis (see, for instance, Cassidy, 2010; Gorton, 2012).

Regulators in peripheral developing countries operate in a context that is different in important ways to that of their counterparts in more advanced economies. As discussed in Chapter 2, many are tasked not only with ensuring financial stability, but also supporting the development of the financial sector and wider economy. While all regulators face an asymmetry of resources and information vis-à-vis the banks that they regulate, in low- and lower-middle-income countries, regulators operate in environments of institutional weakness and, in many cases, acute human and financial resource constraints. This makes it challenging to design and effectively enforce anything but the simplest forms of bank regulation (Abdel-Baki, 2012; Fuchs et al., 2013; Gottschalk, 2016, 2010; Gottschalk and Griffith-Jones, 2006). While this might lead us to expect regulators in low- and lower-middle-income countries to generally oppose the introduction of international standards, particularly the most onerous and complex elements, powerful ideational and reputational incentives may lead regulators to champion adoption, as we explain below.

Banks

Even when regulators have a high level of operational independence on paper, they are rarely fully independent in practice. Studies of financial regulation in advanced industrialized countries, particularly the US, have drawn attention to the ways in which private banks can 'capture' regulators (Johnson and Kwak, 2011; Lall, 2012; Mattli and Woods, 2009; Pagliari and Young, 2014; Stigler, 1971). In the US, for instance, the financial industry exercises a powerful role in regulatory decisions, including through lobbying, campaign contributions, and revolving doors between the industry and regulators (e.g. FCIC, 2011). Fragmentation among regulatory institutions helps the industry exercise this power (Lavelle, 2013).

While much of the literature has conceived of the relationship between the financial industry and state as a one-way street, with banks exercising power over regulators, others have argued that the relationship is one of mutual dependence. The sheer size of the financial sector relative to the rest of the economy in many industrialized economies means that regulatory decisions often reflect the interests of the sector, yet in large and lucrative markets, banks ultimately rely on the goodwill of the regulator to operate (Culpepper, 2015). In many European countries, a series of formal and informal ties between the political system and the banking system[2] enable banks to exercise a significant influence over the regulatory process through their political connections but also make banks receptive to political guidance (Monnet et al., 2014).

The ability of big banks to capture regulators is not limited to industrialized countries. Maxfield (1991) studies Mexico and Brazil and shows how the relative strength of bankers' alliances decisively shapes regulatory policies. In Mexico, a strong alliance between bankers, industry, and the central bank resulted in a set of policies that prioritized bank interests, promoting macroeconomic stability and the free flow of capital. In Brazil, in contrast, a weak alliance of bankers coupled with a strong state-planning authority led to a set of growth-oriented policies, including extensive intervention in financial markets. Pepinsky (2013) makes a similar argument, and shows how powerful financial sectors in Mexico and Indonesia successfully influenced regulatory policies and maintained restrictions on foreign ownership in the banking sector. Boone (2005) shows how strong and relatively autonomous financial sectors in South Africa and Mauritius made regulators more vulnerable to the demands of private finance.

A striking and important difference in low- and lower-middle-income countries is that the size of the banking sector is much smaller relative to the wider economy than in upper-middle- and high-income countries (see Chapter 2). As a result, while individual banks may be influential because they are linked to powerful politicians (discussed below), the financial sector doesn't have the structural power that we see in many advanced economies. Moreover, in a context where the wider economy is underdeveloped and dominated by small informal enterprises and smallholder agriculture, lending to government and state-owned enterprises is central to the business strategy of banks.

In this book we distinguish between *domestically oriented* and *internationally oriented* banks, arguing that they have very different incentives when it comes to banking regulation and the adoption of international standards. The salient feature of domestically oriented banks is that, irrespective of whether they are owned by domestic or foreign shareholders, their business model focuses on the

---

[2] For instance, German public saving banks (Sparkassen and Landesbanken) that held some 33 per cent of the assets of the German Banking sector in 2009 remain owned and controlled by regional governments.

domestic market. As we explain in more detail below, for banks reliant on the domestic market, the adoption of complex international standards has high costs and few benefits. Although domestically oriented banks stand to lose from the implementation of international standards, they rarely had sufficient power to decisively influence regulatory outcomes.

In contrast, internationally oriented banks focus their business strategy on international markets. For reasons we explain below, internationally oriented banks gain reputational advantages from the implementation of international standards and, unlike domestically oriented banks, they are more likely to have the power to decisively shape regulatory outcomes. Where they are present, large, internationally oriented banks shape regulatory outcomes. Yet relatively few low- and lower-middle-income countries have such banks, as they tend to be associated with more developed financial markets. This variation helps explain different responses to international standards.

A striking finding of our empirical chapters is that the presence of foreign banks, particularly those headquartered in Basel Committee countries, does not create pressures to converge on international standards. We might expect international banks to champion convergence as when they have to comply with different regulatory requirements across the jurisdictions in which they operate this can generate uncertainty and complexity, particularly for globally systemically important banks (Bauer and Drevon, 2015). It is also plausible that foreign banks will champion the implementation of international standards to put them at a competitive advantage vis-à-vis smaller domestic banks, as the latter struggle to comply with complex regulatory requirements. Yet, in our case studies, we find no evidence of foreign banks championing convergence on international standards. Where regulators have decided to implement Basel standards, there are examples of foreign banks providing technical assistance to domestic banks, and even to the regulatory authorities, but they haven't been strong advocates for implementation. Indeed, some international banks have cautioned regulators against implementing some of the more complex elements of Basel III, arguing that they are ill suited to their context.[3]

Politicians

Politicians exert influence over regulatory decisions directly, through their policies and oversight of the regulatory authority, and indirectly, through their political connections to banks. As several of our empirical cases powerfully illustrate, the existence of an independent regulatory authority does not preclude the influence of policy or politics. In a vital government institution like the central

---

[3] Interview with senior official from a large pan-African bank, via telephone, June 2015.

bank, senior officials are selected for their expertise, but they are also likely to be appointed on the basis of their broad alignment with the policy objectives of incumbent politicians. The more prevalent the appointment of such 'technopols' (people with a hybrid status as technocrats and politicians—see Domínguez, 1997) in the regulatory agency, the greater the influence that government policy is likely to have over regulatory outcomes. In several countries, the appointment of senior officials in the regulatory authority, including the appointment of central bank governors, is a decision for the executive branch.

While politicians may not take an interest in the complex technical details of international banking standards, they do set the overall policy stance towards the financial sector. Financial sector policies vary substantially across peripheral developing countries. Politicians may adopt an interventionist approach, using a variety of policy instruments to direct the allocation of credit in the economy in line with specific policy objectives. Alternatively, they may pursue policies that allocate credit purely on the basis of market prices, focusing on policy measures to improve market efficiency.

The policy-orientation of governments has important path-dependent effects on the institutional set-up for banking regulation. Where the government has a history of interventionism, often as part of a wider developmental state model, the executive branch is likely to have retained a high level of oversight and control over bank regulation and supervision, and regulatory authorities are likely to have a lower level of independence. In contrast, where the country has pursued a more market-oriented approach, it is more likely to have an autonomous regulator.

In general, it is reasonable to expect that the degree of alignment between international standards and pre-existing regulatory institutions will shape national responses to international standards, as has been shown for the adoption of international standards in advanced countries (Quillin, 2008). Specifically, for peripheral developing countries, we might reasonably expect countries that have historically pursued market-oriented policies and have an independent regulatory authority to be more receptive to the market-oriented Basel standards than countries where governments have historically pursued interventionist approaches.

Over and above this general trend, we explain below why politicians seeking to attract international capital to their country and the creation of an international financial centre may perceive the implementation of banking and other international standards to be a vital part of their country's economic development strategy, leading to a particularly powerful dynamic of convergence on international standards. As Reddy (2010) notes, eagerness to develop a thriving international financial centre is likely to result in an approach to regulation that puts self-regulation by market participants at its heart.

Politicians may also exert influence over regulation to further the interests of specific banks to whom they are politically connected. In countries where economic and political power is highly centralized, banks may be owned by powerful elites and used to further business and political interests. Hutchcroft (1998) shows how, in the Philippines, powerful families with sources of economic income outside of the state were able to dominate politics and the business sector, through family-owned conglomerates. As part of their wider business strategy they set up or acquired ownership stakes in domestic banks, using them to provide credit to their own businesses, and to shore up their connections to politicians. The regulator had very little power to enforce bank regulations vis-à-vis these powerful, politically connected banks (Hutchcroft, 1998).

Powerful politicians may also have direct ownership stakes in banks, or otherwise exercise influence over the business operations of banks in order to shore up their political power. In countries where state-owned banks dominate the banking sector, these banks provide incumbent politicians with a high level of discretionary control over credit allocation in the economy. While this control may be used to pursue policy objectives, as in the developmental state model, it may also be used for political patronage. Arriola (2013) shows how incumbent politicians in several different African countries have used discretionary powers over finance to make credit allocation contingent on political allegiance. While Arriola argues that this is particularly likely to happen when banks are state owned, politicians may also use ownership stakes in private banks to further their political goals. During processes of privatization in the 1980s and 1990s in African countries, bank licenses were often granted in ways that shored up political patronage systems, ensuring enduring links between politicians and banks (Boone, 2005).

Thus, to explain responses of regulators to international banking standards, we need to understand the interests and preferences of regulators, banks, and politicians, as well as the relations between them, a relationship that is often more complex than it may at first appear. While we conceive of bank regulation as a three-way game between regulators, large banks, and incumbent politicians, it is the politicians and regulators that exert the greatest influence over regulatory outcomes. This in turn implies an important role in our explanatory framework for policy ideas about how banks should be regulated; for party politics and political systems; and for the material interests of political elites. This distinguishes our analytical framework from the frameworks that scholars use to explain regulatory outcomes in industrialized economies, in which the business interests of large banks loom large (Culpepper, 2015; Helleiner and Porter, 2010; Lall, 2012; Mattli and Woods, 2009; Oatley and Nabors, 1998; Pagliari and Young, 2014; Singer, 2007; Underhill and Zhang, 2008).

International context

The connections between national politicains, regulators, and banks to international financial players and networks of global financial governance also play an important role in our anlaytical framework. As the interconnectedness of peripheral developing countries with global finance has increased, so too has the responsiveness of national regulations to an array of international interests and actors. There is a long history of engagement between peripheral developing countries, particularly low- and lower-middle-income countries and the World Bank and IMF. Widespread reforms in the 1980s and 1990s under structural adjustment loans, as well as in the wake of the Asian financial crisis, aimed to create regulatory institutions and practices explicitly aligned with the work of the Basel Committee (Hamilton-Hart, 2003; Mathieu, 1998). These reforms were very contentious and often only partially implemented (Killick et al., 1998; Mosley, 2010). Even where they were implemented, they often failed to strengthen the financial sector (Mathieu, 1998). Yet for many developing countries they ushered in a step-change in how the financial sector was structured and regulated,[4] reducing the level of state intervention and creating independent, arm's-length regulatory institutions. This created conditions that were more conducive to, although not sufficient for, the implementation of Basel II and III standards in later years.

More recently, engagement with international private finance has increased. Peripheral developing countries have increasingly opened up to foreign banks and cross-border flows of portfolio finance, and, more recently, governments have tapped into international capital markets to finance their own activities. Increased exposure to international finance renders peripheral developing countries particularly vulnerable to changes in the international environment, whether that is shifts in international credit cycles, or in the regulations that prevail in the financial core (Bauerle Danzman et al., 2017; Rey, 2015). With integration, regulators, banks, and politicians become acutely aware of, and responsive to, the preferences of international investors and credit rating agencies, as well as regulators in other jurisdictions. As we explain below, this engagement generates specific incentives for regulators, banks, and politicians in peripheral developing countries to converge on international banking standards.

Although the exposure of peripheral developing countries to international finance has increased, we should not expect external pressures and incentives to generate uniform responses across peripheral developing countries (Boone, 2005). Peripheral developing countries are embedded in international finance in different ways and to different extents and, as we argue below, domestic political economy dynamics condition countries' responses to these external pressures and incentives.

---

[4] See also Lavelle (2004) who argues that programmes of the International Financial Corporation, World Bank, and IMF were also key in fostering the development of equity markets in developing countries.

Convergence: drivers and political underpinnings

We now turn to the specific factors that drive convergence and divergence. In this section we explain the causal mechanisms that underpin the four factors we identify as providing strong incentives for regulators in peripheral developing countries to converge on international banking standards, and then do the same for the four factors we identify as driving divergence. These drivers of convergence and divergence are summarized in Figure 3.1.

Politicians seeking international capital

Politicians seeking to attract international capital into the financial services sector can be a strong driver of convergence on international banking standards. Following the rapid growth of East Asian countries in the 1970s and 1980s, many other developing countries looked to manufacturing as the pathway 'out of the periphery' (Haggard, 1990). In the past decade the viability of late developers cultivating an export-oriented manufacturing sector has been heavily questioned (e.g. Hallward-Driemeier and Nayyar, 2017). Perhaps in response, politicians are increasingly looking to drive development through the expansion of financial services. In some of our case studies politicians are working hard to position their country as an international hub for financial services, looking to emulate Singapore or Mauritius. In other cases, politicians are championing the adoption of international standards in order to attract international investment into banking, with the aim of increasing competition and reducing the cost of credit

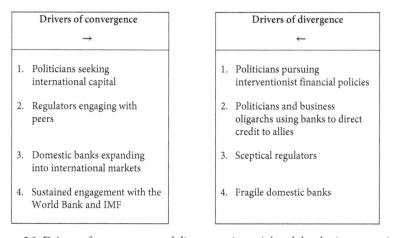

Drivers of convergence	Drivers of divergence
→	←
1. Politicians seeking international capital	1. Politicians pursuing interventionist financial policies
2. Regulators engaging with peers	2. Politicians and business oligarchs using banks to direct credit to allies
3. Domestic banks expanding into international markets	3. Sceptical regulators
4. Sustained engagement with the World Bank and IMF	4. Fragile domestic banks

Figure 3.1 Drivers of convergence and divergence in peripheral developing countries.

to the private sector. This may be part of a drive to liberalize the banking sector and break ties between the banking sector and related patronage structures (Walter, 2008).

The implementation of international banking standards is perceived by politicians as an important mechanism for signalling to potential investors that their banking sector is soundly regulated. Scholars have shown how reputational signalling has become important for developing countries, and moves to give central banks independence were often driven by politicians' desire to signal creditworthiness to international investors, in a context of growing financial interdependence (Ghosh, 2007; Maxfield, 1997). Similar reputational dynamics underpin the implementation of international banking standards. It is hard for international investors, and actors like credit rating agencies that intermediate the relationship between investors and peripheral developing countries, to reliably assess how well a financial sector is regulated. International investors and other market participants appreciate simple metrics such as compliance with international standards for providing a straightforward assessment of national performance that can be easily integrated into risk-return calculations (Mosley, 2003). We find that, for politicians seeking to improve their country's reputation in the eyes of international investors, implementing Basel and other international financial standards is an obvious way to signal commitment to transparency and more stringent regulation.

The incentive to implement Basel standards is particularly strong for countries seeking to establish themselves as financial centres, as they deliberately cultivate their image as secure and stable investment destinations as this enables them to attract a greater volume of lucrative business (Sharman, 2009). The reputational payoffs for compliance with international standards are comparatively high and governments may thus be willing to bear the costs of compliance (Brummer, 2012, p. 147; Ercanbrack, 2015, p. 214).[5] Enhancing its reputation as a sophisticated international financial centre is a major driver for Mauritius' high implementation of Basel II and III, as well as other international financial standards.[6]

In general, the greater the emphasis that politicians place on attracting and retaining international investment in the financial services sector, the stronger the incentives that regulators face to converge on international banking standards.

Domestic banks expanding into international markets

Regulators may also adopt international banking standards to facilitate the expansion of internationally oriented domestic banks into new markets. Relatively few

---

[5] However, for international financial activity that thrives on secrecy and regulatory forbearance, regulators may deliberately opt against adoption of international standards to signal commitment to continuing this approach. See (Goodhart, 2011).

[6] Discussions with senior government officials, Oxford, June 2016.

banks headquartered in low- and lower-middle-income countries have international operations, but this is changing, particularly with the expansion of regional banks across Africa, Asia, and Latin America. While many regional banks are headquartered in upper-middle- and high-income countries, a growing number are located in low- and lower-middle-income countries. In the Africa region, for instance, Togo (a low-income country) is the home supervisor of Ecobank, a major pan-African bank that operates in thirty-six countries, often with a systemically important presence. Similarly, Nigeria and Morocco (both lower-middle-income countries) are the home regulators of major pan-African banks, while Kenya (also lower-middle-income) is the home regulator for several banks that are active across the East African region (Enoch et al., 2015).

For home regulators of these internationally oriented domestic banks, implementation of international standards is an important mechanism for reassuring host regulators that their banks are soundly regulated at the parent level. Because of the risk of cross-border financial contagion, host regulators will seek assurance that a bank is soundly regulated at home before they issue a license allowing a foreign bank to operate in their jurisdiction. International standards can provide an 'epistemic signpost' that reassures host regulators that there is a high quality of regulation and supervision at the parent level (Brummer, 2010, p. 264). In the EU, member states are allowed to restrict access to third-country banks whose home country regimes do not meet EU standards. Similarly, in the US, the Federal Reserve has the authority to issue banking licenses to foreign banks only if they are 'subject to comprehensive supervision or regulation on a consolidated basis by the appropriate authorities in its home country' and if they are 'well-capitalized and well-managed' on a global basis (Alexander et al., 2006, p. 146). In the 2000s, compliance with Basel Core Principles and implementation of the latest Basel standards were the common reference point for EU and US regulators in making these assessments.[7] Thus, while not an explicit condition for market entry, implementation of the international benchmark has been, as a matter of practical regulatory policy, an important mechanism for entering these markets.

There is evidence that, during the 1990s and early 2000s, regulators in emerging economies in Asia adopted Basel standards to help their banks gain entry into European and US markets (Chey, 2007; Ho, 2002). In the Middle East, regulators perceive compliance with the latest Basel standards to be vital for enabling Gulf banks to obtain regulatory legitimacy and approval, particularly in North American and European markets (Ercanbrack, 2015, p. 214).

Even where adoption of Basel standards is not a pre-requisite for market entry, regulators may adopt Basel standards to boost the reputation of their internationally active banks. Knaack (2017) argues that improving the reputation of China's

---

[7] Reliance on Basel as a signal of high-quality domestic banking regulation has waned since the global financial crisis, as both the EU and the US have come to distrust each other's modifications of Basel III.

internationally active banks is an important explanation for China's recent over-compliance with Basel standards, particularly Basel III. The Executive Director of the Reserve Bank of India gave a similar explanation for Basel adoption in India: 'Any deviation [from global standards] will hurt us both by way of reputation and also in actual practice. The "perception" of a lower standard regulatory regime will put Indian banks at a disadvantage in global competition' (Vishwanathan, 2015). As Goodhart (2011, p. 186) notes, soon after the Basel standards were first developed, the Basel Committee found that 'the recommendations and standards developed and intended only for large G10 international banks *became regarded by all other countries, and their banks, as reputationally binding*' [emphasis added].

The implementation of Basel standards may also be supported by locally incorporated banks that are tapping into international credit markets (Alexander et al., 2006; Chey, 2014; Gottschalk and Griffith-Jones, 2006). For banks issuing bonds to finance their operations, their cost of borrowing on international markets is largely determined by their credit ratings. In turn, there is anecdotal evidence that the major international ratings companies consider compliance with the latest Basel standards as being 'positive for bank creditworthiness' (Moody's Investors Service, 2015). For instance, in its assessment of Colombia, Fitch Ratings argued that the country's failure to fully align with Basel III standards meant that 'they trail international peers that use more conservative and globally accepted capital standards' (Wade, 2018).

In general, the higher the number of domestic banks with international operations, the stronger the incentives that regulators face to converge on international banking standards.

Regulators engaging with peers implementing standards

Regulators may also face strong incentives to implement international standards as a result of their engagement with peers in other countries who are already implementing them. Given that regulators in peripheral developing countries face particularly acute constraints in designing financial regulations, we expect them to learn from and emulate the practices of regulators in other countries. In general, the higher the level of engagement that senior officials have with peers who are implementing international standards, the stronger their incentives to follow suit.

Research on the diffusion of global norms provides insights into the specific ways in which transnational networks drive policy transfer, distinguishing between process of learning and emulation. We expect regulators to look to and draw lessons from the experiences of regulators in countries similar to theirs, and to apply these lessons in designing their own policies (Dobbin et al., 2007).

Learning is based on an evidence-based evaluation of practices in other countries and a progressive move from less effective to more effective policies. While this may take place, hard evidence of the efficacy of a policy in another jurisdiction may not always be available. Sociologists have drawn attention to the ways in which policies may still diffuse across borders, driven by a quest for normative acceptance and legitimacy rather than technical efficiency, as policymakers emulate the policies of those they perceive to be leaders in their field.[8] While processes of policy transfer are usually used to describe a move towards more effective policies, this is not inevitable. As Sharman (2010) shows, policy transfer can also be dysfunctional, leading to worse policy outcomes.

Transnational professional networks are a powerful vector for the transmission of regulatory practices around the world. They provide a forum for regulators to discuss the common challenges they face and to learn from each other's experiences, and they can play an important role in shaping regulators' decisions. As Ban (2016) powerfully shows, in Spain and Romania the extent to which bureaucrats engaged with international professional networks promulgating neoliberal ideas greatly shaped the policies these countries pursued. The highly technical and practical nature of the discussions within international financial networks fosters common knowledge and 'shared understandings' among the officials involved, which shape regulatory decisions at the national level (Porter, 2005). Crucially, international standards or norms—like Basel standards—become focal points around which discussions converge and, through this process, become widely accepted as 'best practices' (Simmons et al., 2006). Transnational networks can also be sources of coercive pressure, as Bach and Newman (2010) show in their study of insider-trading legislation: lead regulators backed by significant market power, such as the United States' SEC in securities, may use asymmetries within transnational networks to promote the global export of their domestic policies.

Financial sector regulators are particularly likely to follow decisions made by their peers, as their professional incentives dissuade them from following an experimental approach to regulation and encourage herd behaviour (Romano, 2014). Following 'international best practices' and the practices of successful peers helps insulate regulators from attribution and attendant costs, in the event of a financial crisis at home (Gadinis, 2015, p. 52). In some instances, there may be powerful socialization effects at work within peer networks. Where networks promulgate specific financial standards, non-implementation may result in social reproach from peers for failing to deliver on the group's regulatory programme or shared norms (Brummer, 2012; Martinez-Diaz and Woods, 2009). Engagement in

---

[8] See discussion of this literature in Sharman (2010).

transnational networks is a major driver of the diffusion of Basel II standards across the globe Jones and Zeitz (2019).

Transnational networks are not the only forum through which regulators in peripheral developing countries engage with their peers. Where national authorities supervise internationally active banks, this requires them to be in regular contact with supervisors in other jurisdictions. The existence of home-host communication and cooperation is much easier when there are common regulatory standards and supervisory practices, and this creates a powerful incentive for regulators to converge on and implement international standards (see for instance Cassidy, 2010; Chwieroth, 2010; Gorton, 2012).

In general, the higher the level of engagement in transnational regulatory networks, particularly in networks where Basel standards are actively promulgated, the stronger the incentives that regulators face to converge on international banking standards.

Sustained engagement with the World Bank and IMF

Regular interactions with international financial institutions like the IMF and World Bank, either through lending programmes or technical assistance, can provide strong incentives for regulators to implement international standards. While deep institutional reforms occurred under World Bank and IMF loans in the 1980s and 1990s, the World Bank and IMF have remained closely involved in the design of financial sector reforms in many peripheral developing countries.

In the wake of the Asian financial crisis in the late 1990s, the World Bank and IMF placed greater emphasis on strengthening supervisory capacity in developing countries, making the strengthening of regulation and supervision a condition in loans, and embedding long-term technical advisers in the banking supervision departments of central banks. Since the early 2000s, the IMF, World Bank, and Financial Stability Board have also conducted regular joint reviews of countries' supervisory practices under Financial Sector Assessment Programs (FSAPs), and this includes a review of the compliance with Basel Core Principles. The IMF and World Bank have funded regulators to attend training courses that promote Basel standards. In Africa, two 'AFRITAC' training centres funded by the IMF provide trainings and country-level technical assistance in East and West Africa with the explicit aim of supporting national regulatory authorities to comply with the Basel Core Principles, and to move from Basel I to Basel II and III.

There are more subtle forms of engagement too. As some of our case studies illustrate, there is often a revolving door between the IMF and World Bank and key institutions in peripheral developing countries, including central banks and ministries of finance. It is common for senior officials to spend part of their career in the IMF or World Bank, before returning to more senior posts in their home institutions. In addition to equipping officials with the technical skills to implement international standards, it is reasonable to expect that intense and regular engagement with IMF and World Bank staff leads to the diffusion of norms and ideas, helping to create regulatory institutions where the ideas and beliefs of senior staff are aligned with those prevailing in the IMF, World Bank, and closely related institutions.

Yet the IMF and World Bank have not universally championed the implementation of Basel standards. While the IMF and World Bank have enthusiastically supported compliance with the Basel Core Principles, their advice on the implementation of Basel II and III has been more circumspect. For instance, in its response to a Financial Stability Institute survey, Belize states that it is not implementing Basel II on the direct advice of the IMF (FSI, 2015, p. 4). A close read of FSAP reports reveals other instances in which the FSAP team has actively discouraged the implementation of Basel II, including in Rwanda, Barbados, and Cameroon. As our case studies show, in some instances peripheral countries have proceeded with Basel implementation *against* the advice of the IMF.

In general, we expect regular and extensive engagement with the IMF and World Bank to result in higher levels of implementation of the Basel Framework, although this may fall short of support for implementing the full suite of international standards.

Divergence: drivers and political underpinnings

While the international economic and political context in which peripheral countries are embedded can generate strong incentives for regulators in peripheral countries to implement Basel standards, they often face strong incentives to diverge from them. Four are particularly important: politicians pursuing interventionist financial sector policies, politicians and business oligarchs using banks to direct credit to allies, skeptical regulators, and fragile domestic banks.

Politicians pursuing interventionist financial sector policies

Where governments use interventionist measures to direct credit to specific sections of the economy or particular societal groups, this is likely to create incentives to diverge from the implementation of Basel standards. In many countries around the world, governments intervene in the allocation of credit through price or quantity rules in order to achieve specific policy objectives by providing competitive advantage to certain economic sectors. While often associated with the state-led industrialization strategies of fast-growing East Asian countries, policy-directed lending has been central to industrialization in many advanced countries.

In countries including Japan, South Korea, France, and Germany, a credit-based financial system allowed the state to exert influence over the economy's investment pattern and guide the development of productive sectors (Zysman, 1983; Haggard and Lee, 1995; Woo-Cumings, 1999; Naqvi et al., 2018). In the wake of the global financial crisis there has been a resurgence in interventionist financial policies, including renewed interest in national development banks, as governments have sought to channel credit into productive, longer-term projects.

Interventionist approaches were the norm in peripheral developing countries in the post-independence period, but many governments abandoned them in the 1980s and 1990s, often under the pressure of structural adjustment programmes (Mathieu, 1998). However, governments in some peripheral developing countries are pursuing interventionist financial sector policies, including Ethiopia and Bolivia, countries we examine in this book. In general, interventionist financial sector policies sit at odds with core aspects of the Basel framework.

The Basel Core Principles and Standards are premised on market-based allocation of credit, with the government only stepping in to address market failures. The Basel framework requires a formally independent regulator that operates at arm's length from the institutions it regulates (banks), as well as from the executive and legislative branches of government. Under this framework, the regulator's core role is to ensure the market works effectively by refereeing the allocation of credit by private institutions, and to limit excessive risk-taking. While such an approach is presented as apolitical, as Ghosh (2007) argues, the creation of independent regulatory institutions with narrow mandates is a political decision to prioritize a specific and narrow policy agenda, such as financial stability. In contrast, interventionist financial policies seek to channel credit on the basis of policy priorities rather than market prices, and deliberately seek to disrupt the market allocation of credit. Under such systems the government's core function is not that of referee, but that of a player, selectively allocating credit to specific industries (Zysman, 1983).

The market-orientation of the Basel framework is reflected in the Basel Core Principles, which emphasize the need for supervisors to have operational independence, free from political interference, and the relevant legal powers to ensure compliance. Policy-directed lending and the general use of financial intermediaries as instruments of government policy are identified as distorting market signals and impeding effective supervision (Basel Committee on Banking Supervision, 2012). Basel II standards place even greater emphasis on market actors and price signals than Basel I, with credit ratings agencies and banks accorded central roles in evaluating risks, and the third pillar of Basel II dedicated to improving market discipline, including through new public disclosure requirements. In countries where the government relies extensively on policy-directed lending, the Basel framework is unlikely to be an attractive basis for regulation.

Reformist politicians may promote the implementation of Basel standards as part of a wider agenda to move away from an interventionist to a market-oriented approach to the financial sector. Such moves are likely to provoke opposition from local elites who have been privileged within the existing system (Mosley, 2010). The implementation of Basel I in the developmental states of East Asia, as part of a wider market-based reform agenda, generated substantial resistance (Chey, 2014; Walter, 2008).

In general, the greater the level of interventionist financial policies in a country, the stronger the incentives that regulators face to diverge from international banking standards.

Politicians and business oligarchs using banks to direct credit to allies

Where politicians and business oligarchs use banks to direct credit to their allies, they are likely to oppose the introduction of international standards. Politicians may use their control over banks to allocate credit to political allies, while powerful economic elites may use banks to allocate credit to their own businesses and curry favour with politicians. Where such politically based lending is pervasive, regulation is typically lax, with regulators exercising a high level of forbearance. This may include the non-enforcement of regulations on non-performing loans extended to politically connected individuals, overlooking breaches to single obligor limits and related-party lending, and failing to follow due process when issuing bank licenses.

It is common for regulatory institutions in developing countries to face acute resource constraints, and in some cases this may be intentional. Hutchcroft (1998) explains why the central bank in the Philippines was one of the strongest government institutions and widely respected for maintaining a high level of macro-economic stability, yet it housed a banking supervision department that was weak and where regulatory forbearance was the norm. He argues that this was due to the economic interests and political priorities of the powerful oligarchs. Underlying political economy dynamics also help explain why Singapore and Malaysia had strong regulatory institutions, while in Indonesia they were very weak (Hamilton-Hart, 2003).

Where political lending is pervasive, politicians and powerful economic elites are likely to resist moves to increase the quality of regulation and supervision and allocate more resources to regulators, moves that are required for the implementation and enforcement of international banking standards. In China, for instance, the introduction of Basel I was opposed by powerful groups within the party-state apparatus that benefited from politically directed credit allocation. Implementation only began in earnest after the Asian financial crisis alerted the leadership to the risks associated with an unreformed financial sector (Walter, 2010). In Malaysia and Thailand, powerful family-owned banks strongly resisted disclosure requirements that are an integral part of the Basel framework, as this would have revealed high levels of related-party lending (Walter, 2008).

Our case studies are a reminder that it is important to distinguish conceptually between interventionist financial sector policies, where credit is allocated on the basis of objective policies, and politically directed lending where credit is allocated on the basis of political favours to individuals. These two conceptually distinct phenomena are often conflated in the literature, reflecting an (often implicit) assumption that interventionist policies will be accompanied by high levels of politically directed lending, while systems of market-based credit allocation will be accompanied by low levels of politically directed lending (e.g. Arriola, 2013; Barth et al., 2006). Yet it is equally possible for politically directed lending to be pervasive under market-based systems of credit allocation, and for it to be negligible under interventionist systems, as several chapters in this book highlight.

In general, the more that banks are used by politicians and business oligarchs to allocate credit to allies, the stronger the incentives that regulators face to diverge from international banking standards.

Sceptical regulator

Given all the debate surrounding the appropriateness of Basel standards for low- and lower-middle-income countries, particularly Basel II and III, it is very plausible that the regulatory authority will be a source of resistance to the introduction of international standards, particularly the more complex elements of Basel II and III.

Supervisory capacity is a particularly acute constraint in many developing countries, and can be a major deterrent to moving from relatively simple compliance-based supervision under Basel I to risk-based supervision under Basel II (Beck, 2011; Fuchs et al., 2013; Gottschalk, 2010; Griffith-Jones and Gottschalk, 2016). Even national authorities in developed Basel member jurisdictions have found implementation of the new Basel standards challenging because of human resource constraints, above all the advanced, internal-ratings based approaches of Basel II and the macroprudential elements of Basel III (Bailey, 2014; BCBS, 2013).

The complex approaches of Basel II and III can also exacerbate information asymmetry between supervisors and banks, giving banks greater opportunity to game the regulations. These concerns are even more salient in developing countries, where human and financial resources are scarcer, and where remunerative differences and brain drain to the private sector pose significant challenges for regulatory authorities (Abdel-Baki, 2012; Fuchs et al., 2013; Gottschalk, 2016, 2010; Gottschalk and Griffith-Jones, 2006). Barth and Caprio (2018) argue that the Basel standards are too cumbersome and too costly for countries with small financial sectors, particularly countries with banking systems with total assets of less than US$10 billion.

In particular, we expect regulators to oppose the implementation of components that are irrelevant given the conditions in their financial markets (such as the requirements for counter-party credit risk in countries where banks do not have substantial trading books, and liquidity requirements where there is a shortage of assets that meet definitions of high quality) or overly complex given data availability and resource constraints (such as internal model-based approaches for assessing risk).

It is also plausible that regulators will block the implementation of international standards when this is likely to publicly expose weaknesses in the banking sector, and, in an extreme case, may even lead to banks being closed or trigger a financial crisis, for which they may be held accountable.

In general, the greater the resource constraints and technical challenges associated with implementing international standards, and the weaker the banking sector, the stronger the incentives that regulators face to diverge from implementing international standards.

Fragile domestic banks

Banks with business models focused exclusively on the domestic market in peripheral developing countries are likely to oppose the implementation of complex regulations because of the additional compliance costs this generates. An interesting finding from our empirical studies is that in low- and lower-middle-income countries, this often applies irrespective of whether these banks are foreign-owned or domestically owned. Opposition is likely to be strongest from small, weak banks, for whom the costs of implementation are highest.

In general, and unlike their counterparts in developed countries, banks in most developing countries are expected to be able to easily meet the levels of capital and liquidity required under Basel II and III, although adjustment costs vary greatly depending on the business characteristics of banks, variations in national tax regulations, and the availability of a sufficiently diversified portfolio of high-quality liquid assets.[9] The reason for this is that banks in developing countries typically hold capital well above the minimum international standards as a result of national regulatory requirements and the risky nature of the financial sector in which they operate. This does not mean that capital is necessarily of high quality as other factors, including accounting weaknesses, may put the quality of capital

---

[9] See for instance (Abdel-Baki, 2012; Frait and Tomšík, 2014; Gobat et al., 2014; Kasekende et al., 2011; World Bank, 2013). Another study of Bolivia, Colombia, Ecuador, and Peru suggests that major banks in these countries already meet the Basel III capital adequacy ratios (Galindo et al., 2011).

into question, but it does mean that nominal compliance with the Basel standards ought to be within reach. In Africa, for instance, more than one third of national regulators impose higher capital standards than required under both Basel II and Basel III (Kasekende et al., 2011).

However, the adjustment costs for banks of moving from Basel I to Basel II and III can be extremely high, particularly for smaller banks that have relied on relationship-based lending.[10] In particular, banks need to train staff and upgrade information technology systems to bring their risk management into line with Basel standards. As Rajan and Zingales (2003) explain, in the absence of disclosure requirements and proper enforcement, financing is typically relationship-based. Incumbent financiers use connections to obtain information to monitor loans, and various informal levers of power to cajole repayment. Disclosure and impartial enforcement tend to level the playing field and reduce barriers to an entrance into the financial sector. The incumbent financier's old skills become redundant, while new ones of credit evaluation and risk management become necessary. For banks focused on serving the domestic market, the implementation of international standards, particularly the more complex elements of Basel II and III, entails high costs and few gains.

Local subsidiaries of international banks may have more sophisticated risk-management systems, and greater technical expertise, reducing the costs of compliance relative to small domestically owned banks. We might reasonably expect this to lead foreign subsidiaries to champion the implementation of international standards, in order to gain a competitive edge over domestic banks. Yet our case studies don't bear this out. Instead, the local subsidiaries of international banks are ambivalent or even circumspect about the desirability of fully implementing Basel standards. Even if a bank has the internal systems to readily comply with Basel II and III, the situation in the wider economy, including a lack of readily available credit information and limited access to high-quality liquid assets, may impede compliance. Moreover, the structural features of the wider economy render banking sectors in many low- and lower-middle-income countries highly profitable and lacking in real competition, despite a high number of foreign and local banks (see Chapter 2). In such an environment, there is less incentive for the subsidiaries of international banks to try and use the introduction of complex regulations to gain a competitive edge.

Opposition to the implementation of international standards is likely to be particularly high among banks that are financially weak, poorly governed, or have lent extensively to politically connected clients. Basel implementation

---

[10] Tarullo (2008, p. 167) suggests that the costs to an individual bank of compliance with some of the more complex elements of Basel II (internal model approaches to credit risk) are US$42 million per institution.

is likely to engender particularly strong opposition from banks during an economic downturn.

In general, the higher the prevalence of weak domestic banks, the stronger the incentives that regulators face to diverge from international banking standards.

Pathways to convergence, divergence, and mock compliance

In the sections above, we set out the key actors and the factors that generate incentives for regulators in peripheral developing countries to converge on, or diverge from, international banking standards. A logical implication of the preceding discussion is that in countries where regulators face incentives to converge that are stronger than incentives to diverge, we expect greater levels of convergence on international standards than when incentives to diverge outweigh incentives to converge.

In line with the preceding discussion, we expect *convergence* to be high where a country has traditionally pursued a market-based approach to credit allocation and where the political and business elite pursue a development strategy that prioritizes integration into international finance and the expansion of the financial service sector; where regulators have substantial autonomy and are embedded in an international policy environment that encourages adoption of international standards; and where large domestic banks have a substantial international footprint.

Conversely, we expect *divergence* to be high in cases where a country has a history of interventionist policies towards the financial sector, or where politicians and business oligarchs extensively use banks for political ends; where the regulator is sceptical about the applicability of Basel standards for their local context and does not prioritize engagement in international policy networks that encourage the adoption of Basel standards; and where there are a substantial number of weak and poorly governed domestic banks.

Of course, country contexts are not static. In this section, we explore pathways of convergence and divergence, and explain why trajectories are likely to differ depending on which actor is driving the process. We also discuss the ways in which regulators are likely to respond when they face strong incentives to both converge and diverge, arguing that the outcome is likely to be mock compliance or stalled implementation.

A summary of the argument is reflected in Table 3.1.

Pathways to convergence

Countries can embark on a process of convergence with international standards for different reasons. *Policy-driven convergence* is led by incumbent politicians

Table 3.1 Pathways to convergence, divergence, and mock compliance

Drivers of convergence				Drivers of divergence				Pathway	Outcome
Politicians seeking international capital	Regulators engaging with peers	Domestic banks expanding into international markets	Sustained engagement with the World Bank and IMF	Politicians pursuing interventionist financial policies	Politicians and business oligarchs using banks to direct credit to allies	Sceptical regulator	Fragile domestic banks		
√	–	–	–	–	–	–	–	Policy-driven	Convergence
–	√	–	–	–	–	–	–	Regulator-driven	
–	–	√	–	–	–	–	–	Bank-driven	
–	–	–	√	–	–	–	–	IFI-driven	
–	–	–	–	√	–	–	–	Policy-driven	Divergence
–	–	–	–	–	√	–	–	Politically driven	
–	–	–	–	–	–	√	–	Regulator-driven	
–	–	–	–	–	–	–	√	Bank-driven	
√	–	–	–	√	–	–	–	Politically driven	Mock compliance
–	√	–	–	–	√	–	–	Regulator-driven	

Note: √ denotes the factor driving the process of convergence or divergence

with a strong vision of integrating their countries into global finance and expanding the financial services sector, perhaps with the support of local business elites. Politicians may face resistance from the regulator, particularly if the regulator has limited expertise and resources, and from small domestic banks, particularly if they are used to a lax regulatory environment. For these groups, the costs of adjustment to a new regulatory regime can be very high.

In this scenario, we expect politicians to make bold and ambitious public statements about the implementation of international standards to signal their reformist intentions to international and domestic audiences. However, implementation may be slow and targets frequently missed, as the regulatory authorities and domestic banks resist implementation. This scenario is unlikely to be stable, as politicians can take policy decisions that shift the preferences of the regulatory authority and banks over time. For instance, politicians may decide to reform and strengthen regulatory institutions, including by appointing governors to the central bank that are aligned with their strategy, providing them with additional resources and greater powers. Politicians may also take policy decisions that lead to the internationalization of the banking sector, shifting bank preferences in favour of implementing international standards. Over time we expect the consistent pursuit of convergence by politicians to result in high levels of Basel implementation.

Regulator-driven convergence is led by regulators, and is particularly likely when the regulatory authority has a high level of independence, and when senior officials engage extensively in international policy discussions and aspire to senior positions in international financial institutions organizations. In this situation, the regulatory authority is likely to adopt a normative identity focused on the championing of 'international best practices'.

Where regulators initiate convergence, they are may meet resistance from domestically oriented banks and ambivalence or opposition from politicians. Whether the reform initiative is successful depends on the level of independence the regulator has from the executive branch and whether it has sufficient resources and power to compel banks to comply. If for historical reasons the regulator has substantial independence that is widely respected by politicians, then the regulator may succeed in issuing regulations in line with international standards, and enforcing them.

In situations where banks and politicians form an alliance against regulatory reforms, the regulator may champion an ambitious level of convergence, but is unlikely to be able to follow through. This scenario can persist as a relatively stable equilibrium unless politicians change their policy stance and start to favour the internationalization of the financial sector, or domestic banks expand overseas and press for convergence. Regulators on their own are rarely powerful enough to shape the preferences of the other key actors (politicians and banks).

Bank-driven convergence occurs when large domestic banks champion the implementation of international standards as part of a drive to expand into new international markets. These proposals are likely to be met with opposition from smaller banks, and inertia or opposition from the regulator and politicians. In this situation, individual banks may voluntarily comply with the standards, while they continue to advocate and lobby for formal implementation by regulator. Where these banks have a high level of political influence, they may well succeed in gradually shifting the preferences of politicians and/or the regulator in favour of implementation. In particular, once banks have expanded overseas, home regulators have an incentive to implement international standards in order to facilitate cross-border supervision with host supervisors.

Finally, *IFI-driven convergence* occurs when implementation is championed by the IMF or World Bank. Where these are opposed by regulators, politicians, and banks, little meaningful implementation is likely to occur, unless it is made a condition for accessing financial support, in which case implementation may happen on paper, but is unlikely to fully occur in practice. However, if the regulatory authorities are supportive of implementation, then an alliance between international financial institutions and senior technocrats may be sufficiently powerful to convince politicians to push reforms through.

Pathways to divergence

Unlike processes of convergence, where regulators have to take the active step of aligning with international standards, divergence is the default option. Divergence occurs when a new set of international banking standards is agreed by the Basel Committee, but the regulator takes no steps to align domestic regulations with the new standards. Over time, as the Basel Committee issues more standards, the gap between national regulations and those prevailing at the international level widens, and divergence becomes more pronounced.

It is unlikely a regulator will actively change national regulations so that they are less aligned with international standards. As discussed above, the reputational gains from implementing international banking standards in the eyes of international investors and regulators in other jurisdictions can be substantial. Deliberate decisions to undo regulations based on international standards is likely to be interpreted as a signal of weak prudent regulation, with the attendant risk of capital flight. This is a similar logic to that outlined by Boylan (2001) who explains that newly elected governments will be reluctant to reverse central bank independence lest they pay the high costs associated with transgressing this sort of reputational mechanism: the massive outflow of foreign capital from their economies (Boylan, 2001, p. 57).

Divergence, then, occurs when politicians, regulators and banks are ambivalent towards international standards so there is no champion for implementation, or when one or more of these actors successfully thwarts their implementation. *Policy-driven divergence* occurs when the pursuit of interventionist financial sector policies creates a mismatch between the need for the regulator to ensure that government and state-owned banks make informed, impartial policy-based decisions in the direct allocation of credit, and the role envisaged for the regulator under the Basel framework. When interventionist policies are the main mechanism for allocating credit in the economy, we expect a high level of divergence to occur, and for this to be a relatively stable equilibrium, as regulators, politicians, and banks are all vested in this arrangement. In countries where there is a hybrid approach and only some institutions allocate credit in this way (such as national development banks), the regulator may exempt these institutions from complying with Basel standards, even if other banks are regulated under them. Indeed, governments in advanced and emerging economies have exempted their development banks from full compliance with Basel standards (Castro Carvalho et al., 2017; Hohl et al., 2018).

Politically driven divergence occurs when political and business elites have a vested interest in maintaining an opaque and highly personalized system of credit allocation. This is also likely to be a fairly stable equilibrium as an alliance of political and business elites is likely to have sufficient power to block any initiatives to implement international standards.

Regulator-driven divergence occurs when the regulator seeks to block the implementation of international standards out of concern that they are ill suited to the domestic context. Sceptical regulators are likely to advocate cautious and selective implementation of the standards and tailoring to suit the local context. Even when regulators have relatively little power, and convergence is being driven by politicians and internationally oriented banks, this strategy of selective adoption is likely to be successful. Politicians and banks are looking to use the implementation of the latest international standards as a signal to international investors, credit rating agencies, and regulators in other countries that regulation is sophisticated and effective. Precisely because they are relying on the implementation of standards as a heuristic shortcut for assessing the quality of regulation and supervision, these third parties are unlikely to differentiate between full and selective adoption of the latest international standards.

Bank-driven divergence is likely to occur when a critical mass of domestic banks are weak and poorly governed, and implementation of international standards is likely to publicly expose their fragility. Domestic banks are likely to advocate for a delay in implementation and, where they are particularly fragile, we expect regulators and politicians to support them, fearing reputational, economic, and political fall-out if they proceed with implementation. In situations where regulators want to regulate internationally oriented domestic banks according to international standards, they may opt to create a segmented regulatory regime, where international standards only apply to specific parts of the financial sector. For instance, many members of the Basel Committee exempt smaller banks from the purview of Basel II and III, only applying the full suite of Basel standards to large, internationally active banks (Castro Carvalho et al., 2017).

Mock compliance

Specific sets of dynamics occur when regulators simultaneously face strong and conflicting incentives to converge on and diverge from international standards. In this situation, regulators may issue regulations that are aligned with international standards, but *intentionally* fail to enforce them. Scholars have labelled such situations forms of 'cosmetic' or 'mock compliance' (Chey, 2014, 2006; Walter, 2008).

Politically driven mock compliance occurs when politicians want to implement international standards in order to signal creditworthiness to international investors, yet are concerned that implementation will limit their ability to direct credit for policy or political reasons. *Regulator-driven mock compliance* occurs when the regulator wants to implement international standards in order to support the international expansion of domestic banks and enhance their professional standing in the eyes of their peers, yet is concerned that implementation will expose hitherto undisclosed weaknesses in capital provisioning by domestically oriented banks.

Whether mock compliance is a sustainable strategy depends on the incentives and information available to the third parties to whom implementation is intended to signal sophisticated and robust regulation. Forms of mock or cosmetic compliance can be quite sophisticated and hard to detect without detailed scrutiny of national regulations. Japan, for instance, managed to circumvent the implementation of Basel I standards by maintaining national accounting standards that enabled banks to hold much less regulatory capital than intended by Basel I standards (Chey, 2014). Conversely, in situations where a country has a reputation for lax regulation and widespread regulatory forbearance, claims to be faithfully implementing and enforcing more complex regulations based on international standards are unlikely to persuade third parties unless there is an overhaul of the regulatory institution and a demonstrable change in the incentives of politicians and business elites. Paradoxically, even where mock compliance is suspected, credit rating agencies and even international creditors may not have an incentive to investigate or punish mock compliance: the global financial crisis has exposed the perverse incentives that persist in financial markets, particularly among intermediaries.

Conclusion

This chapter has set out a framework for explaining why regulators in peripheral developing countries respond very differently to international banking standards. It has identified the key actors, drivers of convergence and divergence, and explained how this leads to specific trajectories of convergence on and divergence from international standards, as well as instances of mock compliance.

Table 3.2 Matching case study countries against the explanatory framework

Country	Pathway	Outcome (number of BII and BIII components implemented)
Pakistan	Policy-driven convergence	Ambitious implementation (14)
Rwanda	Policy-driven convergence	Ambitious implementation (10)
Ghana	Policy-driven convergence	Ambitious implementation (8)
WAEMU	IFI-driven convergence	Ambitious implementation (10)
Tanzania	Regulator-driven convergence	Selective implementation (8)
Kenya	Regulator-driven convergence	Selective implementation (7)
Bolivia	Regulator-driven convergence	Selective implementation (5)
Nigeria	Regulator-driven mock compliance	Mock compliance (6)
Angola	Politically driven mock compliance	Mock compliance (5)
Vietnam	Politically driven mock compliance	Mock compliance (3)
Ethiopia	Policy-driven divergence	No implementation (0)

Notes: Ambitious implementation = includes at least one of the more complex components (internal models under Basel II and/or liquidity or macroprudential/liquidity standards under Basel III); Selective implementation = standardized approaches under Basel II and only microprudential capital requirements under Basel III; Mock compliance = on paper, not enforced

In the case study chapters that follow, we use this framework to explore the political economy of Basel implementation in eleven low- and lower-middle-income countries across Africa, Asia, and Latin America. While the real world never maps perfectly onto an abstracted explanatory framework, our case study countries can be classified according to the extent to which they align with the dynamics described above (Table 3.2).

In four cases (Pakistan, Rwanda, Ghana, and West African Economic and Monetary Union (WAEMU) implementation of Basel standards has been ambitious, and included some of the more complex elements of Basel II and/or III. In the first three cases, convergence was the result of politicians perusing policies to attract international capital into the financial services sector. In WAEMU it was the result of sustained engagement with the IMF, and a regulator that was very supportive of Basel implementation. In a further three cases (Tanzania, Kenya, and Bolivia) convergence was championed by regulators and resulted in selective adoption of the standards, with regulators implementing the more straightforward elements of the Basel framework. In three cases (Nigeria, Vietnam, and Angola) we see mock compliance, where international standards are implemented on paper but not enforced. In Nigeria mock compliance is driven by conflicted incentives within the regulatory authority, while in Angola and Vietnam it is driven by conflicted incentives on the part of politicians. Finally, we have one case of divergence (Ethiopia), which is driven by interventionist policies towards the financial sector.

In Chapters 4 to 15 we examine each case in turn.

References

Abdel-Baki, M., 2012. *Forecasting the Costs and Benefits of Implementing Basel III for North African Emerging Economies: An Application to Egypt and Tunisia*, AfDB Economic Brief. African Development Bank.

Alexander, K., Dhumale, R., Eatwell, J., 2006. *Global Governance of Financial Systems: The International Regulation of Systemic Risk, Finance and the Economy*. Oxford University Press, Oxford; New York.

Arriola, L.R., 2013. Capital and opposition in Africa: Coalition building in multiethnic societies. *World Politics* 65, 233–72. https://doi.org/10.1017/S0043887113000051.

Bach, D., Newman, A.L., 2010. Transgovernmental networks and domestic policy convergence: Evidence from insider trading regulation. *International Organization* 64, 505–28. https://doi.org/10.1017/S0020818310000135.

Bailey, A., 2014. *The capital adequacy of banks: Today's issues and what we have learned from the past.* Speech by Mr Andrew Bailey, Deputy Governor of Prudential Regulation and Chief Executive Officer of the Prudential Regulation Authority at the Bank of England, at Bloomberg, London, 10 July 2014. https://www.bis.org/review/r140711e.htm.

Ban, C., 2016. *Ruling Ideas: How Global Neoliberalism Goes Local*. Oxford University Press, New York.

Barth, J.R., Caprio, G., 2018. Regulation and supervision in financial development, in: Beck, T., Levine, R. (Eds.), *Handbook of Finance and Development*. Edward Elgar Publishing, Cheltenham, pp. 393–418. https://doi.org/10.4337/9781785360510.

Barth, J.R., Caprio, G., Levine, R., 2006. *Rethinking Bank Regulation: Till Angels Govern*. Cambridge University Press, Cambridge, England; New York.

Basel Committee on Banking Supervision, 2012. *Core principles for effective banking supervision*. Bank for International Settlements, Basel, Switzerland.

Bauer, G.W., Drevon, F., 2015. 2016 Outlook: Macro Challenges, Regulation Will Offset Improved Fundamentals, *Global Banking*. Moodys Investment Service.

Bauerle Danzman, S., Winecoff, W.K., Oatley, T., 2017. All crises are global: Capital cycles in an imbalanced international political economy. *International Studies Quarterly* 61, 907–23. https://doi.org/10.1093/isq/sqx054.

BCBS, 2013. *The regulatory framework: Balancing risk sensitivity, simplicity and comparability—discussion paper*.

Beck, T., 2011. *Financing Africa: Through the Crisis and Beyond*. World Bank, Washington DC.

Boone, C., 2005. State, capital, and the politics of banking reform in Sub-Saharan Africa. *Comparative Politics* 37, 401–20.

Boylan, D.M., 2001. *Defusing Democracy: Central Bank Autonomy and the Transition from Authoritarian Rule*. University of Michigan Press, Ann Arbor, MI.

Brummer, C., 2010. How international financial law works (and how it doesn't). *Geo. LJ* 99, 257.

Brummer, C., 2012. *Soft Law and the Global Financial System: Rule Making in the 21st Century*. Cambridge University Press, Cambridge; New York.

Cassidy, J., 2010. *How Markets Fail: The Logic of Economic Calamities*, Paperback ed. Penguin Books, London.

Castro Carvalho, A.P., Hohl, S., Raskopf, R., Ruhnau, S., 2017. *Proportionality in banking regulation: A cross country comparison* (FSI Insights on policy implementation No. 1). Bank for International Settlements.

Chey, H., 2014. *International Harmonization of Financial Regulation? The Politics of Global Diffusion of the Basel Capital Accord*. Routledge, New York.

Chey, H.-K., 2006. Explaining cosmetic compliance with international regulatory regimes: The implementation of the Basle Accord in Japan, 1998–2003. *New Political Economy* 11, 271–89. https://doi.org/10.1080/13563460600655664.

Chey, H.-K., 2007. Do markets enhance convergence on international standards? The case of financial regulation. *Regulation & Governance* 1, 295–311.

Chwieroth, J., 2007. Neoliberal economists and capital account liberalization in emerging markets. *International Organization* 61. https://doi.org/10.1017/S0020818307070154.

Chwieroth, J.M., 2010. *Capital Ideas: The IMF and the Rise of Financial Liberalization*. Princeton University Press, Princeton, NJ.

Culpepper, P.D., 2015. Structural power and political science in the post-crisis era. *Business and Politics* 17, 391–409. https://doi.org/10.1515/bap-2015-0031.

Dobbin, F., Simmons, B., Garrett, G., 2007. The global diffusion of public policies: Social construction, coercion, competition, or learning? *Annual Review of Sociology* 33, 449–72. https://doi.org/10.1146/annurev.soc.33.090106.142507.

Domínguez, J.I. (Ed.), 1997. *Technopols: Freeing Politics and Markets in Latin America in the 1990s*. Pennsylvania State Univ. Press, University Park, PA.

Enoch, C., Mathieu, P.H., Mecagni, M., Canales Kriljenko, J., 2015. *Pan-African Banks: Opportunities and Challenges for Cross-Border Oversight*. IMF, Washington, DC.

Ercanbrack, J., 2015. *The Transformation of Islamic Law in Global Financial Markets*. Cambridge University Press, Cambridge, UK.

FCIC, 2011. *The Financial Crisis Inquiry Report: Final report of the National Commission on the Causes of the Financial and Economic Crisis in the United States*, Financial Crisis Inquiry Commission, Washington, DC.

Frait, J., Tomšík, V., 2014. Impact and implementation challenges of the Basel Framework for emerging, developing and small economies. *Comparative Economic Studies* 56, 493–516. https://doi.org/10.1057/ces.2014.31.

FSI, 2015. *FSI Survey—Basel II, 2.5 and III Implementation*. BIS.

Fuchs, M., Losse-Mueller, T., Witte, M., 2013. The reform agenda for financial regulation and supervision in Africa, in: Beck, T., Maimbo, S.M. (Eds.), *Financial Sector Development in Africa: Opportunities and Challenges*. The World Bank, Washington DC.

Gadinis, S., 2015. Three pathways to global standards: Private, regulator, and ministry networks. *American Journal of International Law* 109, 1–57. https://doi.org/10.5305/amerjintelaw.109.1.0001.

Galindo, A., Rojas-Suarez, del Valle, M., 2011. *Capital requirements under Basel III in Latin America: The cases of Bolivia, Columbia, Ecuador and Peru*, Policy Brief. Inter-American Development Bank, Washington DC.

Ghosh, J., 2007. Central bank 'autonomy' in the age of finance, in: Bagchi, A.K., Dymski, G. (Eds.), *Capture and Exclude: Developing Economies and the Poor in Global Finance*. Tulika Books, New Delhi, pp. 39–51.

Gobat, J., Yanase, M., Maloney, J.F., 2014. *The net stable funding ratio: Impact and issues for consideration*. IMF Working Paper WP/14/106, IMF, Washington, DC. https://www.imf.org/external/pubs/ft/wp/2014/wp14106.pdf.

Goodhart, C.A.E., 2011. *The Basel Committee on Banking Supervision: A History of the Early Years, 1974–1997*. Cambridge University Press, Cambridge, UK; New York.

Gorton, G., 2012. *Misunderstanding Financial Crises: Why We Don't See Them Coming*. Oxford University Press, New York.

Gottschalk, R. (Ed.), 2010. *The Basel Capital Accords in Developing Countries: Challenges for Development Finance*. Palgrave Macmillan, Basingstoke, England; New York.

Gottschalk, R., 2016. Assessing capacity constraints for effective financial regulation in Sub-Saharan Africa, in: Griffith-Jones, S., Gottschalk, R. (Eds.), *Achieving Financial Stability and Growth in Africa*. Routledge, London, pp. 61–82.

Gottschalk, R., Griffith-Jones, S., 2006. *Review of Basel II implementation in low-income countries (Report prepared for the UK Department for International Development)*. Institute of Development Studies.

Griffith-Jones, S., Gottschalk, R. (Eds.), 2016. *Achieving Financial Stability and Growth in Africa*. Routledge Taylor & Francis Group, London.

Haggard, S., 1990. *Pathways from the Periphery: The Politics of Growth in the Newly Industrializing Countries*. Cornell Studies in Political Economy. Cornell University Press, Ithaca, NY.

Haggard, S., Lee, C.H. (Eds.), 1995. *Financial Systems and Economic Policy in Developing Countries*. Cornell University Press, Ithaca, NY.

Haldane, A., 2012. *The dog and the frisbee*. Paper by Andrew G. Haldane, given at the Federal Reserve Bank of Kansas City's 36th economic policy symposium, 'The Changing Policy Landscape', Jackson Hole, WY, 31 August 2012. https://www.bankofengland.co.uk/-/media/boe/files/paper/2012/the-dog-and-the-frisbee.pdf?la=en&hash=4DEAA2E6D1698A1A0891153A6B4CE70F308351D7.

Hallward-Driemeier, M., Nayyar, G., 2017. *Trouble in the making? The future of manufacturing-led development*. The World Bank. https://doi.org/10.1596/978-1-4648-1174-6.

Hamilton-Hart, N., 2003. *Asian States, Asian Bankers: Central Banking in Southeast Asia*. Singapore University Press, Singapore.

Helleiner, E., Porter, T., 2010. Making transnational networks more accountable. *Economics, Management, and Financial Markets* 5, 158–73.

Ho, D.E., 2002. Compliance and international soft law: Why do countries implement the Basel Accord? *Journal of International Economic Law* 5, 647–88. https://doi.org/10.1093/jiel/5.3.647.

Hohl, S., Sison, M.C., Sastny, T., Zamil, R., 2018. *The Basel framework in 100 jurisdictions: Implementation status and proportionality practices* (No. No 11), FSI Insights on policy implementation. Bank for International Settlements.

Hutchcroft, P.D., 1998. *Booty Capitalism: The Politics of Banking in the Philippines.* Cornell University Press, Ithaca, NY.

Johnson, S., Kwak, J., 2011. 13 *Bankers: The Wall Street Takeover and the Next Financial Meltdown*, 1st Vintage Books ed. Vintage Books, New York.

Jones, E., Knaack, P., 2019. Global financial regulation: Shortcomings and reform options. *Global Policy.* https://doi.org/10.1111/1758-5899.12656.

Jones, E. and A. O. Zeitz 2019. Regulatory Convergence in the Financial Periphery: How Interdependence Shapes Regulators' Decisions International Studies Quarterly, https://doi.org/10.1093/isq/sqz068

Jones, E., Zeitz, A.O., 2017. The limits of globalizing basel banking standards. *Journal of Financial Regulation* 3, 89–124.

Kasekende, L., Bagyenda, J., Brownbridge, M., 2011. *Basel III and the Global Reform of Financial Regulation: How Should Africa Respond? A Bank Regulator's Perspective.* New Rules for Global Finance, Washington, DC.

Killick, T., Gunatilaka, R., Marr, A., 1998. *Aid and the Political Economy of Policy Change.* Routledge, London; New York.

Knaack, P., 2017. An unlikely champion of global finance: Why is China exceeding global banking standards? *Journal of Current Chinese Affairs* 46, 41–79.

Lall, R., 2012. From failure to failure: The politics of international banking regulation. *Review of International Political Economy* 19, 609–38.

Lavelle, K.C., 2004. *The Politics of Equity Finance in Emerging Markets.* Oxford University Press, Oxford; New York.

Lavelle, K.C., 2013. *Money and Banks in the American Political System.* Cambridge University Press, Cambridge; New York.

Martinez-Diaz, L., Woods, N. (Eds.), 2009. *Networks of Influence? Developing Countries in a Networked Global Order.* Oxford University Press, Oxford; New York.

Mathieu, N., 1998. *Financial Sector Reform: A Review of World Bank Assistance*, OED study series. World Bank, Washington, DC.

Mattli, W., Woods, N., 2009. *The Politics of Global Regulation.* Princeton University Press, Princeton, NJ.

Maxfield, S., 1991. Bankers' alliances and economic policy patterns: Evidence from Mexico and Brazil. *Comparative Political Studies* 23, 419–58. https://doi.org/10.1177/0010414091023004001.

Maxfield, S., 1997. *Gatekeepers of Growth: The International Political Economy of Central Banking in Developing Countries*. Princeton University Press, Princeton, NJ.

Monnet, E., Pagliari, S., Vallee, S., 2014. *Europe between financial repression and regulatory capture*. (Bruegel Working Paper No. 2014/08).

Moody's Investors Service, 2015. *Basel III implementation in full swing: Global overview and credit implications*. Moody's Investors Service.

Mosley, L., 2003. *Global Capital and National Governments*. Cambridge University Press, Cambridge, UK.

Mosley, L., 2010. Regulating globally, implementing locally: The financial codes and standards effort. *Review of International Political Economy* 17, 724–61. https://doi.org/10.1080/09692290903529817.

Naqvi, N., Henow, A., Chang, H.-J., 2018. Kicking away the financial ladder? German development banking under economic globalisation. *Review of International Political Economy* 25, 672–98. https://doi.org/10.1080/09692290.2018.1480515.

Oatley, T., Nabors, R., 1998. Redistributive cooperation: Market failure, wealth transfers, and the Basle Accord. *International Organization* 52, 35–54.

Pagliari, S., Young, K.L., 2014. Leveraged interests: Financial industry power and the role of private sector coalitions. *Review of International Political Economy* 21, 575–610. https://doi.org/10.1080/09692290.2013.819811.

Pepinsky, T.B., 2013. The domestic politics of financial internationalization in the developing world. *Review of International Political Economy* 20, 848–80. https://doi.org/10.1080/09692290.2012.727361.

Porter, T., 2005. *Globalization and Finance*. Polity, Cambridge; Malden, MA.

Quillin, B., 2008. *International Financial Co-Operation: Political Economics of Compliance with the 1988 Basel Accord*, Routledge international studies in money and banking. Routledge, London; New York.

Rajan, R.G., Zingales, L., 2003. The great reversals: The politics of financial development in the twentieth century. *Journal of Financial Economics* 69, 5–50. https://doi.org/10.1016/S0304-405X(03)00125-9.

Reddy, Y.V., 2010. Regulation of the financial sector in developing countries, in: Griffith-Jones, S., Ocampo, J.A., Stiglitz, J.E. (Eds.), *Time for a Visible Hand: Lessons from the 2008 World Financial Crisis*. Oxford University Press, Oxford, UK, pp. 242–52.

Rey, H., 2015. *Dilemma not trilemma: The global financial cycle and monetary policy independence* (No. w21162). National Bureau of Economic Research, Cambridge, MA. https://doi.org/10.3386/w21162.

Romano, R., 2014. For diversity in the international regulation of financial institutions: Critiquing and recalibrating the Basel architecture. *Yale Journal on Regulation* 31.

Sharman, J.C., 2009. The bark is the bite: International organizations and blacklisting. *Review of International Political Economy* 16, 573–96. https://doi.org/10.1080/09692290802403502.

Sharman, J.C., 2010. Dysfunctional policy transfer in national tax blacklists. *Governance* 23, 623–39. https://doi.org/10.1111/j.1468-0491.2010.01501.x.

Simmons, B.A., Dobbin, F., Garrett, G., 2006. Introduction: The international diffusion of liberalism. *International Organization* 60, 781–810.

Singer, D.A., 2007. *Regulating Capital: Setting Standards for the International Financial System*. Cornell University Press, Ithaca, NY.

Stephanou, C., Mendoza, J.C., 2005. *Credit risk measurement under Basel II: An overview and implementation issues for developing countries*, World Bank Policy Research Working Paper. World Bank, Washington, DC.

Stigler, G.J., 1971. The theory of economic regulation. *The Bell Journal of Economics and Management Science* 2, 3. https://doi.org/10.2307/3003160.

Tarullo, D.K., 2008. *Banking on Basel: The future of International Financial Regulation*. Peterson Institute for International Economics, Washington, DC.

Underhill, G.R.D., Zhang, X., 2008. Setting the rules: Private power, political underpinning and legitimacy in global monetary and financial governance. *International Affairs* 84, 535–54.

Vishwanathan, N.S., 2015. *Basel III implementation: Challenges for Indian banking system*. Inaugural address delivered by Mr. N.S. Vishwanathan, Executive Director of the Reserve Bank of India, on the occasion of the National Conference on 'BASEL III Implementation: Challenges for Indian banking system', organized by The Associated Chambers of Commerce & Industry of India with support of the National Institute of Bank Management, Mumbai, 31 August 2015. https://www.bis.org/review/r150917a.pdf.

Wade, J., 2018. Fitch ratings: Closer alignment with Basel III Standards will improve credit profile of Colombian banks. *Finance Colombia*.

Walter, A., 2008. *Governing Finance: East Asia's Adoption of International Standards*, Cornell studies in money. Cornell University Press, Ithaca, NY.

Walter, A., 2010. Chinese attitudes towards global financial regulatory cooperation: Revisionist or status quo?, in: Pagliari, S., Helleiner, E., Zimmerman, Hubert (Eds.), *Global Finance in Crisis: The Politics of International Regulatory Change*. Routledge, London.

Woo-Cumings, M. (Ed.), 1999. *The Developmental State*, Cornell studies in political economy. Cornell University Press, Ithaca, NY.

World Bank, 2013. *Global finance development report 2014: Financial inclusion*. World Bank, Washington DC.

Zysman, J., 1983. *Governments, Markets, and Growth: Financial Systems and the Politics of Industrial Change*, Cornell studies in political economy. Cornell University Press, Ithaca, NY.

PART II

CASE STUDIES

4

Pakistan

Politicians, Regulations, and Banks Advocate Basel

Natalya Naqvi

Introduction

In the 1950s and 60s, Pakistan was held up as the poster-child for late development and state-led industrialization, and considered on a par with South Korea. Since then, the two have followed markedly different development trajectories. Since the 1990s, Pakistan was among a set of developing countries that wholeheartedly implemented IFI sponsored liberalization reform, resulting in a dramatic transformation from a state-led 'developmentalist' model up until the 1970s, to a 'neoliberal' model based on Washington Consensus principles after the 2000s. As part of these reforms, Pakistan transformed its tightly controlled, highly segmented, public bank-dominated financial system into an almost fully privatized, deregulated, and liberalized one by the 2000s. One of the key tenets of Pakistan's new development model is the promotion of services exports, especially financial services, by encouraging the internationalization of the banking sector, making it an especially interesting case to observe the causal mechanisms of adoption of international financial standards. The Pakistani case also shows how liberalization pressures from international financial institutions in one period can create path dependencies, leading to policy-driven convergence over time. Pakistan is also one of the few cases where all three major actors (politicians, regulators, and banks) faced strong incentives to converge on international standards by the 2000s. This led to substantive compliance, compared to cases like Nigeria or Vietnam where one or more of the major actors had conflicting incentives, resulting instead in mock compliance (Table 4.1).

As part and parcel of banking sector internationalization, Pakistan is one of the highest adopters and implementers of Basel I, II, and III and the Basel Core Principles (BCPs), but with different actors driving adoption over time. Starting from a domestically oriented model, over the course of the 1980s to 2000s, Pakistan's politicians were the initial drivers for convergence. Subsequently, regulators pushed for Basel adoption, and finally, once the banks' interests became aligned with those of politicians and regulators, all three major actors pushed for a concerted convergence on Basel standards.

Natalya Naqvi, *Pakistan: Politicians, Regulations, and Banks Advocate Basel* In: *The Political Economy of Bank Regulation in Developing Countries: Risk and Reputation.* Edited by: Emily Jones, Oxford University Press (2020).

Table 4.1 Pakistan: key indicators

Pakistan	
GDP per capita (current US$, 2017)	1,584
Bank assets (current US$)	120.1 bn
Bank assets (% of GDP)	43.1
Stock market capitalization (% of GDP)	28.1
Credit allocation to private sector (% of GDP)	16.5
Credit allocation to government (% of GDP)	28.6
Polity IV score (2017)	7

Note: All data is from 2016 unless otherwise indicated.

Source: FSI Database, IMF (2018); GDI Database, World Bank (2017); Polity IV (2014)

While Basel I and BCP adoption in Pakistan was a result of IMF and World Bank conditionality, over the course of the late 1980s and 2000s, Pakistani politicians, whether civilian or military, increasingly shifted away from prioritizing state-led industrial development, to embrace a more international orientation and championing financial services exports in particular. A liberalized, privatized, and internationalized banking sector was seen as vital to this development strategy, even though the specifics of Basel adoption fell under politicians' radar and were not as politically salient an issue as other reforms like bank privatization. The adoption of international banking standards was seen as important for internationalizing the banking sector, but regulators also made instrumental use of Basel standards to force bank consolidation.

As part of IFI conditionality and financial liberalization, the independence and regulatory power of the Pakistani central bank, the State Bank of Pakistan (SBP), was greatly strengthened. At the same time, internationally oriented politicians began to appoint former IFI bureaucrats to key posts at the SBP, generating strong peer incentives for officials to international standards. By 2000 the SBP took over from the IFIs in becoming the main actor driving through Basel I and then II adoption. Initially this was done against the wishes of the domestic banks, which viewed the adoption of international standards as a heavy burden, but were not politically powerful enough to oppose the SBP, either because they were still in the process of privatization, or were loss-making because of the financial crisis of the 1990s. During this period, foreign banks were the SBP's main partners in pushing forward adoption and helping local banks to implement. By 2007/8, however, the situation dramatically reversed, with the domestic banks taking the lead on adoption, while the SBP lost some of its steam after international financial standards were discredited in Pakistan for failing to stop the global financial crisis. By this point, not only had the highly internationalized domestic private banks incurred massive sunk costs by investing in costly Basel-related infrastructure, but they had emerged as a powerful interest group because of the transfer of ownership to domestic industrial conglomerates or foreign investors, as well as the fact that the new development model's emphasis on financial services placed them at a privileged position in the economy, giving them leverage over the SBP. The banks now saw staying up to date with international standards as a vital signalling mechanism to preserve their global position. For its part, although the SBP was less zealous about Basel III than it had been about Basel II, in order to compensate for Pakistan's FATF blacklisting, it not only went ahead with Basel III adoption, but modified certain elements to make them even more stringent than the original standard. Therefore, in Pakistan after 2007, incentives for convergence were salient for all three sets of major actors, which explains the high degree of adoption and implementation.

The following analysis is based on central bank, IMF, World Bank, and other official documents, speeches of central bank governors, news articles from major local business newspapers, and twenty-seven semi-structured, off-record interviews. The interviews were conducted in Karachi between December 2016 and January 2017, with bank CEOs, CFOs, and risk managers, at large and medium domestic private banks, foreign banks, a domestic public bank, a microfinance institution, current and former senior officials at the central bank, consultancies which specialized in helping banks with Basel implementation, as well as with industry associations Pakistan Banking Association, Pakistan Business Council, and Karachi Chambers of Industry.

Political economic context

Pakistan is a lower-middle-income country with a high degree of external vulnerability due to a periodic balance of payments crisis and a development model that prioritized attracting foreign investment. After the late 1980s, Pakistan's development model began changing wholescale from a 'developmentalist' state-led model based on import substitution industrialization, to a 'neoliberal' model based on 'Washington consensus' principles (Zaidi, 2015). While Pakistan is no longer a primarily agricultural economy, industrial growth has stagnated since the 80s, and the economy has become increasingly services based (Zaidi, 2015).

The financial system

Until the late 1980s, Pakistan had a typically 'repressed' financial system, with a high degree of policy directed lending through public development finance institutions (DFIs), a nationalized commercial banking system, and credit planning (Janjua, 2004, 2003).

Financial liberalization and deregulation began in 1988 under an IMF structural adjustment program (Janjua, 2003). DFIs and policy lending were phased out, and four of the five nationalized commercial banks were privatized with only National Bank of Pakistan (NBP) left in the public sector, entry restrictions on foreign banks relaxed, and bank licensing liberalized (Naqvi, 2018). Significant changes in the regulatory framework were also made. Prior to the 1990s, regulatory functions were shared between the Ministry of Finance, Pakistan Banking Council (PBC), SBP, and the Corporate Law Authority (CLA). On the recommendation of the IMF, in 1997, the PBC was abolished in 1997, making the SBP sole regulator of the banking system (Janjua, 2004).

Post-liberalization financial structure

By the mid-2000s, the financial sector was highly liberalized and almost completely privately owned (Naqvi, 2018). The new 'outward-oriented' development strategy envisioned a financial sector that was highly profitable and internationally competitive in order to contribute to GDP, and in particular to increase financial services exports (Government of Pakistan, 2007; International Trade Centre with Government of Pakistan, 2007). The new strategy depended on attracting foreign investment into the domestic financial sector, as well as encouraging domestic banks to internationalize in order to profit from fees-based activities in their foreign branches. SBP governor Muhammad Yaqub captured this change in strategy in a 1993 speech in which he stated that he was determined to transform the banking industry '[in]to a service industry from a bureaucratic machinery' (Yaqub, 1993, cited in Janjua, 2003, p. 286).

By the 2000s, the post-liberalization Pakistani financial system was highly concentrated, consisting mainly of five large domestic commercial banks, MCB, UBL, HBL, ABL, and NBP, which together account for about 80 per cent of all profits in the banking sector, and 60 per cent of bank deposits (Munir and Naqvi, 2015). These five banks were internationally oriented: although domestic for regulatory purposes, they became partially foreign owned, with majority shareholdings of UBL and HBL being sold to foreign investors (Munir and Naqvi, 2015). These banks also had an extensive historic network of foreign branches in countries ranging from the UK, Europe, and the US, to Asia Pacific, the Middle East, and Africa (HBL UBL, MCB, ABL, NBP company accounts), which catered mainly to the Pakistani diaspora. After bank licensing was deregulated, a variable number of small private banks emerged, but these never managed to capture significant market share, since they could not compete with the extensive branch network of the five large commercial banks. Although the number of foreign banks increased (see Figure 4.1), their activities remained limited to investment banking, or in some cases consumer finance, as they could not compete with the large commercial banks in capturing deposits either. The large increase in foreign ownership of bank assets therefore reflects increased

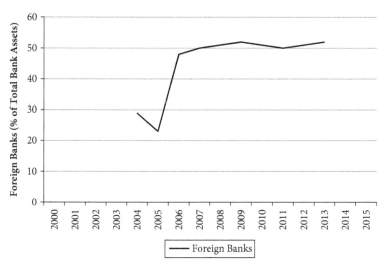

Figure 4.1 Pakistan: foreign ownership in the banking sector.

Source: Claessens and Horen (2014)

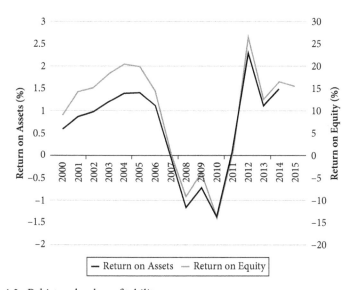

Figure 4.2 Pakistan: bank profitability.

Source: Bankscope and Orbis Bank Focus, Bureau van Dijk (2018)

foreign shareholding of the large five banks rather than the dominance of foreign bank subsidiaries.

Following a period of crisis while they were being privatized, the commercial banks became extremely profitable, especially between 2004 and 2007, and again after the financial crisis (see Figure 4.2). Although real-economy lending had fallen, the banks remained profitable through heavy investments in risk-free but high-yielding government bonds (Naqvi, 2018).

Political economy of governing elites, regulators, and banks

The two main political parties, the PPP and PML-N, which have shared power since the return to democracy in the 1990s, shared a similar 'outward-oriented' financial agenda under the strong influence of the World Bank and IMF. During the 2000s under the military dictatorship of Pervez Musharraf, banking regulation was delegated to the newly autonomous SBP, which carried the pace of financial reforms forward. Since the resumption of democracy under PPP in 2008 and then PML-N in 2013, financial sector policy has not shifted. In comparison to the dramatic changes that have taken place in the Pakistani financial system during the 1990s, especially bank privatization, Basel adoption remains a relatively uncontroversial de-politicized topic, with low visibility in electoral politics.

The domestic banks had little political influence the 1970s and 90s because they were under government ownership, or in the process of privatization. At the same time, institutional reforms under IMF programmes drastically increased the SBP's authority and autonomy, giving it the upper hand in enforcing bank regulation. However, once privatization was completed by the mid-2000s, the situation reversed dramatically.

The highly concentrated five large commercial banks articulated their interests to the SBP through the well-organized Pakistan Bankers Association (PBA). Although the PBA represents both domestic and foreign banks, it is dominated by the large privatized commercial banks. Not only were the banks politically well connected, but the government's strategy of promoting banks' foreign profits also ensured their privileged position in the economy, as did their high profitability from 2004 onwards, increasing their leverage over the SBP.

Pakistan's adoption and implementation of Basel I, II, and III, and the Basel Core Principles

Pre-Basel I financial regulation

Prior to the introduction of Basel I standards in the late 1990s, Pakistani regulators had in place a number of regulations for the purpose of maintaining financial system stability, including strict bank and branch licensing, bank-wise credit ceilings, minimum paid-up capital, and a liquidity requirement (Janjua, 2004, 2003). These regulations began to be phased out as they were replaced with the various Basel Accords, but minimum paid-up capital requirements were maintained and continued to be raised.

Basel I

Pakistan was a relatively late adopter of Basel I, waiting nine years after it was agreed internationally to introduce it into domestic regulation. In 1997, all commercial banks, NBFIs, and foreign banks were instructed to adopt the system of risk-weighted capital in line with the Basel accord through BPRD Circular #36 of 4 November 1997. After a significant delay following the BCBS's 1996 amendment to Basel I to include a capital charge for market risk, the SBP amended the capital adequacy framework, in order to 'align the regulatory capital requirement with the internationally accepted standards and institute a true risk-based capital adequacy framework' in August 2004 (State Bank of Pakistan, 2004).

Basel Core Principles

A few years after the Basel Core Principles were announced by the BCBS in 1997, the SBP made moves to incorporate these into the domestic regulatory framework (State Bank of Pakistan, 2005). In 2003 the SBP issued a 'Handbook for Corporate Governance', which was modelled directly on the Core Principles, as these were considered 'international best practise' at the time (Akhtar, 2006a). The new governance document provided guidelines for bank boards of directors, management, and auditors (see State Bank of Pakistan, 2003).

Basel II

Basel II adoption by Pakistan was extremely fast, showing the SBP's enthusiasm for the new regulations. The SBP issued a 'roadmap' for Basel II implementation in March 2005 via BSD Circular No. 3 2005, less than a year after the BCBS replaced Basel I with Basel II, followed by detailed instructions in June 2006 via BSD Circular #8 of 27 June 2006.

Aside from the speed of Basel II adoption, two other patterns are striking. Firstly, unlike many other peripheral countries, which were selective in their adoption, Pakistan adopted nine out of ten Basel II components, compared to an average of four for non-BCBS member countries (Jones and Zeitz, 2019). Pakistan was ambitious in its adoption, going quickly for the most complex components, including Internal Rating Based (IRB) approaches. In addition, the components were introduced by the SBP in a largely unmodified form, with the instruction document following the original Basel II documents (BCBS, 2004) almost word for word, even giving detailed instructions for the calculation of risk weights for financial instruments that barely existed in Pakistan, such as collateralized OTC derivatives. Basel II regulations in Pakistan were not modified for specialized banks, DFIs, or smaller banks.

Basel III

While Basel III adoption was still high compared to other non-BCBS countries, with Pakistan implementing four out of eight, compared to an average of just one out of eight components by 2015, the SBP took a more gradual approach compared to its speedy adoption of Basel II. Basel III began to be adopted with a three-year delay from when the BCBS issued the new accord in 2010, and the initial set of instructions contained only requirements to implement the core capital, leverage ratio, and capital conservations buffer, as the SBP wanted some time to consult with all the relevant stakeholders about the relevance of elements such as the countercyclical capital buffer, LCR, NSFR, and domestic systemically important financial institutions (D-SIFI). However, this gradual approach was combined with the SBP modifying certain elements of Basel III such as the CAR and capital conservation buffer to make them even stricter than the original requirements (FSI, 2015; State Bank of Pakistan, 2016) (Table 4.2).

Enforcement

Available assessments from IMF FSAPs and Article IV Consultations, World Bank reports, SBP self-assessments, and the US Department of State's Investment Climate Statements, between 1998 and 2017, suggest that although compliance lagged during the initial phases of Basel I and II implementation during the late 1990s and early 2000s because of capacity constraints, especially among small banks, since the mid-2000s compliance with implemented Basel II and III standards has been largely substantive. Pakistan is also judged by the IMF to have achieved 'a degree of compliance with most of the Core Principles' (IMF, 2004, p. 28).

Table 4.2 Pakistan: adoption of Basel standards

Basel component	Adoption	Implementation
Basel I	BPRD Circular 36 of Nov 1997—Credit risk BSD Circular 12 of August 2004—Market risk	Credit risk—1998 Market risk—2004
Basel II	BSD Circular 3 of March 2005 (Roadmap document) and BSD Circular 8 of June 2006 (detailed instructions) (9/10 components)	Standardized approach—2008 Internal-ratings-based approach—2010
Basel III	BPRD Circular 6 of 2013 BPRD Circular 8 of 2016 (4/8 components)	CET-1, CCB, leverage ratio—2013–19 LCR and NSFR—2017–18

Source: Various SBP (State Bank of Pakistan) documents

This was broadly confirmed by interviews with regulators at the central bank, the SBP, and independent consultants. Punishment for non-compliance includes limiting of banking activities, and eventually revoking of banking licences, which suggests that adopted standards were enforced. By the time interviews were conducted in December 2016, both large and small banks were compliant with the Basel II and III provisions mandated by SBP regulations, but three large banks and one medium-size bank had already moved to the advanced approaches of Basel II, which were not mandatory. At the time of the interviews, four banks were compliant with the foundation internal-ratings-based approach, in terms of operational risk; all the large banks had moved to the standardized/alternative standardized approach; while two were trying to implement the advanced measurement approaches (various interviews with consultancies and domestic banks). No exemptions were made in Basel I, II, or III compliance for specialized banks, DFIs, or small banks.

Political economy of Basel adoption

Basel adoption in Pakistan can broadly be divided into three distinct phases, the first being IFI led, the second central bank led, and third private bank led. While Basel I was first introduced to Pakistan as part of a wider regulatory overhaul under various World Bank programmes, the newly strengthened SBP soon took the reins and became an ardent advocate of Basel II. This was despite the fact that banks were initially reluctant because of the high regulatory cost of adoption. The financial crisis proved to be a turning point in the SBP's attitude to international regulatory standards, with the perceived failure of Basel II in preventing the global financial crisis resulting in a much more cautious attitude to adoption. However, by this time, a new advocate for Basel II and then III had emerged; the large internationalized domestic commercial banks that had initially been reluctant adopters of Basel standards. These banks now saw keeping up to date with the most sophisticated international standards as vital to maintaining their global position.

IFI-led adoption of Basel I and BCP (1998–2000)

During this first phase, the World Bank and IMF were the main players in driving through Basel I adoption as part of structural adjustment conditionalities (Janjua, 2004). Following the end of military rule, two main political parties, the centre-left, formerly socialist, Pakistan People's Party (PPP), supported by industrial and rural workers, but also members of the landed elite, and the centre-right, fiscally and socially conservative Pakistan Muslim League-Nawaz (PML-N), which draws its support from influential industrialists and agriculturalists of the most populous Punjab province, have alternated in power over the course of the 1990s. Despite their divergent political stances and constituencies, they have shared a remarkably similar financial agenda, centralized around liberalization and privatization. This was because these civilian governments, especially the PML-N government of 1997, were closely aligned with the IFIs in terms of international economic policy orientation (Zaidi, 2015). For example, full-time finance ministers were rarely appointed during this time, with civilian governments instead relying on advisors from the IMF and World Bank to ensure the implementation of conditionalities (Zaidi, 2015). Although the SBP was involved in the regulatory reform process, it did not have a very strong role in deciding the direction of reform because of its limited regulatory authority in the early 90s (World Bank, 1998). There is no available evidence to suggest that the then still nationalized banking system had an important role to play either. During this time, the main opposition to regulatory overhaul came from the Federation of Pakistan Chambers of Commerce and Industry, who feared that complex regulations would make access to credit more difficult (Janjua, 2004). However, in comparison to the controversial bank privatization programme, which saw many union protests (Munir and Naqvi, 2017), Basel I adoption remained a relatively de-politicized topic, with low visibility in electoral politics.

Adoption of Basel I and Core Principles occurred under the hard conditionalities of the 1997 World Bank Banking Sector Adjustment Loan (BSAL) (World Bank, 1998) and the October 1997 IMF Exchange Credit Fund and Exchange Facility Fund programmes. One of the main 'project objectives' of the World Bank BSAL I, on which release of funds for the next BSAL was conditional, included revising capital adequacy rules to bring them in line with the Basel I minimum CAR of 8 per cent by 31 December 1997 (World Bank, 1998). The IMF programmes included a similar performance criterion to make prudential regulations on capital adequacy consistent with international norms (Wilf, 2017). In the years following, all of the nationalized commercial banks became compliant, with only four of the small banks remaining non-compliant by 2002, while non-compliant DFIs were gradually phased out (Janjua, 2004).

Central bank-led adoption of Basel I and II (2000–7)

During the 2000s, although the IMF and World Bank remained important in influencing Pakistan's financial sector policies, the government, especially the newly independent central bank, took the reins of economic policymaking under the military dictatorship of Pervez Musharraf. Under Shaukat Aziz, a former international investment banker, who was appointed finance minister in 1999, and then prime minister in 2004, the international orientation of the financial sector was consolidated. Aziz's vision revolved around globalizing the banking sector; both through attracting inward foreign investment and through outward internationalization of Pakistani banks. Since the resumption of democracy under the PPP in 2008 and then PML-N in 2013, financial sector policy has remained outward oriented.

During this period banking regulation was delegated to the newly autonomous SBP, which had started taking a much more proactive role in designing financial sector policy as its regulatory powers had been expanded, and autonomy increased under IFI structural adjustment. While the independent central bank had sole authority over financial regulation, its policies were in keeping with the general thrust of Aziz's vision for the financial sector, because SBP governors were appointed by the Federal Government. Basel II adoption was given impetus by the appointment of two SBP governors between 1999 and 2009, Ishrat Hussain and Shamshad Akhtar, who were ardent advocates of adopting Basel II, influenced by their IFI background. While the domestic banks were initially resistant to Basel II implementation because of the heavy costs it would entail, the foreign banks emerged as a key partner in Basel I and II implementation. The SBP had a great amount of leverage over domestic private banks during the early 2000s, as the large banks were still being privatized, and were at times loss-making, limiting their political influence and economic importance.

By the 2000s, the SBP's authority and independence was dramatically increased mainly as a result of IFI conditionalities during the 1990s. On the recommendation of the IMF, the SBP was made the sole regulator of the banking system in 1991, given formal independence from the Ministry of Finance in 1994 (Janjua, 2004). Furthermore, a number of measures were taken to strengthen the regulatory capacity of the SBP under the World Bank FSAL, between 1997 and 1999. An international consultant was hired in order to train the Banking Supervision Department in charge of prudential regulation and identify and recruit qualified supervision staff (World Bank, 1998).

Reflecting governing elites increasing outward orientation after the 1980s, the nature of SBP governors appointed by the Federal Government changed accordingly. Between 1947 and the late 1970s, the first six governors had domestic banking or civil service backgrounds, and the next five governors had only loose affiliations with the IFIs, for instance holdings consultancy assignments, or attending training courses. The appointment of career IMF bureaucrat Muhammad Yaqub in 1993 reflected the clear shift towards outward orientation by the civilian governments of the 1990s. The appointment of Ishrat Hussain in 1999 and then Shamshad Akhtar in 2006, who had previously made their careers in the World Bank and Asian Development Bank, respectively, by the Musharraf dictatorship, reflected the consolidation of the new financial sectors strategy under Shaukat Aziz. This was followed by the appointment of international investment bankers as governors from 2009 onwards (Munir and Naqvi, 2017).

Therefore, the nature and power of the SBP had changed dramatically by the early 2000s, from a nationally oriented developmentalist central bank, to one that was outward looking and deeply embedded in transnational regulatory networks. In particular, by 1999, the institutional reforms that gave it sufficient independence regulatory power had been completed, and coincided with the appointment of Ishrat Hussain who was an aggressive advocate for Basel I and II. At the same time, the commercial banks remained weak, while governing elites shared the SBP's outward orientation, giving the SBP leadership an unprecedented degree of power. This was reflected in the speed with which Basel II was adopted, and the fact that all elements were adopted without modification.

Basel I and II adoption were important for the SBP in the new regime for three complementary reasons. Firstly, and most importantly, with the change in development model and reorientation of financial sector strategy towards improving Pakistani banks global positioning (Dawn, 2007), Basel adoption came to be seen as a necessary signalling tool to attract foreign investors.

Secondly, liberalization of bank licensing in 1991 had led to the proliferation of a large number of small private banks (Zaidi, 2005). These were seen as lacking sufficient scale to become internationally competitive with cross-border banks post-liberalization. According to Hussain, 'The financial institutions [small banks] are neither conducive to positioning Pakistan in the global financial markets nor helpful for efficient intermediation within Pakistan' (Hussain, 2001a). The SBP therefore actively pursued a policy of encouraging consolidation in the banking sector through merger and acquisition during the first decade of the 2000s (Dawn, 2005). Basel I and II regulations proved a useful tool for this policy, as small banks found it much harder to meet the requirements, which then gave the SBP an excuse to revoke bank licenses, or force a merger. Between 2001 and 2006 alone, twenty-one financial institutions were merged or taken over (Akhtar, 2006b).

Finally, in part because of their socialization at the IFIs, top officials at the SBP, especially governors Ishrat Hussain and Shamshad Akhtar, believed that Basel I and then II were better tools for risk management because of their socialization at the IFIs. They thought Basel would become especially important in protecting against the risks of globally interconnected financial markets, as the traditionally closed Pakistani financial system liberalized externally. In line with the thinking of the time, which SBP officials were familiar with because of their strong links with transnational regulatory networks, and in reaction to the previous era of state intervention, the governor believed in the philosophy underlying Basel II, namely that light-touch regulation and market discipline would be more effective in promoting financial stability. For example, according to Ishrat Hussain in a 2001 speech, 'Economic theory and international experience all suggest that the Central Bank should encourage such transparent, disclosure-based and market-based regulation that the financial institutions themselves have the incentive to comply with the regulations for their own protection' (Hussain, 2001b).

This top-down pressure for implementation by SBP governors was complemented by 'peer pressure' on more junior officers in the Banking Policy Review department responsible for Basel implementation from transnational regulatory networks. In particular, SBP officials noted that they had experienced peer pressure from other central banks they interacted with often, including those in Malaysia, Singapore, the Philippines, and Bangladesh, for example through meetings of the FSB Regional Consultative Group for Asia, for which Pakistan has acted as co-chair, or meetings of SAARCFinance, a network of central bank governors of the SAARC region[1] (Financial Stability Board, 2016).

When the Basel II regime replaced Basel I in 2004, the SBP was already well connected to transnational regulatory networks, and keeping abreast of current international developments and 'best practice'. According to an interview with an SBP official responsible for Basel implementation, 'we have constantly been observing international developments. There has been an accepted notion in SBP that all international standards should be complied with until it is seen that there is some kind of negative'.[2] Following international regulators, Ishrat Hussain thought that Basel I had some 'inherent rigidities' that undermined its effectiveness, which were remedied by Basel II (Hussain, 2005).

Meanwhile, the domestic banks, although not opposed to Basel II in principle, were reluctant to adopt the new standards too quickly because of the heavy costs this would entail. A survey conducted by the SBP in 2003 found that the majority of banks (49 per cent) thought that Basel II should not be implemented until 2008, and that the Standardized Approach as opposed to the IRB would be sufficient (State Bank of Pakistan, 2005). Not only did domestic banks initially lack the computerized systems and reliable data that adoption would have required, they also often had to hire expensive foreign consultancies and invest in expensive software infrastructure in order to ensure compliance (interviews with various domestic banks and consultants). In 2004, Ishrat Hussain chastised the domestic banks for lagging behind in implementation: 'I have very little doubt that the foreign banks operating in Pakistan will have any serious problems in making the transition successfully but I remain very much worried about our domestic banks... I see that our large banks have not yet woken up to attract the human resource of the right kind, set up the internal rating systems and the supporting technology' (Hussain, 2004). According to interviewees, the SBP pushed ahead with Basel II adoption despite the banks' complaints: 'Ishrat's response to bank complaints was that if you cannot do this [implement Basel II] then you have no business running a bank and I will find a buyer for you'.[3] Falling behind on adoption also carried severe penalties that included the imposition of heavy fines, limiting of banking activities, and eventually revocation of banking licenses

---

[1] SBP Official, Karachi, 6 January 2017.   [2] SBP Official, Karachi, 6 January 2017.
[3] CEO, Consultancy, Karachi, 27 December 2016.

(Iqbal, 2005). According to interviewees, whereas before the 2000s banks never faced penalties for non-compliance with SBP regulation, under Hussain these penalties were rigorously enforced. During this period, the domestic banks were still in the process of privatization, or were loss-making because of the financial crisis of the 1990s, and so were not politically powerful enough to oppose the SBP.

Initially, therefore, the foreign banks were the SBP's main partner in pushing the Basel agenda through, since they were required by their headquarters to become compliant. The foreign banks wanted domestic banks to implement Basel II both because they were engaged in correspondent banking relationships with the domestic banks, and they found Basel II compliance reassuring in this regard, but also because they did not want to be at a competitive disadvantage to domestic banks.[4] Another important channel through which foreign banks aided Basel II implementation was through the transfer of personnel from early adopting foreign banks such as Citibank, American Express, and Bank of America to domestic banks. After the SBP made Basel II compliance mandatory, many domestic banks poached foreign bank-trained personnel because of the lack of local expertise on Basel II, in order to rush ahead with compliance.[5]

Under Shamshad Akhtar, the drive for Basel II implementation was strengthened. Akhtar was a strong advocate for Basel II, and described it as nothing short of a 'revolution' in risk management (Dawn, 2006). The Pakistan Banks Association (PBA) had to argue with her from time to time to tone down her approach. According to a foreign banker, 'the SBP under Shamshad was so over-ambitious that the PBA's Basel committee had to work with local and foreign banks to help convince her to slow down. The local banks were having a lot of trouble in implementation'.[6]

In particular, while the large banks were more easily able to bear the costs associated with Basel adoption, and could afford to hold the required amount of capital, the small banks felt especially penalized.[7] This was not a concern for the SBP as the policy of banking sector consolidation continued under Akhtar. According to an SBP employee who had worked closely with Akhtar, 'It [Basel II and increases in minimum capital requirements] was a political move—we felt that some people wanted to get banking licenses and we didn't want them to get it, and we thought it would be good if some of the smaller banks that were facing solvency and liquidity problems merged. They protested but we implemented it anyway'.[8]

While Basel II implementation was not a part of IFI conditionality, the IMF praised these developments, arguing that the SBP's establishment of a roadmap for Basel II implementation had contributed to strengthening the regulatory

---

[4] CEO, foreign bank, Karachi, 22 December 2016.
[5] CEO, consultancy, Karachi, 27 December 2016.
[6] CEO, foreign bank, Karachi, 22 December 2016.
[7] Consultancy, Karachi, 20 December 2016.   [8] SBP Official, Karachi, 6 January 2017.

framework and been looked upon favourably by 'the market', citing a narrowing of Pakistan's EMBI spreads relative to its peers as evidence (IMF, 2005).

Bank-led implementation of Basel II and III (2008–present)

The 2008 global financial crisis was another turning point for Basel implementation in Pakistan. Although the SBP's implementation drive lost some steam because Basel II's failure in preventing the global financial crisis discredited the regulations, they were pressured to continue with Basel III implementation, and even over-comply with some components, in order to compensate for the negative reputational shock caused by Pakistan's FATF blacklisting in 2008 and 2010.

Furthermore, by this point the large domestic privatized banks, now owned by domestic conglomerates or foreign investors, had emerged as a key player and had gained leverage over the SBP, both because of political connections and their important position in the economy, given the new development strategy. Since 2004, the profitability of the largest five banks had been very high, strengthening their bargaining position. The five large domestic commercial banks now emerged as the leading advocates for Basel II and III adoption, with some banks even going above and beyond SBP mandated requirements. This was because the large five banks were highly internationalized, and saw keeping up to date with international standards as vital to maintaining and expanding their global position. This was not because they believed it helped them with risk management, but because they saw it as a vital signalling mechanism to reassure international investors and regulators. During this phase, the banks would actively lobby the SBP to offer more advanced approaches, while the SBP preferred a more gradual pace of adoption.

Ironically, at exactly the same time that large banks began to support Basel II adoption, Basel II itself became discredited in the eyes of both Pakistani regulators and banks. This was mainly because they had prevented neither the 2008 global financial crisis nor the 2008 domestic financial crisis experienced in Pakistan at the same time. Basel II was now perceived both as too complex and costly for the 'vanilla' Pakistani banking system. Furthermore, it was also perceived as ignoring some of the most important risks in the Pakistani financial system; excessive concentration of bank portfolios in government securities, which made the whole system very vulnerable to government default, and excess concentration of lending in very few industrial conglomerates (interviews).

After the financial crisis, the SBP's strong drive to implement Basel II lost some of its prior zeal, although by this point most banks were already compliant. A new SBP governor, Salim Raza, was appointed in 2009. Despite his international banking background, he was not as ardent an advocate of the Basel regulations as Hussain and Akhtar had been. In a speech shortly after his appointment, he criticized Basel II regulations for ignoring systemic risk, and for an excessively 'light-touch' approach that was 'in vogue in advanced economies' (Raza, 2009). The banks, on the other hand, suggested that the SBP was no longer keen on moving ahead with the adoption of Basel standards because they themselves did not feel able to regulate the more advanced approaches.[9]

In a reversal from the previous phase of adoption, the main actors driving adoption of Basel II and later III now became the five large privatized domestic commercial banks. While the PBA had previously worked to convince Akhtar to slow the pace of Basel II adoption, it now took an active role in Basel II and III adoption; for example, in 2013, private banks approached the SBP to ask for the adoption of the Alternative Standardized Approach for operational risk, even though the SBP had not offered it in the Basel II instructions (State Bank of Pakistan, 2013), and continued to lobby the SBP to offer more advanced approaches at the time interviews were conducted.[10] This was not due to any belief in the regulatory superiority of the Basel Accords, but due to the market pressures inherent in a globalized and competitive financial environment. The large five banks wanted to maintain their historic network of foreign branches. In addition, Pakistani banks wanted to continue to internationalize by attracting foreign investment and making alliances with foreign banks (interviews with various domestic banks). The large banks believed compliance with the most advanced approaches would signal their relative sophistication to foreign investors and regulators, and set them apart from both their domestic as well as regional rivals in order to improve their international standing: 'SBP pressure is equal across banks but we are trying to go further in order to get recognition from our international partners. We take Basel as an opportunity to up our game'.[11]

Pakistani banks' preferences regarding Basel II shifted significantly after 2007, when Basel Committee members were required to be compliant with Basel II. The large domestic banks came to realize that now that Basel II had become 'best practice' in the developed world, compliance was vital for internationalization in multiple ways (interviews). This continued to be the case after Basel III was introduced in BCBS member countries in 2013. A former SBP governor described the Basel regulations as 'a necessity for Pakistani banks to internationalise'.[12] In addition, most of the substantial work in acquiring appropriate platforms, hiring skilled personnel, and expensive consultancies for Basel II implementation had already occurred between 2004/5 and 2008 under pressure from the SBP.[13] This meant the banks had already incurred huge sunk costs in putting the

---

[9] Risk management, medium domestic commercial bank, 13 January 2017.
[10] CEO medium domestic commercial bank, Karachi, 9 January 2017; Chief risk officer, large domestic commercial bank, Karachi, 28 December 2016.
[11] CEO, medium domestic commercial bank, Karachi, 9 January 2017.
[12] Former SBP Governor, Karachi, 21 December 2016.
[13] Consultancy, Karachi, 27 December 2016.

relevant infrastructures in place, and their incentives for further Basel II and III implementation changed accordingly.

Domestic banks found that compliance was important for their correspondent banking relationships, especially in major trading partner countries. According to one banker, 'Any changes that happen in the west, especially the US, filter to the Pakistani banking sector because of our corresponded banking relationships'. This was because the Basel standards provide a 'common standard that international partners can recognise' which reassured their partners that appropriate risk management systems were in place.[14] Another important reason was the maintenance or expansion of foreign bank branches. In this case, the pressure to become compliant comes from foreign regulators, who required compliance in order to continue operating in their jurisdiction. Banks even reported that some foreign regulators were pressuring them to report components of Basel III such as the LCR and NSFR, before the SBP had even mandated them.[15] However, this only applied to those banks that had branches in jurisdictions that were already Basel III compliant. Those banks that had branches mainly in regions where regulators were not concerned with Basel adoption, such as the Middle East, stated that the maintenance of foreign branches was not a relevant pressure for Basel II and III adoption.[16] Some banks also found compliance helpful when making international alliances with foreign banks. For example, one domestic bank made an alliance with a US bank, whereby the Pakistani bank issued the US banks' credit cards in Pakistan. According to the CEO of this bank, Basel II and III compliance helped them to get the deal, as the US bank had their own due diligence requirements for choosing foreign partners, and 'Basel compliance helps'.[17]

For its part, the SBP was not as eager to implement Basel III as it had been Basel II. In a 2012 speech to the Islamic Financial Services Board in Istanbul, the SBP governor Yaseen Anwar was sceptical about the effectiveness of Basel III and noted that the new complex international regulations were not well suited to the Pakistani financial system because they did not have a high degree of exposure to the complex financial products that were responsible for the 2008 crisis in the first place. He also noted the importance of 'keeping in view our own local legal, regulatory and economic environment' when implementing international standards (Anwar, 2012).

However, because of the international market pressures inherent in an 'outward-oriented' approach to the financial sector, the SBP had to continue keeping up to date with Basel III adoption, and even over-comply with certain components. In particular, the SBP was worried about the negative stigma associated with

---

[14] CRO, large domestic commercial bank, Karachi, 28 December 2016.
[15] Chief financial officer, large domestic commercial bank, Karachi, 21 December 2016.
[16] Risk management, medium domestic commercial bank, Karachi, 13 January 2017.
[17] CEO, medium domestic commercial bank, Karachi, 9 January 2017.

Pakistani banks in the post-9/11 environment, as banks came under scrutiny for terrorism financing, but especially since Pakistan was blacklisted by the FATF between 2008 and 2010 and again from 2012 to 2014. The SBP combined a gradual approach to Basel III adoption with over-compliance since keeping up to date with the latest international standards was seen as an important counterweight to the blacklisting. According to an SBP official, 'with 9/11 the financial sector has been under a lot of scrutiny so Basel helps developing countries establish internationally recognized financial systems. SBP ratios are even higher than Basel requirements. Frankly speaking, it is to demonstrate to the outside world that Pakistani banks are safe and sound because we have a lot of other challenges like the FATF'.[18] It was also expected that it would not be much of a problem for most banks to meet the Basel III requirements, since SBP regulations had already been very stringent, and the capital adequacy ratio for the banking system was already at 14 per cent (State Bank of Pakistan, 2011).

Although the IFIs were no longer the driving factor behind Basel II and III adoption, they continued to support implementation. In 2013 the IMF even asked the SBP to raise the CAR (among other reforms) in exchange for a USD 5bn Extended Fund Facility (InpaperMagazine, 2013). In addition, the IFC now took on a more direct role, because of its direct investments in domestic banks. According to an interviewee at one such bank, 'in 2014 we talked to IFC to invest in us and to give them comfort we wanted to be Basel compliant. Basel was one of the tick boxes for the IFC'.[19] According to interviewees at commercial banks, pressure to implement Basel II and III also comes from the ADB, which now provides much of its financing in Pakistan through private banks rather than through the government. Basel compliance affects the allocations private banks receive from the ADB, since before entering into an agreement the ADB evaluates domestic banks' risk management. If they feel risk management is weak, they will not enter into an agreement with that bank, and being Basel compliant is an important way of allaying these fears.[20]

Conclusion

Pakistan moved from being domestically oriented country during the pre-1980 era, to a 'policy-driven' pathway to Basel adoption due to the shift towards an internationally oriented development strategy by political elites between the late 1980s and early 2000s, in conjunction with IMF and World Bank structural adjustment programmes. However, Basel I and BCP fell under the radar of domestic

---

[18] SBP Official, Karachi, 6 January 2017.
[19] CEO, medium domestic commercial bank, Karachi, 9 January 2017.
[20] Risk management, medium domestic commercial bank, Karachi, 13 January 2017.

politicians, and the initial push for changes in financial regulation came from the IFIs. This was reflected in the slow pace of Basel I adoption, and a lag in bank implementation, especially by smaller and public banks.

As Pakistan's domestic political economy transformed because of the policy-driven financial liberalization reforms initiated during the late 1980s, Pakistan gradually embraced international standards. Politicians championed initial convergence and, in line with the argument in the analytical framework, this policy-driven convergence generated incentives for the regulator and the banking sector to become more internationally oriented over time. By the early 2000s, the newly independent and powerful internationally oriented SBP took the reins for Basel I and II adoption despite difficulties in implementation for small banks. This was reflected in the sudden and wholescale adoption of Basel II, even in the face of initial pushback from the banks.

Finally, by 2007/8, the third major actor, the large private domestic banks, had completed their transformation from nationalized developmental institutions to privately owned, internationally competitive banks. These internationally oriented banks, which saw adoption of the most advanced approaches of Basel II and III as vital to maintaining their internationalized business model, took over as the main driver of convergence. This was in order to maintain their extensive foreign branch network, and to facilitate entry into new markets, to maintain credibility among international investors and partners, as well as to maintain correspondent banking relationships. The 2007/8 crisis discredited Basel II and later III among Pakistani regulators, and threatened to shift Pakistan onto a merely market-driven pathway to convergence, with domestic banks going above and beyond SBP mandated standards. However, the private banks successfully lobbied the SBP to continue keeping up to date with Basel adoption, as did the external shock of FATF blacklisting. Therefore after 2007/8, despite the SBP's more cautious approach, Pakistan continued on its policy-driven pathway to convergence, which was reflected in ambitious Basel standard implementation and voluntary enforcement by banks. As at January 2019, Pakistan had the highest level of convergence on Basel standards among our case study countries and regions.

References

Akhtar, S., 2006a. *Corporate governance' keynote address at the Conference on Corporate Governance.* Pakistan Institute of Corporate Governance and International Finance Corporation, Karachi, Pakistan.

Akhtar, S., 2006b. *Pakistan's financial services sector: A future perspective,* Speech delivered at Pakistan Society Dinner. London.

Anwar, Y., 2012. *International regulatory initiatives to enhance global financial stability,* 9th Islamic Financial Services Board Summit. Istanbul, Turkey.

BCBS, 2004. *Basel II: International convergence of capital measurement and capital standards: A revised framework*. BCBS.

Bureau van Dijk, 2018. *Bankscope and Orbis Bank Focus*. London, Bureau van Dijk.

Claessens, S., Horen, N. van, 2014. *The Impact of the Global Financial Crisis on Banking Globalization*. International Monetary Fund, Washington, DC.

Dawn, 2005. Fewer but stronger banks. *Dawn.com*.

Dawn, 2006. Basel II described as revolution in risk management [WWW Document]. *Dawn.com*. URL http://www.dawn.com/news/210105 (accessed 1.2.19).

Dawn, 2007. Banks role in economic growth recognised. *Dawn.com*.

Financial Stability Board, 2016. *FSB Regional Consultative Group for Asia discusses macroprudential frameworks, financial technology and correspondent banking* [WWW Document]. URL http://www.fsb.org/2016/12/fsb-regional-consultative-group-for-asia-discusses-macroprudential-frameworks-financial-technology-and-correspondent-banking (accessed 1.2.19).

FSI, 2015. *FSI Survey: Basel II, 2.5 and III Implementation* Basel: Financial Stability Institute.

Government of Pakistan, 2007. *Vision 2030*. Government of Pakistan, Islamabad.

Hussain, I., 2001a. *How is Pakistan positioning itself for challenges of globalization?*, Paper presented at the launch ceremony of Human Development in South Asia. Human Development Centre.

Hussain, I., 2001b. *Financial sector in Pakistan: The way forward*, Address at the Forty Ninth Annual General Meeting of Institute of Bankers. Karachi, Pakistan.

Hussain, I., 2004. *Pakistan's financial sector: A roadmap for 2005–2010*, Keynote address delivered at the 54th Annual General Meeting of the Institute of Bankers. Karachi, Pakistan.

Hussain, I., 2005. *Global banking: Paradigm shift*. Regulatory issues, Chairman's Inaugural Address. Federation of Indian Chambers of Commerce and Industry and the Indian Banking Association, Mumbai.

IMF, 2004. *Pakistan: Financial System Stability Assessment* (No. IMF Country Report No. 04/215). IMF, Washington, DC.

IMF, 2005. Pakistan: 2005 *Article IV Consultation and Ex Post Assessment of Longer-Term Program Engagement* (No. IMF Country Report No. 05/409). IMF, Washington, DC.

IMF, 2018. *Financial Soundness Indicators Database*. IMF, Washington, DC.

InpaperMagazine, 2013. IMF for stronger banks. *Dawn.com*.

International Trade Centre with Government of Pakistan, 2007. *Services Exports: National roadmap for Pakistan*. International Trade Centre, Geneva.

Iqbal, S., 2005. Paid-up capital limit raised for banks: Uniform CAR replaced. *Dawn.com*.

Janjua, A., 2003. *History of the State Bank of Pakistan (1977–88)*. State Bank Printing Press, Karachi.

Janjua, A., 2004. *History of the State Bank of Pakistan (1988–2003)*. State Bank Printing Press, Karachi.

Jones, E. and A. O. Zeitz 2019. Regulatory Convergence in the Financial Periphery: How Interdependence Shapes Regulators' Decisions *International Studies Quarterly*, https://doi.org/10.1093/isq/sqz068

Munir, K., Naqvi, N., 2015. Pakistan's post-reforms banking sector. *Economic and Political Weekly* 48, 7–8.

Munir, K., Naqvi, N., 2017. Privatization in the land of believers: The political economy of privatization in Pakistan. *Modern Asian Studies* 51, 1695–726. https://doi.org/10.1017/S0026749X16000585.

Naqvi, N., 2018. Finance and industrial policy in unsuccessful developmental states: The case of Pakistan. *Development and Change* 49, 1064–92. https://doi.org/10.1111/dech.12424.

Polity IV, 2014. *PolityProject*. Center for Systemic Peace.

Raza, S.S., 2009. *Current crisis and the future of financial regulation*, Keynote address at the Annual General Meeting of the Institute of Bankers. Karachi, Pakistan.

State Bank of Pakistan, 2003. *Handbook of Corporate Governance*. State Bank of Pakistan, Karachi, Pakistan.

State Bank of Pakistan, 2004. *Minimum capital requirements for banks/DFIs*, Circular No. 12 of 2004. State Bank of Pakistan, Karachi, Pakistan.

State Bank of Pakistan, 2005. *Roadmap for the Implementation of Basel II in Pakistan*. State Bank of Pakistan, Karachi, Pakistan.

State Bank of Pakistan, 2011. *Majority of banks in Pakistan to meet Basel-III requirements comfortably: Mr. Yaseen Anwar*. State Bank of Pakistan, Karachi, Pakistan.

State Bank of Pakistan, 2013. *Country Paper—Pakistan*. State Bank of Pakistan, Karachi, Pakistan.

State Bank of Pakistan, 2016. *Implementation of Basel III—Liquidity Standards*. State Bank of Pakistan, Karachi, Pakistan.

State Bank of Pakistan, n.d. *Online Economic Database*. Karachi, Pakistan.

Wilf, M., 2017. Market forces or international institutions? The under-emphasized role of IFIs in domestic bank regulatory adoption. *Presented at the Political Economy of International Organizations* (PEIO) 2017.

World Bank, 1998. *Implementation completion report. Islamic Republic of Pakistan. Banking Sector Adjustment Loan* (No. Report no. 18684). World Bank, Washington, DC.

World Bank, 2017. *World Development Indicators*. World Bank, Washington, DC.

Zaidi, S.A., 2005. *Issues in Pakistan's Economy*, second edition. Oxford University Press, Oxford, New York.

Zaidi, S.A., 2015. *Issues in Pakistan's Economy: A Political Economy Perspective*. Oxford University Press, Oxford.

5

Rwanda

Running Without Legs

Pritish Behuria

Introduction

Since the 1994 genocide, the Rwandan Patriotic Front (RPF) government has led
the country through a remarkable economic recovery with annual GDP growth
rates exceeding 6 per cent in most years. The RPF government's economic strategy
is to develop a service-based economy, which includes making Kigali (its capital)
a hub of various kinds—from tourism to ICT—and also for finance. This differen-
tiates Rwanda from the East Asian developmental states and another aspiring
African developmental state (Ethiopia) where financial sectors have been
largely under government control (or owned by local nationals) (Oqubay, 2015;
Wade, 1990). With the aim of becoming a financial sector hub, the RPF government
has transformed its financial sector—liberalizing it and recently committing to
rapidly adopt and implement Basel II and III standards. Since Rwanda's financial
sector remains largely underdeveloped, the government's exuberance for adopting
and implementing the most recent international banking standards seems out of
touch with the capacities and status of the country's financial sector, also contra-
dicting the aim of becoming a developmental state. In its position as a small
country with limited resources, the RPF government has become an uncritical
standard-taker in its financial sector. The government's adoption of Basel
standards signals a commitment to experimentation but highlights the prioritization of meeting (what they perceive as) best practices ahead of dealing with
domestic contextual realities.

This chapter argues that the RPF government's adoption and proposed implementation of Basel banking standards is 'policy-driven' convergence. Rwandan
regulators have limited autonomy and leadership. Rwandan regulators support
Basel adoption because it aligns with a broader economic objective (becoming
a financial sector hub). Yet unlike dynamics in Ghana (another example of
policy-driven convergence), the goal of implementing Basel standards is not a
matter of political contention given that the dominant party (RPF) enjoys relatively uncontested authority. Rwanda's economic leadership (the president and
senior ministers) drives Basel implementation because it is perceived to be an

Pritish Behuria, *Rwanda: Running Without Legs* In: *The Political Economy of Bank Regulation in Developing Countries:
Risk and Reputation.* Edited by: Emily Jones, Oxford University Press (2020). © Oxford University Press.
DOI: 10.1093/oso/9780198841999.003.0005

instrument to achieve larger strategic goals: meeting global best practices, becoming a financial hub, reducing risk in the financial sector, and encouraging East African Community (EAC) harmonization and integration. The prevailing attitude among regulators is to meet standards first and then 'adapt to challenges later'.[1] For Rwanda, this highlights a conflicted development strategy where leadership sets priorities for the economy and feedback is rarely acted upon until failure is proven to have occurred.

For the broader comparative study of Basel adoption in developing countries, Rwanda presents a surprising case among aspiring developmental states in its policy actions in the financial sector. Even though the policy lending that usually characterizes developmental states generates incentives for countries to divergence from international financial standards, in Rwanda incentives to converge outweigh incentives to diverge. Among instances of 'policy-driven' convergence, the Rwanda case demonstrates the difficulties associated with Basel implementation when few actors are placed in a position to contest strategic priorities set by the economic leadership.

Research for this chapter was conducted in June 2017. Forty-six interviews were conducted in Kigali with government officials including the National Bank of Rwanda (BNR)—the financial sector regulatory agency, representatives from all commercial banks (including risk managers), donors (including the World Bank and IMF), and financial sector consultants. This chapter also builds on the author's previous fieldwork experience in Rwanda, which dates back to 2011. It begins with an examination of the political economy of Rwanda's banking sector. It then discusses the evolution of Basel adoption and implementation in Rwanda, followed by a discussion of the political economy of Basel adoption in Rwanda. The chapter concludes by highlighting the impact of policy-driven Basel adoption in Rwanda, describing how target-setting among economic leadership has exposed the weaknesses of the country's financial sector and has imposed limits on the country's developmentalist ambitions.

The political economy of the post-1994 banking sector in Rwanda

Rwanda's financial sector has grown substantially since 1994 and in recent years it has been among the fastest-growing sectors in the country (Behuria and Goodfellow, 2017). Rwanda's development strategy—VISION 2020—prioritized the creation of a knowledge-based economy, with the liberalization of the financial sector perceived to be a foundation on which services-based development

---

[1] Interview, BNR regulator, Kigali, June 2017.

would thrive (Government of Rwanda, 2000). In November 2015, the Rwandan government announced its intention to rapidly and concurrently adopt and implement aspects of Basel II and III banking standards. This occurred at a time when Rwanda's financial sector expanded to eleven commercial banks operating in Rwanda, four microfinance banks, one development bank, and one cooperative bank, as of July 2017. The banking system comprises the largest share of financial sector assets at 66.3 per cent as of June 2016 (National Bank of Rwanda, 2016). Pensions, microfinance institutions, and Savings and Credit Cooperatives contribute the remaining banking sector assets. Though the financial sector remains shallow and underdeveloped, it has expanded considerably from its pre-1994 size (Table 5.1).

Before 1994, there were three active banks in Rwanda: Banque Commerciale du Rwanda (BCR), Bank of Kigali (BK), and Banque Continentale Africaine du Rwanda (BACAR). Union des Banques Populaires du Rwanda later became Banque Populaire du Rwanda (BPR). After the genocide, the government liberalized the commercial banking sector and licensed two new commercial banks— Bank of Commerce, Development and Industry (BCDI) and Banque à la Confiance d'Or (BANCOR). Local Rwandans—closely tied to the RPF—became lead investors in these banks. In 1999, more than forty Rwandan investors and state-owned institutions (which owned a minority share) collectively established a new bank—Cogebanque.

In the early and mid-2000s, elite frictions within the RPF became public (Behuria, 2016; Reyntjens, 2013). During this phase, prominent Rwandan officials in private commercial banks were accused of embezzling funds. These events, and frictions between prominent RPF elites (and pressure from international financial institutions), contributed to decisions to liberalize the financial sector. During this period, commercial banks came close to bankruptcy and senior RPF

Table 5.1 Rwanda: key indicators

Rwanda	
GDP per capita (current US$, 2017)	784
Bank assets (current US$)	2.05 bn
Bank assets (% of GDP)	24.2
Stock market capitalization (% of GDP)	Data not available
Credit allocation to private sector (% of GDP)	21
Credit allocation to government (% of GDP)	4.4
Polity IV score (2017)	−3

Note: All data is from 2016 unless otherwise indicated.

Source: FSI Database, IMF (2018); GDI Database, World Bank (2017); Polity IV (2014)

leadership became increasingly worried about the security of the financial sector.[2] The government recognized its political vulnerability and the limited capabilities that had been associated with relying on domestic elites in the sector and decided to rely on foreign investment in commercial banking, believing that increased competition would secure the sector's growth. Yet through its state-owned bank (Bank of Kigali), the government chose to retain some control over the sector. Since state-, party-, and military-owned enterprises controlled a large share of the economy, the government also retained some control within the financial sector through operating as a large client for commercial banks. Thus, the government did not completely ignore the importance of some degree of state control of the financial sector but it had departed a great deal from the traditional role of the developmental state in the financial sector.

Today, Rwanda's commercial banking sector can be divided into four categories: a state-owned commercial bank (BK), a large international investor-owned commercial bank, several regional or pan-African bank subsidiaries, and one bank collectively owned by several Rwandan investors (*Cogebanque*). As of 2016, government-owned BK retained over 30 per cent of the market share of the domestic financial sector in several indicators including assets (34 per cent), net loans (38 per cent), customer deposits (37 per cent), and equity (39 per cent). Since 1994, the IMF and World Bank has often pressurized the Rwandan government to sell its stake in BK. Government officials have also considered selling shares to international banks or strategic investors.[3] In 2011, BK initiated an initial public offering of 62.5 million dollars on the Rwandan Stock Exchange (RSE).[4] Despite 45 per cent of BK shares remaining in 'free float' on the RSE, the government retains a majority shareholding in the bank in partnership with its institutional partner—the Rwanda Social Security Board (RSSB). Though BK operates as the only state-owned bank in the sector, its role as an instrument for developmental state objectives is unclear. It is often the bank used for strategic investments but it also has among the highest interest rates for loans across the sector. BK continues to be the most profitable and the largest bank operating in Rwanda. According to an I&M Bank official—among BK's largest domestic rivals—'BK is four times our balance sheet'.[5] Though BK dominates the sector, it is relatively small within the region and is barely within the top twenty banks operating in East Africa.[6]

Atlas Mara BPR is the only significant international investor operating in the sector. As of 2016, BPR was the third largest bank in the country (after I&M Bank).

---

[2] Interviews, BNR, Kigali, June 2017.
[3] Interviews, BNR, Ministry of Finance and Economic Planning (MINECOFIN) and BK, Kigali, June 2017.
[4] Currently, shares in four banks are listed on the RSE: BK, I&M, KCB, and Equity.
[5] Interview, I&M Bank, Kigali, June 2017.   [6] Interview, small bank, Kigali, June 2017.

In 2016, Bob Diamond and Ashish Thakkar's investment company—Atlas Mara—completed the purchase of 62 per cent of BPR's shares. This added to their existing presence in Rwanda since Atlas Mara bought the BRD's commercial bank in 2015.[7] Within Rwanda and elsewhere in Africa, Atlas Mara's investments have experienced some initial difficulties. The bank's cost-to-revenue ratio of over 95 per cent was the highest in the country (Mwai, 2017). Atlas Mara has recently imposed significant employment cuts and centralized most of its operations. Headcount has shrunk by 25 per cent in the last year.[8] A restructuring programme has been launched to improve profitability, reverse loss of market share, and shift the business to a more balanced retail and corporate customer base.[9] In 2017, the cost-to-revenue ratio had reduced to 80 per cent.[10] When Atlas Mara took over BPR, they 'had a big surprise with very large numbers of non-performing loans (NPLs). Currently, the bank's NPLs are 12.4 per cent and by the end of the year, the bank's target is to reduce it to 6 per cent (with the average across commercial banks about 5.6 per cent)'.[11]

Several regional banks also operate in Rwanda. Out of such banks, I&M Bank (formerly BCR) has the largest market share. Other regional banks include Equity, KCB, GT Bank, Access Bank, Commercial Bank of Africa, Crane Bank, and Ecobank. *Cogebanque* is the only commercial bank in which Rwandans own a majority share (outside BK).

In comparison to other case studies in the Navigating Global Banking Standards project, Rwanda is relatively unique. The composition of its commercial banking sector includes one large government-owned bank (BK) with most other banks operating in Rwanda as subsidiaries of larger regional or pan-African banks. Though the sector is liberalized, the government remains a significant actor—both through its ownership in the largest bank (BK) but also as the largest customer, with party- and military-owned enterprises remaining large recipients of loans. Though BK is very large within Rwanda, it is miniscule when compared to the size of the parent companies of local Rwandan subsidiaries. Thus, most commercial banks operating in Rwanda are better resourced with more access to capital and expertise than BK. The consequences of the adoption and implementation of Basel II and III banking standards will vary across these different banks and most commercial bank representatives were pessimistic, admitting difficulties associated with implementation in the short term.

---

[7] The BRD had established a commercial bank for a few years. After its sale, its role is restricted to that of a development bank.

[8] Interview, Atlas Mara BPR, Kigali, June 2017.

[9] Interview, Atlas Mara BPR, Kigali, June 2017.

[10] Interview, Atlas Mara BPR, Kigali, June 2017.

[11] Interview, Atlas Mara BPR, Kigali, June 2017.

Rwanda's adoption and implementation of
Basel banking standards

The RPF government has adopted a relatively conservative stance to banking regulation. This has been motivated by its desire to ensure financial sector stability, its position as a standard-taker in global banking regulation, and the hope that the implementation of global financial standards may contribute to making Kigali into a financial sector hub. Basel I standards were implemented in 1998. However, the Rwandan government was relatively slow with officially stating its intention to comply with Basel Core Principles (BCPs) or Basel II and III banking standards. Discussions of formally adopting Basel reforms began in the mid-2000s when the East African Community (EAC) argued for a common stance in relation to Basel standards. Despite limited discussions of formally adopting Basel II and III, Rwanda already complied with more than 80 per cent of BCPs and in some measures (like capital adequacy requirements), and Rwanda's financial standards were much higher than those required in Basel II (Enoch et al., 2015). In 2015, Rwanda was ranked among the most compliant countries in Africa (with regard to BCPs).

In the last two years, the RPF government has formally announced its intention to adopt and implement most Basel II and III requirements. In November 2015, the BNR issued a directive, which required parallel reporting of Basel II capital requirements. By 1 January 2018, all commercial banks in Rwanda had to be fully compliant with Basel II and III (although only elements of both will be part of the regulation). Initially, observers (Andrews et al., 2012) had argued that there would be minimal impact because of already existing conservative regulatory measures in Rwanda. However, the implementation of Basel standards is already forcing commercial banks to significantly alter their operations.

The ambitious adoption of Basel banking standards is even more surprising given the rapid changes that have occurred in the banking sector over the last two decades. After the 1994 genocide, the financial sector was in severe difficulties, with the fleeing members of the previous government stealing over 30 billion francs or two thirds of the monetary base, including cash from the BNR vaults (Addison et al., 2001). The post-1994 government perceived liberalization of the sector to be necessary for stabilizing the economy. Official BNR reports (National Bank of Rwanda, 2011) highlighted the 'direct control' of the financial system as a hindrance to growth. Liberalization of the financial sector and the introduction of a flexible exchange rate system were introduced in the context of three economic stabilization programmes, pushed through by the IMF and the World Bank—the Structural Adjustment Programme (1990), the Enhanced Structural Adjustment Facility-Poverty Reduction and Growth Facility (1998), and the Policy Support Instrument (2010).

Table 5.2 Rwanda: adoption of Basel standards

Basel component	Adoption	Implementation
Basel I	1998	1998 Credit risk No operational or market risk
Basel II and Basel III	November 2015 directive (Adoption) January 2018 (Proposed implementation) 5/10 components (Basel II) 6/8 components (Basel III)	Standardized approach for market risk Revised standardized approach for operational risk and capital buffers (including capital conservation buffer and domestic systemic important bank)

Rwanda began adopting Basel I banking standards in 1998 (Table 5.2). Initially, Basel I was implemented with a focus on credit risk and there was limited attention to banking supervision, operational risk, and market risk. Since the Rwandan financial sector has a very limited range of products, market risk is marginal across commercial banks. An initial motive for adopting Basel banking standards was the decision to harmonize banking standards within the EAC. Within the EAC, Rwanda occupies a relatively unique position. Since Rwanda is land-locked and because it is a comparatively smaller country with a small market, the government perceives EAC integration as essential to access larger markets and to achieve its aim of becoming a services hub. President Kagame has been the leading champion of EAC integration in the region and government officials constantly highlight the importance of regional integration, arguing that 'we have to set an example for integration because without it, there are limits to our growth'.[12] Government officials see regional integration to be particularly significant in terms of the goal of becoming a financial sector hub. Their reasoning relied on two main factors, which they saw as the country's comparative advantage: leadership and domestic security.[13] Though most consultants doubt that such advantages could be enough to make Kigali a financial sector hub, government officials remain committed to the target.

In 1999, the Banking Supervision Department was created within BNR with the aim of streamlining and ensuring an efficient banking sector. The BNR Law of 1981 was revised by the Banks Act of 1999, with BNR issuing several prudential regulations. The regulatory level of commercial banks' share capital went up progressively from Rwf 100 Million to Rwf 300 million in 1995, to Rwf 1.5 billion in 1999 and to Rwf 5 billion in 2006. In 1999, the Rwanda Central Banking Act was

---

[12] Interview, BNR official, Kigali, June 2017.   [13] Interview, BNR official, Kigali, June 2017.

revised to grant BNR independence to formulate and implement monetary policy and ensure financial stability. The 1999 Act was 'strengthened to enhance regulatory frameworks, reduce regulatory forbearance, ensure market discipline and comply with the Basel principles of effective supervision' (Rusagara, 2008, p. 3). In 2003, IFRS-based accounting standards were introduced for the banking sector. In the same year, the CAR was increased from 8 to 10 per cent, the decrease of permissible deduction of accepted collateral from loan-loss provisions from 100 to 70 per cent, and the rules on insider lending, loan management, credit concentration, and the restructuring of the banking sector were strengthened.

To enable the central bank to focus on high-risk banks and high-risk areas in each bank, BNR adopted the Risk Based Supervision (RBS) framework in 2006. Adoption of RBS was to ensure compliance with and implementation of international best practices. A 2007 BNR Law and a 2008 Law on the Organization of Banking (LOB) have further strengthened the BNR's regulatory authority. Since the 2008 LOB was enacted, BNR dedicated time to ensuring all new regulations aligned with the law. During this period, several new banks entered the sector. As a result, new commercial banks hired several BNR officials—including risk managers. The extent of regulation became less of a problem compared to the limited capabilities within BNR since new employees had to be hired once trained employees were hired elsewhere.[14] In the late 2000s, all twelve of BNR's risk managers gave notice within a short space of time and even in 2017, two former BNR officials joined new commercial banks.[15] Consequently, retaining staff continues to pose a significant challenge for BNR.

The Rwandan government has also published two Financial Sector Development Program (FSDP) Strategies, which have been direct responses to two IMF Financial System Stability Assessment (FSAP) reports. After FSAP-1, in 2005, the government developed a strategic plan (2008–12) under FSDP-1. The FSAP-1 (IMF, 2005) recommended that the government take several actions to improve compliance with BCPs. One report (Andrews et al., 2012) claims that over 90 per cent of policy actions in FSDP 1 were completed. IMF (2005) highlighted several weaknesses in relation to enforcement, limited BNR staff, amending the CAR, strengthening regulations on lending, and harmonizing auditing and accounting standards to international levels. In 2007/8, Rwanda's banking sector suffered a crisis, forcing BNR to redesign its prudential regulations on liquidity risk management (Sanya et al., 2012). BNR regulators highlight that during this period, there was a 'liquidity crunch'.[16] This liquidity crisis continued until at least 2010, occurring at a time when several new banks began operations in Rwanda.

---

[14] Interview, commercial bank risk manager, Kigali, June 2017.
[15] Interview, commercial bank, Kigali, June 2017.
[16] Interview, BNR official, Kigali, June 2017.

BNR's banking supervision team 'lost all of their staff', further highlighting the skills shortage within the financial sector.[17]

After FSAP-2 was conducted, FSDP-2 developed a roadmap between 2014 and 2018 while also identifying 437 policy actions. FSAP-2 (IMF, 2011) highlighted that Rwanda's capital adequacy requirements conform to Basel I principles. Though the minimum capital adequacy requirement is 15 per cent in Rwanda, the BNR did not apply a capital adequacy charge for market risk (as of 2011). The IMF (2011) also found several weaknesses in Rwanda's banking sector reforms including the need to speed up the process of introducing prudential regulation on the basis of new laws, strengthening the framework for cross-border supervisory cooperation, increasing the frequency of on-site examinations for the largest banks, and ensuring BNR staff remained updated with the skills and supervisory methods expected of them in relation to new laws and regulations. After FSAP-2, BNR initiated new requirements in banking supervision within commercial banks, calling for the establishment of separate risk departments. This was a significant challenge as there were few bankers within Rwanda with such expertise. In 2012, across the financial sector, the National Skills Survey found that 'the financial services sector has a total skills gap of 6,312 labour units', with over 45 per cent of the gap comprising 'technicians' (Rwanda Development Board, 2012).

The decision to adopt and implement Basel II and III was taken after the FSAP-2 was published. At least in terms of capital adequacy requirements, the average among commercial banks operated above Basel 1 requirements. The capital adequacy ratio (CAR) in commercial banks stood at 13.7 per cent in 2006, 16.2 per cent in 2007, and 15.9 per cent in 2008 (National Bank of Rwanda, 2009). After 2010, Rwanda's CAR has stayed in excess of 20 per cent and is the highest in the region. Figure 5.1 illustrates the evolution of Rwanda's CAR and non-performing loans (NPLs). Commercial bank representatives and BNR officials both admitted that NPLs are much higher and vary significantly among banks, as compared to these official statistics. Atlas Mara BPR, for example, has much higher NPLs than most other banks.

In 2011, BNR required banks to hold core capital of at least 10 per cent of risk-weighted assets and total capital (core plus supplementary capital) of at least 15 per cent of risk-weighted assets. In 2016, several banking standards were above Basel II/III thresholds. For example, the leverage ratio increased at a rate of 1 per cent annually between 2014 and 2016—from 8 per cent to 10 per cent, which was significantly above Basel II/III thresholds (3 per cent) and BNR requirements (6 per cent). The key difference was the introduction of risk-weighting based on the external credit rating of the counterparty. But it was estimated that there would be 'minimal effect due to virtual absence of rated counterparties to the Rwandan banking system' (Andrews et al., 2012, p. 66).

---

[17] Interviews, Rwandan risk managers (government and commercial), Kigali, June 2017.

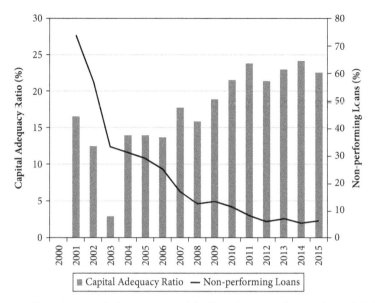

Figure 5.1 Rwanda: capital adequacy ratios (CAR) and non-performing loans (NPLs).
Source: IMF (2018)

In 2013, consultations between economic leadership and BNR led to the establishment of a Basel steering committee, which included key BNR officials and three commercial bank risk managers (who were the most senior Rwandan regulators, two of whom had previously worked in BNR). Most decisions with regard to Basel II and III implementation have been taken after discussions with the committee. Commercial banks have been invited to take part in the consultation process. Though commercial bank representatives agreed that there was consultation, they complained that discussions were 'never reflected in the final document'.[18] The establishment of the Steering Committee was a response to ensure different stakeholders had a voice in Basel adoption and implementation while also ensuring the government made full use of the expertise within the financial sector (which had become concentrated in commercial banks).

BNR decided to adopt Basel II and III rapidly and concurrently. By the end of 2013, a draft of the regulatory framework was in place. In 2014, a kick-off event took place with all managing directors of commercial banks invited. In November 2015, a directive was issued, which required parallel reporting of Basel II capital requirements. At this time, regulators at commercial banks 'did not really know what to do' and there were 'capacity challenges'.[19] As part of the 2015 directive, BNR required banks to hold a minimum total capital of 12.5 per cent of total

---

[18] Interview, commercial bank, Kigali, June 2017.
[19] Interview, commercial bank and consultant, Kigali, June 2017.

risk-weighted assets and to hold 10 per cent of core capital to risk-weighted assets. Banks were also required to hold capital conservation buffers of 2.5 per cent. SIBs were obliged to keep additional systemic capital buffers of 1–3.5 per cent defined for different brackets (National Bank of Rwanda, 2016). As of 2017, it was not clear which banks would be categorized as SIBs (though BK, I&M, and Atlas Mara BPR said they expected to be named SIBs). Most older and medium-sized banks complained about the added burden that would be associated with the capital conservation buffer.[20] One banker said that the buffer would 'penalize all large banks in the sector and restrict attractiveness of the country. The return on equity in the region is already the lowest and it is nearly half of what it is in other East African countries.'[21] Figure 5.2 illustrates the evolution of return on assets (RoA) and return on equity (RoE) in Rwanda. According to respondents from commercial banks, these official statistics overestimate the RoE.[22] In Rwanda, the RoE has been particularly low because even in the fastest-growing sectors, investments have often not reaped profits. For example, in the high-growth tourism sector, there has been a danger of 'over-supply' in hotels with capacity utilization at

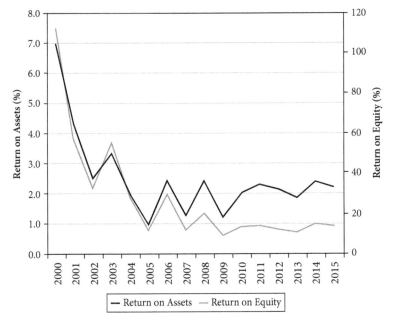

Figure 5.2 Rwanda: rates of return on assets (RoA) and equity (RoE).
Source: Bankscope and Orbis Bank Focus, Bureau van Dijk, 2018

---

[20] Interviews, commercial banks, Kigali, June 2017.
[21] Interview, commercial bank, Kigali, June 2017.
[22] Interviews, commercial banks, Kigali, June 2017.

below 50 per cent (International Growth Centre, 2016). Over one hundred hotels shut down in Kigali between 2013 and 2015 (Gahigi, 2015).

Though Basel II and III implementation would require some changes to capital adequacy requirements, the FSAP-2 (Andrews et al., 2012) estimated that the effect would be minimal on commercial banks. To be Basel III compliant, Rwanda will retain the current 15 per cent total capital ratio (though the EAC agreed minimum standard is 14 per cent) (Government of Rwanda, 2013). Risk management may change significantly, as a result of Basel II and III implementation. 'Earlier, BNR was only concerned with credit risk. Now, there is more of an interest in operational risk and we don't have the systems or data for that in all the banks'.[23] However, for many banks, operational and market risk remain negligible and 'don't really affect' them.[24] Yet the impact will be uneven across commercial banks. For Atlas Mara BPR, which has large numbers of daily transactions, operation and market risk will have an impact.[25] One BNR regulator admitted that 'it may affect growth in lending but the question is how resilient commercial banks are in moving from credit risk to adding operational risk and market risk'.[26]

BNR has now adopted most aspects of Basel III standards with the exception of risk coverage (for counterparty credit risk) and requirements for global systemically important banks (as it has no such banks in its jurisdiction). To improve reporting procedures between commercial banks and the central bank, BNR is establishing an electronic data warehouse. In May 2017, the regulation was issued, although there was a lack of clarity about whether it would be in effect immediately or starting January 2018. There was also some confusion about how the Internal Capital Adequacy Assessment Process (ICAAP) and the Internal Liquidity Adequacy Assessment Process (ILAAP) would be implemented across the financial sector. BNR officials said they were discussing how to implement ICAAPs in relation to risk exposure in the sector and highlighted the lack of skills within the country as a limitation.[27] Some commercial banks were worried about the way ICAAP would be computed. 'There is currently no framework for pillar 1 and my understanding is that there is no standardized framework worldwide for pillar 2. In particular, we are unsure of what parameters to use and there is a major challenge with non-quantitative risk types'.[28] One consultant doubted the feasibility of implementing ICAAP programmes.[29]

In February 2018—a month after all commercial banks had to be compliant with Basel II and III standards—BNR issued a directive, which stated that all banks would have to submit approved annual ICAAP and ILAAP documents for

---

[23] Interview, commercial bank, Kigali, June 2017.
[24] Interview, commercial bank, Kigali, June 2017.
[25] Interview, commercial bank, Kigali, June 2017.   [26] Interview, BNR, Kigali, June 2017.
[27] Interview, commercial bank, Kigali, June 2017.
[28] Interview, commercial bank, Kigali, June 2017.
[29] Interview, consultant, Kigali, June 2017.

review by March 2019, with larger banks having to prepare their first ICAAP and ILAAP documents by July 2018.

Some large banks (like BK and Atlas Mara BPR) were also worried about the implementation of IFRS 9, which all banks had to implement by January 2018. One banker said, 'the impact of IFRS 9 will change the landscape of the market. We have a lot of data constraints and segmentation issues. We aren't privy to high-level macrodata. This impacts how we construct our models. We also don't have good historical data'[30]

Unlike in Ethiopia, the RPF government fails to question donor-led models in the financial sector and nearly every regulator and commercial banker in the country said that there were long-term benefits in enacting Basel reforms. Though scholarship (Gottschalk, 2010) has shown that Basel adoption is not necessarily the best way forward for late developing countries, such arguments have not gained traction with Rwandan banking regulators. The Rwandan government's uncritical stance towards Basel adoption can be interpreted both as a belief in such standards or ideological agreement with market-led reforms. Clearly, international consultants (employed by the IMF) have been influential in setting the parameters on which BNR's regulation would be judged. However, Rwandan bankers—individually and as a group—are detached from regional or international banking networks. There is significant turnover of BNR staff and though some remain involved in discussions of Basel implementation, BNR simply acts as an agency charged with implementing Basel.

Rwanda's policy-driven adoption of Basel banking standards has been ambitious and has progressed without acknowledging negative consequences. The RPF government has enacted such reforms, assuming that it may result in a more secure financial sector. Yet it may have the opposite effect with commercial banks worried about the effect it may have in the short term.

The political economy of Basel adoption

Policy-driven Basel adoption in Rwanda follows closely in line with the project's analytical framework. BNR regulators and banks are domestically oriented and have very limited access to international networks. In contrast, RPF politicians are internationally oriented and their services-based hub development strategy depends on attracting foreign attention and investment. The state-owned bank (BK) has ambitions of expanding in the region in the future but it is not on the horizon in the next few years. Though pan-African banks have a substantial presence in Rwanda, most invested primarily to increase their footprint in the region. Though BPR Atlas Mara is among Bob Diamond's first investments in Africa, its

---

[30] Interview, commercial bank, Kigali, June 2017.

investments are primarily focused on securing the Rwandan subsidiary's financial difficulties in the immediate future. In line with the expectations of the project's framework, Rwanda has adopted Basel banking standards but implementation remains confused and difficult. There is reason to doubt the effectiveness of implementation given BNR's capacity and technology constraints. Commercial banks will also be limited by skills, technology, and finance constraints in their aim to meet Basel requirements. Despite this, BNR officials and even some respondents within commercial banks mentioned that they were preparing for 'full implementation and compliance' by January 2018.[31]

The RPF's economic leadership has been the main driving force behind Basel implementation. RPF economic leadership comprises President Paul Kagame, his economic advisors, the Special Policy Unit in the Office of the President, and key ministers who have led The Economic Cluster and have also worked in leadership roles in BNR, including John Rwangombwa, Francois Kanimba, and Claver Gatete. Rwangombwa is the current BNR governor and has served in this post since 2013. Prior to this post, he was minister of finance. Kanimba is a former BNR governor (2002–11) and was the minister of trade and industry until August 2017 when he was replaced in a cabinet reshuffle. Gatete was the minister of finance from 2012 to 2018 and had previously served as BNR governor from 2011 to 2013. Other leading officials (serving at the rank of minister) in The Economic Cluster include James Musoni (the former minister of infrastructure and minister of finance), Francis Gatare, and Clare Akamanzi.

During Kanimba's stint as BNR governor, a decision was taken to adopt Basel standards and though implementation has only been embraced recently, BNR has retained a conservative stance on regulation since Kanimba took over the position in 2002. Successive governors have retained similar conservatism in their regulation of the financial sector. Thus, the economic leadership has taken the decision to adopt Basel standards but BNR is the agency charged with delivering that goal. BNR has some autonomy in the ways in which Basel standards will be implemented but it will be judged by economic leadership in its task of becoming a leading adopter and implementer of Basel standards.

BNR has always been 'quick to follow international best practices', and since these were the standards that were offered to them, the target was to achieve those standards.[32] Beck et al. (2011) cite this as a common experience among African countries where complex rules are adopted to follow international best practice (and out of fear that they would be penalized, e.g. in the form of higher international borrowing costs), even if those rules are not appropriate to the country's needs. A BNR official said, 'after FSAP-2 in 2011, the benchmarks that they would be assessed on were based on Basel II and III so though they didn't tell us to

---

[31] Interviews, BNR and commercial banks, Kigali, June 2017.
[32] Interview, consultant, Kigali, June 2017.

implement Basel, we would be judged on that basis'.[33] There have been few discussions about the vulnerabilities that may accompany the implementation of Basel banking standards.[34] One IMF official highlighted the uncritical stance that almost all entities operating in the financial sector were taking on Basel implementation: 'As more countries start adopting it, you kind of forget the question of whether it is a good thing or not'.[35]

Though some IMF and World Bank officials claim to have warned the government against implementing Basel banking standards, BNR officials did not remember such warnings.[36] IMF and World Bank officials within Rwanda supported the implementation of Basel banking standards. However, they stressed that discussions of its implementation were 'not high on their agenda'.[37] The IMF, World Bank, and African Development Bank (AfDB) funded training programmes in BNR's bank supervision departments and for risk managers at commercial banks.[38] The IMF has also provided technical assistance for the implementation of Basel banking standards with specific funding for building BNR's supervisory capacities.[39] IFIs have provided access to Basel standards and have influenced the parameters within which banking regulation has occurred. Few alternatives have been provided and the government has not sought other options, thus signalling Rwanda's position as a standard-taker in international financial regulation.

Commercial banks voiced a number of complaints about the implementation of Basel banking standards. However, complaints varied among banks. Though the Rwanda Bankers Association (RBA) exists, banks have not developed a common stance with regard to Basel implementation. Though they acknowledged 'the hurt' that would be experienced in the short term, most said it would be better for the entire sector and their own individual banks in the long term.[40] Most banks complained about the pace at which Basel standards were being adopted. Some bank representatives criticized BNR for 'copy and pasting Basel standards without reflecting on their appropriateness in Rwanda'.[41] Though BNR officials said they were taking a 'flexible' approach to implementing Basel reforms, commercial bankers complained 'there was limited room to manoeuvre' and BNR was 'very punitive'.[42]

Across the sector, there was little resistance to the implementation of Basel reforms. One commercial bank representative said, 'you can't win a fight against your regulator. There's no bank that will do that. Even less in Rwanda'.[43] Larger

---

[33] Interview, BNR, Kigali, June 2017.   [34] Interviews, BNR, Kigali, June 2017.
[35] Interview, IMF, Kigali, June 2017.
[36] Observations made by former World Bank consultant, June 2017.
[37] Interview, IMF, Kigali, June 2017.   [38] Interviews, IMF and World Bank, Kigali, June 2017.
[39] Interview, IMF and World Bank, Kigali, June 2017.
[40] Interviews, commercial banks, Kigali, June 2017.
[41] Interview, commercial bank, Kigali, June 2017.
[42] Interviews, BNR and commercial banks, Kigali, June 2017.
[43] Interview, commercial bank, Kigali, June 2017.

banks were very critical about the implementation of the capital conservation buffer and the additional requirements that would be in place for SIBs. Most banks, which operated as subsidiaries in Rwanda, were not worried about Basel implementation given that their parent companies had either already enforced Basel implementation across their subsidiaries or were in the process of doing so. Two representatives from regional banks mentioned that they had been forced to be compliant with Basel II and III because their parent company had ordered it.[44] However, they were worried about the pressure that would accompany ensuring there were returns on these new investments. Since the return on investments in Rwanda remained low compared to the region, risk managers in commercial banks said it was 'difficult to see how to get return on investment in the current market when we also have to ask for capital injections from our group headquarters'.[45] Another regional bank representative said, 'If I had to raise capital locally, it would be a struggle. Parent companies may give capital but how do we get returns?' Among commercial banks, there was a consensus that the market was 'highly capitalized without potential for gaining significant returns'.[46]

BK—as a majority state-owned bank and the biggest commercial bank in the country—was in a difficult position. BK officials saw Basel implementation as the right way forward in the long term. However, they were worried about the difficulties and financial burden that would accompany implementation in the short term. Though some representatives from commercial banks argued that the BNR 'may overlook some (of BK's) discrepancies', there is no evidence that such partiality is being practised.[47] While EAC harmonization and the implementation of Basel would help BK expand operations abroad, it was not part of BK's strategy to meet Basel banking standards for that purpose. Instead, the government was more hopeful that large foreign banks could choose to invest in Rwanda because of BNR's decision to enact best practices.[48] In some ways, BK had the most to lose from Basel implementation because they could not avail of a parent company's expertise or funds and largely relied on the domestic market for both skills and resources. After the implementation of Basel, the difficulties BK faced had quickly surfaced. To meet the requirement of maintaining high capital buffers—as part of Basel II and III requirements—BK announced that it would list 222.2 million shares on the Rwandan and Nairobi Stock Exchanges, with the aim of raising $67.3 million (Herbling, 2018). This would dilute the Rwandan government's ownership of the country's largest bank, suggesting that Basel implementation had already begun to limit the developmentalist functions of the state. The RPF government was acting against the short-term interest of its own

---

[44] Interviews, commercial banks, Kigali, June 2017.
[45] Interview, commercial bank, Kigali, June 2017.
[46] Interview, commercial bank, Kigali, June 2017.
[47] Interview, commercial bank, Kigali, June 2017.
[48] Interview, former BNR official, Kigali, June 2017.

state-owned bank through which most strategic projects are being financed, highlighting the inconsistencies that have characterized the country's development strategy and the government's attitude to the financial sector (Behuria, 2018).

The composition of the private sector also presents significant challenges to domestic banks in their implementation of Basel reforms. Though regulators may be able to direct banks to change the composition of their loan-books, a more significant problem is that very few companies take up large portions of each bank's loan-book. Difficulties with some investments by large institutions (e.g. the RSSB) contributed to the liquidity crunch in the late 2000s.[49] Even today, there are a 'few big institutions taking up 20 per cent of deposits. If one is in trouble, it is difficult to raise liquidity'.[50] The RSSB itself holds about 40–50 per cent of the liquidity in the banking sector.[51] The concentration of the economy among certain institutions thus increases the economy's vulnerability to liquidity crises. Commercial banks also have limited options to diversify their loan-books and this affects the potential of increasing returns-on-equity.

The Rwandan government's stubbornness and ambition to achieve goals is evidenced in its implementation of Basel standards. Yet the desire to achieve goals within the government apparatus has not left much space for receptiveness to feedback before Basel adoption and implementation, signalling the narrow role that BNR has in implementing policy-driven adoption. Indeed, BNR officials and commercial bankers all anticipate difficulties with implementing Basel. A senior BNR regulator admitted that there 'will be complications and some of it, we will figure it out as we go along'.[52] A commercial banker echoed the BNR regulator's observation by saying 'the approach here seems to be: let's go for it and address issues later'.[53] The 'learn as you go' approach to implementing Basel was in evidence in February 2018 when a new Basel III liquidity measurement regime was rolled out for commercial banks, incorporating Basel III's flagship Liquidity Coverage Ratio (LCR) and Net Stable Funding Ratio (NSFR). The introduction of NSFR requirements has further exacerbated the already existing problems regarding the lack of availability and affordability of mortgages since banks' balance sheets have to now indicate enhanced maturity matching (Vemuru, 2018). Five other liquidity monitoring tools were also issued for banks including maturity mismatch analysis, cashflow projections, stock of liquidity assets, diversification of funding liabilities, and reliance on parent and other subsidiaries. Ecobank publicly stated that 'this is by far the most comprehensive liquidity measurement regime in our coverage basket' and that 'voluminous haggles between banks and BNR' were expected during the implementation phase as balance sheets would have to be rearranged significantly (Ecobank Research, 2018).

---

[49] Interview, BNR, Kigali, June 2017.   [50] Interview, commercial bank, Kigali, June 2017.
[51] Interview, commercial bank, Kigali, June 2017.   [52] Interview, BNR, Kigali, June 2017.
[53] Interview, commercial bank, Kigali, June 2017.

It may be surprising that Rwanda—elsewhere classified as a developmental state or in similar ways (Booth and Golooba-Mutebi, 2012)—is embracing global banking standards. This indicates the high degree of international orientation among Rwanda's economic leadership. For the RPF, the pathway to economic security depends on regional integration and a reliance on international legitimacy in the short and medium term. Given Rwanda's geographical vulnerability and lack of resources, the government has an explicitly externally oriented development strategy, with success depending on regional integration. This has been made clear in Rwanda's embrace of Basel standards and amendments made to the 2008 banking law in 2017, ahead of implementation of Basel standards a few months later. The amendments were justified by the need to harmonize Rwanda's financial system in line with regional and international standards. These included small changes including replacing the title of 'Vice Governor' of BNR to 'Deputy Governor' (to harmonize titles with other East African countries) to larger changes like altering the start and end dates of the financial year and strengthening BNR's Monetary Policy and Financial Stability committees (Kwibuka, 2017).

Rwanda's development path is very different from the kind pursued in East Asia. Though BNR does not impose sectoral lending targets, the central government does pinpoint strategic growth sectors. In Rwanda, most loans have been concentrated in real estate, hotels, and other service sectors. One commercial banker said, 'today, if there is a problem in the real estate sector, banks will suffer. Retail banking is very small and our loan-books are concentrated.'[54] For example, construction and hotels accounted for 45 per cent of BK's loan-book in 2016, with another 40 per cent being allocated for commerce and transport loans. According to one banker, 'this was done strategically and it is a ticking time bomb. In most other countries, the regulator would have seen this as concentration and stopped it.'[55] For a small country like Rwanda, the pursuit of economic development is accompanied by a great deal of instability. That instability is often generated through external pressures but resources are also received from international sources. Thus, the high degree of internationalization has combined with some facets of a developmental state to create a conflicted development strategy, which combines aspects of market-led reforms and strategic state interventions (Behuria, 2018).

Conclusion

The policy-driven pathway to convergence with Basel standards in Rwanda provides interesting contributions to our understanding of why developing countries

---

[54] Interview, commercial bank, Kigali, June 2017.
[55] Interview, commercial bank, Kigali, June 2017.

implement Basel standards. First, it highlights how two aspiring 'developmental states' (Ethiopia and Rwanda) have developed such strikingly different attitudes to Basel adoption and implementation. While Ethiopia and even Bolivia have highlighted clear distinctions between developmental state objectives and Basel adoption objectives, the RPF government has failed to distinguish between such objectives (and the contradictions between them). Another interpretation could be that the RPF government feels that its services-based development strategy requires the adoption of 'best practice' financial standards. Yet the announcement that the government will reduce its shareholding in BK through a public offering on the Kigali and Nairobi stock exchanges highlights how the government's developmentalist ambitions may be at risk. Thus, the implementation of Basel standards has brought into focus the inconsistencies within Rwanda's development project where the government 'want to be all things to everyone.'[56]

Unlike other policy-driven examples, though, the RPF government has demonstrated consistent conservative regulation practices in the banking sector. There is less political contestation compared to Ghana and the rapid adoption of Basel standards has not been opposed. Yet there are severe deficiencies in technical capacity and expertise in the sector and Basel implementation seems largely out of touch with the realities of Rwanda's shallow and underdeveloped financial sector.

There is still a lack of clarity within the banking sector about aspects of the implementation process. The government and commercial banks, in their 2018 annual statements, claim that IFRS 9 has been implemented but in 2017, most commercial banks argued that there was no way this would be possible. The consequences of Basel implementation have already led to a restructuring of the commercial banking sector, with BK's ownership and role in the country set to change. BK will face challenges to Basel implementation given its status as the largest Rwandan bank in a sector where subsidiaries have better-funded and more-skilled parent companies. Atlas Mara BPR already faces significant challenges—particularly in relation to non-performing loans—and will encounter additional difficulties. Other banks may find it much more difficult to receive returns on their new investments in Rwanda where non-performing loans are the highest in the region and return on equity is the lowest.

Basel implementation will undoubtedly bring significant change to Rwanda's financial sector. Yet there is no guarantee that it will help the RPF government achieve its goal of becoming a financial sector hub. Unless feedback mechanisms are integrated within the implementation process, it is likely to result in negative consequences in the short term for banks. Thus, the case of Basel adoption in Rwanda provides us with an interesting snapshot of a small developing country, which is committed to pursuing economic development, trusting the standards of international financial institutions with limited critical engagement. In Rwanda's

---

[56] Interview, consultant, Kigali, June 2017.

ambitious development project, there is little room for BNR and commercial banks to voice criticism (in the planning stages) with regards to the scale of the ambition of the country's economic leadership. The consequences will be borne out in the coming years as banks and the regulator grapple with Basel implementation.

References

Addison, T., Geda, A., Le Billon, P., Murshed, S.M., 2001. *Financial Reconstruction in conflict and 'post-conflict' economies* (Discussion Paper No. 2001/90).

Andrews, A.M., Jefferis, K., Hannah, R., Murgatroyd, P., 2012. *Rwanda: Financial Sector Development Program II*. Ministry of Finance and Economic Planning, Kigali.

Beck, T., Maimbo, S., Faye, I., Triki, T., 2011. *Financing Africa: Through the Crisis and Beyond*. World Bank, Washington, DC.

Behuria, P., 2016. Centralising rents and dispersing power while pursuing development? Exploring the strategic uses of military firms in Rwanda. *Review of African Political Economy* 43, 630–47. https://doi.org/10.1080/03056244.2015.1128407.

Behuria, P., 2018. Learning from role models in Rwanda: Incoherent emulation in the construction of a neoliberal developmental state. *New Political Economy* 23, 422–40. https://doi.org/10.1080/13563467.2017.1371123.

Behuria, P., Goodfellow, T., 2017. The disorder of miracle growth in Rwanda: Understanding the limitations of transitions to open ordered development, in: Pritchett, L., Sen, K., Werker, E. (Eds.), *Deals and Development: The Political Dynamics of Growth Episodes*. Oxford University Press, Oxford.

Booth, D., Golooba-Mutebi, F., 2012. Developmental patrimonialism? The case of Rwanda. *African Affairs* (Lond) 111, 379–403. https://doi.org/10.1093/afraf/ads026.

Bureau van Dijk, 2018. *Bankscope and Orbis Bank Focus*. London, Bureau van Dijk.

Ecobank Research, 2018. *Rwanda Central Bank Rolls Out Basel III Liquidity Measurement Regime*. Proshare.

Enoch, C., Mathieu, P.H., Mecagni, M., Canales Kriljenko, J., 2015. *Pan-African Banks: Opportunities and Challenges for Cross-Border Oversight*. IMF, Washington, DC.

Gahigi, M.K., 2015. How Rwanda became the land of a hundred hotel auctions. *Quartz Africa*.

Gottschalk, R., 2010. *The Basel Capital Accords in Developing Countries: Challenges for Development Finance*. Palgrave Macmillan, Basingstoke.

Government of Rwanda, 2000. *Rwanda Vision 2020*. Government of Rwanda, Kigali.

Government of Rwanda, 2013. *Final Report: Rwanda Financial Sector Strategy 2013–2018*. Government of Rwanda, Kigali.

Herbling, D., 2018. Bank of Kigali Seeks $67 Million in Offer That Dilutes State. *Bloomberg*.

IMF, 2005. *Financial Systems Stability Assessment.* IMF, Washington, DC.

IMF, 2011. *Financial Systems Stability Assessment.* IMF, Washington, DC.

IMF, 2018. *Financial Soundness Indicators Database.* IMF, Washington, DC.

International Growth Centre, 2016. *Raising exports and attracting FDI in Rwanda.* IGC, London.

Kwibuka, E., 2017. Parliament passes new Bill governing BNR. *The New Times,* Rwanda.

Mwai, C., 2017. Atlas Mara founder dispels rumours of possible buyout. *The New Times.*

National Bank of Rwanda, 2009. *Annual Report on Financial Stability 2008.* Government of Rwanda, Kigali.

National Bank of Rwanda, 2011. *Annual Report.* Government of Rwanda, Kigali.

National Bank of Rwanda, 2016. *Annual Financial Stability report June 2015 to June 2016.* Government of Rwanda, Kigali.

Oqubay, A., 2015. *Made in Africa: Industrial Policy in Ethiopia.* Oxford University Press, Oxford.

Polity IV, 2014. *PolityProject.* Center for Systemic Peace.

Reyntjens, F., 2013. *Political Governance in Post-Genocide Rwanda.* Cambridge University Press, Cambridge.

Rusagara, C., 2008. *Financial Sector Development Program: The Case of Rwanda.* IMF, Washington, DC.

Rwanda Development Board, 2012. *Rwanda Skills Survey 2012: Financial Services Sector Report.* Government of Rwanda, Kigali.

Sanya, S., Mitchell, A.E.W., Kantengwa, A., 2012. *Prudential liquidity regulation in developing countries: A case study of Rwanda* (Working Paper No. 12/20). IMF, Washington, DC.

Vemuru, V., 2018. *Project information document-integrated safeguards data sheet: Development response to Displacement Impacts Project—P164101* (No. PIDISDSA24990). World Bank, Washington, DC.

Wade, R., 1990. *Governing the Market: Economic Theory and the Role of Government in East Asian Industrialization.* Princeton University Press, Princeton, NJ.

World Bank, 2017. *World Development Indicators.* World Bank, Washington, DC.

6

Ghana

Reformist Politicians Drive Basel Implementation

Emily Jones

Introduction

On the face of it, the trajectory of Basel implementation in Ghana is puzzling. Ghana has a reputation as an open economy with a government that is quick to adopt international norms, yet it was relatively slow to implement international banking standards. The Ghanaian government has pursued a series of financial sector reforms since the late 1980s in close collaboration with the World Bank and IMF, with a relatively high presence of foreign banks. Ghana was an early implementer of Basel I, but attempts to move towards Basel II in the mid-2000s faltered. The IMF assessed Ghana as having a low level of compliance with the Basel Core Principles relative to other countries in Sub-Saharan Africa (Marchettini et al., 2015, p. 28). This pattern changed dramatically in 2017 when the government embarked on a radical reform of the banking sector, implementing major elements of Basel II and III and catapulting Ghana to among the most ambitious implementers of Basel standards among our case study countries.

This chapter attributes the stop-start nature of Basel implementation in Ghana to different interests and policy ideas among Ghana's two main political parties, which meant that the approach to international banking standards varied according to which political party was in power. In common with many developing countries, Ghana adopted Basel I as the result of World Bank driven reforms in the 1990s. While the adoption of Basel I was externally driven, the more recent drive for Basel II and III adoption was domestic and came from politicians of the New Patriotic Party (NPP). The NPP sought to turn Ghana into an international financial services hub and perceived the adoption of international standards as vital for pursuing this vision. Strikingly, the IMF pushed back against early moves towards Basel II implementation in the 2000s, advising the Government of Ghana not to proceed with Basel II until it had addressed fundamental weaknesses in its basic supervision. The NPP government pressed ahead but implementation stalled when the government changed in 2009 and the National Democratic Congress (NDC) assumed office. It was only after

Emily Jones, *Ghana: Reformist Politicians Drive Basel Implementation* In: *The Political Economy of Bank Regulation in Developing Countries: Risk and Reputation.* Edited by: Emily Jones, Oxford University Press (2020).
© Oxford University Press. DOI: 10.1093/oso/9780198841999.003.0006

the NPP regained power in early 2017 that the implementation of Basel standards resumed in earnest, as part of a radical reform of the banking sector.

The different approaches of the NDC and NPP towards international banking standards reflects differences in their ideas about the role of the financial sector in development as well as the material interests of the businesses groups they are aligned with. As a party the NPP has deliberately set out to position Ghana as a financial services hub for the West Africa region, seeking to attract international investors into the financial sector and develop strong domestic banks and financial firms that can capitalise on the sector's expansion. In contrast, NDC prioritised directing credit to productive sectors of the economy and supporting indigenous banks; the implementation of a complex and costly set of international standards was simply not a priority.

The fact that convergence is policy-driven is surprising because such regulatory decisions fall under the exclusive mandate of Ghana's central bank (the Bank of Ghana), which has a high level of formal independence from the executive branch and hence from political parties. Yet close scrutiny shows that, in practice the central bank has become increasingly responsive to changing policy agendas. Since the early 2000s it has become the norm for central bank governors and their deputies to step down within a few months of a new political party assuming office, even when their official terms have not ended. In tandem, it has become commonplace for senior technocrats at the central bank to leave office or be moved. The politicization of government institutions has been observed in other areas too (Appiah and Abdulai, 2017; Gyimah-Boadi and Yakah, 2012). While some argue that this undermines the quality of central bank decisions, others argue that it makes the institution more accountable to Ghana's democratically elected leaders.

Despite being the target of these various regulatory initiatives, banks have not played a major role in shaping the trajectory of Basel implementation in Ghana. In the context of a highly profitable and so-far weakly supervised banking sector, foreign banks would not derive any competitive advantage from the implementation of more complex regulatory standards. Meanwhile, domestic banks are yet to venture overseas in a meaningful way, so they have little reason to support implementation of more cumbersome regulations. Although implementation entails substantial costs for these banks, they have not been a source of strong opposition to implementation, perhaps because they have not expected rigorous enforcement.

Although both political parties have taken different approaches to the adoption of international banking standards, the actual supervision and enforcement of banking regulation has historically been lax under both parties. This only started to change after 2016 when a snap audit of the banking sector (required as part of a new loan arrangement with the IMF) revealed fragility and poor corporate governance of several banks, Following its election in 2017, the NPP government made a series of moves to strengthen supervision and enforcement.

The analysis in this chapter is based on a review of the secondary literature, official documents, media reports, and twenty-one semi-structured interviews conducted in Accra in March 2016 and April 2017. Interviews were conducted with current and former representatives from the Bank of Ghana and Ministry of Finance, senior representatives from eight banks (headquartered in Ghana, other African countries, and the UK), an international accounting firm, a representative of the Ghana Association of Bankers, a member of the Board of the Bank of Ghana, a member of the Monetary Policy Committee, and an MP serving on the Parliamentary Finance Committee. Interviews are not directly attributed, in order to preserve the anonymity of participants.

The next sections explain the wider political economy context and Ghana's adoption of Basel standards and compliance with Basel Core Principles, and then explains the political economy of Basel implementation. The chapter concludes by situating the findings and arguments in the wider literature on political economy dynamics in Ghana.

Political economy context: mutual dependence between banks and government

Ghana has a middle-sized economy relative to others in Sub-Saharan Africa, and is renowned within the region for its vibrant democracy. It experienced high growth rates in the 2000s, partly as a result of the worldwide commodity boom and international debt relief, and has achieved one of the best records of poverty reduction in Sub-Saharan Africa. In 2011, it moved into the category of lower-middle-income countries and has a GDP per capita of close to US$1,400 (Table 6.1).

Despite high growth and attempts to diversify its economy, Ghana remains heavily reliant on the export of primary commodities including gold, cocoa, and,

Table 6.1 Ghana: key indicators

Ghana	
GDP per capita (current US$)	1,641
Bank assets (current US$)	10.17 bn
Bank assets (% of GDP)	27.3
Stock market capitalization (% of GDP)	11.7
Credit allocation to private sector (% of GDP)	19.7
Credit allocation to government (% of GDP)	10.4
Polity IV score	8

Note: All data is from 2017 unless otherwise indicated.

Source: FSI Database, IMF (2018); GDI Database, World Bank (2017); Polity IV (2014)

following recent discoveries, petroleum. As a result of macro-economic shocks relating to commodity dependence, as well as high levels of pre-election spending, successive governments have struggled with rising public sector indebtedness. In 2015 the IMF and the World Bank declared Ghana to be at 'high risk of debt distress' and the Ghanaian government entered into an extended credit facility arrangement with the IMF (IMF and World Bank, 2015).

The banking sector has grown rapidly since 2000, with total assets increasing from just under US$4 billion (22 per cent of GDP) in 2005, to more than US$10 billion (27.3 per cent of GDP) in 2017. The nature of the banking sector has also changed as the result of policy reforms. The first wave of reforms occurred in the late 1980s and early 1990s under a World Bank Financial Sector Adjustment Programme (FSAP) which restructured distressed banks, reformed bank regulation and supervision, and opened the banking sector to new entrants (Antwi-Asare and Addison, 2000; Aryeetey, 2003; Aryeetey et al., 1997). A second wave of reforms in the early 2000s included the introduction of universal banking, which allowed banks to engage in commercial, development, merchant, and investment banking without the need for separate licenses (Quartey, 2005).

The reforms led to a substantial adjustment in bank ownership patterns (Table 6.2). In the 1990s the banking sector was dominated by government-owned banks and by 2017 government-owned banks only controlled one fifth of assets. Domestic private banks expanded to fill the space, with their market share increasing to one third of assets in 2017. Since the early 2000s, about half of banking sector assets have been controlled by foreign-owned banks. Although the share of foreign ownership has remained relatively stable, European banks have ceded share to recent entrants from Nigeria and South Africa. The dramatic NPP-led consolidation of the banking sector during 2017 and 2018, which cost the taxpayer more than GhC12billion (more than US$2billion), led the number of banks to decline from thirty-four in mid-2017 to twenty-three at the end of 2018 (Bank of Ghana, 2019; Dontoh, 2019).

Table 6.2 Ghana: changing patterns of bank ownership

	2010		2017	
	Number of banks	% of total assets	Number of banks	% of total assets
Government-controlled	5	28.9	3	16.6
Domestic privately controlled	7	17.7	11	32.2
Foreign privately controlled	14	53.4	17	51.3

Source: Author's calculations based on data from IMF databases (2018)

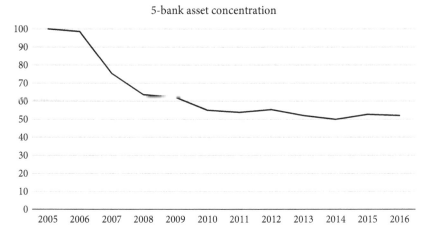

Figure 6.1 Ghana: banking sector concentration .

Source: Global Financial Development Database, World Bank (2018a)

Banks in Ghana have business models that rely overwhelmingly on the domestic market, with domestic assets accounting for more than 90 per cent of the sector's assets (Bank of Ghana, 2017a). Only one Ghanaian bank operates internationally.[1]

Early banking reforms in Ghana were heralded as one of the most successful in Africa (IMF, 1999a). Yet, as in other countries, the reforms have not fulfilled their ambitions of creating a competitive banking industry that lends to the private sector. Despite an increase in the number of banks and the corresponding reduction in market concentration (Figure 6.1), Ghana's banking sector remains uncompetitive, short-term, and expensive, with unusually high interest rate spreads and profits (Adjei-Frimpong et al., 2016; Biekpe, 2011; Buchs and Mathisen, 2005). Like the banking sector in many other African countries, it is also very profitable (Figure 6.2). Since the global financial crisis, return on equity in global banking has hovered around 8-10% while it has been twice as high in Africa (Chrionga et al. 2018) Although lending to the private sector increased to just above 20 per cent of GDP in 2015, this was well below the average of 29 per cent for Sub-Saharan Africa (Figure 6.3).

High interest rate spreads, highly profitable banks, and a low level of lending to the real economy are arguably due to the government's reliance on the banks as a source of short-term finance (Figure 6.3). A strong appetite of successive governments for domestic borrowing has led banks to invest heavily in high-yielding short-term government securities. Between 1998 and 2003, for example, government securities accounted for 25 per cent of bank assets, while net loans were only 34 per cent (Buchs and Mathisen, 2005). Similarly, in mid-2018, government

---

[1] Fidelity Bank opened a wholly owned subsidiary in Malaysia in 2012.

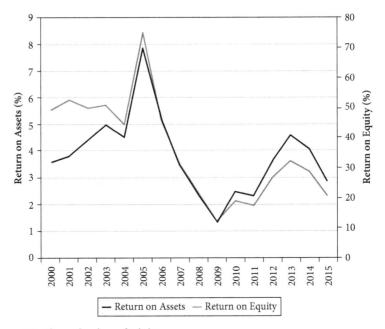

Figure 6.2 Ghana: bank profitability.

Source: Bankscope and Orbis Bank Focus, Bureau van Dijk (2018)

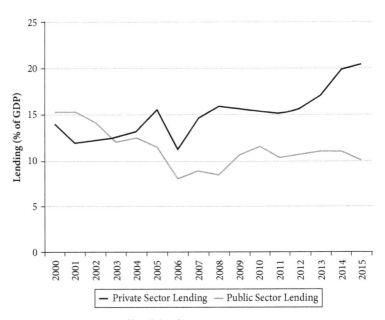

Figure 6.3 Ghana: patterns of bank lending.

Source: World Bank (2018b, 2017)

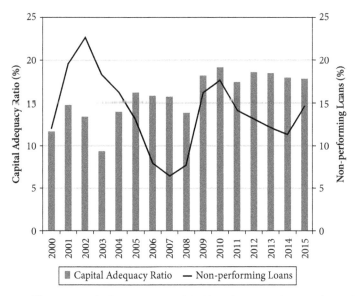

Figure 6.4   Ghana: capital adequacy ratios (CAR) and non-performing loans (NPLs).
Source: Financial Soundness Indicators Database, IMF (2018)

bills and securities accounted for 36 per cent of bank assets, while net loans were only 33 per cent (Bank of Ghana, 2018a).

The dominance of short-term, high-yielding government securities on the books of Ghana's banks has contributed to banks being relatively safe, well capitalized, and highly liquid. Average levels of capital have substantially exceeded the prudential requirement of 10 per cent of risk-weighted assets (Figure 6.4) and capital adequacy and liquidity levels in Ghanaian banks have been well above regional peers. However, the quality of assets in the banking sector has varied, with spikes in the level of non-performing loans (NPLs) (Figure 6.4). NPLs have been caused by a mix of macro-economic shocks and arrears in government payments to contractors. They have plagued all types of banks, including reputable international ones (IMF, 2011a).

While concerns had been raised about the high levels of NPLs, it was only when the IMF demanded an asset quality review of all banks in 2016 as part of a loan package that it became clear that headline figures masked a high level of variation at the level of individual banks. Crucially, the asset quality review used a more stringent approach to loan classification than had been the norm. Historically, the Bank of Ghana had not required banks to classify loans as nonperforming if they originated from government or had a government guarantee (Bank of Ghana, 2016). When reviewed under the stricter prudential standards, eight banks were found to be insolvent, illiquid, or both, and a series of corporate governance failures and regulatory breaches were revealed (Bank of Ghana, 2018a).

The results triggered a slew of reforms, first under the NDC (2015–16) and then under the NPP (2017 onwards). Reforms included new legislation, new regulations in areas ranging from minimum capital requirements to corporate governance, the closure of seven banks, and mergers between banks that couldn't meet the new minimum capital requirements.

Interviews in 2016 revealed a lax supervisory environment. Banking supervision, carried out by the Banking Supervision Department of the Bank of Ghana, was by several interviewees to be relatively weak, with supervisors always playing 'regulatory catch-up'.[2] Interviewees noted that the Bank of Ghana faced significant shortages in the number of supervisors with the requisite expertise. Supervisors were reported to rely heavily on auditors' reports, but, as auditors were reported to have a very cosy relationship with the banks, interviewees intimated that the under-reporting of NPLs was common. Moreover, when they detected problems, supervisors were often reluctant to initiate any action, particularly when banks were politically connected.[3] Investigations following the IMF-promoted audit revealed a series of regulatory breaches, corporate governance failures, insider dealings, and accounting and financial improprieties, and led the Bank of Ghana to close seven banks during 2017-8. As part of wider reforms to the sector, the Bank of Ghana created an Office of Ethics and Internal Investigations to strengthen the quality of supervision (Bank of Ghana, 2018b).

Ghana's adoption and implementation of the Basel banking standards

Since its first Financial Sector Assessment Programme (FSAP) in the late 1990s, the government has been under pressure from international financial institutions to improve its compliance with the Basel Core Principles. Ghana was relatively quick to adopt and implement Basel I. Yet, despite making moves to implement Basel II as early as 2004, it was only in January 2019 that elements of Basel II and III came into force (Table 6.2).

Basel Core Principles

Since the 1990s, Ghana has been criticized by the IMF and World Bank for weak compliance with the Basel Core Principles. Ghana's banking regulation and supervisory practices were first evaluated against the Basel Core Principles in the late 1990s (IMF, 1999a). A joint IMF–World Bank FSAP evaluation in 2000 found

---

[2] Interviews with senior government officials and representatives of private banks, Accra, March 2016.
[3] Interview with private sector representative, Accra, 21 March 2016.

Ghana to be 'largely compliant' with the Basel Core Principles, but highlighted a series of legal changes needed to bring the Ghanaian framework 'closer to international practices'. The FSAP team criticized the Bank of Ghana's limited independence and stressed the need for supervisors to 'act more aggressively in enforcing prudential standards as they had instead tended to favour moral suasion' (IMF, 2003).

The level of compliance with the Basel Core Principles declined during the 2000s. Another FSAP was conducted in 2010 and assessed Ghana to be non-compliant or materially non-compliant with fourteen of the twenty-five Basel Core Principles—substantially below the average in the sub-region (IMF, 2011b, p. 49). It found that, despite the financial sector reforms of the 2000s, financial stability risks had heightened, non-performing loans were high, and commercial banks' internal controls and risk management practices had not kept pace with the industry's growth and changing risks. Even a moderate deterioration in the asset quality of banks would have led to the insolvency of several banks (IMF, 2011b; Marchettini et al., 2015, p. 28). The Bank of Ghana disputed the IMF's assessments, judging itself to be non-compliant or materially non-compliant with eight of the Core Principles, not the fourteen identified by the IMF (Bank of Ghana, 2013).

Basel I, II, and III

Ghana was an early adopter of Basel I, adopting prudential regulations based on the standard in 1989, only a year after they had been agreed by the Basel Committee. Ghana's Banking Act (1989) introduced capital adequacy requirements at 6 per cent of risk-weighted assets. These requirements were modelled on Basel I, although the Bank of Ghana's criteria for risk-weighting assets were simpler, with only two categories of risk weights rather than a spectrum (World Bank, 1994, p. 54). The Bank of Ghana's capital adequacy requirement was lower than the 8 per cent stipulated in Basel I but, because the method for calculating capital adequacy ratios was more conservative, in practice banks were required to maintain capital levels in excess of the Basel minimum (IMF, 2003, 1999b; World Bank, 1994).[4] From 1992, the Bank of Ghana started to implement Basel I to assess credit risk; from 1998 it introduced an assessment of operational risk; and from 2000 it started to assess market risk (focusing on the foreign exchange exposure of banks).[5]

---

[4] The Bank of Ghana standards apply higher risk weights for some assets, such as interbank loans, and because fixed assets and certain investments are deducted from both the numerator and the denominator of the ratio (IMF, 2003).

[5] Interview with government official, Accra, 17 March 2016.

The Bank of Ghana also looked like it would be an early adopter of Basel II. Ghana was one of the first countries in Sub-Saharan Africa to initiate risk-based supervision, as a precursor to implementing Basel II (Dosoo, 2006). The Bank of Ghana Act (2004) provided for risk-based supervision and all banks were required to implement risk-based management practices from 2007 (Bank of Ghana, 2007). In 2007, the Bank of Ghana undertook a series of preparatory steps towards implementation of Basel II including a readiness and gap analysis of banks, identifying champions in the banking sector to lead implementation efforts, and preparing guidelines for the calculation of the minimum capital requirements. It set a target date of 2010 for the full implementation of Basel II (Bank of Ghana, 2015; IMF, 2009).

Following extensive consultations, the Bank of Ghana and local banks mutually agreed to adopt the Basel II standardized approaches for credit, operational, and market risk (IMF, 2009). A joint committee comprising Bank of Ghana officials and representatives from the banks was formed to oversee Basel II implementation, and the committee met quarterly to discuss progress (IMF, 2009).

If these plans had come to fruition, Ghana would have been an early adopter of Basel II among our case study countries. But implementation was 'placed on hold' for six years from 2009 to 2015 (Bank of Ghana, 2015).[6] It was only in 2015 that implementation resumed, although at a slow pace. The Banks and Special Deposit-Taking Institutions Act (2016) provided the Bank of Ghana with enhanced powers to resolve banks and laid the foundations for the implementation of Basel II (Asiama, 2017) and the Bank of Ghana announced 2017 as the new target date for full implementation (Business and Financial Times, 2017b; PWC, 2016). However interviews in 2016 suggested that it was unlikely to happen as neither the regulator nor the banks appeared to be ready. A banking survey carried out by PricewaterhouseCoopers in early 2017 revealed that the majority of banks did not have a detailed plan for how to transition to Basel II and were waiting on the Bank of Ghana to issue guidelines (PWC, 2017).

In a move that took banks and observers by surprise, in September 2017, the Bank of Ghana announced that all banks had fifteen months to meet a three-fold increase in minimum capital requirements, which rose from GhC120 million (approx. US$25 million) to GhC400 million (approx. US$80 million). This was quickly followed in November 2017 with the issuance of new draft capital requirements based on core elements of both Basel II and Basel III. Following a consultation period with banks, the Capital Requirements Directive was issued in June 2018 and came into effect in January 2019 (Bank of Ghana, 2018c). The directive required all banks to comply with the capital requirements of Basel II (the standardized approaches to credit, operational, and market risk) as well as the capital-related requirements of Basel III (Table 6.3).

---

[6] This was confirmed in interviews.

Table 6.3 Ghana: adoption of Basel standards

Basel component	Adoption	Implementation—issuance of regulations and guidelines	Implementation—regulations and guidelines take effect
Basel I (modified)	Banking Act 1989	Credit risk—1992 Operational risk—1998 Market risk—2000	
Risk-based supervision (precursor to Basel II)	Banking Act 2004	2007 for all banks	
Basel II	Bank of Ghana has requisite powers under Banking Act 2004 and 2016	June 2018—Capital Requirements Directive • Credit risk—standardized approach • Operational risk—standardized approach • Market risk—standardized approach	Entered into force 1 January 2019
Basel III	Bank of Ghana has requisite powers under Banking Act 2004 and 2016	June 2018—Capital Requirements Directive • Basel III definitions of capital • Capital conservation buffer • Countercyclical buffer • Leverage ratio • D-SIB	Entered into force 1 January 2019

The political economy of Basel standards in Ghana

Four sets of actors are central to explaining Ghana's response to the Basel framework: the regulator (Bank of Ghana); the IMF and the World Bank; Ghana's two main political parties (the NDC and NPP); and its banks.

In its capacity as regulator and supervisor of banks, the Bank of Ghana has the mandate to decide whether and how much of the suite of international banking standards to adopt, implement, and enforce. The Bank of Ghana, along with the Ministry of Finance, has a reputation for being a strong and effective government institution, with a high level of technical expertise. Although formally independent, it is heavily influenced by party politics. Crucially, it has become the norm for central bank governors and deputies to step down within a few months of a change in government, under considerable pressure from the incoming government, to make room for the appointment of governors who are closely linked to the incoming party. These links are illustrated in two instances when central bank governors have later been appointed as the country's vice president when the political party that they served under regained power.

As an institution, the Bank of Ghana has cultivated strong links with the international policy community of the international financial institutions, generated through successive IMF and World Bank-supported financial sector reform programmes. There is a 'revolving door' at the level of senior staff: all five central bank governors that were in office between 2000 and 2018 previously worked for the IMF, World Bank, or African Development Bank. The Bank of Ghana is also closely linked to its peer regulators within Africa through its participation networks of supervisors, and has particularly strong bilateral relations with the Central Bank of Nigeria. It is also engaged in the Financial Stability Board's Regional Consultative Group for Africa, and closely engaged in international policy discussions at the Bank of International Settlements.

Below I trace the political economy dynamics behind Ghana's stop-start implementation of international banking standards and the role of the Bank of Ghana, politicians from the two main political parties, the IMF and World Bank, and domestic and foreign banks. The analysis is split into four chronological periods, each with distinct dynamics.

World Bank in the driving seat: PNDC and NDC era (1980s to 1999)

Following the economic and financial crises in the 1980s, financial sector reforms started in earnest in 1987 under a World Bank Financial Sector Adjustment Programme (FINSAP). In addition to restructuring, privatizing, and liberalizing the banking sector, the reforms sought to improve Ghana's banking regulations and supervisory capabilities. Bank of Ghana and World Bank officials in consultation with 'banking, accounting and other professional bodies in Ghana and abroad' drafted a new banking law, and provisions were '*broadly patterned upon those of the Basel guidelines*' (emphasis added, World Bank, 1995, p. 5). The Basel I standard was adapted to suit Ghana's relatively simple banking sector and the low level of supervisory resources in the Bank of Ghana, with only two categories of risk weights (0 per cent and 100 per cent) rather than a spectrum (World Bank, 1994, p. 54).

Implementation of Basel I standards started in earnest in 1992, with the introduction of assessments of credit risk, and this was followed by the introduction of assessments for operational risk in 1998 and market risk (foreign exchange exposure) in 2000.[7]

While there are few documents verifying the politics of banking sector reform during this period and few interviewees could recollect details, the available evidence suggests that the World Bank and the IMF played a crucial role in introducing Basel I and the Basel Core Principles to Ghana.

---

[7] Interview with government official, Accra, 17 March 2016.

Bank of Ghana drives through Basel reforms: NPP era (2001–8)

The IMF, World Bank, and donor community continued to exert influence over policy reforms in Ghana in a variety of policy areas during the 2000s, with varying efficacy (e.g. Abdulai and Hulme, 2015; Whitfield, 2010). A fantasticating aspect of financial sector reforms was that the NPP pursued a vigorous reform agenda that was sometimes at odds with the IMF.

The NPP's drive for financial sector reforms reflected a specific mix of interests and policy ideas. The NPP is widely perceived to be a party that supports the business class, with strong international connections, and several of its most prominent financiers have come from the financial sector. Upon its election in 2001, the NPP government proclaimed that it would usher in a 'golden age of business' and its three policy priorities were improved governance, extensive government divestiture, and the development of an efficient financial sector with proper supervisory standards.

The NPP government's vision for the financial sector, as articulated in the 2003 Financial Sector Strategic Plan, was to diversify, grow, and *globalize* Ghana's financial system (Mensah, 2015). The strategic plan set out a vision for 'a financial sector that is…fully integrated with the global financial system and supported by a regulatory system that promotes a high degree of confidence' (Ministry of Finance and Economic Planning, 2003).

A cornerstone of the NPP's vision for the banking sector was to position Ghana as a financial services hub for the West African region. The NPP government perceived an opportunity because Ghana's two main competitors were weak: Nigeria had a much larger financial market but its regulatory and legal institutions were weak and it lacked policy credibility, while Cote d'Ivoire suffered from political instability.[8] In line with this vision, the NPP government introduced new laws that, *inter alia*, raised minimum capital requirements, permitted the issuance of universal banking licenses, and increased the level of independence of the central bank (Biekpe, 2011; IMF, 2011b).

Reforms were led by Paul Acquah, governor of the central bank, who had been deputy director of the IMF's Africa Department, and was recruited by the NPP to head up the central bank. Interviewees repeatedly stressed the pivotal role he played in driving through financial sector reforms. According to one interviewee who was privy to discussions in the top echelons of the NPP government, Acquah 'had a vision [for the financial sector] and he sold it to the NPP leadership…it was a vigorous reform agenda that sought to liberate the economy'.[9] Scrutiny of the policy documents at the time bears this out: the vision and rationale for a financial

---

[8] Interview with former government official, Accra, 22 March 2016, interview with former government minister, Accra, 22 March 2016.
[9] Interview with former government minister, Accra, 22 March 2016.

services hub was articulated in greatest detail by Paul Acquah and his senior officials. They argued that creating a financial services centre would help insert Ghana into the international financial system, opening the economy up to cross-border capital flows and global financial markets (Acquah, 2007; Bank of Ghana, 2008).

Acquah's financial sector vision was strongly supported by the president and key ministers, and followed an agenda that was closely aligned with the interests of the NPP's financial supporters, whose capital was invested in the financial services sector.[10] It was also supported by international private investors, who honoured Acquah with the Emerging Markets award for the African Central Bank Governor of the Year in 2005 (Hammond, 2005). The implementation of Basel II and other international standards was seen as vital for attracting international investors into the financial sector. As one former official who had worked closely with Acquah explained, 'If you have adopted best practices, they [investors] will be attracted. Investors like to see good practices'.[11] The standards were also perceived to be important for managing the increased risk that would come with closer integration into global finance.[12]

In preparation for Basel II, officials at the Bank of Ghana assessed the risk management systems of banks, and found them to be extremely weak. As a former official of the Bank of Ghana noted, 'Their systems were really simple—the banks just looked to see if the borrower had collateral or not. At most they assessed credit risk. For anything complex, international banks sent the analysis to their headquarters to do'.[13]

The Bank of Ghana set a target date of 2007 for implementing a risk-based supervisory approach as a precursor to the full implementation of Basel II (Dosoo, 2006). The Bank of Ghana was aware that a shift to risk-based supervision and then to Basel II would be demanding. Ghanaian regulators received extensive technical support from the IMF, the World Bank, and the West African Institute for Financial and Economic Management (WAIFEM).[14] The Bank of Ghana also sent staff to the UK and Canada to study their approaches to risk-based supervision (Bank of Ghana, 2004). It decided to emulate the Canadian approach and for several years the Canadian government provided technical assistance to support Basel II implementation.[15]

While the NPP's interest in financial sector reforms broadly aligned with the priorities of the IMF and other major donors, the NPP's determination to

<hr>

[10] Financial supporters included Databank Ltd, a local financial services company whose CEO would become the Minister of Finance under the NPP government in 2017.
[11] Interview with former government official, Accra, 22 March 2016.
[12] Interviews with senior government officials, Accra, 17 and 22 March 2016.
[13] Interview with former government official, Accra, 22 March 2016.
[14] Interview with government official, Accra, 17 March 2016.
[15] Interviews with government official, 17 March 2016, and former government official, 22 March 2016, Accra.

implement Basel II received push-back. The IMF reportedly tried to deter the Bank of Ghana from implementing Basel II, arguing that it was too ambitious and that Ghana should focus on complying with the Basel Core Principles.[16] However, as one interviewee explained, the governor and senior officials had a different view: '[Their] philosophy was that because Ghana's financial system is still quite simple, now is the time to play with concepts so that we are ready when the financial system gets more complex. [Ghana's] financial sector is developing fast'.[17]

The Bank of Ghana went ahead despite the IMF's reservations, setting a target for the full implementation of Basel II by 2010 (IMF, 2009). It undertook a series of preparatory steps, including conducting a readiness and gap analysis of banks, identifying champions in the banking sector who would lead implementation efforts, preparing guidelines for the calculation of the minimum capital requirements for pillar 1 for credit, operational, and market risk, and designing Basel II reporting formats (Bank of Ghana, 2015).

Strikingly, throughout this period there was no appetite among foreign or domestic banks for Basel II implementation. Foreign banks operate as locally incorporated subsidiaries and are regulated under the purview of the Bank of Ghana. Although foreign banks would have been able to comply with Basel II standards more easily than domestic banks, in Ghana's highly profitable banking sector they had no incentive to capitalise on this advantage. Only one domestic bank operates internationally, and only since 2012 when it opened a subsidiary in Malaysia. Although some domestic banks were raising international finance and seeking international credit ratings, this did not translate into support for Basel implementation. Interviews with such domestic banks revealed that while they were strong advocates of the move to adopt IFRS standards, as they perceived this would dramatically improve their creditworthiness in the eyes of foreign investors, they did not perceive investors or credit ratings agencies to have any interest in Basel implementation.[18]

IMF in the lead under the NDC (2009–16)

Following elections, an NDC government assumed office in January 2009 with a markedly different vision for the financial sector. The NDC is a social democratic party and its financial sector strategy focused on encouraging lending to priority sectors of the economy including agriculture, industry, and fisheries (NDC, 2008). The party's elite have a much stronger nationalist tradition than the NPP, seeking to protect and support indigenous businesses, and are less connected to international

---

[16] Interview with senior government official, Accra, 21 March 2016.
[17] Interview with former government official, Accra, 22 March 2016.
[18] Interview with senior bank representatives (Ghanaian bank), Accra, 17 March 2016.

policy circles and the international investment community. While its financial supporters operate in a range of economic sectors, they are much less involved in the financial sector than those connected to the NPP.

Although there is passing mention in the NDC's 2008 manifesto to creating a financial services hub (NDC, 2008), interviewees made it clear that the NDC did not share the NPP's ambition of globalizing Ghana's banking sector. In particular the NDC was critical of the NPP's moves to further liberalize the banking sector. As a senior NDC figure explained during an interview, 'Paul Acquah [the central bank governor under the NPP] thought "capital was capital" and issued lots of foreign bank licenses... but it isn't safe to have all the banking sector in foreign hands... Two Nigerian banks entered in this way—they were poorly regulated and he let them in'.[19] Financial sector reforms continued under the NDC but at a slower pace, and the implementation of Basel II standards stalled.

The dramatic shift in the pace of reforms illustrates the impact of party politics and a change in policy priorities on the ostensibly independent central bank. The incoming NDC government reportedly perceived the Bank of Ghana to be overly aligned with the previous NPP administration. Paul Acquah stepped down and was replaced by Kwesi Amissah-Arthur who had previously served as the NDC's deputy finance minister and was widely perceived to be a close ally of the President. Senior officials who had worked closely with Governor Acquah felt under pressure to leave, even including those who were not politically aligned.[20] Those who had acquired expertise on Basel II and championed its implementation left, and enthusiasm for Basel II implementation among the technical officials waned. Many of the remaining officials were 'risk-averse and thought the standards were too advanced for Ghana', while others had lost faith in the Basel standards following the global financial crisis.[21]

This shift in the pace of Basel II implementation is clearly reflected in correspondence between the Government of Ghana and the IMF. In the 2009 Letter of Intent to the IMF written while Acquah was still in office, the Government of Ghana committed to implementing the Standardized Approach of Basel II by 2010 (IMF, 2009). Once Acquah had left, the IMF encouraged the Bank of Ghana to slow down Basel II implementation. As one interviewee explained, 'when Paul Acquah left, the IMF came in and wanted to put the brakes on [Basel II implementation]. They didn't get the rationale'.[22] The IMF's (2011a) report states that: 'The planned adoption of the standardized approach of the Basel II framework *should not proceed* without meeting certain pre-conditions. The transition to Basel II will require sound project management by the [Bank of Ghana], including

---

[19] Interview with senior banking sector representative, Accra, 21 March 2016.
[20] Interview with former government official, Accra, 22 March 2016.
[21] Interview with senior government official, Accra, 21 March 2016.
[22] Interview with former government official, Accra, 22 March 2016.

extensive technical analysis and some policy decisions' (emphasis added, IMF, 2011b, p. 24). Following a highly critical Financial Sector Assessment Programme report, the IMF wanted the Bank of Ghana to focus on improving compliance with the Basel Core Principles before moving onto Basel II.

The NDC had a much less clearly defined financial sector strategy than the NPP and, although the new team at the central bank had some experience with the IMF, their professional links were much less extensive than those of the outgoing team. Together with the loss of technical expertise, interviewees argued that these differences resulted in the IMF having much greater influence over Ghana's financial sector reforms. As a former NPP Minister explained, 'During Paul Acquah's time the IMF was cautious as they knew Paul had experience with the IMF. [The] IMF would listen because they knew Paul had done his homework...Now the team is weak and they don't push back'.[23]

Under pressure from the international community, the NDC government reversed steps that the NPP had taken to establish Ghana as an offshore financial centre. In 2009 Ghana underwent a peer-review by the inter-governmental Group Against Money Laundering in West Africa (GIABA), which revealed numerous shortcomings in Ghana's implementation of Financial Action Task Force (FATF) standards, judging Ghana to be 'compliant' or 'largely compliant' with only five of the forty-nine standards (GIABA, 2009). Shortly after, the OECD warned Ghana of the risks of becoming a tax haven (Mathiason, 2010). Following this criticism from the international community, the Bank of Ghana withdrew the only offshore banking license it had issued, held by Barclays Bank, and took steps to improve its compliance with FATF standards. As the governor explained: 'At a time that Ghana was gaining a reputation for laundry, we did not want to confirm this misperception' (Dogbevi et al., 2011).

When Ghana entered into an IMF Extended Credit Facility Arrangement in 2015 following a macro-economic crisis, the IMF took the opportunity to pressure the government to improve the quality of supervision in the banking sector and increase compliance with the Basel Core Principles. The IMF Programme included a series of structural benchmarks aimed at overcoming the weaknesses that had been flagged in the 2010 FSAP, including a requirement that the government would complete an asset quality review of banks and introduce new legislation to increase the central bank's independence and improve prudential supervision (IMF, 2015, p. 74).

The IMF's push for an asset quality review is significant, as loan classification had been an source of tension between the Bank of Ghana and the IMF for many years (IMF, 2011b). Crucially, the Ghanaian authorities did not classify loans as non-performing if the loan originated from the government on the basis that

---

[23] Interview with former government minister, Accra, 22 March 2016. This view was corroborated in interviews with senior officials in the Bank of Ghana.

ultimately 'the government will pay'.[24] In a context where banks were heavily exposed to the government, interviewees explained how severe fiscal imbalances had led to erratic government payments and the build-up of arrears to contractors and other private sector companies, and this in turn posed a major source of risk for the banking sector.[25] However, the Bank of Ghana was reluctant to punish individual banks for problems that ultimately originated from the government's persistent fiscal problems.

In line with the conditions attached to the IMF financing agreement, the IMF and Bank of Ghana undertook a joint asset quality review of all banks in 2015. In the words of one interviewee, this 'snap audit' was 'very revealing'. It showed that 'the auditors were in bed with the banks', the level of non-performing loans in many banks was substantially higher than had been reported, and the risk management systems of many banks were very weak.[26] The IMF criticized the Bank of Ghana for its regulatory forbearance, particularly with regard to the impairment of loans originating from state-owned companies. Following a second asset quality review that revealed several banks to be severely undercapitalized, the government and the IMF agreed that the Bank of Ghana would review banks' recapitalization and restructuring plans, and initiate resolution procedures for banks found to be unviable (IMF, 2016).

As per the IMF loan conditions, the government also passed two new banking sector acts in 2016. The Banks and Specialized Deposit-Taking Institutions Act, 2016 (Act 930) provided the Bank of Ghana with greater independence and enhanced powers to resolve banks that are deemed to be unviable, while the Ghana Deposit Protection Act, 2016 (Act 931) introduced a new deposit insurance scheme. Perhaps because these changes have made Ghana more compliant with Basel Core Principles, the IMF started to strongly support a move to Basel II, providing technical assistance and supporting the Bank of Ghana in its aim to implement Basel II by mid-2017 (IMF, 2016).

NPP resumes office and implements Basel II and III (2017–present)

Following elections in late 2016, the NPP resumed office and the central bank governor and both deputies stepped down, reportedly under pressure, and despite not completing their scheduled terms in office.[27] The NPP appointed Ernest Addison as the new governor. He had been a senior official at the central bank

---

[24] Interview with senior government official, Accra, 15 March 2016.
[25] Interview with senior bank representative (foreign bank), Accra, 17 March 2016.
[26] Interview with government official, Accra, 17 March 2016.
[27] The governor stepped down in March 2017 (three months into the new administration), one deputy governor in July 2017, and the other in December 2017.

during the previous NPP administration and had left to work at the African Development Bank when the NDC assumed office.

The change of government ushered in a shift in financial sector strategy as, once again, the NPP's election manifesto prioritized repositioning Ghana as an international financial services centre, citing Mauritius as a model (NPP, 2016). This vision was championed by Ken Ofori-Atta, the newly appointed Minister of Finance, an investment banker who had worked for Morgan Stanley and founded Ghana's leading investment banking group. In repeated public appearances, Ofori-Atta emphasized the government's determination to turn Ghana into an international financial services hub, citing Singapore as an example (Business and Financial Times, 2017a). In the 2017 budget statement he set out a vision for positioning Ghana as an international financial services centre, so that it would become the preferred headquarters for all international banks operating in the sub-region, and the hub for financial technology and payment systems, and international private equity and venture capital firms (Ofori-Atta, 2017). In early 2018 Ofori-Atta led a delegation of senior politicians and officials to Singapore and Hong Kong 'to study best practices to inform Ghana's plan to become a regional financial services hub' (Ministry of Finance, 2018).

As before, while the NPP government continued with banking sector reforms agreed with the IMF, it was more ambitious than the NDC had planned to be and the IMF demanded. The NPP government sought structural changes in the banking sector, rather than simply improving the performance of the existing banks. An important first move by the NPP government was to impose far higher minimum capital requirements in a deliberate move to spur the consolidation of the banking sector. Announced in September 2017, the new requirement of GhC400 million (approx. US$80 million) was almost double that which had been planned under the NDC (Bank of Ghana, 2017b; Dzawu, 2017). While justified as a move to improve the resilience of the financial sector, analysts noted that smaller local banks would struggle to raise the capital needed to comply and would either need to exit or merge. In public speeches Ofori-Atta, the finance minister, and Ernest Addison, central bank governor, explained that they wanted to stimulate the creation of large Ghanaian-owned banks to ensure that Ghanaians directly benefited from the positioning of the country as an international financial services hub (Business and Financial Times, 2017a). The example of Nigeria was frequently invoked in policy and media discussions, where consolidation in the banking sector in the 2000s led to the creation of large banks that expanded overseas and acquired a major share of the regional market.

While foreign banks were able to meet the new capital requirements relatively easily, local banks petitioned the president for an extension of the deadline, but it was not granted. The Bank of Ghana revoked the licences of seven domestic banks (closing two and amalgamating assets of five others into a new government-owned consolidated bank). The bank closures, voluntary winding-up of another bank, and several mergers resulted in the number of banks in operation shrinking from thirty-four in 2017 to twenty-three at the end of 2018. Leading figures in the NDC criticized the NPP's approach, with the former finance minister arguing that the bank closures and related job losses were unnecessary. The NDC would have supported the small indigenous banks to recapitalize, rather than closing them down (Appiah, 2018).

Alongside the consolidation exercise, a raft of regulatory reforms were implemented to bring Ghana in line with international standards. As the central bank governor explained, 'the global financial system is continually evolving and Ghana cannot continue to lag behind in transforming its banking sector in line with international standards and practices' (Ablordeppey, 2017). A new Capital Requirements Directive (June 2018) incorporated major elements of Basel II (the standardized approaches to credit, operational, and market risk), as well as the capital-related elements of Basel III, and banks were given only six months to comply (Bank of Ghana, 2018c). The Bank of Ghana also issued new guidelines on financial reporting to ensure common standards in line with IFRS 9 (June 2017), a new directive on corporative governance based on Basel Core Principles (May 2018, revised in December 2018), revisions to anti-money laundering guidelines (July 2018), and a directive on the voluntary winding-up of financial institutions (September 2018).[28]

The reforms were widely welcomed by international investors and the international policy community. The issuance of the new Capital Requirements Directive was deemed 'positive' by Moody's (Ashiadey, 2018), while Governor Addison reported that the banking reforms contributed to Standard and Poor's decision to upgrade Ghana's long-term rating from B- to B (Addison, 2018). Meanwhile, the IMF's Managing Director praised the banking sector reforms as 'courageous steps' (Lagarde, 2018). For the first time, some of the larger banks also offered public support for the reform agenda and implementation of international standards, arguing that it would help them access international capital. As a senior executive from a locally incorporated foreign bank argued, 'To ensure that Ghana becomes and remains an important global player on global financial markets, our markets must also conform to international standards. Other African markets including Nigeria are in the process of getting their laws amended to improve their adherence to international norms and we need to ensure that we are not left behind in our bid to attract and retain capital' (Owusu Kwarteng, 2018).

Implementation of the regulatory reforms is expected to be challenging. In 2016, interviewees had been sceptical that Basel II could be implemented easily, suggesting that many domestic banks as well as the Banking Supervision

---

[28] A list of directives is available at: https://www.bog.gov.gh/supervision-a-regulation/banking-acts-and-directives.

Department of the Bank of Ghana did not have the requisite capacity.[29] A survey of banks revealed that while international banks already reporting under Basel II and III expected a relatively easily transition, domestic banks anticipated shortages of expertise, the need to upgrade information technology systems, and challenges in securing the high-quality data required by the Bank of Ghana (PWC, 2017).

The Bank of Ghana was keen to emphasize that it intended to enforce the new regulations. Many of the weaknesses revealed in Ghana's banking sector by the IMF-driven audit were due to regulatory breaches, rather than weaknesses in the regulatory framework per se. Supervision and enforcement by the Bank of Ghana had been lax and banks were found to have obtained licenses through false pretences, circumvented single obligor limits, concealed related party exposures, and mis-reported financial data. To safeguard the reforms, the central bank governor emphasized the need for strict enforcement, and greater levels of regulatory and supervisory vigilance (Addison, 2018). As the deputy governor explained, 'the culture of regulatory forbearance that once prevailed will not be countenanced' (Annerquaye Abbey, 2018) and the Bank of Ghana created an Office of Ethics and Internal Investigations to improve the quality of supervision and enforcement.

The focus of the NPP's reforms was on ensuring financial stability and improving the reputation of the sector in the eyes of citizens and international investors. Much less attention has been paid to increasing bank lending to the productive economy. As discussed in Chapter 2, critics of the Basel standards argue that implementation may deter banks from lending to the private sector for productive investments. A survey of bank executives in 2017 revealed that they anticipated reducing their lending to high-risk sectors including agriculture, real estate, and downstream energy in order to comply with the new Basel II and III regulations. As Ghana's financial sector remains heavily bank-based, this prompted concerns that some sectors of the real economy might be negatively affected by the implementation of Basel standards (PWC, 2017).

These expectations appear to be borne out in the data, which shows that the immediate reaction of banks to the new regulations was to reduce the volume of lending to the real economy and increase holdings of government securities. Between October 2017 and 2018, the share of bank assets comprising net advances (loans) reduced from 36 per cent to 29 per cent, which resulted in a 15 per cent contraction of credit to the private sector in real terms. Meanwhile, banks dramatically increased holdings of government securities (Bank of Ghana, 2018d). However, the NPP government hoped that the consolidation of the banking sector would create larger banks that can more readily finance major projects, and it has taken steps to restructure the state-owned National Investment Bank and Agricultural Development Bank to support industrialization and agricultural

---

[29] Interview with senior bank representative (foreign bank), Accra, 16 March 2016, interview with private sector representative, Accra, 21 March 2016.

development. Whether the reforms lead to higher levels of investment in the productive sectors of the economy remains to be seen.

Conclusion

In Ghana, the IMF has exerted a strong influence over bank reforms throughout the period under review. Yet the drive to converge on international standards came from a small group of NPP politicians and closely aligned officials in the Bank of Ghana. For the NPP government, positioning Ghana as an international financial services centre has been a priority, and implementation of the latest international banking standards has been perceived as central to attaining this goal. This vision was not shared by the NDC, and implementation of international standards stalled when it was in office. This difference between the two political parties with respect to the adoption of international standards stemmed from differences in policy agendas and material interests.

The policy differences between the two political parties were reflected in regulatory decisions because the Bank of Ghana is less immune to political changes than the formal legal framework suggests. While the central bank has a high level of independence on paper, governors and deputy governors routinely resign, reportedly under pressure, within a few months of the election of a new political party. As some interviewees argued, this arguably makes the central bank more accountable to the electorate than the IMF-driven model of independence, which seeks to insulate the central bank from party politics.[30] Neither the foreign nor internationally oriented domestic banks advocated for Basel implementation and, although small domestic banks opposed some elements of the reform agenda, their complaints went unheeded.

This analysis of the politics of banking regulation speaks to the wider literature on political dynamics in Ghana. Ghana's politics has been described as competitive clientelist as the distribution of power is diffuse and political parties compete in tightly fought elections by prioritizing policies that distribute spending among voters (e.g. Abdulai and Hickey, 2016; Whitfield, 2011). In many issue areas this leads the main parties to converge on very similar policy agendas (Abdulai and Hickey, 2016; Whitfield, 2018, 2011). While this is the first research to systematically examine the politics of financial regulation, other studies have also revealed how ideational differences and the orientation of the NPP towards international capital have resulted in policy divergences, including in the oil sector (Abdulai, 2017; Hickey et al., 2015; Mohan et al., 2018). An interesting area for future

[30] E.g. interview with former government minister, Accra, 22 March 2016.

research is to tease out the conditions under which policy divergence occurs between the two main parties.

The Ghana case study provides two important insights for this volume. First, it shows the importance of policy ideas in shaping the responses to Basel standards. The main driver for implementing Basel standards has been the development strategy of the NPP, a party with strong ideological and material connections to international finance, and a vision for repositioning Ghana as a financial services hub for West Africa. A similar vision is shared by politicians in Pakistan, Rwanda, and Kenya. Second, it suggests that a high level of foreign bank presence will not necessarily create incentives for the implementation of Basel standards. Foreign banks in Ghana are domestically oriented, with highly profitable business models that, like local banks, depend on investing heavily in short-term government securities. As domestic banks have yet to expand overseas, there are no strong market incentives to advocate for Basel standards, although this may change with the consolidation of the banking sector. If this leads to the creation of large, internationally active banks, as it did in Nigeria and Pakistan, this may generate market incentives for convergence on international standards.

References

Abdulai, A.-G., 2017. The political economy of regional inequality in Ghana: Do political settlements matter? *The European Journal of Development Research* 29, 213–29. https://doi.org/10.1057/ejdr.2016.11.

Abdulai, A.-G., Hickey, S., 2016. The politics of development under competitive clientelism: Insights from Ghana's education sector. *African Affairs*. https://doi.org/10.1093/afraf/adv071.

Abdulai, A.-G., Hulme, D., 2015. The politics of regional inequality in Ghana: State elites, donors and PRSPs. *Development Policy Review* 33, 529–53. https://doi.org/10.1111/dpr.12124.

Ablordeppey, S.D., 2017. Banks' new minimum capital to reflect their risk exposure. 11 August, *Graphic Business*, Accra. https://www.graphic.com.gh/business/business-news/banks-new-minimum-capital-to-reflect-their-risk-exposure.html.

Acquah, P., 2007. *Ghana at 50: The achievements, challenges of the financial services sector and expectations of the next 50 years.* Speech at Annual Dinner of the Chartered Institute of Bankers (Ghana), 15 December. Accra, Ghana.

Addison, E., 2018. *Address by Dr Ernest Addison, Governor, Bank of Ghana.* Speech at Annual Dinner of the Chartered Institute of Bankers (Ghana), 1 December. Accra, Ghana. https://www.bog.gov.gh/privatecontent/Speeches/GOVERNOR'S%20SPEECH%20-%20CIB%20DINNER%20DANCE%202018.pdf.

Adjei-Frimpong, K., Gan, C., Hu, B., 2016. Competition in the banking industry: Empirical evidence from Ghana. *Journal of Banking Regulation* 17, 159–75.

Annerquaye Abbey, R., 2018. No turning back on banking reforms—central bank. *Business and Financial Times*, Accra, Ghana, 25 April. https://thebftonline.com/2018/headlines/no-turning-back-on-banking-reforms-central-bank/#.

Antwi-Asare, T.O., Addison, E.K.Y., 2000. *Financial Sector Reforms and Bank Performance in Ghana*. Overseas Development Institute, London.

Appiah, D., Abdulai, A.-G., 2017. *Competitive clientelism and the politics of core public sector reform in Ghana*. ESID Working Paper No. 82, The University of Manchester, UK. http://www.effective-states.org/wp-content/uploads/working_papers/final-pdfs/esid_wp_82_appiah_abdulai.pdf.

Appiah, E., 2018. Gov't had ¢20bn plan to avert 'needless' bank collapse—Terkper. *JOY FM News*, 4 September. https://www.myjoyonline.com/business/2018/September-4th/govt-had-20bn-plan-to-avert-needless-bank-collapse-terkper.php.

Aryeetey, E., 2003. Recent developments in African financial markets: Agenda for further research. *Journal of African Economies* 12, ii111–52. https://doi.org/10.1093/jae/12.suppl_2.ii111.

Aryeetey, E., Nissanke, M., Steel, W.F., 1997. Financial market fragmentation and reforms in Ghana, Malawi, Nigeria, and Tanzania. *World Bank Economic Review* 11, 195–218. https://doi.org/10.1093/wber/11.2.195.

Ashiadey, B.Y., 2018. Moody's backs Bank of Ghana's new Capital Requirement Directive. *Business and Financial Times*, 4 July. https://thebftonline.com/2018/headlines/moodys-backs-bank-of-ghanas-new-capital-requirement-directive.

Asiama, J., 2017. *Bank of Ghana's monetary policy in 2017*. Speech by Johnson P. Asiama, 2nd Deputy Governor of the Bank of Ghana, Kempiski Hotel, Accra, Ghana, 11 January 2017. https://www.bog.gov.gh/privatecontent/Speeches/Monetary%20Policy%20_%202017%20-%20Fin.pdf.

Bank of Ghana, 2004. *Annual Report 2004*. Bank of Ghana, Accra.

Bank of Ghana, 2007. *Developments in Banks and Non-Bank Financial Institutions (Annual Report and Accounts)*. Bank of Ghana, Accra.

Bank of Ghana, 2008. *Offshore Banking and the Prospects for the Ghanaian Economy*. Research Department, Accra.

Bank of Ghana, 2013. *Assessment of BOG's Compliance with the BCPs*. Bank of Ghana, Accra.

Bank of Ghana, 2015. *Basel II Implementation—Ghana*. Bank of Ghana, Accra.

Bank of Ghana, 2016. *Transcript of the Press Conference of the Monetary Policy Committee, held on July 18, 2016*. Bank of Ghana, Accra.

Bank of Ghana, 2017a. *Banking Sector Report—July 2017* (No. Vol. 2.3). Bank of Ghana, Accra.

Bank of Ghana, 2017b. *Notice to the Banks and the General Public: Notice No. BG/GOV/SEC/2017/19, New minimum paid up capital*. Bank of Ghana, Accra.

Bank of Ghana, 2018a. *Banking Sector Report: July 2018*. Bank of Ghana, Accra.

Bank of Ghana, 2018b. *Bank of Ghana Establishes Ethics and Internal Investigations Unit to Strengthen Good Governance within the Bank (Press Release)*. Bank of Ghana, Accra.

Bank of Ghana, 2018c. *Capital Requirements Directive*. Bank of Ghana, Accra.

Bank of Ghana, 2018d. *Banking Sector Report—November 2018*. Bank of Ghana, Accra.

Bank of Ghana, 2019. *Update on Banking Sector Reforms (Press Release)*. Bank of Ghana, Accra.

Biekpe, N., 2011. The competitiveness of commercial banks in Ghana. *African Development Review* 23, 75–87. https://doi.org/10.1111/j.1467-8268.2010.00273.x.

Buchs, T.D., Mathisen, J., 2005. *Competition and Efficiency in Banking: Behavioral Evidence from Ghana*. International Monetary Fund, Washington, DC.

Bureau van Dijk, 2018. *Bankscope and Orbis Bank Focus*. Bureau van Dijk, London.

Business and Financial Times, 2017a. Ofori-Atta pushes for Ghana as an international financial centre. *Business and Financial Times*, 14 August. https://www.myjoyonline.com/business/2017/August-14th/ofori-atta-pushes-for-ghana-as-an-international-financial-centre.php.

Business and Financial Times, 2017b. BoG to implement Basel II/III in 2017. *Business and Financial Times*, 7 December. https://www.ghanaweb.com/GhanaHomePage/business/BoG-to-implement-Basel-II-III-in-2017-399102.

Chironga, Mutsa et al. (2018) *Roaring to life: Growth and Innovation in African Retail Banking* McKinsey Available here: https://www.mckinsey.com/~/media/McKinsey/Industries/Financial%20Services/Our%20Insights/African%20retail%20bankings%20next%20growth%20frontier/Roaring-to-life-growth-and-innovation-in-African-retail-banking-web-final.ashx

Dogbevi, E.K., Emmanuel, K., Quandzie, E., 2011. There is perception of money laundry, low interest in Ghana's offshore banking—BoG. *Ghana Business News*, February 23. https://www.ghanabusinessnews.com/2011/02/23/there-is-perception-of-money-laundry-low-interest-in-ghanas-offshore-banking-bog.

Dontoh, E., 2019. Ghana settles banking cleanup as most lenders meet demands. *Bloomberg Markets*, 4 January. https://www.bloomberg.com/news/articles/2019-01-04/ghana-settles-banking-cleanup-as-most-lenders-meet-new-demands.

Dosoo, L.V.L., 2006. *Risk-based supervision*. Keynote address by Mr Lionel Van Lare Dosoo, Deputy Governor of Bank of Ghana, at the 'Regional seminar on risk-based supervision', Accra, 24 April. https://www.bis.org/review/r060824g.pdf.

Dzawu, M.M., 2017. Ghana's banks need more capital than its markets can provide. *Bloomberg Markets*, 4 October. https://www.bloomberg.com/news/articles/2017-10-04/ghana-s-banks-need-more-cash-than-its-markets-can-provide.

Food and Agriculture Organization, 2015. *Country fact sheet on food and agriculture policy trends*. FAO, Rome.

GIABA, 2009. *Mutual evaluation report: Ghana.* GIABA.

Gyimah-Boadi, E., Yakah, T., 2012. *Ghana: The limits of external democracy assistance.* UNU-WIDER Working Paper 40/2012, UNU-WIDER, Helsinki. https://www. wider.unu.edu/publication/ghana-0.

Hammond, E., 2005. Paul Acquah is African Central Bank Governor of the Year. *Ghana Web.*

Hickey, S., Abdulai, A.-G., Izama, A., Mohan, G., 2015. *The politics of governing oil effectively: A comparative study of two new oil-rich states in Africa.* ESID Working Paper No. 54, University of Manchester. https://papers.ssrn.com/sol3/papers. cfm?abstract_id=2695723.

IMF, 1999a. *Ghana: Enhanced structural adjustment facility policy framework paper 1999–2001.* IMF, Washington, DC.

IMF, 1999b. *Ghana: Selected issues (IMF Staff Country Report No. 99/03).* IMF, Washington, DC.

IMF, 2003. *Ghana: Financial system stability assessment update, including reports on the observance of standards and codes on the following topics: Banking supervision, insurance regulation, and securities regulation.* IMF, Washington, DC.

IMF, 2009. *Ghana: Letter of intent, memorandum of economic and financial policies, and technical memorandum of understanding.* IMF, Washington, DC.

IMF, 2011a. *Ghana: Financial system stability assessment update, IMF Country Report.* IMF, Washington, DC.

IMF, 2011b. *Ghana: Financial system stability assessment update, IMF Country Report No. 11/131.* IMF, Washington, DC.

IMF, 2015. *Ghana: Request for a three-year arrangement under the extended credit facility; staff report; press release; and statement by the Executive Director for Ghana.* IMF, Washington, DC.

IMF, 2016. *Ghana: Letter of intent, memorandum of economic and financial policies, and technical memorandum of understanding.* IMF, Washington, DC.

IMF, World Bank, 2015. *Ghana: Request for a three-year arrangement under the extended credit facility—Debt sustainability analysis.* IMF, Washington, DC.

Lagarde, C., 2018. *Ghana: Planting economic seeds for future prosperity.* IMF, Washington, DC.

Marchettini, D., Mecagni, M., Maino, R., 2015. *Evolving banking trends in Sub-Saharan Africa: Key features and challenges* (No. 15/8). IMF African Departmental Paper.

Mathiason, N., 2010. Tax haven risks corruption, OECD warns Ghana. *Guardian,* 19 January. https://www.theguardian.com/business/2010/jan/19/ghana-oecd-tax-haven-warning.

Mensah, J.M.K., 2015. *Banking regulatory framework in Ghana: 'Strengths, Weakness, Opportunities and Threats'* (SSRN Scholarly Paper No. ID 2572976). Social Science Research Network, Rochester, NY.

Ministry of Finance, 2018. *Monthly newsletter: February 2018*. Accra.

Ministry of Finance and Economic Planning, 2003. *Financial sector strategic plan*. Accra.

Mohan, G., Asante, K.P., Abdulai, A.-G., 2018. Party politics and the political economy of Ghana's oil. *New Political Economy* 23, 274–89. https://doi.org/10.1080/13563467. 2017.1349087.

NDC, 2008. *NDC Manifesto 2008*. NDC, Accra.

NPP, 2016. *Change: An agenda for jobs (New Patriot Party Manifesto for Election)*. NPP, Accra.

Ofori-Atta, K., 2017. *The Budget Statement and Economic Policy of the Government of Ghana for the 2018 Financial Year*. Government of Ghana.

Owusu Kwarteng, G., 2018. Bank of Ghana needs our support. *Graphic Business*.

Polity IV, 2014. *PolityProject*. Center for Systemic Peace.

PWC, 2016. *Ghana Banking Survey*. PWC, Accra. https://www.pwc.com/gh/en/assets/ pdf/2016-banking-survey-report.pdf.

PWC, 2017. *Risk-based minimum regulatory capital regime: What it means for banks in Ghana (2017 Ghana Banking Survey)*. PWC, Accra. https://www.pwc.com/gh/en/ assets/pdf/2017-banking-survey-report.pdf.

Quartey, P., 2005. *Financial sector development, savings mobilization and poverty reduction in Ghana*. World Institute for Development Economics Research 32.

Whitfield, L., 2010. The state elite, PRSPs and policy implementation in aid-dependent Ghana. *Third World Quarterly* 31, 721–37. https://doi.org/10.1080/01436597.2010. 502692.

Whitfield, L., 2011. *Competitive clientelism, easy financing and weak capitalists: The contemporary political settlement in Ghana*. DIIS Working Paper 2011:27, Copenhagen. http://pure.diis.dk/ws/files/110319/WP2011_27_Competitive_ Clientelism_Ghana_web.pdf.

Whitfield, L., 2018. *Economies after colonialism: Ghana and the struggle for power*. Cambridge University Press, New York.

World Bank, 1994. *Ghana financial sector review: Bringing savers and investors together* (No. 13423-GH). World Bank, Washington, DC.

World Bank, 1995. *Project completion report, Republic of Ghana, Financial Sector Adjustment Credit I*. World Bank, Washington, DC.

World Bank, 2017. *World Development Indicators*. World Bank, Washington, DC.

World Bank, 2018a. *Global financial development database* [WWW Document]. URL https://datacatalog.worldbank.org/dataset/global-financial-development (accessed 24.11.18).

World Bank, 2018b. *International Financial Statistics*. World Bank, Washington, DC.

7

West African Economic
and Monetary Union

Central Bankers Drive Basel Under IMF Pressure

Ousseni Illy and Seydou Ouedraogo

Introduction

The West African Economic and Monetary Union (WAEMU)[1] adopted Basel II
and III standards simultaneously on 24 June 2016, and started implementing them
from January 2018 with a transitional period of one and a half years. Considering
the weak development of the financial sector in the Union and its poor connectedness to the international financial system, this reform was unexpected. How
can we explain WAEMU's decision to align itself with international standards?

In this chapter, we explain the political economy of banking reform and the
adoption of international banking standards—and Basel standards in particular—
in WAEMU. Our findings show that a leading role was played by the supranational Central Bank of West African States (BCEAO), pressured by the IMF,
while governments and domestically oriented banks did not show any support for
Basel standards or public opposition to their implementation.

Internationally oriented and well connected to peer regulators, the BCEAO
used its dominant position in banking regulation at the domestic level to champion
the adoption of international standards, including Basel I, II, and III. Central
bank governor Alassane Ouattara, a former Director of African department at the
IMF, played a prominent role in the adoption of Basel I and is said to be the
'godfather' of the supranational regulation and supervision reform including
the Banking Commission.[2] The multinational dimension of the BCEAO reinforces
its power by insulating it from political pressure, giving it significant room for
manoeuvre.

---

[1] WAEMU is a regional economic community encompassing Benin, Burkina Faso, Côte d'Ivoire,
Guinea-Bissau, Mali, Niger, Senegal, and Togo, sharing a single currency, the CFA Franc, issued by a
common central bank, the Central Bank of West African States (known by its French acronym,
BCEAO).

[2] Interview with central bankers, BCEAO, Dakar (March 2016).

Ousseni Illy and Seydou Ouedraogo, *West African Economic and Monetary Union: Central Bankers Drive Basel
Under IMF Pressure* In: *The Political Economy of Bank Regulation in Developing Countries: Risk and Reputation.*
Edited by: Emily Jones, Oxford University Press (2020). © Oxford University Press.
DOI: 10.1093/oso/9780198841999.003.0007

At the same time, the BCEAO is under the influence of the IMF and has experienced enormous pressure to adopt Basel II and III standards, and the impact studies and drafting of the new regulations have been conducted under IMF technical assistance, through AFRITAC West. IMF Managing Director Christine Lagarde explicitly recommended the 'move to Basel II and III which would allow alignment to international standards' (Lagarde, 2015). This position towards WAEMU, which is in sharp contradiction with its recommendations to other low-income countries (including the case studies identified in this book), is intriguing—even to some BCEAO officials.

WAEMU is an example of regulator-driven convergence. The adoption of Basel standards is championed by a regulator with strong links to international policy communities, while governments and domestically oriented banks do not play an active role, complicating the implementation and enforcement of the new regulations.

The methodology of the study combined a review of literature and an analysis of various reports and documents from several stakeholders including the IMF, the BCEAO, and the Banking Commission. Furthermore, interviews were conducted in five countries[3] with officials and former officials of the BCEAO, the Banking Commission, national authorities, private bank executives, diplomats, and experts. In total, thirty-eight people were interviewed in thirty-two semi-structured interviews, conducted from January 2016 to December 2017.

This chapter describes the political economy context of WAEMU (Table 7.1), including the evolution of the financial sector. It then discusses the adoption, implementation, and enforcement of Basel standards in WAEMU, before examining the factors behind convergence on international banking standards in the Union. It ends with a brief conclusion.

Table 7.1 WAEMU: key indicators

WAEMU

GDP per capita (current US$)	756
Bank assets (current US$)	3.25 bn
Bank assets (% of GDP)	29.915
Stock market capitalization (% of GDP)	39.34
Credit allocation to private sector (% of GDP)	24.05
Credit allocation to government (% of GDP, 2014)	5.62
Polity IV score (2017)	5

Note: All data is from 2016 unless otherwise indicated.

Source: FSI Database, IMF (2018); GDI database, World Bank (2017); Polity IV (2014)

---

[3] Benin, Burkina Faso, Côte d'Ivoire, Senegal, and Togo.

Political economy context

Economic and financial conditions

Seven of the eight WAEMU countries are classified as low income, while Côte d'Ivoire is lower-middle income. Their economies are dominated by a few export crops including cocoa, cotton, and coffee, as well as natural resources, gold, oil, uranium, phosphate, and bauxite. Their financial systems remain underdeveloped even compared to the average of the Sub-Saharan Africa region. A huge difference used to exist between WAEMU's and the Sub-Saharan African region's ratios of private sector credit to GDP, but WAEMU's performance has improved during the past decade and is now close to the continent's average (Figure 7.1).

Despite increasing financial development, lending to the economy remains an important challenge. Banks provide a third of their total loans (35 per cent in 2015) to the governments, mainly through governments' bonds. Huge sectorial asymmetries exist in credit allocation. In 2015, 32.2 per cent of total loans were provided to trade activities and 32 per cent to services. The industrial sector accounted for 17.4 per cent and only 3.6 per cent of loans were dedicated to the agricultural sector. The remainder of the loans were devoted to mining, construction, and other activities. In addition, 68.8 per cent of these loans were extended as short-term credit (BCEAO, 2016a).

As in most developing countries, banks dominate the financial sector in WAEMU. The regional stock market (Bourse Régionale des Valeurs Mobilières—BRVM), based in Abidjan, remains embryonic. The number of companies listed

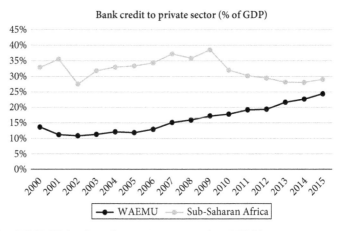

Figure 7.1 WAEMU: bank credit to private sector (% of GDP).

Source: World Bank (2017)

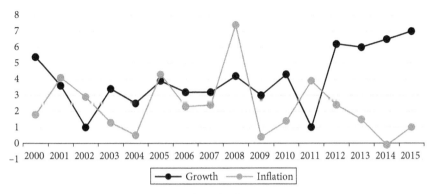

Figure 7.2 WAEMU: economic growth and inflation (%).
Source: BCEAO (2015b and 2012)

on the BRWM is about forty, the same as Accra's stock market. The microfinance sector accounts for 13.9 million clients (September 2014) compared to the banking sector which has only 8 million personal banking accounts. However, deposits collected by microfinance institutions amount to only 6.3 per cent of bank deposits and their total credit is about 7 per cent of bank loans (BCEAO, 2015a). Mobile banking is also growing rapidly (36 million accounts in 2016) (BCEAO, 2016b).

WAEMU's banking sector operates in a context of low inflation. Indeed, changes in consumer prices were close to zero in 2014 and 1 per cent in 2015. A difficult decade culminated in a political crisis in 2011 in Côte d'Ivoire, the Union's foremost economy, after which the region enjoyed high economic growth, reaching 7 per cent in 2015 (Figure 7.2).

Historical evolution of WAEMU's financial sector

Major changes have occurred in the financial sector in WAEMU during the past three decades. Like other countries in Sub-Saharan Africa, WAEMU countries were hit by a severe banking crisis towards the end of the 1980s that nearly destroyed the entire banking sector. It is estimated that one third of banks in the region were in difficulties in 1988 and a quarter of extended credit was unrecoverable (Powo Fosso, 2000). The crisis has had huge consequences for households, firms, and the States more broadly. For instance, the cost borne by States is estimated to be equivalent to 17 per cent of GDP in Benin and Senegal, and close to 25 per cent in Côte d'Ivoire (Caprio and Klingebiel, 1996).

With reforms put in place in the early 1990s, the banking sector has returned to profitability and been growing rapidly. However, non-performing loans (NPLs) still present a significant challenge (Figure 7.3).

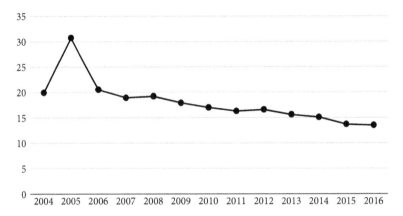

Figure 7.3 WAEMU: non-performing loans (NPLs) (% total loans).
Source: BCEAO (2016b)

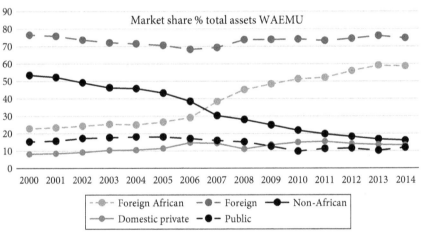

Figure 7.4 WAEMU: patterns of bank ownership.
Source: Ouédraogo (2017)

Bank ownership, bank concentration, and competition

After a period of decline, the number of banks has risen from fifty-four in 1996 to ninety-two in 2005 and 112 by 2015. New entrants are mainly African banks that have challenged the previous dominance of European banks. As in other regions of Africa, the rise of pan-African banks (PABs) is one of the most important developments in WAEMU's financial sector in the last decade. Foreign African banks took the lead in market share from non-African and European and American banks in 2006 and grew to having about 60 per cent of total assets in the region. Public and private domestic banks remain in the minority (Figure 7.4).

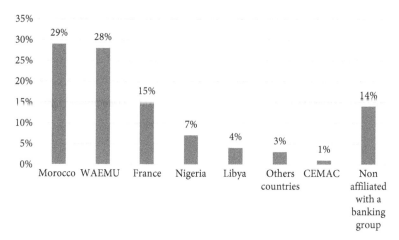

Figure 7.5 WAEMU: bank market share by bank origin.
Source: BCEAO (2014)

Moroccans lead the banking sector and control 29 per cent of total assets. Banks from WAEMU control 28 per cent, and French banks have 15 per cent of the market, followed by Nigerian banks with 7 per cent.

The Union's banking sectors are domestically oriented, and its banks do not access international markets. The various players carry different interests and strategies, but their business models remain largely domestically oriented (Figure 7.5).

Banks operate in markets with limited competition. While the number of players has risen steadily and banking concentration has fallen sharply over the last fifteen years (Figure 7.6), it remains high relative to several countries in Sub-Saharan Africa, including Ghana, for example.

In relation to market concentration, bank profitability is very important (Ouédraogo, 2013). Despite a high level of NPLs (about 14.2 per cent of total loans in 2015), the banking sector provided a return on equity of about 14 per cent in 2015.

Banking regulatory and supervision set-up

The regulatory and supervision set-up of WAEMU's banking sector is quite complex, with at least four types of bodies involved. Among these are the Council of Ministers, the BCEAO, the Banking Commission, and the national authorities (ministers of finance). The first two are normally in charge of the initiation and adoption of banking regulations. However, as we will see, they are also involved to some extent in the supervision process. The Banking Commission and the National authorities are entrusted with supervision more broadly.

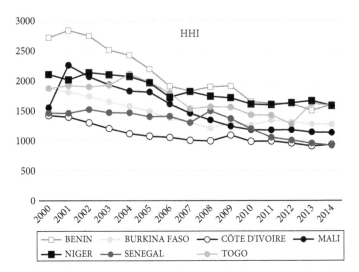

Figure 7.6 WAEMU: bank concentration Herfindahl-Hirschman Index (HHI).
Source: Calculations based on data from BCEAO (2014b)

The Council of Ministers and the BCEAO

The Council of Ministers is principally responsible for monetary policy and banking regulation. It is composed of ministers of finance of member states. It is worth mentioning that France, which has a seat on the board of the BCEAO and the Banking Commission, is not represented on the Council of Ministers. The Council is normally assisted in its mission by the BCEAO.[4] However, according to the Treaty establishing the WAMU, the BCEAO may also initiate regulations by itself. Nonetheless, the adoption of those regulations lies with the Council. In practice, most regulations are initiated and prepared by the BCEAO, in collaboration with members states (ministers of finance), and transmitted to the Council for adoption.

The Council of Ministers works under the authority of the Conference of Heads of States and Government, which is the highest governing body of WAEMU. The Conference does not intervene directly in the regulation process.

The Banking Commission and national authorities

The Banking Commission was created in 1990, in response to the failure of the national authorities that were then in charge of banking supervision in member states. It comprises nineteen members (commissioners): representatives of states (eight), a representative of France as the guarantor of the CFA Franc, independent

---

[4] See Article 17 of the Treaty establishing the West African Monetary Union (WAMU).

commissioners (nine), and the governor of the BCEAO, who presides over the institution. The Secretariat of the Commission is in charge of the technical work, notably supervision. It is assured by the BCEAO, which provides all of its staff.

The Commission is mandated to supervise all banks and related credit institutions operating in WAEMU's member states. This includes issuing and withdrawing banking licences; supervising credit institutions; placing administrative measures and sanctions against credit institutions and their managers for wrongful acts; and appointing provisional administrators or liquidators for troubled banks.

In some of these areas, the Commission shares powers with the finance ministers. This is the case in banking licence. For issuing banking licence, the application of the candidate is instructed by the Commission but the final decision lies with the finance minister of the member state concerned. However, the minister cannot issue a licence where the Commission has given a negative opinion. The same procedure is observed on licence withdrawal: the decision is taken by the Commission but its implementation belongs to the finance minister.

Basel adoption, implementation, and enforcement

Basel I

International banking standards were introduced in WAEMU for the first time in 1991, following the financial crisis of the 1980s.

This occurred in two phases: in 1991, the 'core capital' requirement of Basel I (Tier 1 capital) was adopted. Later, in 1999, the capital adequacy ratio was upgraded to 8 per cent, as recommended by the Basel Committee. Although other reforms of the regulatory framework were introduced later,[5] the minimum capital requirement to address credit risk remained the same.

Basel II and III

Initial moves towards Basel II adoption date back to 2004. However, the process never resulted in concrete reforms until the agreement on Basel III was reached by the Basel Committee in 2010. Therefore, the BCEAO decided to adopt Basel II and III concurrently.

---

[5] In 2007, the banking regulation was amended to increase minimum share capital from 1 to 5 billion CFA Francs. Another amendment in 2015 raised the minimum share capital to 10 billion CFA Francs.

The process started in 2013, with technical assistance coming from the IMF (BCEAO, 2014a). Qualitative and quantitative impact studies were conducted in 2014 and 2015.[6] The process was completed and on 24 June 2016 the Council of Ministers finally adopted Decision n°013 establishing the new prudential standards of WAEMU. A transitional period was set up for banks to adapt to the new standards. Consequently, the regulations entered into effect from 1 January 2018, and full implementation of some elements is extended until 2022.

The new regulations are largely inspired by Basel II and III standards. For instance, the definition of regulatory capital is taken exactly from Basel III.[7] Furthermore, contrary to the previous regime, where capital adequacy requirements covered only credit risk, the new legislation also includes operational and market risks, and a standardized approach is retained for all risks (Basel II).

The minimum total regulatory capital adequacy ratio has been raised to 9 per cent[8] of risk-weighted assets, which is higher than Basel III (8 per cent). Moreover, common equity tier 1 capital must be at least 5 per cent of risk-weighted assets, while the Basel III threshold is 4.5 per cent. Tier 1 capital must be at least 6 per cent, as recommended by Basel III. Unlike most low-income jurisdictions, WAEMU has also adopted two novel liquidity ratios from Basel III, namely the Liquidity Coverage Ratio and the Net Stable Funding Ratio (Table 7.2).

Basel Core Principles (BCPs)

Neither the BCEAO nor the Banking Commission has ever undertaken an assessment study of its regulatory and supervisory framework with the BCPs. A World Bank and IMF Financial Sector Assessment Programme (FSAP) was conducted on WAEMU in 2008. However, the report was never published on the websites of these institutions, and our efforts to obtain a copy have failed. Therefore, it is difficult to ascertain whether WAEMU banking framework complies with the BCPs.

Anti-Money Laundering/Combating Financing of Terrorism (AML/CFT) and International Financial Reporting Standards (IFRS)

Actions on AML/CFT started in 2003 in WAEMU when the Council of Ministers adopted the Uniform Act on money laundering on 20 March. In 2008, another uniform act was adopted on financing terrorism. These legislations were criticized for not taking sufficient account of international standards (IMF, 2011). They were

---

[6] Interview with central bank officials, BCEAO, Dakar (March 2017).
[7] See Decision n°013, Title II, Chapter 1.   [8] This ratio is currently set at 8 per cent.

Table 7.2 WAEMU: adoption of Basel standards

Basel component	Adoption	Implementation
Basel I	Prudential regime 1990 and 1991	1991
Basel II	Dispositif Prudentiel applicable aux banques et établissements financiers de l'Union monétaire ouest-africaine à compter du 1er janvier 2000—*Credit risk, Standardized Approach (SA)* Décision n°013/24/06/2016/CM/UMOA portant Dispositif Prudentiel applicable aux établissements de crédit et aux compagnies financières de l'Union Monétaire Ouest Africaine—*Market and operational risks, SA*	Credit risk, SA—1 January 2000 Market and operational risks, SA—January 2018
Basel III	Décision n°013/24/06/2016/CM/UMOA portant Dispositif Prudentiel applicable aux établissements de crédit et aux compagnies financières de l'Union Monétaire Ouest Africaine: - *Definition of capital* - *Capital adequacy requirements* - *Capital conservation buffer* - *Single large exposure limit* - *Leverage ratio* - *Liquidity coverage ratio* - *Net stable funding ratio*	In force since 1 January 2018

Source: BCEAO (2016c)

therefore revised in 2015 in a new merged Uniform Act on 'Combating money laundering and financing of terrorism in WAEMU', which has been transposed into domestic laws in all member countries.[9] The new legislation is in line with the Financial Action Task Force's (FATF's) recommendations on AML/CFT.

In addition, a new banking chart of accounts was passed by the BCEAO in 2016 aimed at convergence with global financial reporting standards, including IFRS.[10]

Implementation issues

Implementation and compliance with regulations, the prudential regime in particular, have always been a concern in WAEMU. Almost all IMF staff reports on the region since 2011, including the latest one (2017), have raised the issue. According to the 2017 report, 'the conditions in the banking sector remain challenging' and

---

[9] Contrary to the prudential regime, which is directly applicable, uniform acts must be incorporated into domestic law before being enforceable.
[10] Interview with BCEAO officials (Dakar, March 2017).

'the current rules—despite being less strict than the newly introduced ones—are not effectively enforced' (IMF, 2017, p. 17).

This non-compliance may be explained by several factors. First, the Banking Commission has a notable lack of capacity. As of 2015, the Secretariat of the Commission was composed of 120 staff members, of which less than half were dedicated to supervision activities (BCEAO, 2015c). This staff had to supervise more than one hundred banks in eight countries. The second factor is 'regulatory forbearance', mainly for economic and political reasons. Indeed, the Banking Commission sometimes refrains from taking prudential action when state-owned banks make politically sensitive loan decisions.

The political economy of Basel adoption in WAEMU

The analytical framework in this book helps us grasp the role and motivations of each actor in setting banking regulation in WAEMU and their responses to international standards. In this context, the essential actors are the BCEAO, the IMF, banks, governments, and politicians. The BCEAO is the dominant player at the domestic level and is internationally oriented. Under the influence of the IMF, it played a decisive role particularly in the adoption of Basel I in the early 1990s and the recent adoption of Basel II and III. The other actors do not show preferences favourable to the recent Basel norms, or an active opposition. The banks, without forming a homogeneous group with respect to their preferences for regulation, have various reservations but have not coordinated resistance to the adoption of Basel II and III. Governments and political parties seem to be the least concerned and essentially passive.

The BCEAO's international orientation
and peer regulator networks

The BCEAO is internationally oriented, a position that can be identified at several levels, especially in the training and appointments of the Bank's executives and leaders, as well as the international network of regulators in which the BCEAO participates.

While a large part of its staff is trained in its own centre at the Centre Ouest Africain de Formation et d'Etudes Bancaires (COFEB), French academics and experts make up most of the body of trainers, and many of the COFEB speakers from the BCEAO have been trained in IMF training of trainers' courses, and relay the direct intervention of IMF experts.[11] French research and training centres are

---

[11] Interview with central bank official, BCEAO, Ouagadougou (December 2017).

part of the COFEB's Scientific Council in charge of 'assisting the Governor of the BCEAO in defining the orientations and modalities of the training policy' and 'deliberating on the organization and programs training sessions' (BCEAO, 2017, p. 7).[12]

Governor Alassane Ouattara (1988–90), a former Director of the Africa Department of the IMF (current President of Côte d'Ivoire), represents this international orientation of the BCEAO well. He has played a leading role, as shown below, in the reform of regulation and the institutional framework of banking supervision at the end of the 1980s. His successors have all spent the essential part of their careers at the BCEAO and have maintained this international orientation.

The BCEAO invests heavily in its large network of regulators around the world. Supervisory colleges of cross-border banks that operate in WAEMU including Nigerian, Moroccan, and even the Union's own banks (notably Ecobank and Orabank) are the most important peer regulators network to which the BCEAO is connected. It has developed special relations with the Moroccan banking authorities. Indeed, in addition to sharing the same working language, Moroccan banks have been the leaders in WAEMU for a few years now. The governors of the two Central Banks performed reciprocal working missions, and Bank Al-Maghrib is a technical partner assisting the BCEAO in the adoption and implementation of Basel II and III standards. The Moroccan Central Bank also participated in the exchange seminar on the draft texts of both sets of standards.

The BCEAO and the Banking Commission are also stakeholders in several other regional and international supervisory networks. The WAEMU Banking Commission participates in three groups of banking supervisors: the Group of Francophone Banking Supervisors (GSBF), the Community of African Banking Supervisors (CABS), and the Supervisory Committee for West and Central African Banks (CSBAOC) (BCEAO, 2016b). Launched in 2004, the GSBF aims to 'develop at a high level the cooperation between its members so that the exchange of experience and information promotes the spread of best practices and the convergence of prudential approaches to common problems'. The international regulatory reforms related to Basel II and III are the main topics of the group's work, which aims to facilitate their implementation. The CABS was established more recently, in 2013, with the objective, among others, to 'Capitalize on the experience of African Central Banks that have implemented Basel II' (COBAC, 2015). The CSBAOC was created in 1994 and brings together more than a dozen African countries, and organizes several meetings and training seminars for the benefit of its members. Nigeria is the member country that has gone furthest in adopting recent Basel standards.

---

[12] The Centre d'études et de recherches sur le développement international (CERDI, France) and the Institut Bancaire et Financier International (IBFI) of the Banque de France are members of the COFEB Scientific Council. They are also historic and closed partners of BCEAO.

In addition, the BCEAO was a member of the Basel Consultative Group (BCG) and was its only direct representative of an LIC. Nearly all other members are from upper-middle-income class or higher, and none of them African. WAEMU was also a member of the Core Principles Liaison Group (CPLG), organized in 1998 and 2006 by the Basel Committee as a forum for the exchange of experiences to promote the implementation of the fundamental principles for effective banking supervision.

The BCEAO: the dominant player in banking regulation at the domestic level

The BCEAO is the most influential player at the domestic level in terms of banking regulation. Four key factors give it this position, discussed below.

Firstly, beyond the formal independence of the BCEAO, its sub-regional nature protects its ability to issue regulation from the pressures and games of political interest. Moreover, the banking sector, particularly regulation, is almost absent from the political debate in WAEMU countries. Politicians and governments have little control over the sub-regional level.

Secondly, in practice, the effective division of labour of banking regulation assigns the BCEAO a leading role. As noted before, the Bank initiates legislation, prepares the draft in collaboration with member states, and submits it to the Council of Ministers for adoption. It has significant influence on the Council because often it is composed mainly of technocrats that previously worked in international financial and economic institutions including the IMF, the UNDP, and in many cases the BCEAO itself. Indeed, several finance ministers are seconded BCEAO executives who return at the end of their political mandate.

Thirdly, the BCEAO has significant technical, financial, infrastructural, and material resources. Interviews with national authorities explicitly reference this technical capacity of the BCEAO. A senior national authority figure said, 'our governments show little interest in the reforms related to Basel II and III. They seem to delegate everything to the BCEAO by technical insufficiency. Thus, even the consequences of these standards on economies are seldom discussed'.[13]

This technical precedence and leadership in the reform process is all the more asserted as WAEMU member governments often have a weak vision for banking. A closer look at seven development plans[14] of the WAEMU member countries reveals the lack of attention given to the issue, most notably in a failure to address banking supervision and particularly regulation. Indeed, no development plan explicitly mentions the issue of banking regulation at all. The interviews confirm

---

[13] Interview with a WAEMU country minister of Trade and Industries (March 2017).
[14] All WAEMU countries excluding Guinea Bissau.

limited knowledge on the part of the member states on international banking standards and related issues.[15]

Finally, the BCEAO and the Banking Commission exhibit significant authority over banks. The interviews with bankers repeatedly stressed an asymmetric power relationship. Several officials testified: 'they (the BCEAO) invited us to tell us what they decided, it was not a consultation',[16] 'they do what they want';[17] 'they will decide what they want but we know there will be problems in the application that they will have to consider'.[18]

The IMF's influence in WAEMU countries

The IMF has significant sway over WAEMU member countries. Since the financial crises of the 1980s, WAEMU members have signed onto programmes with the IMF and the World Bank. From traditional adjustment programmes (SAPs) to the current extended credit facility (ECF) programmes, their cooperation with the IMF has been continuous. Several ECF programmes have succeeded each other in each country. The conditionalities that accompany them do not mention the aspects of banking regulation, but these remain at the core of relations between the IMF and the BCEAO. In addition, as mentioned previously, the IMF uses its technical assistance to the BCEAO as a channel of influence and pressures the adoption of international standards.

Regulator-driven adoption of Basel I: the leadership of Governor Ouattara of the IMF

Going back to Basel I adoption and the creation of the Banking Commission in the 1990s, one may recall the leading role that the then governor and former IMF staff member, Alassane Ouattara, played in enacting reforms. He championed the adoption of Basel I and the tightening of supervision by creating the Banking Commission. The governor of the BCEAO, Tiemoko Koné, recalled his role as the 'main architect' of the reforms and 'designer of the Banking Commission of WAEMU', for which he was dubbed the 'godfather' of the Commission (Koné, 2015).[19]

Indeed, Mr Ouattara came to lead the Bank at a critical time when the region was experiencing one of the worst banking crises in its history. The crisis served as a permissive context—its costs paved the way to taking strong measures, notably

---

[15] Interviews with ministers in WAEMU (March and May 2017).
[16] Interview with pan-African banker at Dakar (March 2017).
[17] Interview with Ivorian Banker, Abidjan (March 2017).
[18] Interview with African banker at Ouagadougou (April 2017).
[19] Interviews with BCEAO officials, Dakar (March 2017).

the reinforcement of the BCEAO's prerogatives in banking regulation and the replacement of National Commissions with a sub-regional banking commission. Supranational centralization constituted a structural change that repositioned the BCEAO in its relationship with the states in relation to banking.

Adopting Basel II and III: the BCEAO under the pressure of the IMF

The BCEAO's crucial role in adopting Basel II and III must be highlighted. These reforms were top-down, as there was no demand for them on the ground and banks are still struggling to abide by existing rules.

The BCEAO officials' interviews have displayed their appropriation of international standards and mention several motivations for the transition to Basel II and III.[20] Indeed, for them, the emergence of cross-border banks and the influence of international banks leave the WAEMU member states vulnerable. They also mention the need to harmonize regulations in order to interact with foreign banks that have implemented and are subjected to the new Basel standards. Thus, the reform will have 'great benefits including the contribution that Basel II and III will make to the soundness of financial institutions'.[21]

The international orientation of the BCEAO and its supranational dimension are crucial in understanding the adoption of Basel II and III. They explain both the receptivity and permissiveness of the BCEAO to IMF pressures to adopt both sets of standards and its room for manoeuvre vis-à-vis domestic actors.

Since starting banking reforms, the BCEAO has relied on the support of the IMF. The IMF has not only pushed hard for the transposition of international standards, but has also offered the technical assistance required for preliminary studies and capacity building—both for training actors and even for writing the law. Indeed, the officials in charge of the project at the BCEAO appear to have benefited from the support of the IMF throughout the process of the reform. The West Africa Regional Technical Assistance Center, AFRITAC West, has contributed throughout the project.[22]

Qualitative and quantitative studies recommended the transition to Basel II and III. These studies are mentioned in AFRITAC West's 2014/15 activity report, which refers to missions to the BCEAO by a team reinforced with an IMF-hired expert on the transposition of Basel II and III to WAEMU (Afritac Ouest, 2015). The report specifies the following results: 'a) Drafting of a study on the readiness of banks to transition to Basel II and Basel III; b) completion of a capital impact assessment as part of the transposition of Basel III; c) formalization of guidelines for the implementation of supervision on a consolidated basis and the subjection

---

[20] Interviews with BCEAO officials, Dakar (March 2017).
[21] Interviews with BCEAO officials, Dakar (March 2017).
[22] Interview with BCEAO officials, Dakar (March 2017).

of banking groups controlled by unregulated holding companies; d) preparation and training of banks for the impact assessment on capital requirements (Pillar 1 of Basel II)' (Afritac Ouest, 2015, p. 29). However, their results are not published. The draft texts developed were sent to the IMF and the World Bank[23] before being adopted by the Council of Ministers in June 2016.

Prior to the completion of the impact study, during the conference she hosted at the BCEAO headquarters in January 2015 on the theme of financial inclusion, the Managing Director of the IMF, Christine Lagarde, recommended the adoption of a regulatory framework 'based on adequate capital requirements for banks, sound prudential standards and strong enforcement of these standards as they are fundamental pillars of the stability of the financial sector. There is room to consolidate all these pillars in the region and the ongoing efforts to move to Basel II/Basel III are extremely encouraging...this passage to Basel II, Basel III which will also bring it closer to international standards' (Lagarde, 2015).

This explicitness of the position held by the IMF is very surprising because it is contrary to its position on other low-income countries whose cases are examined in this book, including the better financially developed Ghana. Indeed, the adoption of Basel II and III standards is not overtly recommended in all low-income countries.

The evidence of IMF influence and pressure is further supported by private banks and some BCEAO officials. Private bank executives cited, among others, the sustained presence of AFRITAC/IMF staff and experts during seminars and training they received in preparation for Basel II and III.[24] On the part of the BCEAO, even though the term 'pressure' is not openly mentioned, some of the executives we met recognize the 'central role' of the IMF in the process.[25] Some stated clearly that: 'It is the IMF that is pushing.'[26] A high-ranking national authority indicates that 'the Central Bank relays the position of the IMF in order to be well graded by it.'[27]

IMF pressure is not limited to the adoption of Basel II and III; it has also aimed at a broader set of international standards. Recently, the Executive Directors of the IMF 'encouraged' the authorities of WAEMU 'to speed up the reform agenda, *particularly the implementation of Basel II and Basel III*, to strengthen risk-based supervision, to align prudential limits with international standards and best practices, to enforce existing prudential rules to reduce NPLs, and to avoid regulatory forbearance' (IMF, 2016, p. 2, emphasis added).

---

[23] Interviews with BCEAO officials, Dakar (March 2017).
[24] Interview with African bankers, Ouagadougou (April 2017).
[25] Interview with BCEAO officials, Dakar (March 2017).
[26] Interview with BCEAO officials, Dakar, March 2017 and Abidjan (January 2016).
[27] Interview in Abidjan (March 2017).

The BCEAO has been receptive to these recommendations by the IMF, and always committed itself to their implementation. It is striking that the law adopted in June 2016 retains all these recommendations verbatim—from the risk concentration threshold and the classification of loans as non-performing to capital requirements. In addition, the transition to IFRS standards is expected to be in the new accounting plan currently in the works. Through pressure from the IMF and its peer networks, the BCEAO takes the local lead and then tries to 'sell' the reform to the other stakeholders, namely governments and private banks.

The BCEAO's network of regulators constitutes frameworks for learning and disseminating information about international standards to the banking authorities of WAEMU. As the Banking Commission itself points out in its 2014 report, 'discussions on international reforms, such as Basel II, Basel III or the new accounting framework, are also at the heart of the work [of the Bank Supervisory Groups] and aim to facilitate their implementation' (BCEAO, 2014a, p. 66).

Interviews with officials of the BCEAO and current and former officials of the Banking Commission support the hypothesis of peer emulation in the adoption of international standards. For the BCEAO, these groups are primarily places of information and learning through shared experience. In addition, cooperation encourages the adoption of seemingly more advanced standards that have been implemented by the supervisors of foreign banking groups. From this point of view, the interviews confirm that the relationship with Morocco was particularly favourable to the adoption of the new standards.[28] BCEAO executives emphasized the delay with which certain jurisdictions in WAEMU participated in the various colleges of supervisors, thus underlining one of the motivations for the ongoing reforms.[29] However, the interviewees also clearly indicated that the influence of the IMF is the most decisive.[30]

The position of the WAEMU banks

The adoption of Basel II and III in WAEMU has not been met with enthusiasm amongst banks. Yet they also did not show outright defiance, probably because of the BCEAO's position of power but also because of the nuances in their positions. Interviewees gave several indications on shared positions regarding 'the busy agenda' and 'the tight scheduling' of the reform, but highlighted the divergences of opinion on the opportunities of the reform, costs of transposition, and inherent competitive benefits.

---

[28]   Interviews with BCEAO officials, Dakar (March 2017).
[29]   Interviews with BCEAO officials, Dakar (March 2017).
[30]   Interviews with BCEAO officials, Dakar (March 2017).

Strikingly, all bank executives interviewed, be they from public, domestic, pan-African banks, or international banks, agreed on the fact that the reform agenda is very demanding. Indeed, the bankers consider that the combined adoption of Basel II and Basel III, with the addition of the new banking accounting plan, is carried out on a 'very tight schedule' and demands from them 'a lot of resources'.[31] These reforms require human resources that are very limited in practice, even in international banking groups—especially since in many cases, 'it's the same teams that are in charge of these projects'.[32] The reform 'requires a tedious standardization of all human resources of banks', including commercial teams in international banks. International banks are therefore providing timid support for the reform and it is difficult to see any genuine initiative on their part in favour of adopting the new international standards.[33]

The 'very tight timing of the reform'[34] was one of the main concerns expressed by the banking sector during the consultation process prior to the adoption of Basel II and III. FABEF's scientific committee strongly advocated for and obtained an extension of the implementation deadline, initially set for January 2017 in the draft texts and finally decided on for 1 January 2018.

If a consensus is established on the timing of the reform, the opportunity the reforms present is assessed differently by different banks. International banks whose parent companies are governed by Basel II and/or III generally consider the reforms as favourable to the sector as a whole, unlike domestic banks. For example, an official from a Moroccan bank said, 'It's the agenda that is more troublesome than the objectives'.[35] This statement was confirmed by that of another executive of a French bank.[36] Banks with no affiliation to any banking group, as well as those with no experience of Basel II and III, are strongly against the reforms: 'if this reform were in place, our bank would have never been able to exist and have the journey that it had'; the reform 'will prevent local initiatives like ours to take place in the banking sector'.[37]

In addition, the cost of transposing standards to the local context is also not estimated similarly by the different categories of banks. Large banking groups affiliated with parent companies that are already regulated on the basis of these new standards report benefiting from their learning and previous experiences. They pool the expenses of the different institutions in teams coordinated at the regional level—a fact that proves to be the case for the French, Moroccan, and Nigerian banking groups. Banking groups from WAEMU do the same, although

---

[31] Interviews with bankers, Lomé (December 2016); Cotonou (December 2016); Dakar (March 2017); Abidjan (April 2017); Ouagadougou (April 2017).
[32] Interviews with bankers, Dakar (March 2017); Ouagadougou (April 2017).
[33] Interviews with bankers, Lomé (December 2016); Dakar (March 2017); Ouagadougou (April 2017).
[34] Interviews with bankers, Dakar (March 2017); Ouagadougou (April 2017).
[35] Interview with executive of Moroccan bank in Ouagadougou (April 2017).
[36] Interview with executive of French bank Abidjan (April 2017).
[37] Interview with executive of WAEMU bank, Ouagadougou (April 2017).

they do not all have Basel II/III experience. They face much higher costs than the large banking groups, which are also their main competitors.[38] Unaffiliated institutions with no relevant experience pay the highest costs to meet the new standards. Many of them have had difficulty meeting the standards already in place.

However, real difficulties are apprehended by all the banks. Foreign organizations highlight the challenges that the entire industry is confronted with in implementing the new regulatory standards. The requirement to upgrade computer systems is particularly difficult. Indeed, one main operator manages most of the banks' ICT system in the region; the ability of this supplier to satisfy the demand of all firms is questioned.[39] The constraints are also relative to the banking environment, including the dysfunctions of judicial services in WAEMU member countries, the ecosystem of banks that is marked by a highly developed informal sector, and very pressing information problems, among other factors.

Certainly, the international banks recognize that the reform could be in their favour, and that it would eventually put all banks on an equal footing. French banks in particular have often explained their decline and the emergence of African banks by citing the stronger regulatory requirements imposed on them by their parent company in Basel III.[40] Banks placed under the control of Moroccan groups indicate that their customers complain about the cumbersome nature of their new credit procedures because of the reorganizations introduced by parent companies.[41] Yet these new procedures now give them a lead over competitors in implementing Basel II/III.

In sum, international banks have comparative advantages in implementing the new regulatory standards, and could profit from their domestic competitors; however, they do not seem to have pushed for the reforms, of which they emphasize the tight timing, the important costs induced, and the constraints posed by the context of application. If local banks accuse them of having contributed to the reform process, they still concede the decisive role of the IMF and France, which would serve the European banks.[42]

A role for France?

France has a singular position in the monetary and banking institutions of the WAEMU member countries. A former colonizing power, it has representatives on

---

[38] Interviews with executive of WAEMU bankers in Lomé (December 2016); Dakar (March 2017); Abidjan (April 2017); Ouagadougou (April 2017).

[39] Interviews with executives of French bank, Ouagadougou (April 2017); Abidjan (April 2017).

[40] Interviews with executive of French bank, Ouagadougou (April 2017).

[41] Interviews with executive of Moroccan bank, Ouagadougou (April 2017).

[42] Interviews with executives of WAEMU banks, Lomé (December 2016); Benin (December 2016); Dakar (March 2017); Abidjan (April 2017); Ouagadougou (April 2017).

the BCEAO board of directors and on the Banking Commission. France's influence on monetary and banking issues has often fuelled controversy.

The premise of France's influence on the Basel II/III adoption process is therefore based on its colonial legacy and on the decline of French banks in the region. Indeed, they have lost their market leadership and explain their decline, in part, based on the advantage their competitors derive from the margins of manoeuvre afforded to them by the less stringent regulatory constraints they are subject to.[43]

In our research, France's role does not come to the fore—indeed, most discussions have converged on the prominent role of the IMF. While the executives of the central bank and the Banking Commission recognize the 'important contribution of the IMF', they do not recognize any particular action in France.

However, local banks do assign a role to France. One banker said, 'it is France who wants the reform for the benefit of its banks'.[44] Another added: 'this reform serves the interests of French banks first and foremost'.[45] These points of view converge on views transmitted by French banks to French diplomatic circles in Africa.[46] Indeed, according to interviews, these diplomatic circles suggest French banks think that 'they do not operate on the same footing as African banks' because of the stronger regulatory requirements to which their parent companies must adhere.

In addition, several bank officials consider there to be an alliance between the IMF and France in favour of banking reform,[47] but this is unsupported by evidence. As mentioned above, however, the IMF's recommendations for the adoption of Basel II and III in WAEMU are remarkable. In addition, apart from the presence of France in WAEMU's monetary and banking bodies, it should be noted that it is one of the main donors of AFRITAC West—indeed the second biggest donor after the EU in 2014. It is also interesting that the person responsible for supervision and bank restructuring at AFRITAC West has always been a former official of the Banque de France or the French Treasury.

All in all, further investigation is needed to inform a possible role France holds in adopting Basel II and III standards in the WAEMU member states.

Conclusion

WAEMU is an example of IFI-driven convergence on international standards, with an internationally connected regulator advocating implementation under pressure from international financial institutions. Based on interviews and

---

[43] Interviews with French diplomats and executive of French bank, Ouagadougou (April 2017).
[44] Interviews with executive of WAEMU bank, Ouagadougou (April 2017).
[45] Interviews with executive of WAEMU bank, Dakar (March 2017).
[46] Interviews with French diplomats and executive of French bank, Ouagadougou (April 2017).
[47] Interviews with executive of WAEMU bank, Ouagadougou (April 2017).

scrutiny of formal documents, the evidence shows the decisive role of the BCEAO in the adoption of Basel II and III. The supranational dimension that gives the BCEAO more leeway vis-à-vis local players, and its extensive links to the international policy community, reflected in participation in peer regulator networks and in the training of its executives, explains the regulator's preference for Basel standards.

The IMF also played a decisive role in WAEMU. While the IMF and World Bank have been present in other cases and driven financial sector reforms, the WAEMU case stands out in the extent to which the IMF exerted significant pressure for WAEMU to implement Basel II and III, in contrast to its recommendations in other low-income countries and regions. In addition, the BCEAO benefited from IMF technical assistance in conducting reforms and drafting new banking standards. Other actors, both governments and banks, showed no appetite for international banking standards. The role of the IMF, and possible links with France, deserves greater exploration.

In line with the analytical framework, the reforms undertaken by the BCEAO, without the support of the banks, may lead to significant difficulties in implementation. A good proportion of banks, especially those not belonging to a banking group, already had difficulties in complying with the less stringent regulations set by Basel I. The WAEMU case, like Rwanda, is an example of regulations moving in ways that are out of step with the realities of a shallow and underdeveloped financial sector.

References

Afritac Ouest, 2015. *Activity report 2014/2015*. Afritac Ouest, Dar es Salaam, Tanzania.

BCEAO, 2012. *Statistics yearbook, 2012*. Banque Centrale des États de l'Afrique de l'Ouest, Dakar, Senegal.

BCEAO, 2014a. *Annual report*. Banque Centrale des États de l'Afrique de l'Ouest, Dakar, Senegal.

BCEAO, 2014b. *Bilans et comptes de résultats des établissements de crédit de l'UMOA, 2002–2014*.

BCEAO, 2015a. *Situation du secteur de la microfinance dans l'UMOA au 30 septembre 2015, note trimestrielle*. Banque Centrale des États de l'Afrique de l'Ouest, Dakar, Senegal.

BCEAO, 2015b. *Statistics yearbook, 2015*. Banque Centrale des États de l'Afrique de l'Ouest, Dakar, Senegal.

BCEAO, 2015c. *Rapport annuels de la Commission bancaire*. Banque Centrale des États de l'Afrique de l'Ouest, Dakar, Senegal.

BCEAO, 2016a. *Annual yearbook, 2005–2016*. Banque Centrale des États de l'Afrique de l'Ouest, Dakar, Senegal.

BCEAO, 2016b. *Rapport annuels de la Commission bancaire*. Banque Centrale des États de l'Afrique de l'Ouest, Dakar, Senegal.

BCEAO, 2016c. *Textes transposant les dispositions de Bâle II et Bâle III dans L'UMOA*. Banque Centrale des États de l'Afrique de l'Ouest, Dakar, Senegal.

BCEAO, 2017. *COFEB diploma official brochure*. Banque Centrale des États de l'Afrique de l'Ouest, Dakar, Senegal.

Caprio, G.J., Klingebiel, D., 1996. *Bank Insolvencies: Cross-Country Experience* (No. Policy Research Working Paper 1620). World Bank, Washington, DC.

COBAC, 2015. *African banking supervisors group* [WWW Document]. URL http://www.sgcobac.org/jcms/baz_6001/en/groupe-des-superviseurs-bancaires-africains (accessed 21.1.19).

IMF, 2011. *Staff Report on WAEMU*. International Monetary Fund, Washington, DC.

IMF, 2016. *Staff Report on WAEMU*. International Monetary Fund, Washington, DC.

IMF, 2017. *Staff Report on WAEMU*. International Monetary Fund, Washington, DC.

IMF, 2018. *Financial Soundness Indicators Database*. International Monetary Fund, Washington, DC.

Koné, T., 2015. *Speech on the occasion of the 25th anniversary of the Banking Commission 10th of December 2015*. Banque Centrale des États de l'Afrique de l'Ouest, Abidjan.

Lagarde, C., 2015. *Christine Lagarde sur la thème: 'L'intégration financière au service d'une croissance inclusive'*. BCEAO.

Ouédraogo, S., 2013. *Concentration bancaire, profitabilité et développement financier bancaires dans l'UEMOA* (No. Revue d'économique et monétaire de la BCEAO, N°1). Dakar, Senegal.

Ouédraogo, S., 2017. *Bank ownership, foreign bank origin and lending in West Africa*. Princeton University, Oxford-Princeton Global Leaders Fellow Colloquium.

Polity IV, 2014. *PolityProject*. Center for Systemic Peace.

Powo Fosso, B., 2000. *Les déterminants des faillites bancaires dans les pays en développement: le cas des pays de l'Union économique et monétaire Ouest-africaine (UEMOA)*. Ouagadougou.

World Bank, 2017. *World Development Indicators*. World Bank, Washington, DC.

8

Tanzania

From Institutional Hiatus to the Return of Policy-Based Lending

Hazel Gray

Introduction

Despite a consistent commitment to the adoption of international banking standards from the outset of its financial reforms in the late 1980s, Tanzania only finished implementing risk-based supervision in 2009, and opted for selective implementation of Basel II and III standards beginning in 2017. Amongst the countries featured in this volume, therefore, Tanzania is a relatively slow and cautious adopter of international banking standards. Over the past thirty years, Tanzania has been through a fundamental institutional transformation of its banking sector, with a far-reaching shift away from state control towards the creation of a private market-oriented banking sector that until recently has been dominated by foreign banks. Yet, despite twenty years of high growth and global integration, Tanzania is one of the least-banked countries in the world (World Bank, 2017). Although Tanzania has one of the highest number of banks in Africa and one of the most profitable banking sectors on the continent, the economy remains cash-based. While Tanzania has been slow to implement and enforce international banking standards, the IMF has consistently described Tanzania's regulatory system as being in reasonably good shape for its level of economic development (IMF, 2018, 2017a, 2010, 2004).

Tanzania's approach to international banking regulation has undergone two distinct phases. From 1995 to 2008, the enormous institutional shifts occurring within Tanzania's banking sector led to a regulatory hiatus. This was evident from the significant disjuncture between its formal commitment to adopting Basel and the actual pattern of implementation and enforcement. During the second period, from 2009 to 2017, regulation took greater priority, as risk-based supervision was finally implemented and the country moved on to adopt and implement elements of Basel II and III. However, this period was also characterized by the emergence of a more selective approach to Basel adoption—new regulations for segments of

Hazel Gray, *Tanzania: From Institutional Hiatus to the Return of Policy-Based Lending* In: *The Political Economy of Bank Regulation in Developing Countries: Risk and Reputation.* Edited by: Emily Jones, Oxford University Press (2020). © Oxford University Press. DOI: 10.1093/oso/9780198841999.003.0008

the banking and financial sector were introduced that were outside the Basel framework. This brought the informal practices of enforcement into closer alignment with the formal regulatory framework.

In this chapter, I explain how changes in the preferences and relative power of the three key actors—regulators, banks, and politicians—shaped the pattern and pace of Basel adoption over the period under study. During the first period, Tanzania had a predominantly policy-driven approach to adoption that was shaped by the decisive victory of pro-liberalization politicians and the high level of influence from the IFIs on Tanzania's emerging regulatory system. Yet the challenges of implementing an entirely new type of regulatory relationship from scratch should not be underestimated. The kind of policy-based lending that had been practised during Tanzania's socialist period was off the political agenda by the 1990s, but a few recent cases of grand corruption involving senior figures within the state and banking sector suggest that some groups may have had an interest in maintaining a loose regulatory environment. The domestically oriented commercial banks were powerful compared to regulators and politicians. Both foreign and domestic banks retained very high profitability during this period of regulatory hiatus, and they had no interest in pushing for faster implementation of international banking standards. These preferences led to a strong professed commitment to implement Basel but weak implementation in practice during the first period (Table 8.1).

The preferences of regulators, banks, and politicians all changed during the second period, from 2009 onwards. The changing preferences of the regulator were the result of two key factors: first, the appointment of a new internationally oriented governor at the Bank of Tanzania (BoT), and second, the influence of regional commitments to regulatory harmonization within the EAC, which provided a hard deadline of 2018 for the implementation of elements of Basel II and III. The banking sector's preferences also changed as the large foreign banks began to champion Basel adoption—partly a result of pressures from

Table 8.1 Tanzania: key indicators

Tanzania	
GDP per capita (current US$, 2017)	936
Bank assets (current US$)	8.9 bn
Bank assets (% of GDP)	18.8
Stock market capitalization (% of GDP)	Data not available
Credit allocation to private sector (% of GDP)	14.4
Credit allocation to government (% of GDP)	5.3
Polity IV score (2017)	3

Note: All data is from 2016 unless otherwise indicated.

Source: FSI Database, IMF (2018); GDI Database, World Bank (2017); Polity IV (2014)

parent banks and concerns about AML compliance. In addition, changes in the composition of the banking sector that had developed from the end of the 2000s led to greater competition within the sector. The large banks were interested in enforcing Basel, and especially the higher capital requirements, partly as a way of forcing consolidation among smaller banks. Over the same period, politicians' commitment to deep liberalization faltered and demands for policy-based lending returned. This resulted in a move away from the blanket adoption of Basel and towards attempts to tailor regulation for different segments of the banking sector. Thus, in the second period, Tanzania moved from policy-driven convergence, which didn't result in implementation, to regulator- and market-driven convergence, which has led to selective implementation of Basel II and III. While it is hard to perfectly align Tanzania with one of the trajectories set out in the analytical framework, the central role of the regulator leads it to exhibit dynamics of regulator-driven convergence.

The evidence presented in this chapter is based on twenty interviews with government officials, BoT employees, representatives of commercial and government banks, representatives of international development organizations, and academics in Tanzania, most of which took place from March to July 2017. Secondary sources include government publications, official reports of international institutions, grey literature produced by private sector consultants in the financial sector, project appraisal documents, annual reports, and other publications of the commercial banks and court cases.

I start with an overview of the political and economic context in which banking regulation has been implemented. I then trace the changing approach to Basel over time, demonstrating the early adoption, but also its slow and cautious implementation until the end of the 2000s, and the shift in the pace and nature of implementation in the 2010s. The core political economy argument is presented in the fourth section, which shows why Tanzania experienced a shift from policy-driven to a regulator- and market-driven preferences for Basel implementation. To conclude, I argue that the appearance of the banking sector as relatively well regulated and stable is partly a reflection of the minimal role that it has played, at least thus far, in supporting a more fundamental economic transformation within the domestic economy. This points to the mismatch between the characteristics of risk in highly financialized economies that are the focus of international banking standards, compared to the risks that are inherent in the processes of economic transformation of a country with ambitious plans for industrialization.

Economic and political context

Until the mid-1980s, Tanzania was a centrally planned economy with restrictions on the private sector while a significant proportion of the economy was under direct government ownership. After a period of economic decline, a structural adjustment package was signed with the IMF in 1986, putting Tanzania on a path towards economic liberalization and privatization. This was accompanied by political reforms that led to the introduction of multiparty elections in 1995— although Tanzania has consistently remained under the rule of one dominant party, the ruling Chama Cha Mapinduzi (CCM). Growth rates started to pick up from the end of the 1990s and Tanzania experienced an uninterrupted period of high growth for the next twenty years (Figure 8.1).

Economic growth in this period was driven by rising foreign and domestic investment and the emergence of a mining sector, growing by around 15 per cent per year by the early 2000s (Bank of Tanzania, 2004). But despite economic expansion and growing exports and imports, the economy remained largely delinked from the global financial system. Most Tanzanians still worked within the cash-based rural economy and the urban informal sector. Despite rapid urbanization and growing manufacturing output, the country remained one of the least industrialized in the world. Insufficient structural change and employ-ment creation meant that while experiencing the longest period of economic growth in its history, Tanzania's poverty rates remained intransigently high over the 2000s.

Tanzania's banking sector, meanwhile, experienced an enormous transformation since the early 1990s, with the break-up of the mono-banking system and the proliferation of commercial banks, a majority of which were foreign-owned for most of the period under study. During the socialist period, the banking sector consisted of six state-owned banks that provided credit in accordance with National Credit Plans (Bank of Tanzania, 2016b). Economic crisis and misman-agement led to a very high level of non-performing loans (NPLs), reaching 77 per cent of the total loans of the largest bank, the National Bank of Commerce, by 1995 (World Bank, 1995). Reforming the banking sector was central to Tanzania's structural adjustment process initiated in 1986, in response to pressure and loan conditionality from the IMF and World Bank. The Banking and

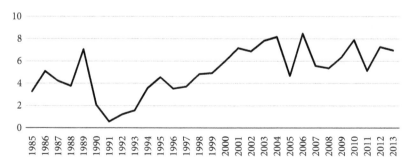

Figure 8.1 Tanzania: GDP percentage growth (1985–2013).
Source: Bank of Tanzania (2016b, 2004)

Financial Institution Act (BFIA) implemented in 1991 and the Bank of Tanzania Act of 1995 set the legal foundations for a new kind of private and market-oriented banking sector.

Like most other low-income countries, Tanzania has retained a bank-dominated financial sector with a very small stock exchange and insurance sector. The only other significant financial actor over the period has been pension funds, accounting for 10 per cent of GDP and around 27 per cent of total financial sector assets (IMF, 2016). From the mid-1990s, Tanzania pursued a very liberal approach to bank licensing in order to foster competition in the financial sector. This generated significant growth of foreign and private banks—so much so that by the end of the 2000s, Tanzania had one of the highest numbers of licensed banks on the continent. By the mid-2000s foreign banks had become dominant, but there was an expansion of locally owned banks towards the end of the decade—the majority of which were small community banks (see Figure 8.2). Compared to the start of the reforms, government control of the banking sector declined dramatically, following the break-up and privatization of the National Bank of Commerce (NBC), the National Microfinance Bank (NMB), and Cooperatives and Rural Development Bank (CRDB). Five new domestic banks were established from 2005, but the growth of domestic banks in this period mainly reflects the rise in small community banks serving particular regions.

Despite the rise in the total number of banks in the 2000s, Tanzania's banking sector has remained highly concentrated. The three largest banks in Tanzania, the NMB, the NBC, and CRDB, accounted for over 65 per cent of total banking

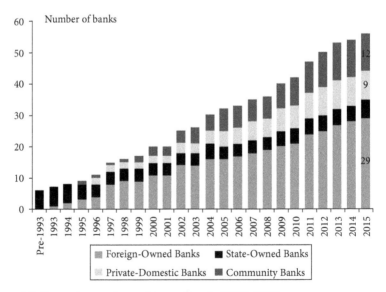

Figure 8.2 Tanzania: number and type of banks (1996–2017).
Source: IMF (2017, p. 8)

sector assets across the 2000s (IMF, 2010). These institutions all originated from the privatization of the dominant state-owned banks. Industry concentration was also reflected in the narrow lending profile of the large banks, which continue to lend primarily to the government and to serve a limited number of large multinational and domestic companies. Despite the expectation that greater competition would lead to a vital expansion of credit, rates of private credit to GDP remained stubbornly low in the first period of banking sector reform, rising from 5 per cent to 17 per cent of GDP from 2003 to 2015 (IMF, 2010; World Bank, 2017)—well below the regional average of 21 per cent (Nyantalyi and Sy, 2015). One reason for this was the availability of low-risk, highly lucrative government securities. The large banks dominated the government securities market, holding around 40 per cent of these assets. With zero risk weights and an interest rate of around 15 per cent, they had little incentive to extend credit to the private sector. Smaller banks, which did not operate so extensively in these markets, relied on being able to borrow from these larger banks, thus pushing up interest rates. Overall in the 2000s, Tanzania had the second highest margin spreads in the region after Malawi (IMF, 2010). Fundamental weaknesses in the state institutions that underpin financial markets, such as an effective commercial court and judicial system, were also key factors in the low level of lending by commercial banks to the private sector.

The insularity of the banking sector allowed banks to retain very high levels of liquidity in the 2000s and this was one of the causes of the fall in the level of NPLs. Dollarization, which was high across the whole sector (around 30 per cent of total deposits and total loans), was particularly concentrated in the largest banks where dollar deposits were 41–62 per cent by the end of the 2000s (IMF, 2010). Tanzania retained capital controls across the 2000s, and only started to take steps towards liberalizing its capital account after the EAC Common Market Protocol was ratified in 2010. The global financial crisis and the economic downturn led to an increase in NPLs across banks of all sizes (Figure 8.3).

Given most of the population has historically had little access to banking, one of the most dramatic changes to occur to Tanzania's financial sector in recent years has been the rapid rise of mobile phone-based financial services since 2008. By 2015, Tanzania caught up with the front-runner, Kenya, in terms of the scale of mobile money services available.

Tanzania's overall policy approach to the financial sector has undergone a marked shift from a policy of rapid general liberalization in the 2000s to a more targeted approach to addressing financial inclusion and promoting policy-based lending through development finance institutions in the 2010s. Characteristics that are frequently associated with clientelism, such as high levels of NPLs and the extension of loans without sufficient collateral, have not been prevalent amongst the systemically important banks over the 2000s. However, the grand corruption scandals that were a feature of Tanzania's political economy in the last

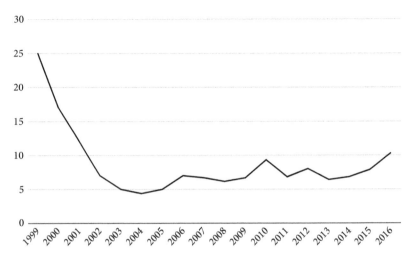

Figure 8.3 Tanzania: non-performing loans (NPLs) (% of total loans).
Source: Bank of Tanzania (2016b, 2004)

two decades exposed links between politicians and elements of the banking sector that suggest a more complex relationship between banking and politics underneath the surface.

Basel adoption, implementation, and enforcement

Since the liberalization of the banking sector in the early 1990s, Tanzania has formally been committed to implementing Basel standards (United Republic of Tanzania, 2000). The major regulations contained in the 1991 Banking and Financial Institutions Act were in line with the Basel Core Principles and the Act introduced a minimum capital requirement of 8 per cent of total assets, which was in line with the spirit of Basel I (United Republic of Tanzania, 1991). However, as risk weights were not included, this requirement acted as a leverage ratio in which all assets were assigned 100 per cent—meaning Tanzania's capital requirements were actually more stringent than required by Basel. The Act also set a range of other restrictions, such as collateral requirements for large loans, aggregate large loan limits, and fixed asset ceilings for banks, that were more restrictive than Basel I requirements.

Reforms to the institutions of banking supervision started in 1992 when the BoT upgraded its Supervision Unit into the Directorate of Banking Supervision. In Tanzania's first FSAP of 2003, the country was deemed to have put in place the foundations of a good supervisory system—but with a need for extensive amendments to law and regulation, banking supervision policy, capacity building within the BoT, and a move to risk-based supervisory practices (IMF, 2004). Following the first FSAP, the legal framework for banking regulation underwent significant changes from 2003 to 2009. The Bank of Tanzania Act, 2006 and the Banking and Financial Institutions Act, 2006 set up the foundations for a more stringent and independent supervisory system (United Republic of Tanzania, 2006). The Deposit Insurance Fund was established and licensing became the sole preserve of the BoT, reducing the potential for political involvement in decision-making. The first steps towards introducing risk-based supervision were taken in 2004 with a survey of the existing risk management framework in banks and non-bank financial institutions (Bank of Tanzania, 2010), which led to the implementation of risk-based supervision on a pilot basis in 2006. In 2007, the BoT published a Risk-Based Supervision Manual, and Capital Adequacy Regulations were published in 2008. This was followed the next year by the implementation of risk-based charges. The general willingness to adopt Basel standards in principle was evident in the fact that the BoT signalled its intention to move forward with Basel II adoption and implementation as early as 2004, even before risk-based supervision had been implemented (Bank of Tanzania, 2004), and a working

Table 8.2 Tanzania: adoption of Basel standards

Basel component	Adoption	Implementation
Basel I	Banking and Financial Institutions Act 1991 Banking Act (Amendment) 1993 (capital adequacy ratio brought into line with Basel)	
Risk-based supervision	Adopted with the Banking and Financial Institutions Act (2006)	The banking and financial institutions (capital adequacy) regulations, 2008
Basel II	Credit risk SA, operational risk, market risk adopted with the banking and financial institutions regulations (capital adequacy) Regulations 2014 Pillar II—Risk Management Guidelines for Banks and Financial Institutions, 2010	Operational risk was implemented in 2017 after a three-year moratorium announced in the banking and financial institutions capital adequacy (amendment) regulations 2015
Basel III	Capital conservation buffer of 2.5% adopted the banking and financial institutions (capital adequacy) regulations, 2014	Implemented in August 2017 announced in the Monetary Policy Statement June 2017

group was established to draw up plans for the implementation of staged elements of Basel II and III (Table 8.2).[1]

Despite the significant efforts to build up the legal framework for supervision, Tanzania's second FSAP in 2009 found that there were significant weaknesses in compliance by the commercial banks and in monitoring and enforcing prudential rules by the BoT (IMF, 2010). Significantly, the actual implementation of a risk-based approach was lacking entirely. This was partly the result of poor record-keeping and capacity constraints at the BoT (IMF, 2010). The FSAP review identified that three banks were undercapitalized, prudential limits had been exceeded for a number of the banks with large single exposures, and loan-to-deposit ratios were in breach in eleven banks. The BoT had shown significant regulatory forbearance in pressing these institutions to address their capital shortfall.

As the fourth section below explains, after 2009 the pace of Basel adoption and enforcement changed in important ways as Tanzania decided to combine the adoption of elements of Basel II and III and push forward with implementation by 2018. This began with improving the risk-based supervisory system in the early 2010s. Several weaknesses in data and the recording of risk-based supervision practices that were identified in the 2009 FSAP were resolved with the introduction of a fully automated reporting system in 2014. Consolidated Supervision Regulations were also issued in 2014, and a pilot examination of one commercial bank was undertaken in 2016.[2] In 2014, a directive to introduce capital requirements for operational risk from Basel II was issued, but commercial banks were given a three-year phase-in period. The operational risk charge became effective in 2017. Tanzania also committed to implementing Pillar 2 of Basel II, consisting of the Internal Capital Adequacy Assessment Process (ICAAP) by commercial banks and the Supervisory Evaluation and Review Process (SREP).

By the end of 2018, Tanzania's capital adequacy requirements were based on Basel I definitions and risk-weightings with some additions (IMF, 2018). Elements of Basel III were introduced in 2017 and 2018, including a revised definition of capital, a capital conservation buffer, and a leverage ratio (Bank of Tanzania, 2016a; IMF, 2018; Ng'wanakilala, 2017). (The BoT committed to revising the capital definition to bring it in line with the Basel III definition by 2018, but argued that they would need to adapt this to Tanzania's specific banking context (IMF, 2017a).) Over this period, a tailored approach to Basel adoption also started to emerge in formal terms, with a new regulatory framework for investment banks introduced in 2011 (Bank of Tanzania, 2011) and plans to develop specific supervisory regulations for Community Banks (FurtherAfrica, 2016). Regulations targeted specifically towards the larger systemic banks were also under consideration, in particular an additional Pillar 2 capital buffer of 2.5 per cent of risk-weighted assets for systemically

---

[1] Interview, Bank of Tanzania, Dar es Salaam June 2017.
[2] Interview, Bank of Tanzania, June 2017.

important banks (IMF, 2017a). Another sign of a tailored approach was in the adoption of a simplified liquidity ratio that was not equivalent to Basel III, but arguably was better suited to the country context and regulatory capacity (Bank of Tanzania, 2014). The BoT also continued to reform its supervisory system to meet Basel Core Principles in the areas that were identified as deficient in the 2009 FSAP, and they are now committed to being fully compliant by 2018.[3]

Money laundering regulations were identified as a particular area of concern in Tanzania, given high reported levels of money laundering in the country despite measurement difficulties arising from the predominantly cash-based nature of the economy (Goredama, 2003). Despite introducing an Anti-Money Laundering Act in 2006, Tanzania was 'blacklisted' and subject to FATF's monitoring process for AML/CTF compliance from 2009 to 2014 (FATF, 2017). In this period, several cases of money laundering were brought to court, but by 2016 no one had been prosecuted, highlighting the difficulties of enforcing the strengthened legislation (Fjeldstad and Heggstad, 2014).

Tanzania's general eagerness to adopt international standards was also evident in its early adoption of international accounting standards; IFRS was adopted in 2004 for all private sector business entities. But again, the actual enforcement of these accounting standards was low. In 2014, the National Board of Accountants and Auditors adopted the demanding IFRS 9 standards without amendments. While the larger and foreign-owned banks had already prepared to conform to these standards in line with their parent companies, many of the smaller banks struggled to prepare themselves for the new capital requirements by the 2018 deadline.

Political economy of Basel standards in Tanzania

As expected, Tanzania's regulatory practices have converged with global standards over time. Its path of adoption, implementation, and enforcement, however, has been shaped by the relative power as well as the preferences of the key actors involved in the financial sector. The political economy features influencing these preferences have evolved over time, so I first explain the early adoption and slow implementation of the first period from 1995 to 2008, and then set out the reasons for a change in the approach to Basel in the second period.

---

[3] Interview, Bank of Tanzania, Dar es Salaam 2017.

High adoption; weak implementation and enforcement (1991–2008)

A striking feature of Tanzania's experiences of Basel has been the early and consistent willingness to signal adoption of the standards. This was in large part due to the influence of IFIs on Tanzanian politicians and regulators from the start of the reform process, when the foundations of a new kind of banking sector were being established. However, at the outset of the reform process, the commitment of regulators and politicians to this approach was not a foregone conclusion. Even after the first structural adjustment agreement was signed in 1986, there were considerable differences of opinion between politicians within the ruling party about the appropriate role of the state in the economy. Some of the most acute ideological struggles occurred over the direction of banking sector reform. The ex-governor of the BoT, Charles Nyirabu, was committed to market liberalization and was Chair of the Presidential Commission of Enquiry (PCE) into the monetary and banking system set up in 1989. Their report, published in 1991, strongly supported the IFI agenda of banking sector liberalization and privatization. However, factions within the ruling party continued to strongly resist reforms throughout the 1990s, the most contentious issue being the privatization of state-owned banks.

To circumvent opposition within the ruling party, the World Bank decided to give the government considerable discretion over the pace and form of privatization (Adams, 2005). Initially the pace of reform was very slow and subject to considerable political contestation (Mwakikagile, 2010) but a pivotal moment came in 1997 when the Board of the National Microfinance Bank vetoed the government's proposals for privatization. In response, President Mkapa intervened and replaced the entire Board, signalling his strong support for the privatization process (Cull and Spreng, 2011). By the end of the 1990s, the debates over the direction of reform had been decisively won by the liberalizers and international best practices were embraced as the standard to which the new banking sector should aspire.

Over the next twenty years, the IFIs played a very significant role in shaping Tanzania's approach to banking supervision, through loan conditionality and technical assistance. The periodic FSAPs were particularly important in setting the agenda of action on Basel implementation.[4] The limited domestic financing options available to the government meant that disbursement conditions on IFI loans were a powerful lever of reform. For example, in the process of deciding how the National Bank of Commerce should be privatized, Amani et al. found that 'Tanzanian policymakers had selected an option that they had been led to believe the World Bank preferred because they believed that such a choice would

---

[4] Interviews, large commercial bank, Tanzania Bankers Association, Dar es Salaam, 2017.

simplify subsequent negotiations with the Bank on these issues' (2005, p. 33). The IFIs' influence on the regulator meant that from very early on, the 'spirit was to adopt international standards'.[5] Initially, however, IFI loan tranche releases were linked to the approval of plans and enactment of legislation, rather than actual implementation (World Bank, 1995).

As privatization got under way, the IFIs turned their attention to strengthening supervisory capacities at the BoT. The first Financial Institutions Development Project (FIDP) that ran from 1991 until 1996 facilitated the establishment of 'most of the basic skills for supervising banks' within the BoT (World Bank, 2000, p. 13). The focus on strengthening supervision was increased in the FIDP II from 2000 to 2006 (World Bank, 2000). Technical assistance was enhanced by the establishment of the IMF East Africa Regional Technical Assistance Centre (AFRITAC) in 2002, based within the BoT in Dar es Salaam. AFRITAC played a key role in providing technical assistance to the Bank for Basel adoption, in particular for the move to risk-based supervision in the 2000s (Chatterji et al., 2013), and subsequently in drafting regulations for Basel II and III implementation (IMF, 2017b).

The period of regulatory hiatus in the 2000s was not the result of a rejection of international standards in principle, but reflected the challenges of constructing a set of market-based regulatory institutions from scratch as well as a lack of incentives to push for greater adoption in a system that served the material interests of a number of powerful groups. Despite the dominance of foreign banks, the banking sector was domestically oriented and did not need to signal creditworthiness to international investors, nor were the domestic banks interested in entering foreign markets.[6]

Enduring links between the banking sector and powerful politically connected figures also influenced the extent of banking regulation enforcement. In the 2000s a series of grand corruption scandals linking politicians and local and international business caused political reverberations within the ruling party (Gray, 2015). Some of the most important scandals occurred within the banking sector and involved the incumbent governor of the BoT, Dr Daud Bilali, as well as a previous governor, Dr Idris Rashidi (IMF, 2018, 2017a, 2010, 2004). A number of commercial banks were embroiled in these scandals as significant funds were moved in and out of their accounts. While no commercial bank was taken to court as a result of these scandals, one did agree to a Deferred Prosecution Agreement with the UK Serious Fraud Office (Serious Fraud Office and Standard Bank Plc, 2015).

Despite these connections, some of the signals of clientelism—such as a high level of NPLs, or bank failures due to overstretched capital—that were seen in other countries in this study (notably Angola) were not evident in formal records in Tanzania. Clientelist practices are always opaque, but the very serious lack of

---

[5] Interview, Bank of Tanzania, July 2017.
[6] Interviews, Tanzania Bankers Association and large commercial bank.

reliable bank-level data on NPLs identified by the IMF in 2010 (IMF, 2010) further obscures the actual practices of lending and supervision in Tanzania in the 2000s. Further, the profitability of most of the banking sector, coupled with a lenient approach to the enforcement of capital requirements on the smallest banks, led to a very low level of bank failure in this first period.

The handful of bank failures in the early 2000s was mainly linked to the failure of the foreign parent companies but raised important issues about political discretion over licensing. Poor bank licensing practices were evident in a chain of decisions that led to a bank being closed down as a result of international money laundering concerns in 2017. This chain started with the Greenland Bank Tanzania Ltd which was established in 1995 and was a subsidiary of Greenland Bank (Uganda) Ltd. The parent bank was closed down by the Bank of Uganda after concerns about its banking practices and when the Tanzanian subsidiary was audited it was found to be insolvent. It was placed under compulsory liquidation and its assets were subsequently sold to Delphis Bank (T). Delphis Bank (T) was a subsidiary of the Kenyan Delphis Bank which became embroiled in a banking scandal involving Kenyan politicians and Kenyan and Tanzanian businesses (Dowden, 1993). It was closed down in 2003 and its main assets were quickly sold by the Deposit Insurance Fund to the Federal Bank of the Middle East Limited (FBME). The central bank was reported to have offered the FMBE quick access to gaining a banking licence, three branches, and premises and staff, and allowed FMBE to be operational in Tanzania within a few months (TanzaniaInvest, 2006).

The FMBE was looking to move its headquarters from the Cayman Islands following more stringent restrictions on the banking sector there (Financial Crimes Enforcement Network, 2016). FMBE became the largest bank in Tanzania, owning over 20 per cent of banking assets by the end of the 2000s. Despite holding the largest market share and having its headquarters in Dar es Salaam, it remained an overseas bank and held 90 per cent of its assets in Cyprus and mainly served wealthy Russian clients (Financial Crimes Enforcement Network, 2016). In 2014 the Financial Crimes Enforcement Network identified the Bank as a concern for money laundering (Financial Crimes Enforcement Network, 2016). It was subsequently blacklisted and a few weeks later, the Tanzanian headquarters were put under statutory management by the BoT. The failures to adequately regulate one of the largest banks in Tanzania for over a decade suggest that there were significant weaknesses in the regulatory system.

In summary, during this first period, Tanzania can be described as an example of policy-driven convergence. This was a result of the influence of the international financial institutions in shaping the preferences of both regulators and politicians. Nevertheless, the actual implementation of international standards and enforcement of all banking regulation was quite weak. This was due to both technical and practical challenges of constructing new market-oriented supervisory institutions from scratch. During the regulatory hiatus that ensued, poor enforcement may also have served to facilitate some of the clientelism that occurred within the political system in the 2000s. Commercial banks had no interest in demanding faster Basel implementation and the high profitability and insularity of the banking system created a stable and relatively low-risk banking sector that generated huge profits for the banks but with limited developmental impact.

2009–17: Faster Implementation and Enforcement, Emergence of Differentiated Rules for Supervision

During the next period, Tanzania continued to signal strong support for adopting key elements of Basel but in addition the pace of implementation and nature of enforcement changed in important ways over the 2010s. In this period, Tanzania can be characterized as having a regulator- and market-driven approach to implementation. The global financial crisis that unfolded from 2008 played a key role in triggering a series of changes in incentives at the international level that influenced all the actors. Changing approaches to the role of the market and state in development also affected the preferences of politicians and generated pressures for the creation of a more tailored approach to Basel implementation.

Two key factors in combination led to changes in the preferences of the regulators towards a faster pace of implementation of Basel in the 2010s. The first was a change in the top leadership at the BoT. After the grand corruption scandals under Governor Bilali, President Kikwete selected a highly respected technocrat, Professor Benno Ndulu, to take on the position of governor at the BoT from 2008. Although Beno Ndulu shared a similar background to Bilali in terms of his experience of working in an international financial institution, he was seen to be a governor who could restore the reputation of the bank and bring greater independence to decision-making.[7] He had been a few years in advance of Kikwete at the University of Dar es Salaam and interviewees reported that Kikwete held his professionalism in high regard.[8] Governor Ndulu's approach to the banking sector was pro-market and he demonstrated his ability to oppose demands from politicians for policies that he disagreed with, for example resisting calls for Tanzania to follow Kenya in introducing interest rate caps in 2016 (The Citizen, 2016a). His pro-market approach was also evident in his decision to allow the mobile money market in Tanzania to develop initially with minimal regulation (African Business, 2017).

The second key factor that influenced the preference of the regulator was the emergence of a stronger agenda on harmonization of banking regulation across

[7] Interview, consultant and former Bank of Tanzania official, Dar es Salaam, April 2017.
[8] Interview, consultant and former Bank of Tanzania official, Dar es Salaam, April 2017.

the region that emanated from the East African Community. The initial commitments to establishing an EAC custom union, common market, and monetary union was established in the EAC Treaty of 2000s but the agenda only started to take a concrete form from the end of the 2000s. The most important EAC commitments on economic harmonization was the Common Market Protocol that was ratified in April 2010. The agreement envisaged the phased liberalization of trade in financial services and the elimination of restrictions on the free movement of capital. In 2013, this was followed by the EAC Monetary Union Protocol which committed all members to the creation of a single currency by 2024 and the establishment of the preliminary elements of a regional financial architecture by 2018. Technical and financial support from the IFIs also shifted from national governments to supporting the harmonization agenda at the level of the EAC. A new project funded by the World Bank to promote harmonization, the First Financial Sector Development and Regionalization Project for East African Community (EAC) to establish the foundation for financial sector integration among EAC Partner States, started in 2011 and was eight years in length.[9]

The Monetary Affairs Committee, consisting of the governors of the central banks of member states, had responsibility for overseeing the financial harmonization agenda. Ndulu was firmly ensconced within international professional networks that supported the implementation of international banking regulation and he maintained close professional ties with the other governors on the Committee. While the MAC set the agenda, the details of implementation were determined by the MAC Finance sub-committee. The Tanzanian delegation was a group of officials from the BoT and the Ministry of Finance. It was tasked with developing country-level action plans for harmonizing banking regulation and moving forward with implementing Basel II and III.

While the top leadership at the bank was more actively supportive of Basel implementation than in the 2000s, other actors within the bank and government remained more cautious about the need for a faster implementation of Basel.[10] Tanzania had a history of slow financial reforms compared to Kenya and Uganda, typified by its resistance to opening its capital account, and Kenya and Uganda also proceeded towards Basel II and III adoption at a much faster pace than Tanzania. Nevertheless, the roadmap for harmonization was an important factor in leading to a more rapid pace of implementation of Basel compared to the 2000s. For example, when Kenya and Uganda adopted increased capital charges in 2014 in line with Basel II, this was an impetus to Tanzania to move forward with

---

[9] Component 2—Harmonization of Financial Laws and Regulations and component 3—Mutual Recognition of Supervisory Agencies were particularly pertinent.
[10] Interview, Ministry of Finance, Dar es Salaam, July 2017.

implementation.[11,12] The consequences of these two factors in combination was that the preferences of the regulator supported a faster implementation of Basel II and III.

Preferences of the large commercial banks also changed in the second period. A significant reason for this was the greater pressure to conform to international banking standards emanating from the 'parent' banks of foreign commercial banks in Tanzania. The large banks were all concerned to improve AML compliance in Tanzania and saw Basel adoption as an important component in achieving this. In addition, a number of the larger banks were concerned about the rapid growth in the number of small commercial banks operating in Tanzania.[13] While the average capital reserves in the banking sector were consistently higher than Basel standards, many of the smaller banks, and in particularly the Community Banks, were operating with much lower levels of capital. Moving to introduce the higher capital requirements contained in Basel II and III was therefore seen as a desirable way to drive consolidation within the banking sector in Tanzania (The Citizen, 2016b).

The larger commercial banks lobbied for faster Basel adoption through the Tanzania Bank Association (TBA). They established a sub-committee of the TBA called the Joint Committee on Regulation, Compliance and Risk. This was made up of the five largest banks. The purpose of the sub-group was to participate in the planning process for Basel adoption and they engaged in a regular dialogue with the BoT on specific aspects of Basel adoption.[14] These large banks also influenced the BoT's approach by running training programmes and sharing technical expertise on issues such as correspondent banking and AML compliance.[15] However, the large influential banks were also in agreement that aspects of Basel II, such as internal ratings models, were not appropriate for the Tanzanian banking sector and they did not lobby for these to be included in the roadmap for Basel adoption.[16] Thus, the combined interests of the larger banks and the institutionalized channels of influence played an important role in moving Tanzania towards a more rapid but selective implementation of Basel II and III.

While the changing preferences of the regulators and the commercial banks help to explain Tanzania's more rapid, but selective, move to adopt and implement Basel II and III after 2009, preferences of politicians also changed in ways that encouraged a more tailored approach to Basel implementation and banking regulation to emerge. Tanzania started to return to a more statist approach

[11] Interview, Bank of Tanzania, July 2017.
[12] The Bank of Tanzania issued a moratorium of three and five years for commercial banks and community banks to fully comply with the minimum capital requirements following lapsing deadlines in Kenya and Uganda.
[13] Interviews, commercial banks, Dar es Salaam, April, July 2017.
[14] Interviews, Tanzania Bankers Association, commercial banks, July 2017.
[15] Interviews, commercial banks, April and July 2017.
[16] Interviews, commercial banks, IMF, Dar es Salaam, April and July 2017.

to economic policy, reflected in the adoption of five-year planning documents, a focus on industrialization, and a return to some elements of policy lending by state banks.

The kind of directed policy lending that had been at the core of the banking system during the socialist period was not viable as many of the potential financial control mechanisms of the state were no longer available. Nevertheless, growing doubts about benefits of the liberalization agenda led to political demands for a more active policy agenda on promoting financial inclusion and directed credit for priority sectors. The more interventionist approach first came into evidence in the wake of the global financial crisis in 2009, when the government introduced a stimulus package through the commercial banks and agreed to guarantee financial institutions for loans where repayment had become difficult because of the global downturn. The Ministry of Finance started to play a more active role in the development of financial sector policy, and the Tanzania Financial Stability Forum was established in March 2013, bringing together financial regulators as well as the BoT and finance ministry representatives to oversee financial stability and regulation. A National Financial Inclusion Framework was launched in 2013.

This new approach culminated in the introduction of a more tailored approach towards the regulation of development and community banks in Tanzania. In 2010 the BoT commissioned a consultant to start working on establishing a supervisory framework for DFIs, including specific prudential regulations (Bank of Tanzania, 2010). The Association of African Development Finance Institutions had already developed a document setting out unique prudential standards, guidelines, and ratings system for African Development Banks that had been adopted in 2008 (African Development Bank, 2009), and provided the basis for Tanzania's new system.[17] Development Finance Institutions Regulations were issued in 2011.

As a result, Tanzania Investment Bank was split into two parts—a non-deposit-taking financial institution, the Tanzanian Investment Bank Development Bank, and a deposit-taking bank called Tanzania Investment Bank Corporate Finance Ltd. TIB Corporate Bank Limited gained its commercial bank licence in 2015. In 2015 the Tanzania Agricultural Development Bank also gained a licence under the new Act. The IMF had consistently opposed the establishment of development banks in Tanzania (IMF, 2010, 2004) but the creation of specific regulation in the 2010s brought a closer alignment between the formal systems of regulation and actual practices.

Another example of the emerging tailored approach towards finance was the increased pressure on pension funds to invest in priority sectors in the 2010. Aside from the development banks, Tanzania's main vehicles of policy lending after liberalization had been the pension funds. In the 2000s, these had been operating with very little oversight. In 2005 the IMF found that 'there is no law

---

[17] Interview, development finance institution, Dar es Salaam, July 2017.

or regulatory body monitoring financial reporting by pension fund' (World Bank, 2005, p. 7). In the 2000s, the investment portfolios of the pension funds were not particularly targeted to priority sectors (IMF, 2010). However, funds were encouraged to provide investment for industrial projects (Ubwani, 2016). The significance of this was that there was less pressure on commercial banks to engage in directed lending.

The other area of banking regulation that underwent significant change after 2010 was the enforcement of regulation on the community banks. Community banks had been established in Tanzania since 2003 when the Banking and Financial Institutions Act was amended to give powers to the BoT to prescribe lower capital threshold for the establishment of regional and community banks. Throughout the 2000s, these banks had low profitability and poor asset quality, very high overhead costs with large boards, and a higher proportion of NPLs (IMF, 2016). Community banks were identified as the least compliant groups with international accounting standards, and they often failed to comply with credit risk disclosure requirements (World Bank, 2005). Despite these problems, no community bank was closed down for a lack of capital until the mid-2010s. The IMF argued that the BoT had exercised considerable regulatory forbearance in dealing with these banks. The BoT may have taken a more lenient approach because these banks were seen as critical for promoting a more inclusive banking sector and addressing the urgent needs of financial inclusion.[18]

From the mid-2010s, stricter regulations and enforcement were introduced on community banks. New minimal capital requirements were introduced in 2015, increasing from Tsh250 million ($154,036) to Tsh2 billion ($1.23 million). Community banks were given five years to address the capital shortfall that many were facing when operational risk charges were introduced in 2012. The decision to take a much stronger approach to poorly performing banks was set out by the new President John Magafuli in 2017 (All East Africa, 2017). Mbinga Community Bank was closed in May 2017 and a further five community banks were shut down in January 2018. This represents a major shift in approach to poorly capitalized community banks in Tanzania.

Thus, during this second period preferences of the regulator, large banks and politicians led to a faster pace of Basel implementation and greater enforcement. This was combined with a move to a more tailored approach to Basel that led to selective adoption of Basel II and III and the formalization of different regulatory systems for development banks (and pension funds). Overall, this brought greater alignment between de facto regulation and de jure practices in the sector. Despite the strengthening of formal institutions, there was still evidence of areas of regulatory forbearance (IMF, 2018). More stringent capital demands entailed by Basel II and III were introduced at a time when the economy was slowing

---

[18] Interviews, retired Bank of Tanzania officials, Dar es Salaam, July 2018, January 2019.

down and NPLs were rising in banks of all sizes. This led to a much more challenging environment for banks overall. The continued willingness to adapt the formal regulatory system was in evidence in 2018 when the BoT issued a circular for loan classification and restructuring to give regulatory relief to banks in the face of rising levels of NPLs (IMF, 2018).

Conclusion

Despite the fact that international banking standards were designed to address the challenges of banking systems that bear little resemblance to Tanzania's banking system in the 1990s, Tanzania sought to implement Basel standards from the outset of its reform process. This was a result of the influence of IFIs on the preferences of politicians and regulators. Their formal commitment to adopt these standards did not, however, lead to an effective implementation of standards and indeed the regulatory framework was very weak across the 2000s. This was partly a reflection of the enormous technical and practical challenges of implementing a new regulatory system but also reflected the preferences of the commercial banks and some powerful groups of politicians whose interests were not served by stronger implementation.

From 2008 these underlying preferences changed in important ways. A number of shocks played a role in shaping these new preferences: the global financial crisis, the AML blacklisting, as well as the grand corruption scandals of the 2000s led to greater pressure to move forward with Basel II and III implementation and to push for greater enforcement. At the same time, changing ideas about the role of banks in Tanzania's development led to a formalization of distinct regulations for directed lending through development finance institutions and social security funds. This helped to bring the actual practices of regulation into closer alignment with the formal supervisory system. As the 2010s draw to a close, it appears that Tanzania has entered a new phase of regulation in the banking sector, with stricter enforcement of regulations. This has been accompanied by a more statist approach to the banking sector but so far this has gone hand in hand with a continued commitment to implementing Basel standards. The problem for countries like Tanzania that have ambitious plans for economic development is that Basel was designed primarily for the banking sectors of the richest countries in the world. Creating a system of banking regulation that can promote sustainable industrialization will require a much more fundamental rethink about the nature of risk and banking supervision than has taken place so far within Tanzania and beyond.

References

Adams, J., 2005. *The right approach to the right policies: Reflections on Tanzania, in: At the Frontlines of Development: Reflections from the World Bank*. World Bank Publications, Washington, DC.

African Business, 2017. Benno Ndulu, Governor of Tanzania's central bank. *African Business Magazine*.

African Development Bank, 2009. *Prudential Standards, Guidelines and Rating System for African Development Banks and Finance Institutions*, Association of African Development Finance Institutions. Tunisia, Africa Development Bank Group.

All East Africa, 2017. Tanzania: JPM Orders Closure of Poor Performing Banks. *All East Africa*.

Amani, H.K.R., Wangwe, S.M., Rweyemamu, D., Aiko, R., Wanga, G.G., 2005. Understanding economic and political reforms in Tanzania, in: *Understanding Economic Reforms in Africa: A Tale of Seven Nations*. Palgrave, Basingstoke, pp. 205–36.

Bank of Tanzania, 2004. *Directorate of Banking Supervision Annual Report 2004*. Bank of Tanzania, Dar es Salaam.

Bank of Tanzania, 2010. *Directorate of Banking Supervision Annual Report 2010*. 14th Edition. Bank of Tanzania, Dar es Salaam.

Bank of Tanzania, 2011. *Directorate of Banking Supervision Annual Report 2011*. 15th Edition. Bank of Tanzania, Dar es Salaam.

Bank of Tanzania, 2014. *The Banking and Financial Institutions Liquidity Management Regulations 2014*. Government Notice No. 293. Bank of Tanzania, Dar es Salaam.

Bank of Tanzania, 2016a. *Directorate of Banking Supervision Annual Report 2016*. 20th Edition. Bank of Tanzania, Dar es Salaam.

Bank of Tanzania, 2016b. *50th Anniversary of the Bank of Tanzania: Evolution of the Role and Functions of the Bank of Tanzania*. Bank of Tanzania, Dar es Salaam.

Chatterji, S., Woodbridge, R., Gray, J., Lo Moro, P., 2013. *IMF East Africa Regional Technical Assistance Center (East AFRITAC). Independent Mid-Term Evaluation Phase III: October 2009 to date (Volume I: Final Report)*. Consulting BASE.

Cull, R., Spreng, C.P., 2011. Pursuing efficiency while maintaining outreach: Bank privatization in Tanzania. *Journal of Development Economics* 94, 254–61. https://doi.org/10.1016/j.jdeveco.2010.01.010.

Dowden, R., 1993. Kenya 'political' banks come under scrutiny: Complaints from IMF and aid donors prompt inquiry after export swindle. *The Independent*.

FATF, 2017. *Improving Global AML/CFT compliance: On-going process* [WWW Document]. URL http://www.fatf-gafi.org/countries/a-c/afghanistan/documents/fatf-compliance-february-2017.html (accessed 19.11.18).

Financial Crimes Enforcement Network, 2016. *Imposition of Special Measure Against FBME Bank Ltd., Formerly Known as the Federal Bank of the Middle East Ltd., as a*

Financial Institution of Primary Money Laundering Concern. Jamal El-Hindi, Washington, DC.

Fjeldstad, O.-H., Heggstad, K., 2014. Capital flight from Africa—with a little help from the banks, in: *Fuga de Capitais e a Política de Desenvolvimento a Favor Do Mais Pobres Em Angola* [Capital Flight and Pro-Poor Development Policy in Angola]. CEIC/NCA, Luanda.

FurtherAfrica, 2016. Bank of Tanzania works on new community bank regulations. *FurtherAfrica.*

Goredama, C., 2003. *Money laundering in East and Southern Africa: An overview of the threat,* ISS Paper 69. Institute for Security Studies, South Africa.

Gray, H.S., 2015. The political economy of grand corruption in Tanzania. *African Affairs* (Lond) 114, 382–403. https://doi.org/10.1093/afraf/adv017.

IMF, 2004. Tanzania: *Financial System Stability Assessment, including Reports on the Observance of Standards and Codes on Banking Supervision* (IMF Country Report No. 03/241). International Monetary Fund, Washington, DC.

IMF, 2010. *United Republic of Tanzania: Financial System Stability Update* (IMF Country Report No. 10/177). International Monetary Fund, Washington, DC.

IMF, 2016. *United Republic of Tanzania, Selected Issues—Macro-Financial Issues* (IMF Country Report No. 16/255). International Monetary Fund, Washington, DC.

IMF, 2017a. *United Republic of Tanzania: Sixth Review Under the Policy Support Instrument and Request for a Six-Month Extension of the Policy Support Instrument— Press Release,* Staff Report and Statement by the Executive Director for the United Republic of Tanzania. International Monetary Fund, Washington, DC.

IMF, 2017b. *East Africa Regional Technical Assistance Centre (East AFRITAC) Mid-Year Report FY 2017.* International Monetary Fund, Washington, DC.

IMF, 2018. *Financial System Stability Assessment: United Republic of Tanzania* (IMF Country Report No. 03/241). International Monetary Fund, Washington, DC.

Mwakikagile, G., 2010. *Nyerere and Africa: The End of an Era.* New Africa Press, Pretoria, South Africa.

Ng'wanakilala, F., 2017. UPDATE 1: Tanzania central bank announces new capital rules for banks. *Reuters.*

Nyantalyi, E.B., Sy, M., 2015. *The banking system in Africa: Main facts and challenges.* African Economic Brief, African Development Bank, Chief Economist Complex 6.

Polity IV, 2014. *PolityProject.* Center for Systemic Peace.

Serious Fraud Office, Standard Bank Plc, 2015. *In the Crown Court at Southward in the matter of s. 45 of the Crime and Courts Act 2013* (No. Case No: U20150854). Royal Courts of Justice, London.

TanzaniaInvest, 2006. FBME Tanzania Interview. *TanzaniaInvest.*

The Citizen, 2016a. Tanzania keeps close eye on Kenya's interest rates cap impact. *Daily Nation.*

The Citizen, 2016b. Kimei: Banking sector needs mergers and acquisitions. *The Citizen*.

Ubwani, Z., 2016. JPM: Invest in factories, not buildings. *The Citizen*.

United Republic of Tanzania, 1991. *The Banking and Financial Institutions Act*. United Republic of Tanzania, Dar es Salaam, Tanzania.

United Republic of Tanzania, 2000. *Letter of Intent of the Government of Tanzania to the IMF*. United Republic of Tanzania, Dar es Salaam, Tanzania.

United Republic of Tanzania, 2006. *The Banking and Financial Institutions Act*. United Republic of Tanzania, Government Printers, Dar es Salaam, Tanzania.

World Bank, 1995. *Memorandum and Recommendation of the President of the International Development Association to the Executive Directors on a Proposed Credit in the Amount Equivalent to SDR 7.5 Million to the United Republic of Tanzania for a Financial Institutions Development Project*. Report No. P-6479-TA. World Bank, Washington, DC.

World Bank, 2000. *Implementation Completion Report United Republic of Tanzania Financial Institutions Development Project (Credit No. 2771-TA)*. Private Sector and Finance Economic Management and Social Policy Department Africa Region, Report No.: 20252. World Bank, Washington, DC.

World Bank, 2005. *Report on the Observance of Standards and Codes (ROSC) Tanzania Accounting and Auditing, April 1, 2005. 35188*. World Bank, Washington, DC.

World Bank, 2017. *Tanzania Economic Update: Money Within Reach. Extending Financial Inclusion in Tanzania* (The World Bank Group Macroeconomics and Fiscal Management Global Practice, Africa Region Issue 9). World Bank, Washington, DC.

9

Kenya

'Dubai' in the Savannah

Radha Upadhyaya

Introduction

Two words reoccur when people describe the Kenyan financial and banking sector in recent years: ambitious and innovative. Kenya's banking system made huge strides between 2003 and 2015, both in terms of overall financial depth and financial inclusion. However, efficiency, measured in terms of interest rate spreads, remains a major concern (Upadhyaya and Johnson, 2015). The rise of mobile banking (MPesa) and local banks following an agency banking model have led to the transformation of both the payments and credit landscapes (Heyer and King, 2015).

Kenya was an early adopter of Basel II and III relative to other cases in this book. It has taken a selective approach, implementing some elements of Basel II and III, in a manner broadly consistent with selective adoption in other peripheral developing countries (Jones and Zeitz, 2017). This chapter sets out the level of adoption of Basel standards in Kenya in detail, and then traces the drivers of this adoption. It argues that Kenya's high level of adoption of Basel standards is due to the alignment of government (politicians and regulators), banking sector, and donor interests. These groups share the view that financial growth, stability, and financial inclusion are priorities for economic development, and essential to the achievement of the country's Vision 2030 goals—and the implementation of Basel standards is perceived to be critical to meeting these objectives. Unlike its neighbours Tanzania and Ethiopia, which take a more interventionist approach to the financial sector and have been cautious about implementing Basel standards, Kenya has always followed a capitalist path and there is little commitment to government-led industrial policy.

In this chapter, we show how Kenya's adoption of Basel standards has been driven by the regulator and supported by both politicians and banks. The regulator, the Central Bank of Kenya (CBK), has a high level of independence in both theory and practice. It has strong links to the international policy community and is very receptive to international policy ideas. Since 2003, the incumbent politicians have also been internationally oriented and keen to adopt the latest

Radha Upadhyaya, *Kenya: 'Dubai' in the Savannah* In: *The Political Economy of Bank Regulation in Developing Countries: Risk and Reputation.* Edited by: Emily Jones, Oxford University Press (2020). © Oxford University Press.
DOI: 10.1093/oso/9780198841999.003.0009

international standards. Meanwhile, as the banking sector is relatively well capitalized, there has been little opposition to Basel Adoption from banks, with some international and large local banks being mildly in favour of it. There is evidence to suggest that enforcement of regulations may have been lax before 2015, but this may be due to capacity issues and not a form of mock compliance. While more stringent application of the rules since 2015 has met with some resistance from banks and politicians, the commencement of other international regulations like IFRS9 reporting standards means that banks see increased compliance with international standards as a fait accompli. In terms of our analytical framework, Kenya is an example of regulator-driven convergence.

The analysis draws chiefly on primary sources: a systematic review of regulatory texts, central bank publications, newspapers, and policy documents; and sixteen interviews conducted between April and December 2017 with CBK employees, ex-central bank regulators, ex-Treasury officials, policy experts on the financial sector, ex-Monetary Policy Committee officials, compliance professionals at banks, representatives of the Kenya Bankers' Association, and experts from the World Bank. Interview data is cited in ways that preserve the anonymity of interviewees.

Political economy context: the evolution of Kenya's banking sector

Kenya is one of the largest economies in Sub-Saharan Africa and a regional hub in East Africa, and is known for its vibrant but fragile democracy. In 2013, Kenya was classified as a lower-middle-income country, after rebasing its GDP (Handjiski et al., 2016).

The economy is still largely dependent on agriculture, which contributed to 30 per cent of GDP in 2015 (KIPPRA, 2016). While manufacturing growth is sluggish, the services sector has been performing well, and the depth of the financial sector and stock market capitalization are very high compared to other countries with the same level of GDP, both in the region and across the world (see Table 9.1).

At the time of independence, Kenya was one of the few African countries to already have a diversified banking sector with both foreign and local banks and an established stock market (Upadhyaya, 2011). Unlike many developing countries, in Kenya there was no wholesale nationalization of banks after independence. International and local private banks continued to operate, though state-owned banks and development finance institutions were established (Upadhyaya and Johnson, 2015). This reflects the international orientation of the Kenyan government that has persisted since independence. The banking sector has gone through a series of reforms, which began with the liberalization of interest rates and exchange rates in the 1990s (Ndung'u and Ngugi, 1999). However, by 2000, the sector remained extremely fragile: the ratio of non-performing loans (NPLs)

Table 9.1 Kenya: key indicators

Kenya	
GDP per capita (current US$, 2017)	1508
Bank assets (current US$)	31 bn
Bank assets (% of GDP)	43.8
Stock market capitalization (% of GDP, 2014)	50
Credit allocation to private sector (% of GDP)	32.7
Credit allocation to government (% of GDP)	13.7
Polity IV score (2017)	9

Note: All data is from 2016 unless otherwise indicated.

Source: FSI Database, IMF (2018); GDI Database, World Bank (2017);
Central Bank of Kenya, (2015); Handjiski et al. (2016); Polity IV (2014)

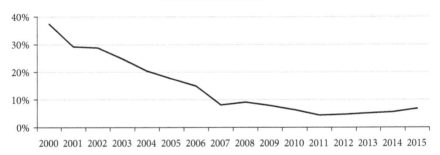

Total NPL / Total Loans

Figure 9.1 Kenya: non-performing loans (NPLs) (% total loans).
Source: Central Bank of Kenya (2015, 2014, 2014, 2002)

for three government-owned banks ranged from 42 per cent to 72 per cent
(Upadhyaya and Johnson, 2015). Since then, banking regulations and guidelines
have been continuously amended to strengthen supervision and regulation
(Dafe, 2014). The main changes have been the introduction of guidelines requir-
ing banks to conform to the various capital stipulations in line with the Basel
Capital Accord, and restricting lending to insiders to 20 per cent of core capital
(Central Bank of Kenya, 2000).[1]

The most significant impact of strengthening regulation and supervision has
been on the quality of banking assets. The overall NPL ratio has reduced significantly from 2000 to 2012 from a high of 37 per cent to 5 per cent, though there has
been a slight increase thereafter to 6.8 per cent by 2015 (Figure 9.1). This can
partly be attributed to weaker macroeconomic conditions, but also to more stringent application of regulations.[2] Between 2007 and 2014, the banking sector in

---

[1] This is discussed in more detail in the next section.
[2] This is discussed in more detail in the next section.

Kenya was relatively stable with only one bank failure. However, in 2015, three banks were put under CBK statutory management, testing the reputation of other private banks (Ngugi, 2016).

There has also been an improvement in banks' capital adequacy ratios (see Figure 9.2). The ratio of total capital to total risk-weighted assets increased from 17 per cent (in 2000) to 23 per cent (in 2012) and then reduced to 19 per cent (in 2015), still staying above the required minimum ratio of 14.5 per cent (Central Bank of Kenya, 2015). Interest rate spreads decreased from 14.24 per cent in 2000 to 7.8 per cent in 2005, but have remained steady since then—economists and policymakers generally agree that the interest rate spread in Kenya is high.[3] The banking sector in Kenya has a low concentration by regional standards, with an HH index of 0.05 in 2012 (see Figure 9.3), and a spread of ownership between foreign-, local-, and government-owned banks (Upadhyaya and Johnson, 2015). However, profitability of the banking sector has been steadily increasing and the return on assets has risen from 0.8 per cent in 2000 to 3.5 per cent in 2011, with a slight drop to 2.9 per cent in 2015. This shows that sustained interest rate margins and spreads have allowed banks to maintain high profit margins. The other key challenges relate to the high level of bank assets in government securities,

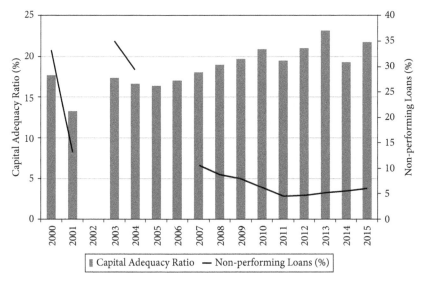

Figure 9.2 Kenya: capital adequacy ratios (CAR) and non-performing loans (NPLs).
Source: Financial Soundness Indicators Database, IMF (2018)

---

[3] In September 2016, MPs passed a law capping the interest rate spread. Thereafter there has been a drying-up of credit to the private sector which can be attributed to both the rate cap and general economic and political uncertainty. It is still unclear whether this cap will be lifted by Parliament.

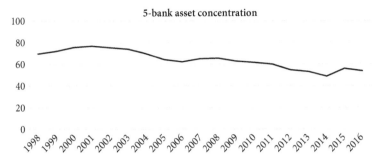

Figure 9.3 Kenya: banking sector concentration (asset share of the five biggest banks).
Source: Global Financial Development Database, World Bank (2018)

a low level of credit to key sectors including agriculture and infrastructure, and low overall savings (Upadhyaya and Johnson, 2015).

Kenya has become an inspiration globally because of the huge strides it has made in financial inclusion. The population that is included in formal finance has jumped from 26.7 per cent in 2006 to 75.3 per cent in 2016 (Central Bank of Kenya, Kenya National Bureau of Statistics, and FSD Kenya, 2016). This can largely be attributed to the rise of mobile money, and Equity Bank and other local banks following the agency banking model (Johnson and Arnold, 2012).

Basel adoption, implementation, and enforcement

While Kenya was a relatively late adopter of Basel I, it has made significant efforts to adopt and implement Basel II and Basel III and to comply with the Basel Core Principles. This section explains that while the level of adoption and implementation is high, the international standards have been adapted to suit the particular needs of the Kenyan banking sector.

Basel I adoption

Kenya began implementing Basel I in the early 1990s. Some of these requirements were included in the Banking (Amendment) Act of 1994, including the reduction of the ratio of single borrower limit to core capital from 100 per cent to 25 per cent (Central Bank of Kenya, 1996, 1995). In response to a spate of bank failures by 1998, several changes were brought into force in 1999, including detailed guidelines on provisioning and regulatory ratios based on Basel I (Central Bank of Kenya, 1999). Thus, while Kenya started the process of adopting some of the Basel requirements as early as 1994, the main requirements regarding ratios were only adopted in 1999.

Basel II adoption

In 2006, the CBK issued new prudential guidelines. While these guidelines do not mention Basel regulations explicitly, the changes were designed to strengthen Kenyan regulations in line with Basel I in preparation for Basel II. The main changes included highlighting differences between core capital (Tier 1) and supplementary capital; defining four risk weights for classifying balance sheet assets (the standardized approach to credit risk); and the definition of conversion factors for interest rate and exchange rate contracts based on residual maturity periods for market risk (Central Bank of Kenya, 2006).

The Basel Committee had noted that the implementation of Basel II may not be a priority for non-members like Kenya (Mwega, 2014). However, CBK documents revealed that in 2007 and 2008, it was developing a framework and preparing the prerequisite supervisory infrastructure to implement Basel II. In 2008, the CBK carried out a Basel II implementation survey that highlighted that the key challenges to implementation were the lack of both human resources and sufficiently advanced IT systems. The CBK noted that many of the relevant institutions did not have requisite five-year data to use for their internal models (Central Bank of Kenya, 2008). This survey was probably a major factor in the CBK's decision to not make internal models compulsory, but to instead recommend that banks use the standardized approach to credit risk; however, with Kenya, government securities were given a zero rating even though they are not AAA risk rated.[4]

New prudential guidelines were issued in 2013, and included many elements of Basel II and some of Basel III (see Table 9.2). The main additions to the credit risk regulations were rules on operational and market risk. In both cases the standardized approach was implemented.[5] The 2013 prudential guidelines also specify liquidity requirements, but Kenya has not adopted the liquidity coverage ratio that is part of Basel III. In 2013 the CBK also issued risk management guidelines and developed a risk-based framework for supervision. While banks were required to report their financial statements on a quarterly basis since 2006, stress testing of banks for supervision has been done since 2015. However, the ICAAP reporting which was in the 2013 guidelines was only enforced in 2017.

Basel III adoption

The CBK, while continuing to implement Basel II, made a series of changes to ensure that Kenya was also moving towards adopting elements of Basel III, with the most significant modifications being implemented in 2013.

---

[4] Interview 7—Senior Manager, accounting firm, Nairobi, 16 May 2017.
[5] Operational risk-weighted assets equivalent is calculated as 15 per cent of average gross income for three years multiplied by 12.5 (inverse of 8 per cent). Interview 7—Senior Manager, accounting firm, Nairobi, 16 May 2017.

Table 9.2 Kenya: adoption of Basel standards

Basel component	Adoption	Implementation
Basel I	Credit risk-weighted ratios—1994 onwards	1999
Basel II (5 out of 10 components)	2013 onwards - Risk management guidelines - Standardized approach to credit, operational, and market risk	1 January 2014 (1-year adjustment period built into guidelines). CBK 2013 pg. 124
Basel III (2 out of 8 components)	- Capital conservation buffer—2013 - Stringent definition of capital	- 1 January 2015

Source: Authors' summary from Central Bank reports and interviews

The main change in relation to Basel III was the inclusion of a capital conservation buffer of 2.5 per cent applicable to all banks (Central Bank of Kenya, 2013), which they were given twenty-four months to comply with (Central Bank of Kenya, 2013, p. 88). The CBK has decided not to implement several elements of Basel III, including contingency capital ratios, the Basel III liquidity ratios, and countercyclical macroprudential regulations,[6] all of which were perceived by the regulator as less relevant to the Kenyan banking system.[7] Unlike some countries, the Kenyan central bank decided not to make exceptions for small banks or development finance institutions.

Compliance with Basel Core Principles

In 2002, a regulation self-assessment revealed that Kenya had fully complied with twelve of the twenty-five Basel Core Principles. The CBK's report notes that it had not fully implemented twelve other core principles, while one was seen as irrelevant to the Kenyan context (Central Bank of Kenya, 2002).[8] In the FSAP 2009 Update conducted by the World Bank, the BCP Detailed Assessment Report stated that the CBK had 'made substantial progress in addressing the deficiencies highlighted in the 2003 FSAP' (World Bank, 2013).[9]

---

[6] Interview 6—Former Treasury official, Nairobi, 9 May 2017; Interview 11—Senior Banker, pan-African Bank, Nairobi, 19 May 2017.

[7] Interview 14—Senior Official, Central Bank of Kenya, Nairobi, 14 August 2017.

[8] In 2002, the requirement of the CBK to ensure that banks adequately control market risks was considered not to be applicable in the Kenyan environment, but by 2007 it was included in the CBK's roadmap to implement Basel II.

[9] The WB's 2005 Financial Sector Assessment report which is based on 2003 FSAP of Kenya mentions that an assessment of compliance with Basel Core Principles was done, but the result is not

Overall, Kenya has made significant progress in adopting and implementing the Basel principles, especially compared to other African countries (Marchettini et al., 2015). In particular, the CBK has stood out for its high level of operational independence, substantial powers, and engagement in consolidated supervision (Central Bank of Kenya, 1997).[10] Continuous improvements have meant that the number of principles that were assessed as Compliant or Largely Compliant increased from sixteen in 2003 to eighteen in March 2013 (World Bank, 2013).

All this means that Kenya is a relatively high adopter of Basel II and Basel III, and exhibits a high level of compliance with the Basel Core Principles. Furthermore, it has the legal authority to ensure its regulations are enforced.[11] This said, there is evidence that despite good adoption of the regulations, enforcement did not happen in full, particularly before 2015, which interviewees suggest was the result of a lack of resources rather than lack of intent and therefore not a form of mock compliance.

The political economy of Basel adoption, implementation, and compliance

This section discusses the specific contextual factors that resulted in the international orientation of politicians, regulators, and banks, and allowed their interests to align in support of Basel implementation.

Politicians

In 2003, Mwai Kibaki succeeded Daniel arap Moi to become the third president of Kenya, as head of the NARC—the National Rainbow Coalition. In the early years, the government had a broad mandate and there was a lot of optimism. This sense of hopefulness was captured in the chants of 'Yote yawezena bila Moi (everything is possible without Moi)' (Murunga and Nasong'o, 2006), and provided the impetus for a drive to change both the structures of government and the relationship between the government and private sector.

Under Kibaki's government, Kenya embarked on an ambitious programme of reform. Financial sector reform constituted a key part of the government's commitment to growth, which included the Economic Recovery Strategy for Wealth

discussed in the report that is available online. We have not found a copy of any report based on the 2009 FSAP on the WB web page.

---

[10] Interview 14—Senior Official, Central Bank of Kenya, Nairobi, 14 August 2017.
[11] Interview 1—KBA official, Nairobi, 4 April 2017; Interview 2—former Senior Banker, foreign-owned bank, Nairobi, 5 April 2017.

and Employment Creation (ERS) (Republic of Kenya, 2003) and the Kenya Vision 2030 (Republic of Kenya, 2007). The ERS explicitly acknowledged that a vibrant financial sector was necessary in order to mobilize the domestic resources necessary for investment, but equally recognized that the performance of the financial sector was constrained by the high level of NPLs prevalent in 2002 (Republic of Kenya, 2003, p. 15). Furthermore, both Treasury and central bank officials had internalized some of the messages coming from IFIs that the two goals of financial stability and financial inclusion were intertwined and crucial for development and growth.[12],[13] In this context, the goals of international standards like Basel, which seek to improve the regulation, supervision, and risk management of banks, matched those of the government in its attempt to clean up the banking sector.

Unlike many developing countries, in Kenya successive governments have not pursued an industrial policy that includes directed lending to specific industries. Instead, bank lending in Kenya has remained market-driven, and Basel regulations are seen to be supporting banks' own efforts rather than in conflict with government policy.[14] Recent government documents, including the Sector Plan for Financial Services 2013–17, are explicit in saying that the rationale for following international standards is to increase stability within the banking sector: 'The CBK used the BIS and IMF defined financial soundness indicators to monitor and evaluate the soundness of financial institutions' (Republic of Kenya, 2003, p. 7).

The international orientation of government policy is also highlighted by the close involvement of international consulting firms in the development of the national economic strategy, and the policy intention to turn Nairobi into a financial services hub.[15] While there was broad consultation with Kenyan citizens when developing Vision 2030, it was openly acknowledged that international consulting firms like McKinsey were strongly involved in its development, as well as the roadmaps to achieving its goals (Wakiaga, 2015).

The plan to turn Nairobi into a regional finance hub lay at the heart of Vision 2030, in plans to establish the Nairobi International Financial Centre. The Kenyan government views the Nairobi International Financial Centre as a key development tool to increase investment and create employment (Republic of Kenya, 2013). While academics have highlighted that the impact could be negative for development (Waris, 2014), the government's commitment to this project has been steadfast. In July 2017, President Uhuru Kenyatta signed the Nairobi International Financial Centre Act, providing the legal framework to facilitate its development (Mwaniki, 2017).

---

[12] Interview 6—former Treasury official, Nairobi, 9 May 2017.
[13] Treasury and ministry of finance are used interchangeably.
[14] Interview 14—senior official, Central Bank of Kenya, Nairobi, 14 August 2017.
[15] Interview 1—KBA official, Nairobi, 4 April 2017; Interview 13—senior banker, large privately owned local bank, Nairobi, 14 September 2017.

Interviews and newspaper articles revealed that this policy goal was a key driver of recent moves to implement Basel II and III standards. As an interviewee noted, 'If we want Nairobi as a financial hub, players must a have a certain status'.[16] When launching the draft bill for the NFIC, the Cabinet Secretary to the National Treasury, Henry Rotich, reiterated that a key source of competitive advantage for the NFIC is that 'Kenya has a robust *legal and regulatory framework based on international best practices*' (Rotich, 2016). Speaking at the launch of the Capital Markets Authority Strategic plan in July 2018, Rotich again reiterated the government's commitment to establish the Nairobi International Financial Centre before the end of 2018 (Amadala, 2018). Thus, while the early impetus for Basel adoption came from the desire to clean up the banking sector, more recent moves have been motivated by the desire to create an internationally recognized financial hub.

Regulator: the Central Bank of Kenya

While the international orientation of the government provided a favourable policy context for adoption, it was the regulator—the Central Bank of Kenya—that was the driving force behind the implementation of Basel and other international banking standards. Crucially, and in contrast to many other case studies in this book, the CBK has enjoyed a high level of autonomy in setting regulations, which has given it the leeway needed to adopt and implement Basel standards.

This trend was entrenched under Kibaki, a very hands-off president who respected independent offices including that of the Central Bank Governor, and gave Treasury and central bank officials the space to drive regulatory reforms.[17] One interviewee stressed that President Kibaki 'gave a free hand which ensured reforms took off'.[18] Still, there was definitely some pushback from the politicians, particularly to the independence of the central bank. This quote from Cheserem's autobiography highlights some of the tensions:

At the time of my appointment as Governor in July 1993, the office of Governor did not have safety of tenure...I faced a lot of resistance in my quest for CBK independence. A number of people, especially those in government, questioned the wisdom of granting independence to the bank.   (Cheserem, 2006, p. 93)

The length of time it took to entrench the independence of the governor, between 1997 and 2006, shows the process was not easy, but nevertheless it did happen.

---

[16] Interview 1—KBA official, Nairobi, 4 April 2017.
[17] Interview 10—senior manager, financial sector donor, Nairobi, 18 May 2017.
[18] Interview 13—senior banker, large privately owned local bank, Nairobi, 14 September 2017.

Furthermore, the independence of all government institutions was strengthened under the very progressive Constitution that was passed in Kenya in 2010.[19]

Compared to many of the case studies in this book, the Kenyan regulator has substantial autonomy over the country's banks. Although several politicians do own banks, these are smaller organizations often referred to as 'Tier 3' banks within Kenya, and they do not have the level of political clout required to push back against regulatory changes.

That said, regulators are not completely unencumbered by politics. There is evidence of regulatory forbearance before 2015, as stricter enforcement of regulations only after Dr Patrick Njoroge took office in June 2015 led to the closure of three banks in late 2015 and early 2016. There is also evidence that politicians are trying to push through changes in the CBK Act in order to reduce the powers of the governor—but so far these efforts have not been successful (Some and Ngirachu, 2017).

International orientation of the central bank

The CBK viewed the implementation of international standards as integral to the broader goals of economic development. A regulator notes, the 'Adoption of BCPs or global standards will enable Kenya [to] achieve aspirations of Vision 2030 which include: improving financial stability; enhancing efficiency in delivery of credit and other financial services; promoting East African Community financial services integration to facilitate trade, enable cross-border operations and movement of capital; and achieving a well-functioning financial system safeguarding the economy from external shocks, and establishing Kenya as a leading financial centre in Eastern and Southern Africa.'[20]

Three specific factors help to account for the CBK's determination to implement Basel standards. First is the extreme fragility of the banking sector in the early 2000s; second, the view that improved regulation is essential to fostering growth within the financial sector; and third, the internationally oriented nature of CBK governors, who have been influenced both by the IFIs and their peers.

The fragility of the banking sector, reflected in very high levels of NPLs and several bank failures in 2004/5, provided the initial impetus for Basel implementation. There was widespread agreement among regulators that an inclusive and stable financial system was needed to support economic growth (Republic of Kenya, 2003). Reformist technocrats within the CBK viewed international standards as an aspiration worth achieving, and they perceived adherence to these standards as a basis for ensuring financial stability and inclusion.[21] This perspective is captured in a speech by the CBK governor Ndung'u, who in a speech to banks

---

[19] Interview 3—former senior official, CBK, Nairobi, 27 April 2017.
[20] Interview 14—senior official, Central Bank of Kenya, Nairobi, 14 August 2017.
[21] Interview 4—former CBK MPC member, Nairobi, 4 May 2017.

in 2013 noted: 'As you expand and innovate, it behoves you to ensure that adequate risk management is employed. It is with this in mind that the central banks have continuously adapted international best practices to ensure that financial stability is maintained' (Ndung'u, 2017). In the Kenyan context, international standard setting bodies were a source of ideas, rather than a source of pressure.[22]

To understand why successive central bank governors have been keen to implement international standards, it is instructive to examine their career trajectories and the extent to which they are connected to international policy debates throughout their careers, their engagement in transnational professional networks, and their participation in international training programmes. Examining the careers of central bank governors reveals that nearly all of them have a high level of embeddedness in international networks and close ties with IFIs (Table 9.3). Prior to his appointment as governor, Micah Cheserem worked for a multinational corporation outside Kenya. He notes in his autobiography that he agreed with many of the ideas promoted by the IMF and World Bank. 'Some people in government accused me of being too close to the IMF. I readily agreed with them. I do not deny that I was close but I must say that I accepted their conditionalities only if they made economic sense' (Cheserem, 2006, pp. 123, 124).

Dr Andrew Mullei worked for the IMF between 1974 and 1981, with a short stint at the UNECA in 1978. Dr Njuguna Ndung'u, while not working directly for the IMF or World Bank, worked for many years for the African Economic Research Consortium, which was funded by the World Bank but was also a forum for researchers across the world to come together to exchange ideas on economic development issues. Dr Patrick Njoroge, who began his term in 2015, had also worked for the IMF since 1995. The one exception was Nahashon Nyagah, who grew through the ranks of the CBK. During his short tenure he did not carry out many changes in regulation, but he was instrumental in developing the bond market.[23]

Table 9.3 Kenya: level of embeddedness of central bank governors

Name	Tenure	Level of embeddedness in international networks
Mr Micah Cheserem	1993–2001	High
Nahashon Nyagah	2001–3	Low
Andrew Mullei	2003–7	High
Njuguna Ndung'u	2007–15	High
Patrick Ngugi Njoroge	2015–Incumbent	High

---

[22] Interview 3—former senior official, CBK, Nairobi, 27 April 2017.
[23] Interview 13—senior banker, large privately owned local bank, Nairobi, 14 September 2017.

The central bank governors and senior staff have further been engaged in transnational professional networks, particularly since the start of Governor Ndung'u's tenure. There were several cross-border visits between the central bank governors of East Africa, which led to an exchange of ideas and declarations of intent to adopt international best practices.[24] The CBK is also involved in several international networks, including the Financial Stability Board (FSB) through the FSB's Regional Consultative Group for Sub-Saharan Africa, the Financial Action Task Force (FATF) through the Eastern and Southern Africa Anti-Money Laundering Group (ESMAALG), and the Association of African Central Banks.[25]

The CBK staff have also been exposed to high levels of international training on regulatory issues.[26] The role of the IMF's East Africa Technical Assistance Centre (East AFRITAC) should be highlighted here. East AFRITAC has been recognized in several of the CBK reports as providing training, particularly on regional supervision (Central Bank of Kenya, 2014). Membership of these transnational professional networks and participation in international training courses provide fertile ground for the exchange of ideas and emulation of international best practices.

Government engagement with IFIs

Although not in the driving seat, the IMF, the World Bank, and DFID have played an instrumental role in Kenya's implementation of Basel standards. Since the Kibaki government took office in 2003, the government has worked closely with the IMF and World Bank. Alongside Vision 2030 and other government economic blueprints, the two institutions developed the Financial and Legal Sector Technical Assistance Programme (FLSTAP), a broad-based lending programme to assist the Kenyan government in identifying weaknesses in the financial sector. The FLSTAP was agreed between the World Bank and the government in 2004,[27] and was based on the Financial Sector Assessment Programmes (FSAPs) that were conducted by the WB and IMF in 2003 and again in 2009. The broad agenda of the World Bank, which is captured in the publication 'Making Finance Work for Africa', centres on its view that stability, certainty, and transparency are cornerstones for an efficient financial system (Honohan and Beck, 2007). Interviews support the idea that politicians and regulators in Kenya took on the World Bank's

---

[24] Interview 2—former senior banker, foreign-owned bank, Nairobi, 5 April 2017.
[25] Interview 14—senior official, Central Bank of Kenya, Nairobi, 14 August 2017.
[26] Interview 13—senior banker, large privately owned local bank, Nairobi, 14 September 2017.
[27] FLSTAP stands for Financial and Legal Sector Technical Assistance Project, which was a lending programme of the World Bank.

position, which helps to explain their desire to incorporate financial growth, financial stability, and financial inclusion in broader economic goals.[28]

Interviews also revealed that in 2003, there was a willingness on the part of the Kenyan government to work with IFIs in a way that had not been the case for a long time.[29,30] There was an explicit recognition that the high level of NPLs in government-owned banks was not sustainable (Republic of Kenya, 2003).

It is clear that the World Bank, the IMF, and other donors like DFID played an instrumental role in the adoption of international banking standards in Kenya.[31] Many of the changes made to ensure compliance with the Basel Core Principles and implement Basel standards were brought in by the Government of Kenya and funded through the FLSTAP.[32] DFID co-funded this programme as part of its support to private sector development, and because it was seen as integral to attaining financial inclusion. This reflected a wider emphasis placed by the UK government on the implementation of international financial standards, as the Prime Minister of the UK at that time, Gordon Brown, was at the forefront of the global move towards Reporting on Standards and Codes.[33]

Although there was some disagreement between the government and World Bank on the privatization of government-owned banks, there was genuine enthu-siasm among government officials for the regulatory agenda of the FLSTAP.[34] Some interviewees explained that the IFIs initially tried to push through regulatory reforms via consultants, but after they changed tactics and developed the capacity of Kenyans within the Treasury and central bank, the project took off.[35] While the World Bank and IMF did not drive adoption of the standards, the CBK took their recommendations seriously, and 'implementation of the 2003 recommendations resulted in ceding of operational supervisory powers from the Ministry of Finance to CBK. And the 2009 FSAP recommendations led to the development of a legal and regulatory framework for consolidated supervision.'[36]

---

[28] Interview 6—former Treasury official, Nairobi, 9 May 2017; Interview 14—senior official, Central Bank of Kenya, Nairobi, 14 August 2017.

[29] Interview 10—senior manager, financial sector donor, Nairobi, 18 May 2017.

[30] There was a recognition that at a very low level of inclusion, higher inclusion can lead to increased stability as banks have a larger depositors base. But, in turn, inclusion needs stability as increased stability allows depositors to trust banks (Interview 6—former Treasury official, Nairobi, 9 May 2017).

[31] Interview 10—senior manager, financial sector donor, Nairobi, 18 May 2017; Interview 5—senior World Bank official, Nairobi, 9 May 2017.

[32] Interview 6—former Treasury official, Nairobi, 9 May 2017; Interview 3—former senior official, CBK, Nairobi, 27 April 2017; Interview 5—senior World Bank official, Nairobi, 9 May 2017; Interview 4—former CBK MPC member, Nairobi, 4 May 2017.

[33] Interview 10—senior manager, financial sector donor, Nairobi, 18 May 2017.

[34] Interview 10—senior manager, financial sector donor, Nairobi, 18 May 2017; Interview 12—for-mer senior official, World Bank, Oxford, 8 June 2017.

[35] Interview 10—senior manager, financial sector donor, Nairobi, 18 May 2017.

[36] Interview 14—senior official, Central Bank of Kenya, Nairobi, 14 August 2017.

Adopting Basel capital standards was seen by the IFIs as one part of the broader institutional architecture needed to improve the financial system.[37] Other important tools included the building of a credit registry, regulations for microfinance institutions, and Savings and Credit Cooperatives, which were also enacted during this period.[38] The development of the credit registry was seen as key to helping reduce NPLs in the system.[39] A project implementation report dated 2013 stated that fifteen Kenyan laws had been drafted and passed with the support of this project (World Bank, 2013). The World Bank and IMF were also key to providing training on Basel, discussed below. Other institutions such as DFID and FSD Kenya were important in providing support for other regulations related to the financial sector.

Therefore, while the CBK was the driving force as a regulator in ensuring adoption of Basel standards, IFIs played an important role alongside it. They were keen to support the broader reform of the financial sector, and their recommendations were crucial to providing information and capacity-building on these issues.

Role of the East African Community

In some countries, including Rwanda, regional integration dynamics have provided impetus for the implementation of international standards. Although Kenya has played a leading role in the development of the East African Community, this does not appear to have been a motivator for Basel implementation.

Central banks from three East African countries have been cooperating with each other to ensure joint supervision of banks. The East African Community web page states: 'With this regard, moving towards legal and regulatory harmonization against the international standards known as the Basel Core Principles (BCPs) is critical to achieve an effective functioning of a single market in banking services' (East African Community, n.d.). In practice, however, interviews indicated that there was little evidence that the EAC was a driving force in adopting Basel. One interviewee reflected that 'Kenya is the driver of standards and there are so many trade conflicts between the East African Community members that issues like Basel are not pushed at EAC level.'[40] There is a lot of positive goodwill at the very top level with governors of the different East African countries meeting in different forums, but lower down and at the EAC secretariat there doesn't seem to be any movement.[41]

---

[37] Interview 3—former senior official, CBK, Nairobi, 27 April 2017.
[38] Interview 3—former senior official, CBK, Nairobi, 27 April 2017.
[39] Interview 5—senior World Bank official, Nairobi, 9 May 2017.
[40] Interview 15—financial sector consultant and former senior banker, foreign-owned bank, Nairobi, 13 December 2017.
[41] Interview 1—KBA official, Nairobi, 4 April 2017.

Market factors

The evidence gathered from interviews suggests that while international or private banks did not lobby for Basel standards to be adopted—because complying with these standards would be resource-intensive—they were not averse to it either. To understand the reaction of banks in Kenya, it is helpful to examine the composition of the banking sector when each set of Basel standards was introduced (Table 9.4). When Basel I and II were introduced, the largest banks by asset share were foreign- and government-owned (FOB and GOB, respectively). International banks were already at different stages of adopting Basel II and III, because of their head office reporting requirements, so the introduction of these standards in Kenya did not pose problems for them.[42] KCB, a GOB, reflects the broad improvement in NPLs reflected in the Kenyan banking sector between 2005 and 2012 and the introduction of a risk management framework in line with international best practices was a key reason for this reduction.[43] The government partially privatized the bank and hired two CEOs with experience from foreign-owned banks—Gareth Terry Davidson and Martin Oduor-Otieno—to head a turnaround and expansion strategy. A reading of Martin Oduor-Otieno's biography shows that the government and board viewed a reduction in NPLs as essential to KCB's expansion strategy (Muluka et al., 2012). While there is no specific reference to Basel, it is highlighted that one of the key reasons why Martin Oduor-Otieno was selected to join KCB was because 'He had the special advantages that he was overseeing projects in Barclays which revolved around getting the multinational operations in Africa to adopt higher governance standards, brought about by Sarbanes-Oxley Act. This, as well as the introduction of International Financial Reporting Standards, meant that his recruitment into KCB would raise the bank's operations to *international best practices*. That international exposure was also important to a bank that wanted to *branch across borders*' (Muluka et al., 2012, p. 148).

By 2010, when Basel III started to be introduced, there had been a major shift in ownership due to the rise of local privately owned banks (LPOBs), including Equity Bank. Crucially, large local banks like Equity Bank were expanding regionally and they viewed adopting international standards as aligned with their interests.[44] As of the end of 2014, eleven Kenyan banks had subsidiaries across branches within the EAC region and South Sudan. The key banks were: KCB, Equity Bank, Cooperative Bank, Imperial Bank, Diamond Trust Bank, CBA, NIC, and I&M (Central Bank of Kenya, 2014; Irungu, 2015).

---

[42] Interview 2—former senior banker, foreign-owned bank, Nairobi, 5 April 2017; Interview 8—senior banker, foreign-owned bank, Nairobi, 16 May 2017.
[43] Interview 16—former senior banker, government-owned bank, Nairobi, 5 April 2018.
[44] Interview 1—KBA official, Nairobi, 4 April 2017; Interview 3—former senior official, CBK, Nairobi, 27 April 2017.

Table 9.4 Kenya: top three banks at different stages of Basel adoption

	Introduction by Basel Committee	Adoption and implementation in Kenya	Top three banks in Kenya (at beginning of implementation)
Basel I	1988	1994 onwards but mainly 1999	Barclays Bank (FOB) Standard Chartered (FOB) KCB (GOB)
Basel II	2004	2006–13	Barclays Bank (FOB) Standard Chartered (FOB) KCB (GOB)
Basel III	2010	2013 onwards	KCB (GOB) Equity (LPOB) Cooperative (LPOB)

Banks expanding across the region viewed a domestic regulatory architecture based on international standards as a 'defence mechanism' that allowed them to expand into other jurisdictions without suspicion.[45] As articulated by the CEO of one private bank, 'One fear we have as we expand is that regulation will be different in different jurisdictions. One therefore wonders if we will be treated differently and we therefore prefer to work within the international best practice regulation'.[46] These newly emerging banks also expected the implementation of Basel standards to make it easier to develop and retain correspondent relationships with foreign banks.[47] As Kenyan banks have expanded regionally, the CBK has set up supervisory colleges to strengthen cross-border banking supervision. These colleges manage the risks posed by Kenyan banks' presence abroad and base their work on the Basel Core Principles (Republic of Kenya, 2012).

A recent study on the credit risk approaches in Basel II and on the enhancement of capital quality and the introduction of capital buffers in Basel III found that the implementation of these requirements in 2013 led to a drop in bank capital ratios, particularly due to the inclusion of market risk and operational risk in calculating capital requirements. However, since the majority of banks in Kenya were above the minimum 14.5 per cent ratio, the impact of the increase in capital due to these requirements was not significant (Ambasana, 2015). The fact that Kenyan banks were well capitalized because of steady increases in capital requirements from 1998 onwards helps explain why banks in Kenya have not opposed some of the more complicated Basel II requirements.

---

[45] Interview 3—former senior official, CBK, Nairobi, 27 April 2017.

[46] Remarks by Mr John Gachora, CEO of NIC Bank at KBA/SOAS/UoN conference, Nairobi, 8 December 2017.

[47] Interview 1—KBA official, Nairobi, 4 April 2017; Interview 2—former senior banker, foreign-owned bank, Nairobi, 5 April 2017; Interview 4—former CBK MPC member, Nairobi, 4 May 2017.

Interviews showed that smaller banks were generally well capitalized, but struggled with adopting the risk-based guidelines mainly because of human resource constraints.[48] As one respondent remarked, in 2006 when it became mandatory for all banks to have a risk manager, there were only three qualified risk managers in Kenya and over forty banks.[49] Some regulations like the Internal Capital Adequacy Process (ICAAP) have been requirements since 2013, but the CBK only began enforcing them in 2017. There is some evidence that smaller banks found it harder to develop these reports than larger banks because of their systems' inability to generate client-specific data.[50] However these smaller banks were not strong enough to push back on these regulations. Overall, then, the CBK was not constrained by the banks in its push for adoption of Basel.

Conclusion

Kenya is a selective adopter of Basel standards. It has not adopted the standards fully but selected those parts of Basel II and Basel III that are relevant to its circumstances.[51] In terms of our analytical framework, the dynamics in Kenya illustrate how regulator-driven convergence can lead to implementation when supported by politicians and banks. Perhaps because the regulator has greater institutional capacity than in countries like WAEMU and Rwanda, so understands the challenges posed by Basel standards, it has taken a more selective approach to implementation.

The regulator received strong support from the politicians and wider government. Politicians from the main parties, as well as senior government officials, are strongly steeped in a market-led view of economic development, and they staunchly support the internationalization of the financial sector, which they believe is at the heart of the development process. As a result, even when governments have changed, key projects like the creation of the Nairobi International Financial Centre have been carried through. This has led them to support the CBK's implementation of international standards, including Basel. The international orientation of successive central bank governors and their embeddedness in international networks highlights the role of ideas in driving Basel adoption and implementation. IFIs, particularly the IMF and World Bank, have been instrumental, providing information and training about the adoption of

---

[48] Interview 2—former senior banker, foreign-owned bank, Nairobi, 5 April 2017.
[49] Interview 2—former senior banker, foreign-owned bank, Nairobi, 5 April 2017.
[50] Interview 8—senior banker, foreign-owned bank, Nairobi, 16 May 2017; Interview 9—senior banker, small privately owned local bank, Nairobi, 17 May 2017; Interview 13—senior banker, large privately owned local bank, Nairobi, 14 September 2017.
[51] This is in contrast to Pakistan, another high adopter where many regulations were brought in word for word.

standards to receptive regulators. Meanwhile, the banks are well capitalized, and their ambition to become regional players has meant that they have not opposed the introduction of international banking standards.

References

Amadala, V., 2018. Nairobi set to host Africa's latest financial hub—Rotich. *The Star*, Kenya.

Ambasana, J., 2015. *The implementation of Basel II and III and the implications on the banking industry in Kenya*. University of Warwick.

Central Bank of Kenya, 1995. *Annual Report and Financial Statements July 1994–June 1995*. Central Bank of Kenya, Nairobi.

Central Bank of Kenya, 1996. *Annual Report and Financial Statements July 1995–June 1996*. Central Bank of Kenya, Nairobi.

Central Bank of Kenya, 1997. *Annual Report and Financial Statements July 1996–June 1997*. Central Bank of Kenya, Nairobi.

Central Bank of Kenya, 1999. *Annual Report and Financial Statements July 1998–June 1999*. Central Bank of Kenya, Nairobi.

Central Bank of Kenya, 2000. *Prudential Guidelines 2000*. Central Bank of Kenya, Nairobi.

Central Bank of Kenya, 2002. *Bank Supervision Annual Report 2002*. Central Bank of Kenya, Nairobi.

Central Bank of Kenya, 2006. *Prudential Guidelines 2006*. Central Bank of Kenya, Nairobi.

Central Bank of Kenya, 2008. *Bank Supervision Annual Report 2008*. Central Bank of Kenya, Nairobi.

Central Bank of Kenya, 2013. *Prudential Guidelines 2013*. Central Bank of Kenya, Nairobi.

Central Bank of Kenya, 2014. *Bank Supervision Annual Report 2014*. Central Bank of Kenya, Nairobi.

Central Bank of Kenya, 2015. *Bank Supervision Annual Report 2015*. Central Bank of Kenya, Nairobi.

Central Bank of Kenya, Kenya National Bureau of Statistics, and FSD Kenya, 2016. *The 2016 FinAccess household survey*. CBK, KNBS, FSDK, Nairobi.

Cheserem, M., 2006. *The Will to Succeed: An Autobiography*. Jomo Kenyatta Foundation, Nairobi, Kenya.

Dafe, F., 2014. *Walking a tightrope progress in balancing multiple central bank objectives in Kenya, Nigeria and Uganda*. Deutsche Gesellschaft für Internationale Zusammenarbeit (GIZ), Bonn.

East African Community, n.d. *Regional banking—An overview* [WWW Document]. URL https://www.eac.int/financial/banking (accessed 26.11.18).

Handjiski, B., Sanghi, A., Bogoev, J., Larbi, G.A., Angelique, U., Randa, J., Kiringai, J.W., Chege, P.N., Whimp, K., Gubbins, P.M., Mistiaen, J.A., Farole, T., Nishiuchi, T., Battaile, W.G., Van Doorn, R., Saez, J.S., Hollweg, C.H., Cirera, X., Mogollon, M.P., Dowdall, G.F.I., Onder, H., 2016. *Kenya—Country economic memorandum: from economic growth to jobs and shared prosperity* (No. 103822). World Bank, Washington DC.

Heyer, A., King, M., 2015. Introduction, in: Heyer, A., King, M. (Eds.), *Kenya's Financial Transformation in the 21st Century*. FSD Kenya, Nairobi, Kenya, pp. 1–14.

Honohan, P., Beck, T., 2007. *Making Finance Work for Africa*. World Bank, Washington DC.

IMF, 2018. *Financial Soundness Indicators Database*. IMF, Washington, DC.

Irungu, G., 2015. Central Bank, IMF to step up cross-border banks supervision. *Business Daily Africa*.

Johnson, S., Arnold, S., 2012. Inclusive financial markets: Is transformation under way in Kenya? *Development Policy Review* 30, 719–48. https://doi.org/10.1111/j.1467-7679.2012.00596.x.

Jones, E., Zeitz, A.O., 2017. The limits of globalizing Basel banking standards. *Journal of Financial Regulation* 3, 89–124.

KIPPRA, 2016. *Kenya Economic Report 2016: Fiscal Decentralization in Support of Devolution*. Kenya Institute for Public Policy Research and Analysis (KIPPRA), Nairobi, Kenya.

Marchettini, D., Mecagni, M., Maino, R., 2015. *Evolving banking trends in Sub-Saharan Africa: Key features and challenges* (No. 15/8). IMF African Departmental Paper.

Muluka, B., Okello, R., Orlale, D., 2012. *Beyond the Shadow of My Dreams—Martin Oduor-Otieno—A Biography*. MvuleAfrica Publishers, Nairobi.

Murunga, G.R., Nasong'o, S.W., 2006. Bent on self-destruction: The Kibaki regime in Kenya. *Journal of Contemporary African Studies* 24, 1–28. https://doi.org/10.1080/02589000500513713.

Mwaniki, C., 2017. Nairobi finance hub closer to reality as Uhuru signs law. *Business Daily Africa*.

Mwega, F.M., 2014. *Financial regulation in Kenya: Balancing inclusive growth with financial stability* (No. Working paper 407). ODI.

Ndung'u, N., 2017. *Practitioner's insight: M-Pesa, a success story of digital financial inclusion*. Blavatnik School of Government, Oxford.

Ndung'u, N.S., Ngugi, R.W., 1999. Adjustment and liberalization in Kenya: The financial and foreign exchange markets. *Journal of International Development* 11, 465–91.

Ngugi, B., 2016. Moody's says CBK lacks capacity to handle new crisis. *Business Daily Africa*.

Polity IV, 2014. *PolityProject*. Center for Systemic Peace.

Republic of Kenya, 2003. *Kenya: Economic recovery strategy for wealth and employment creation, 2003-2007*. Ministry of Planning and National Development, Government of Kenya, Kenya.

Republic of Kenya, 2007. *Kenya Vision 2030 (Popular Version)*. Vision 2030, Nairobi.

Republic of Kenya, 2012. *Budget statement for the fiscal year 2012/2013 (1st July-30th June)*, Ministry of Planning and National Development, Government of Kenya, Nairobi, Kenya.

Republic of Kenya, 2013. *Financial services 2013-2017: Kenya Vision 2030*. Vision 2030, Nairobi.

Rotich, H., 2016. Centre key in making Nairobi a regional hub. *Business Daily Africa*.

Some, K., Ngirachu, J., 2017. How plan to kick out CBK boss failed. *Daily Nation*.

Upadhyaya, R., 2011. *Analyzing the sources and impact of segmentation in the banking sector: A case study of Kenya*. Department of Economics School of Oriental and African Studies (SOAS), University of London.

Upadhyaya, R., Johnson, S., 2015. Evolution of Kenya's banking sector 2000-2012, in: Heyer, A., King, M. (Eds.), *Kenya's Financial Transformation in the 21st Century*. FSD Kenya, Nairobi, Kenya, pp. 15-61.

Wakiaga, P., 2015. Kenya launches ambitious plan for industrial transformation. *The East African*.

Waris, A., 2014. *The creation of international financial centres in Africa: The case of Kenya*. U4 Anti-Corruption Resource Centre, CMI, Bergen, Norway.

World Bank, 2013. *Kenya—Financial and Legal Sector Technical Assistance Project* (No. ICR2726). The World Bank.

World Bank, 2017. *World Development Indicators*. World Bank, Washington, DC.

World Bank, 2018. *Global financial development database* [WWW Document]. URL https://datacatalog.worldbank.org/dataset/global-financial-development (accessed 24.11.18).

10

Bolivia

Pulling in Two Directions: The Developmental State and Basel Standards

Peter Knaack

Introduction

Bolivia had plans for one of the most ambitious implementations of Basel standards among lower-middle-income countries around the world. A novel financial services law promulgated in 2013 established the legal framework for a wholesale adoption of Basel II, including all advanced internal model-based components, and elements of Basel III. Among our case studies, Pakistan is the only other country where the regulator has taken such an ambitious approach. It is puzzling to see such a wholehearted embrace of Basel standards by a left-wing government that follows a heterodox approach to economic policymaking. Domestically oriented and opposed to the neoliberal stance of its predecessors, the current administration espouses a developmental state model that employs quantitative lending targets and interest rate caps to promote economic growth and financial inclusion. Why would a government want to combine such financial interventionism with such an ambitious plan to adopt Basel standards?

Building on archival research and interviews with twenty-six regulators, bankers, politicians, and financial experts in Bolivia, this chapter shows that Bolivia's case is an instance of regulator-driven convergence on Basel standards. Bolivia's financial regulatory agency is embedded in transnational technocratic networks with regulators in the region and in advanced Basel member jurisdictions, an institutional environment that fosters peer learning and emulation. Bolivian regulators regard Basel as the gold standard in prudential regulation, and they played an important role in drafting the law. As the draft law changed hands from regulators to politicians, interventionist policy instruments were grafted onto the prudential regulatory framework. The result is a rather unique combination of measures that aim to achieve two different policy goals: financial stability and inclusive growth. The latter is not a priority for regulators from the rich jurisdictions that dominate the Basel Committee, but it is an essential prerogative for developing countries around the world. Bolivia's policy innovation—whether

Peter Knaack, *Bolivia: Pulling in Two Directions—The Developmental State and Basel Standards* In: *The Political Economy of Bank Regulation in Developing Countries: Risk and Reputation.* Edited by: Emily Jones, Oxford University Press (2020). © Oxford University Press. DOI: 10.1093/oso/9780198841999.003.0010

deliberate or not—therefore merits attention by regulators in other countries that seek to chart a path towards financial sector development that delivers on both resilience to economic shocks and inclusive growth.

At the same time, this study finds a significant implementation gap as only a small subset of Basel II and III components is currently in force. This gap can be attributed to regulatory capacity constraints and a lack of demand for the more complex Basel components by market actors and the government. This chapter also shows that the process of policy innovation underlying the new law has not occurred without friction. The tension between politicians and technocrats in the policymaking process led to unintended consequences that may be detrimental to financial inclusion and financial stability in the future.

This introduction is followed by a description of the key features of Bolivia's political and economic system that provide the background for the development of the new Financial Services Law (FSL). The next section identifies the current state of Basel standards adoption and implementation in Bolivia. The fourth section presents an analysis of the political economy of Basel adoption in the country, highlighting in particular the relationships between a transnationally embedded regulator, a government focused on state-led domestic development, and a banking sector with few international incentives for Basel adoption. The concluding section derives lessons learned from the case study.

Political economy context: evolution of Bolivia's banking sector

Shaken by a financial crisis and political turmoil at the beginning of the twenty-first century, the Bolivian economy has experienced a remarkable period of stability, sustained growth, and significant improvement of social indicators over the last decade. GDP growth has averaged around 5 per cent per year since 2006, and GDP per capita has doubled to over $3000 in current dollar terms (ca. $7000 PPP; see Table 10.1). During this period, both the poverty rate and income inequality have fallen. This is especially noteworthy in a country where elite cohesion has historically constrained the capacity of the state to extract and redistribute wealth (Fairfield, 2015).

Like many other lower-middle-income countries, Bolivia's financial services sector is bank-dominated. Few private companies are listed on domestic securities markets, and local exchanges serve as venues for the issuance of debt rather than equity (S&P Global Ratings, 2016). Public companies are the main issuers of securities, and domestic pension funds are the dominant actors on the buy side.

The banking sector is vibrant, and market concentration is not high (see Figure 10.1). About a dozen universal banks manage close to 70 per cent of deposits and 60 per cent of loans in Bolivia. Three banks that cater specifically to small and medium enterprises (SMEs) account for a further 5 per cent of the

Table 10.1 Bolivia: key indicators

Bolivia	
GDP per capita (current US$, 2017):	3,393
Bank assets (current US$):	18.6 bn
Bank assets (% of GDP):	54.9
Stock market capitalization (% of GDP, 2012):	15.9
Credit allocation to private sector (% of GDP):	64
Credit allocation to government (% of GDP):	0.9
Polity IV score:	7

Note: All data is from 2016 unless otherwise indicated.

Source: FSI Database, IMF (2018); GDI Database, World Bank (2017); Polity IV (2014)

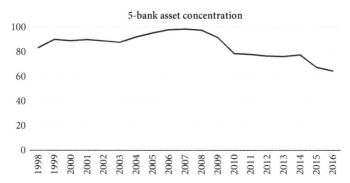

Figure 10.1 Bolivia: banking sector concentration (asset share of the five biggest banks).
Source: World Bank, Global Financial Development Database

market share. The rest of the financial services sector includes close to one hundred small-scale cooperatives and development finance institutions that tend to specialize in microfinance.

The only state-owned commercial bank, Banco Union, has grown at high speed, expanding its loan portfolio by an average rate of 34 per cent per year during 2007–13. The bank operates on a lower net interest margin and lower profitability than its private competitors. It has grown to become Bolivia's second-largest bank with a 10 per cent market share (Moody's Global Credit Research, 2013). Foreign banks play a very limited role, as the overwhelming majority of Bolivia's banking sector is domestic-owned (see Figure 10.2). One of the three foreign-owned banks is part of a private banking conglomerate headquartered in neighbouring Peru. The other two are subsidiaries of state-owned Brazilian and Argentine banks, with a very small market share.

Commodities represent four fifths of Bolivia's exports, and the super-cycle of the early 2000s has produced a windfall for private agriculture business, the state-owned hydrocarbon sector, small-scale mining cooperatives, and others.

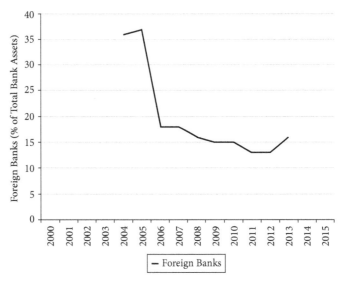

Figure 10.2 Bolivia: foreign bank assets (% of total bank assets).
Source: Claessens and Van Horen (2014)

Supported by macroeconomic stability and the commodities boom, Bolivia's financial system expanded massively in recent years, with credit growth rates of 18 per cent per annum from 2008 to 2014 (S&P Global Ratings, 2016). The favourable economic context allowed banks to maintain capital buffers comfortably above regulatory limits and write off sour loans from the financial crisis at the beginning of the century (Figure 10.3).

Moreover, the last decade was a period of outstanding profitability for Bolivia's banks, with return on equity peaking at over 21 per cent in 2007, and remaining high throughout the global financial crisis (GFC) (Figure 10.4).

The election of Evo Morales and his Movement for Socialism Party in 2005 marked the end of a long neoliberal phase in the Bolivian political economy. The first indigenous head of state in a majority-indigenous country, Morales set out to reduce dependence on the Bretton Woods Institutions, implement redistributionist economic policies, and forge economic and political ties with fellow left-wing governments in the region, in particular Hugo Chavez's Venezuela. The economic outlook of the Morales administration is much more domestically oriented than that of its predecessors. Rather than seeking to attract foreign investment, the new government increased the role of the state in the economy. Within months of assuming office, Morales nationalized the country's hydrocarbon sector, forcing resident multinationals into renegotiations of assets and contracts with the state.

Morales' rise to power coincided with the beginning of the commodities super-cycle. The favourable global environment provided the government with the opportunity to dramatically increase social spending while implementing a

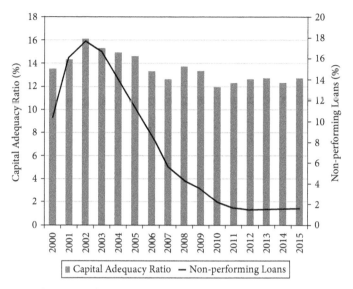

Figure 10.3 Bolivia: capital adequacy ratios (CAR) and non-performing loans (NPLs).
Source: International Monetary Fund (IMF)

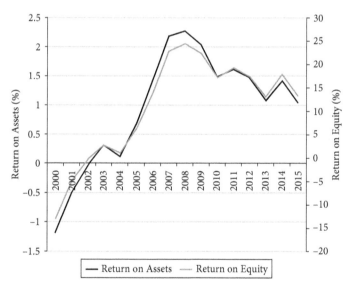

Figure 10.4 Bolivia: rates of return on assets (RoA) and equity (RoE).
Source: Bankscope and Orbis Bank Focus, Bureau van Dijk (2018)

prudent macroeconomic policy, which combined balanced budgets, a stable exchange rate, growing foreign exchange reserves, and low inflation. The Bolivian economy has remained remarkably stable to date, weathering the GFC and the precipitous fall of commodity prices in recent years while many neighbouring countries have fallen into recession.

Private Bolivian banks have been immensely profitable over the last decade, but relations with the governing elite are tense. This is because the government has issued a series of interventionist financial policies to channel some of the sector's profits towards social purposes. In 2012, it imposed an additional 12.5 per cent income tax on financial entities whose returns on equity exceeded 13.0 per cent. In addition, all banks have to pay 6 per cent of pre-tax profits into a guarantee fund destined for social purposes. Finally, Bolivia's financial regulator issued a rule in December 2015 that requires all banks to retain 50 per cent of net profits as a capital buffer. In response, private banks complained about the 'stigmatisation of profits', without much of a result (ASOBAN, 2015).

Bolivia's financial regulator prides itself on its relatively high degree of professional sophistication. Currently headed by a former Morales cabinet minister, the regulatory agency is clearly aligned with the financial policies of the government, but it self-identifies and operates as a technocratic organization of considerable independence.

One distinguishing feature of Bolivia's banking system is the breadth of its financial market. With microfinance institutions at the top of world rankings and significant increases in financial access despite low population density and difficult geography, Bolivia is at the forefront of a global movement towards financial inclusion (Ekka et al., 2010). Microfinance entities provide over 30 per cent of total credit in the country, and the number of borrowers grew by 70 per cent in the period of 2008–15. The microfinance sector operates within the perimeter of prudential supervision, and non-performing loan ratios are as low as those of the banking sector more broadly. Moreover, Bolivian microfinance institutions have made significant efficiency gains that allowed them to lower average interest rates from 65 per cent in 1992 to just below 20 per cent in 2015 (Ekka et al., 2010; Heng, 2015; McGuire et al., 1998).

In sum, Bolivia's financial sector has experienced a period of sustained growth in a stable macroeconomic environment that has allowed banks to clean up their balance sheets and make substantial profits. In this favourable environment, the government has seized the opportunity to gear the financial services sector towards a more pronounced social purpose, albeit with some unintended consequences. Both the governing elite and market actors tend to be domestically oriented, and foreign public and private actors play a rather subdued role in the Bolivian political economy.

Bolivia's implementation of Basel banking standards

Bolivia's regulator had plans for one of the most ambitious Basel implementation strategies among lower-middle-income countries around the world. The new FSL of 2013 provided the legal framework for a wholesale adoption of Basel II and even parts of Basel III. According to the law, Bolivia has adopted all ten components of Basel II and two out of eight of the Basel III components. Yet only a small subset of these Basel rules is currently in force.

In the 1990s and 2000s, Bolivia's banking system was subject to the Banking and Financial Entities Law. Issued in 1993 and modified in 2001, the law incorporated capital requirements and risk-weighting methods based on Basel I, and required banks to hold higher levels of capital than the international standards require. Bolivia has been an over-complier with Basel standards, in that its prudential rules require banks to hold Tier 1 capital equivalent to 7 per cent of risk-weighted assets, and an additional 3 per cent of Tier 2 capital.

Supervision of the Bolivian financial system was under the purview of the Superintendencia de Bancos y Entidades Financieras until 2009. Like many regulatory agencies in Latin America, the Superintendency featured a high degree of organizational autonomy, a salient professional identity, and strong links to technocratic peers abroad (Jordana, 2011). Only one year after Basel II was finalized, the Superintendencia issued the rules to implement the Basel II standardised approach to credit risk (SBEF, 2005). Many organizational characteristics of the Superintendencia were carried over to its successor agency, the Autoridad de Supervisión del Sistema Financiero (ASFI).

Bolivia's financial supervisors received a positive assessment from international financial institutions. In the 2011 Financial Sector Assessment Program (FSAP), the last one undertaken to date, the IMF and World Bank commended Bolivian authorities for significant improvement in financial supervision. Bolivia was judged to be compliant or largely compliant with nineteen out of twenty-five Basel Core Principles, including key aspects such as capital adequacy and provisioning. The IMF and the World Bank even suggested that the supervisor had gone too far in financial sector transparency, and recommended easing reporting requirements for small financial institutions in order to reduce their administrative burden. On the other hand, the international authorities noted deficiencies in anti-money laundering rules and urged ASFI to move towards a risk-based approach to financial supervision, taking into account market, operational, and interest rate risk, among others (IMF and World Bank, 2012).

The FSL of 2013 incorporated many of the FSAP recommendations. It established the legal framework for the regulation of target markets and operational risk. Moreover, the law gave banks permission to use both the standard and the internal ratings-based approaches for the calculation of credit, market, and operational risk (Estado Plurinacional de Bolivia, 2013a, para. 35f). Banks are free to develop internal rating models, but must submit them to the ASFI for approval. The new law maintained the previous requirements of 7 per cent Tier 1 and an additional 3 per cent Tier 2 capital, but it implemented a stricter definition of capital in line with the new Basel III standards. Banks are required to maintain a 10 per cent capital adequacy ratio as mentioned above, but the Executive branch has the authority to increase capital requirements 'in line with official recommendations of the Basel Committee' (Estado Plurinacional de Bolivia, 2013a, para. 417). In addition, the ASFI can apply a conservation buffer of up to 2 per cent at its discretion, bringing the total capital requirement to a maximum of 12 per cent of risk-weighted assets. This capital buffer can be used as a counter-cyclical measure by the regulator—even though it does not follow the technical prescriptions of the Basel Committee, it is designed to serve the macroprudential purpose associated with the counter-cyclical buffer of Basel III. In fact, counter-cyclical loan-loss provisioning rules have been in place since 2008, pre-dating the latest Basel Accord (S&P Global Ratings, 2016). While the new law did not incorporate Basel III liquidity ratios, it carried over pre-existing requirements and obliges banks to provide the regulator with evidence that 'adequate' liquidity buffers are maintained. In sum, other than a modified version of a counter-cyclical buffer and a stricter definition of capital, the law did not adopt any components of Basel III.

Regarding prudential supervision (Pillar 2), the IMF and the World Bank commended Bolivia in 2011 for improving risk supervision with a new inspection manual for on-site inspections. The ASFI also counts on an off-site information sharing system that obliges banks to submit data for ongoing surveillance. Even though Bolivia's supervisory system is compliant with most Basel Core Principles, it is unclear to what extent ASFI staff have the capacity to validate the internal capital allocation techniques of supervised banks in line with Basel II and III. All universal banks are audited and publicly listed, but the small scale and limited range of actors in Bolivia's stock market may limit the effectiveness of market discipline (Pillar 3) (Table 10.2).

Somewhat unusually, the FSL stipulates the exact risk weights and capital requirements for credit risk, rather than leaving the elaboration of such rules to the regulator. While risk weights for most asset classes would meet Basel II SA equivalence criteria, credit to SMEs and microcredits are subject to more lenient risk weights of 50–75 per cent, depending on 'payment capacity' to be determined

Table 10.2 Bolivia: adoption of Basel standards

Basel component	Adoption	Implementation
Basel I	Banking and Financial Entities Law 1993	1993
Basel II	Credit risk SA—Circular 492/2005 Credit, market, and operational risk: SA and advanced approaches—FSL 2013 (10/10 components)	Credit risk SA—2005 Market risk, operational risk SA—no rules issued Advanced approaches—no rules issued
Basel III	Definition of capital, counter-cyclical buffer—FSL 2013 (2/8 components)	Rules for both components in force since 2013

by the regulator (AESA Ratings, 2013; Estado Plurinacional de Bolivia, 2013a, para. 418). Additional measures to enhance financial stability include the establishment of a deposit insurance scheme, a credit registry, enhanced anti-money-laundering rules, and new financial consumer protection provisions. Therefore, the FSL broadly represents an ambitious adoption of Basel II, and a selective adoption of Basel III rules.

The law, however, does not represent a coherent move towards the kind of strictly regulated market-based financial system that Basel Committee best practices envision. Instead, the FSL contains a series of policies that pull in the opposite direction. In order to steer the financial system towards inclusive growth, it stipulates several interventionist measures. The law promotes financing of so-called 'productive sectors', including agriculture, mining, construction, and manufacturing—but not commerce. Banks have to dedicate a percentage of their credit portfolio (currently 50–60 per cent) to productive sectors and social housing. Moreover, credit to these sectors is subject to interest rate caps, currently 6 per cent for large, 7 per cent for small, and 11.5 per cent for micro-enterprises. Deposit rates are also subject to interest rate caps (Estado Plurinacional de Bolivia, 2014, 2013b). Furthermore, the law obliges banks to channel a portion of profits towards social purposes that are to be specified by decree. Currently, banks are required to direct 6 per cent of pre-tax profits to a so-called guarantee fund that is designed to complement or replace collateral for loans in productive sectors or social housing. Thus, borrowers in these sectors have the opportunity to take out a loan without a down-payment or pledging collateral if they qualify.

The combination of Basel-compliant prudential standards and interventionist policies in the FSL can be interpreted in two ways. It could be seen as building on the recognition that classic risk management tends to constrain financial inclusion and growth prospects in the real economy. Banks that exclusively follow prudential goals have an incentive to lend to big firms with large collateral and buy government debt, rather than providing credit for riskier market segments such as SMEs and lower-income households. Thus, only a combination of both prudential and social objectives could move financial intermediaries towards the financial possibility frontier (IMF, 2012), achieving greater financial depth, reach, and breadth while respecting the limits of financial sustainability (Yujra, 2016). A second interpretation is that financial stability and inclusive growth are largely incompatible goals, and their incorporation into the same law merely reflects the bounded rationality of lawmakers.

Even though the FSL formally adopts all Basel II and some Basel III components, implementation is much less ambitious. As of mid-2017, ASFI has not issued capital requirement guidelines for market and operational risk. All banks currently use the standard approach for measuring credit risk. None has submitted internal risk-based models for regulatory approval, and only a few large banks have even considered taking steps in this direction. Thus, while the legal

248 THE POLITICAL ECONOMY OF BANK REGULATION

framework is in place for the more sophisticated components of Basel standards, the implementation of these components is much more limited to date.

The political economy of Basel implementation in Bolivia

What explains Bolivia's embrace of Basel II and III standards in the context of its developmental state and domestically oriented banking sector? This section argues that the Bolivian case is an instance of regulator-driven Basel adoption. It shows that financial regulators played a key role in this process, while the domestically oriented government provided support merely for instrumental reasons. Market actors were ambivalent at most. Outward-oriented and involved in transnational technocratic networks, Bolivian regulators have championed the incorporation of Basel II and III into the FSL. In particular, financial regulators' direct involvement in drafting the law paved the way for the adoption of the more advanced components of Basel standards. The gap between formal Basel adoption and implementation can in turn be attributed to a combination of regulatory capacity constraints and a lack of demand both from the banking sector and the government.

However, rather than merely copying Basel provisions off the shelf, the FSL represents an innovative approach that seeks to combine prudential regulation on the one hand and state interventionism on the other, in order to foster productive development and financial inclusion. The combination of these two goals under the umbrella of development-oriented financial regulation is clearly not a priority for the Basel Committee, but it may serve as a model for the adoption of banking standards in other low- and lower-middle-income countries. However, this section also shows that regulatory practice in the wake of the promulgation of the FSL has produced unintended consequences for financial inclusion. It argues that this phenomenon is a consequence of the tension between technocrats and politicians in policy implementation, even though it is not directly related to the Basel standards themselves.

In the decades before Morales' Movement for Socialism came to power, Bolivia's governing elite shared a neoliberal outlook on economic governance, privatizing state-owned companies and seeking to generate a market-friendly regulatory environment. Several of the major banks were owned by the families that also controlled large shares of Bolivia's agribusiness, and the role of the banking sector in general was to provide financial services for the dominant domestic private commodities producers. The governing elite was thus not outward-oriented in terms of its ambitions to establish Bolivia as a regional financial centre, but it tended to follow the policy recipes written in Washington, London, and Brussels at the time.

This changed drastically when Evo Morales won the national elections in 2005. A major achievement of his government was the drafting of a new constitution in 2008/9. It enshrines the rights of the indigenous people by declaring Bolivia a pluri-national state, and it lays the foundations for a more interventionist role of the state in the economy. Much legislative action in recent years was driven by the need to update Bolivia's laws in order to bring them in line with the philosophy underlying its new constitution. Among them, the FSL of 2013 presents significant changes from its predecessor. It emphasizes the social role of financial services in the country, including universal access and support for integral development. The role of the state is that of the 'rector of the financial system', an entity that participates actively and directly in the design and implementation of measures to improve and promote financing within the productive sector, in order to support productive transformation, employment creation, and equitable income distribution (Estado Plurinacional de Bolivia, 2013a, paras. 7, 94).

It is puzzling that a government with a heterodox economic outlook and a clear domestic orientation would be a major champion of Basel standards. In fact, we are not aware of any other jurisdiction that combines ambitious Basel adoption and financial interventionism to the extent Bolivia does.

In line with what would be expected from a left-wing government, the Morales administration did regard Basel standards as a market-indulging policy recipe of neoliberal extraction, at least initially. When the new government took power in January 2006, the Superintendency had just implemented the novel Basel II Standard Approach to credit risk. Moreover, the agency had created an office dedicated to full Basel II implementation, building regulatory capacity in order to assess and authorize the use of internal ratings-based models in the near future. However, interview partners recall that such implementation efforts stalled as soon as the Morales government took power.[1]

In spite of the political U-turn that the rise of Evo Morales engendered, the Superintendency remained outward-oriented. The agency did not take any further steps towards Basel II implementation, but it continued to engage with regulators abroad in consultation and technical training. Bolivia's financial regulator is a member of the Latin American Banking Supervisory network, ASBA. Crucially, ASBA is a hemispheric rather than a regional organization, and its forty-one member agencies include the Federal Reserve, the Federal Deposit Insurance Corporation (FDIC), the Office of the Comptroller of the Currency (OCC) (all US agencies), and the Central Bank of Spain. These regulatory agencies from the US and Spain host frequent workshops under the ASBA Continental Training Program, which brings together banking regulators for seminars on topics such

---

[1] Interviews with regulators (former and current), La Paz, 15 and 22 March 2017.

as risk and liquidity management, banking resolution, stress testing, and Pillar II supervisory practices (ASBA, 2017).

Technocratic networks that involve US-trained experts have played an important role throughout modern Latin American history. In the 1920s, a commission led by Princeton Economist Edwin Kemmerer advised several Andean countries on financial institution reform. Bolivia is among the 'Kemmerized countries', and traces of the 'money doctor's' reforms can still be found today (Drake, 1989). From the 1970s onwards, the 'Chicago Boys' and other technocratic networks played a crucial role in designing and implementing neoliberal reforms in several Latin American countries, in addition to and beyond the structural adjustment programmes of the World Bank and the IMF (Centeno and Silva, 1998; Teichman, 2001).

In the world of financial regulation, ASBA has arguably played an important role in dispensing technical knowledge and enthusiasm for Basel standards across Latin America. When the Basel-based Financial Stability Institute conducted a survey in July 2004, only a month after the finalization of Basel II, regulators in 70 per cent of respondent countries expressed their willingness to implement the new standard domestically within three to five years (FSI, 2004).

Even though the Morales administration did not champion Basel II implementation, the Superintendency continued to engage in technical upgrades, following international best practices. An ASBA report from 2008 shows, for example, that Bolivia is a leading jurisdiction in credit risk management in the region, having developed an advanced portfolio classification scheme that lays the foundation for internal ratings-based approaches (ASBA, 2008, p. 17f).

The organizational shift from the Superintendency to the ASFI as the central financial authority in 2009 is not associated with significant changes to the professional identity and transnational embeddedness of regulators in Bolivia. Interview partners recall that at the height of the GFC in 2009, ASFI leadership called the validity of Basel standards into question.[2] But regulators soon returned to a pro-Basel stance, and the 2011 FSAP commended the ASFI for 'aligning its regulatory and supervisory framework with international standards' (IMF and World Bank, 2012, p. 21).

In 2011, Bolivia's Ministry of the Economy and Public Finances decided to develop a new law to govern the financial services sector in congruence with the novel constitution. It awarded a consultancy for drafting the outlines of the new legal framework to a former top regulator with a career in the ASFI and the central bank. A technocrat by training rather than a politician, the consultant incorporated the entirety of the prudential regulatory provisions that make Bolivia a high adopter of Basel II and Basel III today. His decision was driven

---

[2] Interview with former regulator, La Paz, 13 March 2017.

less by strategic considerations of signalling to foreign investors or domestic stakeholders and more by a genuine conviction that Basel banking standards represent the best approach to safeguarding a banking system, whether in advanced or developing economies.[3] A Bolivian regulator interviewee employed a nautical metaphor to express this consensus among his peers, asserting that 'for us regulators Basel is the North'.[4]

The law retains many elements of the draft written by the consultant regulator. In particular, all references to Basel and the unusual stipulation of risk weights remained unchanged. Interview partners in Bolivia advanced different reasons for this phenomenon. Some argued that regulatory provisions stayed intact because legislators and ministerial staff lack the technical capacity to fully understand them.[5]

Other respondents asserted that the government welcomed the adoption of sophisticated Basel elements because it would signal a commitment to financial stability. Key officials in the Morales administration arguably felt the need to engage in such signalling because several stakeholders openly criticized the interventionist measures contained in the FSL.[6] As indicated in the section above, the law includes provisions for interest rate caps and directed lending to certain sectors of the economy—measures that are uncommon in market economies. Economic actors from within the country and abroad voiced their scepticism. For example, a global credit ratings agency stated that 'the regulator's focus has shifted somewhat to support social and developmental policies rather than ensuring the financial system's stability' (S&P Global Ratings, 2016, p. 9). For the same reasons, another ratings agency changed the outlook for the Bolivian banking system to negative (Mendoza, 2014). Even the Confederation of Private Entrepreneurs of Bolivia, some of whose members do benefit from the above measures, criticized the law for leading to inefficient capital allocation, concentration risk, and financial fragility (CEPB, 2013).

The relationship between Bolivia's government and the Bretton Woods Institutions has been tense in recent years. Along with several of his peers in the region, President Morales has denounced the IMF in particular for imposing a neoliberal agenda onto developing countries. For years, Bolivian authorities have publicly rejected IMF concerns and any criticism of domestic economic policies. Article IV Consultations continue in all regularity but appear to be rather acrimonious exercises. In the latest such consultation, the Bolivian government

---

[3] Interview with former regulator, La Paz, 20 March 2017.
[4] Interview with former regulator, La Paz, 20 March 2017.
[5] Interviews with former regulators and private sector representatives, La Paz, 13 and 20 March 2017, and via Skype, 30 October 2017.
[6] Interviews with current and former government officials, current regulators, La Paz, 17 and 22 March 2017, and via Skype, 2 and 11 April 2017.

'questioned if the IMF should make policy recommendations for Bolivia' at all (IMF, 2016, p. 19).

In turn, the World Bank and the IMF have expressed concerns regarding the interventionist measures of the FSL (World Bank, 2011). The IMF in particular has suggested Bolivia's prudential and development policies are a zero-sum game where state intervention for social purposes is creating market distortions that inevitably contribute to financial fragility (IMF, 2016, 2015, 2014). The last FSAP of 2011 encouraged Bolivian financial authorities to strengthen risk-based supervision, but the report refrained from recommending the adoption of Basel II or III provisions (IMF and World Bank, 2012). However, both the World Bank and the IMF have welcomed the prudential regulatory provisions of the new law (Heng, 2015).

Even though foreign and even domestic investors have played a subdued role in Bolivia's political economy to date, the government was not completely oblivious to their concerns. After governing Bolivia for almost a decade and successfully steering the country through the GFC, the Morales administration had established a track record that made it much less vulnerable to shifts in investor sentiment than Brazil's Luiz Inácio Lula da Silva upon taking office in 2003, for example. Nevertheless, the imprimatur of Basel may have helped to allay concerns that the Morales administration would embark on a path of financial populism with the FSL.

Market actors have been neither champions nor opponents of the Basel components that are currently in force. Bolivia's financial services sector is domestically oriented and not concerned with the reputational benefits of a regulatory upgrade to the more complex elements of Basel II and III. Conversations with banks' risk managers reveal that Bolivia's banks do not associate an upgrade to internal ratings-based models with higher profitability or any other competitive advantage.[7] Moreover, they do not keep separate loan and trading books. In interviews, regulators refer to such low complexity of bank operations as the main reason why Basel II rules on market risk do not need to be written in yet.[8] Adjustment costs to the prudential regulatory provisions of the FSL have been negligible to date. The new law retains the pre-existing capital adequacy ratio requirement of 10 per cent (above Basel standards). It adopts the stringent capital definition of Basel III, but this change barely affects banks because most of their Tier 1 capital is composed of equity and retained earnings (Galindo et al., 2011). Domestic banks did voice opposition to the interventionist elements of the FSL, but their weak political position did not allow them to exert any significant influence in the development of the legal text.[9]

---

[7] Interviews with senior bank officials, La Paz, 14 and 23 March 2017.
[8] Interviews with regulators, La Paz, 21 March 2017.
[9] Interview with senior bank official, La Paz, 23 March, and government officials, La Paz, 14 March, and via Skype, 11 April 2017.

Foreign banks play a marginal role in the domestic market. Two of them are state-owned with headquarters in Brazil and Argentina, respectively. Their business model revolves around serving home country clients in their business in the neighbouring country, and neither has plans to expand towards a significant Bolivian customer base. Because they are headquartered in jurisdictions that are members of the Basel Committee, they are subject to consolidated supervision under Basel III. But again, Bolivia does not feature prominently in their banking business, and lobbying for Basel III implementation in the country would not significantly change their competitive position. Foreign banks have thus been indifferent towards Basel adoption in Bolivia, but it is noteworthy that they did not object to the interventionist measures of the FSL such as the interest rate caps and directed lending. During the period in which Bolivian lawmakers developed the FSL, both Argentina and Brazil were ruled by left-wing governments that shared a critical attitude vis-à-vis neoliberal policies and an affinity for a developmentalist economic model with the Morales administration. Unlike their domestic private peers, the state-owned foreign banks thus did not voice opposition to any element of the FSL.

Furthermore, a look at the balance sheet of Bolivian banks reveals that the sector is relatively self-contained. The large universal banks do not tend to rely on cross-border funding, and the banking sector as a whole is in a net creditor position (S&P Global Ratings, 2016). Foreign investors do play a role in the provision of capital for microfinance institutions, including NGOs. But the transparency and risk management expectations these actors bring to the table bear only a tenuous relationship with Basel banking standards, chiefly because of significant differences in risk management technology between commercial banks and microfinance institutions.

For decades, Bolivia's banking system was vulnerable to volatility in foreign capital markets because a large portion of both its deposits and loans were denominated in US dollars. Macroeconomic instability in general and the hyperinflationary period of the mid-1980s had undermined citizens' trust in the local currency. However, over the last decade financial authorities have instituted a series of policies to de-dollarize the financial sector. The central bank raised reserve requirements for dollar-denominated deposits by a factor of three. Furthermore, the de facto peg to the dollar from 2006 onwards, along with consistently low inflation rates, has boosted public confidence in the boliviano as a store of value. Consequently, the share of dollar-denominated deposits fell from 94 per cent in 2002 to 15.6 per cent by 2016, with dollar loans experiencing a fall from 97 per cent to 3 per cent in the same period (IMF, 2016; S&P Global Ratings, 2016).

Domestic regulators have played an important role in adopting foreign rules at home, a process Dolowitz and Marsh (2000) call policy transfer. Yet the FSL is not merely an instance of policy transfer by technocrats embedded in transnational regulatory networks. Rather, its peculiar grafting of interventionist policies on prudential regulatory provisions represents a departure from the conservative, prudential approach of Basel. Inherent in this policy innovation is the recognition that the Basel Committee has a mandate to maximize the resilience of the banking sector among its overwhelmingly high-income member jurisdictions, and little incentive to take low-income country prerogatives into account (BCBS, 2013; Jones and Knaack, 2019). In interviews, Bolivian regulators have confirmed that they do not expect Basel standards to foster inclusive financial development in their country.[10] For example, SME and lower-income households are key actors in economic development, yet their access to credit in developing countries is severely constrained. This is because they represent relatively high-risk clients, especially in countries with deficiencies in collateral markets and the rule of law. Under these conditions, it is prudent for banks to minimize their exposure to this market segment and focus on large companies and government securities instead. A policy framework that addresses this issue with interventionist measures, while safeguarding prudential supervision, can be understood as an innovative depart-ure from global best practices, rather than an incomplete policy transfer.

Even though legislators and ministerial officials did not alter Basel provisions, political involvement and modification led to unintended consequences in the application of the interventionist measures of the law. The lending quotas and inter-est rates set by the Executive branch have been effective in channelling bank loans to the so-called productive sector (Estado Plurinacional de Bolivia, 2014, 2013b). However, the majority of businesses in the Bolivian economy are small or even micro-enterprises in the commercial and services sector. In line with the law and the decrees that specify it, microcredit to such 'un-productive' sectors is discouraged by the lending quota and the interest rate caps that financial institutions must meet (Ekka et al., 2010; Heng, 2015; Moody's Global Credit Research, 2013) (Figure 10.5).

As a consequence, credit to SMEs has stagnated, and microcredit lenders have reduced their client base since 2015 (ASOBAN, 2017, 2015; ASOFIN, 2017; ICBE Data, 2014). This reduction in financial inclusion is at odds with a financial ser-vices law that is explicitly designed to 'promote integral development', 'facilitate universal access to financial services', and 'assure the continuity of the services offered' (Estado Plurinacional de Bolivia, 2013a, para. 4). In order to address the unintended consequences of this market intervention, regulators could adjust the current lending quotas and interest rate caps, at least in principle. The draft provi-sions of the FSL envisioned these parameters to be set by the central bank. Such decisions could thus be taken with a certain degree of isolation from the political process, according to technocratic principles. However, ministerial intervention in the development of the law transferred the authority to change these key prices to the newly created Financial Stability Council (FSC), an organ of high political

---

[10] Interview, current regulators, La Paz, 21 March 2017.

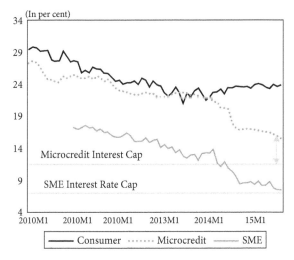

Figure 10.5 Bolivia: interest rate caps.
Source: Heng (2015)

visibility. Its decisions are subject to scrutiny by the population in ways that may be counter-productive. For example, a rise in the interest rate cap for microcredit to productive sectors from 11.5 per cent to 18 per cent may help sustain the business model of microfinance institutions and support financial inclusion, but could be interpreted by the opposition as a 'sell-out to the banks'. Even though the FSC can adjust rates and lending targets at each of its quarterly meetings, it has not changed them once in its two years of operation (Figure 10.6).

In sum, Basel adoption in Bolivia's FSL can be understood as a largely regulator-driven process. Market actors lack external incentives to champion any ambitious adoption of the Basel standards. Similarly, the country's governing elite are domestically oriented. They devised the FSL to implement interventionist financial policies that are designed to foster economic development and financial inclusion. Further, the government is no supporter of advanced Basel II and III implementation. Rather, and to the extent that they were actually capable of a full technical appraisal, lawmakers may have retained the more sophisticated Basel components in the legal text as a signal of prudential integrity to stakeholders who criticized the interventionist measures of the law. The divergence between the provisions of global banking standards in the FSL and the apathy of domestic actors has therefore created an implementation gap, which remains wide because of both demand and supply constraints: market actors show little need for the use of advanced risk models. Interview partners also pointed out that the ASFI currently lacks the regulatory capacity to assess and approve internal ratings-based models.[11]

---

[11] Interviews with former regulator and senior bank officials, La Paz, 13, 21, and 23 March 2017.

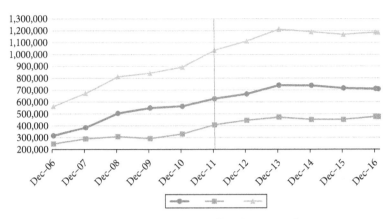

Figure 10.6 Bolivia: number of borrowers, small and microcredit institutions.

Note: ASOFIN: Association of Microfinance Entities (Asociación de Entidades Financieras Especializadas en Micro Finanzas de Bolivia); FINRURAL: Association of Development Finance Institutions (Asociación de Instituciones Financieras de Desarrollo)

Sources: ASFI, ASOFIN, FINRURAL

In its combination of prudential and interventionist measures, the Bolivian approach to financial regulation deviates from global 'best practices'. It incorporates the policy goal of inclusive financial development that is of utter relevance for developing countries but not for the Basel Committee. Some observers would doubt that Basel II and III are supportive of or even compatible with the financial policies of a developmental state. The Bolivian experiment seeks to chart a new path of combining both, which will inform this debate. There are early indications that the FSL entails unintended negative consequences for financial inclusion, but this outcome would be attributable to the institutional setup of interventionist policies, not the Basel standards.

Conclusion

The Bolivian case can be understood as an instance of regulator-driven convergence on international standards. The analysis highlights the active role of technocrats in international policy transfer. Even when banking regulators have no direct contact with the Basel Committee, they are embedded in transnational networks, updating their knowledge of global standards through conferences and technical training courses organized by regional organizations or Basel member agencies. This study also lends empirical support to the conjecture that a gap between de jure adoption and de facto implementation opens when Basel standards do not have domestic champions. As long as neither the government nor market actors see much benefit to incorporating the more sophisticated components of Basel II and III, implementation is likely to remain highly selective.

It would be a mistake, however, to interpret the gap between the number of Basel components in the legal framework and the ones in force as an instance of mock compliance. Walter (2008, p. 32f) states that mock compliance occurs when two conditions are met: signalling compliance and substantive non-compliance. In the Bolivian case, there is no evidence for substantial non-compliance with the standard approach to Basel II. The ASFI has shown no signs of regulatory forbearance to date, although the stringency of supervision, especially of state-owned Banco Union, certainly deserves the attention of analysts in the future.

Rather than mock compliance, Bolivia's implementation gap may be understood as a strategic device with two potential purposes. First, it could serve as a non-costly signal of regulatory stringency and sophistication. The reputational benefits of an ambitious adoption may materialize even when Basel II and III rules are not in force (yet). Second, an encompassing adoption of Basel II and III components may influence the relationship between the government and the regulatory agency. Because legal changes are cumbersome and subject to political negotiations, regulators may consider it advantageous to grant themselves considerable room for manoeuvre to implement individual Basel components as they see fit, without having to consult lawmakers.

Further research is needed to assess the plausibility and effectiveness of either strategy. In addition, more work is necessary to identify the conditions under which the prudential standards of Basel II and III are compatible with interventionist policies designed to promote inclusive financial development, as they appear to be in the Bolivian case to date.

References

AESA Ratings, 2013. *Proyecto de un nuevo marco regulatorio.*

ASBA, 2008. *Sound Management and Supervision Practices for Credit Risk in the Americas.*

ASBA, 2017. *Continental Training Program* [WWW Document]. URL http://asbasupervision.com/en/training/program (accessed 9.2.17).

ASOBAN, 2015. *Memoria 2015.*

ASOBAN, 2017. *Situacion de la Banca y la Economia* (Internal Document).

ASOFIN, 2017. *Impactos no deseados sobre los bancos que atienden a la micro y pequena empresa* (Internal Document).

BCBS, 2013. *Charter.* Bank for International Settlements, Basel.

Bureau van Dijk, 2018. *Bankscope and Orbis Bank Focus.*

Centeno, M.A., Silva, P. (Eds.), 1998. *The Politics of Expertise in Latin America*, 1998 edition. Palgrave Macmillan, New York.

CEPB, 2013. *Ley de Bancos: Propuestas y lineamientos.*

Claessens, S., Van Horen, N., 2014. Foreign banks: Trends and impact. *Journal of Money, Credit and Banking* 46, 295–326.

Dolowitz, D.P., Marsh, D., 2000. Learning from abroad: The role of policy transfer in contemporary policy-making. *Governance* 13, 5–23.

Drake, P.W., 1989. *The Money Doctor in the Andes: The Kemmerer Missions, 1923–1933.* Duke University Press, Durham, NC.

Ekka, R.K., Wenner, M.D., Campion, A., 2010. *Interest Rates and Implications for Microfinance in Latin America and the Caribbean.* Inter-American Development Bank.

Estado Plurinacional de Bolivia, 2013a. *Ley de Servicios Financieros No 393.*

Estado Plurinacional de Bolivia, 2013b. *Decreto Supremo No 1842.*

Estado Plurinacional de Bolivia, 2014. *Decreto Supremo No 2055.*

Fairfield, T., 2015. *Private Wealth and Public Revenue.* Cambridge University Press, Cambridge.

FSI, 2004. *The implementation of the new capital adequacy framework in Latin America.*

Galindo, A., Rojas-Suarez, L., del Valle M., 2011. *Capital requirements under Basel III in Latin America: The cases of Bolivia, Colombia, and Peru* (Policy Brief IDB-PB-137). Inter-American Development Bank.

Heng, D., 2015. *Impact of the New Financial Services Law in Bolivia on Financial Stability and Inclusion* (Working Paper No. 15/267). IMF.

ICBE Data, 2014. *IBCE : Regulación de tasas modifica en parte la calificación de 2 bancos.* IBCE.

IMF, 2012. *Enhancing Financial Sector Surveillance in Low-Income Countries: Financial Deepening and Macrostability* (IMF Policy Paper). IMF.

IMF, 2014. *Bolivia: Staff Report for the 2013 Article IV Consultation.*

IMF, 2015. *Bolivia: 2015 Article IV Consultation.*

IMF, 2016. *Bolivia: 2016 Article IV Consultation.*

IMF, 2018. *Financial Soundness Indicators Database.*

IMF, World Bank, 2012. *Bolivia—Financial sector assessment* (No. 72071). The World Bank.

Jones, E., Knaack, P., 2019. Global financial regulation: Shortcomings and reform options. *Global Policy* 10, 193–206. doi: 10.1111/1758-5899.12656.

Jordana, J., 2011. The institutional development of the Latin American regulatory state, in: Levi-Faur, D. (Ed.), *Handbook on the Politics of Regulation.* Edward Elgar, Cheltenham, pp. 156–70.

McGuire, P.B., Conroy, J.D., Thapa, G.B., 1998. *Getting the Framework Right: Policy and Regulation for Microfinance in Asia.* The Foundation for Development Cooperation [u.a.], Brisbane.

Mendoza, L., 2014. *Moody's alerta sobre riesgos normativos para la banca en Bolivia* [WWW Document]. eju.tv. URL http://eju.tv/2014/08/moodys-alerta-sobre-riesgos-normativos-para-la-banca-en-bolivia (accessed 11.12.18).

Moody's Global Credit Research, 2013. *Bolivia's financial reform: Increased regulation will hurt banks' profitability.*

Polity IV, 2014. *PolityProject.* Center for Systemic Peace.

S&P Global Ratings, 2016. *Banking Industry Country Risk Assessment: Plurinational State of Bolivia.*

SBEF, 2005. *Circular 492/2005.*

Teichman, J.A., 2001. *The Politics of Freeing Markets in Latin America: Chile, Argentina and Mexico*, 1st edition. The University of North Carolina Press, Chapel Hill, NC.

Walter, A., 2008. *Governing Finance: East Asia's Adoption of International Standards.* Cornell University Press, Ithaca, NY.

World Bank, 2011. *Bolivia Financial Sector Notes: Assessing the Sector's Potential Role in Fostering Rural Development and Growth of the Productive Sectors.*

World Bank, 2017. *World Development Indicators.* World Bank, Washington, DC.

Yujra, R., 2016. *Nueva visión de la gestión integral de riesgos: Más allá de la ortodoxia.* ASOFIN Boletin Mensual 161.

11

Nigeria

Catch 22: Navigating Basel Standards in Nigeria's Fragile Banking Sector

Florence Dafe

Introduction

If there is one word that has been used extensively since the mid-2000s to characterize Nigeria's banking sector, it is the term 'potential'. Financial industry experts, be they international consultants, financial journalists, or bankers, have hailed the size of Nigeria's banking sector, its international expansion, and the adoption of global standards like Basel II and IFRS. That said, there is broad agreement among both public authorities and financial industry experts that Nigeria's banking sector is far from realizing its potential. The banking sector has witnessed significant and extended periods of fragility since the 1990s; Nigeria's regulators have been slow to implement and enforce Basel standards and mock compliance has been an important feature of the engagement with Basel standards in Nigeria. What explains this gap between aspiration and reality on the ground, which is so characteristic of Nigeria's economy in general? This chapter explores why Nigeria's banking regulators, the Central Bank of Nigeria (CBN) and the National Deposit Insurance Corporation (NDIC), moved to adopt Basel I, II, and III but were slow to implement and enforce, and how this is related to the fragility in Nigeria's banking sector.

Two factors, namely conflicted preferences and the international-connectedness of regulators, help to explain Nigeria's engagement with Basel standards. The adoption and implementation of Basel II, which is the main focus of this chapter, has primarily been driven by regulators with strong links to international finance. The two CBN governors who most pushed for the adoption of Basel II—Joseph Odele Sanusi, who was in office from 1999 to 2004 and Sanusi Lamido Sanusi, who was in office from 2009 to 2014—had both had careers in the management of internationally active Nigerian banks before joining the CBN. For the former, Basel adoption was imperative for the international expansion of Nigerian banks. For the latter, Basel II was the best available practice to manage risks in the

Florence Dafe, *Nigeria: Catch 22—Navigating Basel Standards in Nigeria's Fragile Banking Sector* In: *The Political Economy of Bank Regulation in Developing Countries: Risk and Reputation.* Edited by: Emily Jones, Oxford University Press (2020). © Oxford University Press.DOI: 10.1093/oso/9780198841999.003.0011

Nigerian banking sector. Senior staff in CBN and NDIC, who attended training courses on Basel standards run by international consultants and foreign regulators like the US, considered Basel II the most appropriate set of regulatory standards to make Nigeria's large, internationalized banking sector more stable.

While Basel II adoption was not a salient issue among Nigeria's domestically oriented politicians, Nigeria's internationally oriented banks welcomed the implementation of Basel II, which began in 2013. These international banks consider Basel II an important means to enhance their competitiveness and signal soundness to markets, regulators, and their peers in the international and domestic arena. In addition, the banks hope that a later move from standardized approaches to advanced internal rating-based components will allow them to reduce their capital charges.

Given the support for the adoption of Basel II among Nigerian regulators and bankers, why the slow movement towards implementation and weak enforcement? The evidence presented in this chapter suggests that this is because Nigerian regulators have conflicting preferences. On the one hand, Nigerian regulators promote Basel II because they consider it the best available set of rules for Nigeria's large and internationally expanding banking sector. On the other hand, regulators are reluctant to move faster on implementation and enforcement because if they do, several fragile banks would have to be restructured, if not resolved, and could therefore no longer play their envisaged role in supporting economic development by providing employment and access to finance for the private sector. Nigerian regulators are concerned about the developmental costs of bank resolutions because the CBN has a formal mandate to support the country's economic development. In addition, bank interventions are politically difficult because Nigerian politicians, often lobbied by the banks, tend to oppose them, supposedly to ensure the banks' contribution to economic development. Reluctant enforcement of prudential regulation perpetuates, however, the weakness of a banking sector that is already fragile because of its exposure to a volatile oil sector. All this is, in the words of a financial sector expert, a catch-22 situation.[1] As mock compliance is driven by the conflicted preferences of regulators, it is a case of regulator-driven mock compliance.

The chapter is based on official documents by Nigerian authorities and international financial institutions (IFIs), local press reports, and twenty-three semi-structured interviews. The interviews were conducted with regulators, bankers, financial industry experts from the private sector, academia, the donor community, and IFIs in Abuja, Lagos, and London.

---

[1] Interview, financial industry expert, Lagos, 22 September 2017.

Large, international, and fragile: banking in Nigeria since the 1990s

Three features of Nigeria's resplendent and complex political economy seem to bear particular importance for developments in Nigeria's banking sector. First, the size of the economy. In 2012 Nigeria overtook South Africa as Africa's largest economy, not least because of significant growth in telecommunications, banking, and construction sectors. However, in 2016 Nigeria's per capita income was merely about 2500 US$. Thus, it falls into the World Bank's category of lower-middle-income countries (Table 11.1).

Second, oil has been at the centre of economic accumulation in Nigeria since the 1970s. While in 2013 oil only made up 13 per cent of GDP, it accounted for over 95 per cent of exports and three quarters of government revenue (IMF, 2017a). Because of oil-induced boom and bust cycles, oil dependence has been a continuous source of economic volatility and vulnerability. Another consequence of oil abundance is the limited reliance on IFIs like the World Bank and international donors more generally. For instance, official development assistance averaged a mere 0.5 per cent of GNI between 2010 and 2015, and Nigeria has not borrowed from the International Monetary Fund (IMF) since the 1980s. As a result, donors and IFIs do not hold sway in Nigeria. A former official concludes, for instance, that 'Nigeria had very few IMF programs and even when there was one, there was only little influence'.[2] Another important consequence of oil dependence is the central role of the state in the economy. Owing to the public ownership of oil and gas reserves, the state has access to significant amounts of oil revenues. As a result, businesses seek to either do business with the state or to benefit from public financial assistance, for instance in the form of subsidized credit.

Table 11.1 Nigeria: key indicators

Nigeria	
GDP per capita (current US$, 2017)	1969
Bank assets (current US$)	81.7 bn
Bank assets (% of GDP)	20.2
Stock market capitalization (% of GDP)	8.8
Credit allocation to private sector (% of GDP)	15.7
Credit allocation to government (% of GDP)	5.8
Polity IV score (2017)	7

Note: All data is from 2016 unless otherwise indicated.

Source: FSI Database, IMF (2018); GDI Database, World Bank (2017a); Polity IV (2014)

---

[2] Interview, former IFI official, Lagos, 8 September 2017.

The third important feature of Nigeria's political economy is that the state has used its resources and central position to intervene significantly in the economy. Activist policies have been employed to support the development and diversification of the economy as well as to redistribute oil rents to certain constituencies to foster political support.

The above features of Nigeria's political economy—size, oil-, and state-centred economic development—are epitomized by Nigeria's banking sector. Nigeria has, at least in absolute terms, the second largest banking sector in Sub-Saharan Africa, just behind South Africa. Both assets and profits accounted for about a quarter of the region's total in 2014 (EY, 2015).

The banking sector, which in 2017 consisted of twenty-two commercial banks and five investment banks (referred to as merchant banks), has other notable features. One is domestic ownership. Only four commercial banks are foreign-owned. Their headquarters are in South Africa, Togo, the United Kingdom, and the United States, respectively. In 2011, 75 per cent of commercial banking assets were held by domestic, privately owned banks (IMF, 2013a).

This highlights another characteristic, namely private ownership. Domestic, privately owned banks emerged in large numbers in the wake of Nigeria's financial sector liberalization, which was an element of Nigeria's Structural Adjustment Programme (SAP) which lasted from 1986 until 1992. By the early 1990s, the number of banks amounted to more than a hundred because of profitable business opportunities arising from arbitrage opportunities in money markets and parallel foreign exchange markets as well as from fraudulent activities such as pyramid schemes.[3] The number of banks only shrank because of bank failures in the 1990s, and the CBN's decision to increase the minimum capital requirement twenty-five-fold in 2004 in an effort to create larger and well-capitalized banks. The 2004 reform reduced the number of banks from eighty-nine to about twenty-five banks, all of which were privately owned. While three banks came under state-ownership in the wake of Nigeria's systemic banking crisis in 2009 to 2011, these banks have since been resolved. Government-ownership does, however, prevail in Nigeria's seven specialized development banks. These banks provide subsidized credit for segments of the economy which are considered a priority for development, such as small and medium enterprises (SMEs).

Nigeria's banks also stand out in the region through their international orientation. As Figure 11.1 shows, about a dozen Nigerian banks have major operations in Sub-Saharan African countries, with Nigerian subsidiaries holding more than 20–30 per cent of deposits in Benin, Gambia, and Sierra Leone (IMF, 2017b). In addition, some of the leading banks have opened subsidiaries and representative offices outside Africa, notably in the US, UK, and Dubai.

---

[3] For an excellent analysis of how the process of financial liberalization rendered the Nigerian banking sector the locus of rent-seeking see Lewis and Stein (1997).

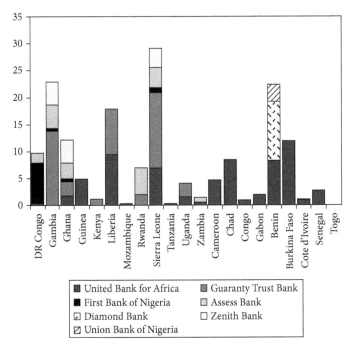

Figure 11.1 Nigeria: banks' share of deposits abroad, 2013 (%).
Source: IMF (2017a)

Where Nigeria's banking sector is lagging behind is the provision of access to finance to Nigeria's private sector. On average, bank credit to the private sector as a share of GDP amounted to about 14 per cent between 2011 and 2016, which is below the Sub-Saharan African average of 29 per cent (World Bank, 2017b) (see Figure 11.2). Lack of competition, as indicated by the fact that five banks held on average 60 per cent of banking assets between 2011 and 2015, might partly explain the limited lending. More important seems to be, however, that it is both profitable and safe to lend to the government.

Moreover, as Table 11.2 shows, a dominant share of bank credit is allocated to the oil sector, highlighting the dominance of oil in the economy. In sum, Nigeria's banking sector is suggestive of a negative relationship between oil abundance and development outcomes and thus of a resource curse in the financial sector.[4]

The centrality of oil has not only shaped lending patterns in Nigeria but also contributed considerably to the vulnerability and fragility of the banking sector. As in the case of Angola, oil dependence has been a source of financial distress. An important cause of Nigeria's systemic banking crisis of 2009 was that the banking sector had significant investments in the oil sector, which were negatively

---

[4] For empirical evidence on the resource curse in finance see Beck et al. (2011) and Bhattacharyya and Hodler (2014).

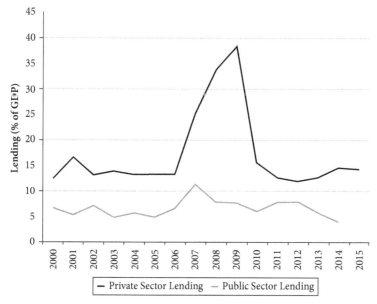

Figure 11.2 Nigeria: Public and private sector lending.
Source: World Bank (2017a)

Table 11.2 Nigeria: sectoral distribution of credit

Sector	June 2016		December 2016	
	₦ billion	Share of total (%)	₦ billion	Share of total (%)
Oil and gas	4511.34	28.78	4890.91	30.02
Manufacturing	2030.67	12.95	2214.98	13.59
Governments	1386.61	8.84	1376.89	8.45
General	1363.54	8.70	1324.10	8.13
General commerce	1071.57	6.83	1038.92	6.38
Information and communication	960.85	6.13	859.16	5.27
Real estate activities	737.96	4.71	820.32	5.03
Finance and insurance	692.94	4.42	737.65	4.53
Power and energy	685.23	4.37	726.29	4.46
Construction	609.68	3.89	633.62	3.89
Agriculture, forestry, and fishing	482.71	3.08	529.06	3.25
Transportation and storage	458.85	2.93	452.19	2.78

Source: Redrawn from CBN (2017a)

affected when oil prices declined in 2008. The decline in oil prices since 2014 has also been a major factor underlying the distress in the banking sector, which is evident in the increase in non-performing loans (NPLs) shown in Figure 11.3. In early 2017, there were officially three undercapitalized banks. These banks had a ratio of minimum capital to risk-weighted assets (CAR) below 8 per cent and accounted

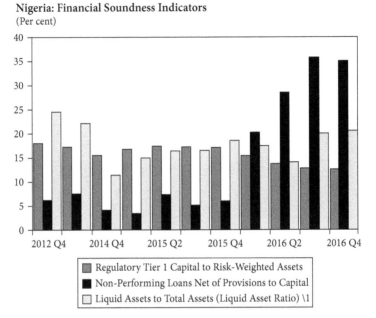

Nigeria: Financial Soundness Indicators
(Per cent)

Legend:
- Regulatory Tier 1 Capital to Risk-Weighted Assets
- Non-Performing Loans Net of Provisions to Capital
- Liquid Assets to Total Assets (Liquid Asset Ratio) \1

Figure 11.3 Nigeria: financial soundness indicators (%).
Source: IMF (2017b)

for 5 per cent of assets (IMF, 2017b). While on average CARs in the commercial banking sector amounted to 15 per cent in 2016, the same figure was about 3 per cent among small banks. In times of low oil prices, financial distress does not only arise because NPLs to the oil sector increase but also because government entities and businesses in other sectors find it difficult to service their loans because their revenues are highly dependent on a booming oil sector. That said, the banking sector distress in the 1990s and late 2000s was not only linked to oil price drops but also to mismanagement and fraud (Apati, 2012; Lewis and Stein, 1997).

The strong role of the state in the economy, facilitated by the state's command of oil revenues, is also visible in the financial sector. The state's developmental strategy, which envisages that banks support economic development and diversification, is best epitomized by the CBN. The CBN has a mandate not only for promoting price and financial stability but also for supporting economic development. From the perspective of the CBN, the role of the central bank in a developing economy must be different from and more activist than the role of a central bank in advanced economies.[5] An important part of the CBN's activities is therefore to support the activities of development finance institutions, through the provision of financial resources and administering some of the schemes for the provision of

---

[5] See for instance Sanusi (2010) or Emefiele (2014).

subsidized credit. The IMF and the World Bank have repeatedly criticized these activities but have had little influence on the CBN because the state is not dependent on their financial assistance.[6]

Basel standard adoption, implementation, and compliance in Nigeria

As Table 11.3 shows, Nigeria has been an early adopter of Basel standards. In 1990, amidst an environment of increasing banking sector distress, the CBN introduced a minimum CAR of 7.5 per cent. Two years later, the CBN brought the CAR more in line with Basel I and required banks to hold a minimum CAR of 8 per cent, with at least half of that being first-tier capital or paid-up share capital and reserves (World Bank, 1994). To position the Nigerian banks for the introduction of Basel II, the CBN increased the minimum CAR to 10 per cent in 2003 (CBN, 2003). This ratio is still in place and was even raised to 15 per cent for Nigerian banks with international authorization in response to Nigeria's banking crisis in 2009/10. While the current levels of minimum CARs exceed Basel standards, the definition of eligible elements for capital in Nigeria diverges from international rules. The Financial Sector Assessment Programme (FSAP) of the IMF and World Bank highlighted in 2012, for instance, that in Nigeria Tier 1 capital is defined to include

Table 11.3 Nigeria: adoption of Basel standards

Basel component	Adoption	Implementation
Basel I	CBN Circular 1990	Various CBN circulars, notably CBN Circular BSD/11/2003 1990 minimum CAR of 7.5% 1992 minimum CAR of 8% 2003 minimum CAR of 10%
Basel II	CBN banking supervision annual report 2000 CBN banking supervision annual report 2001 speech by CBN Governor Sanusi 2002	2013 CBN circular BSD/DIR/CIR/ GEN/LAB/06053, in force since 2014 Credit risk: Standardized approach Market risk: Standardized approach Operational risk: Basic indicator approach advanced approaches—no rules issued
Basel III	2013 Framework for the regulation and supervision of domestic systemically important banks in Nigeria	2014 (BSD/DIR/CON/LAB/07/026) D-SIB minimum CAR of 15%

[6] For such criticism see for instance IMF (2011) and IMF (2013a).

statutory reserves and reserves for SMEs even though they do not meet the requirement of being available immediately to absorb losses.

The extent to which Basel I was enforced in the 1990s and 2000s varied over time and is difficult to assess with precision. While the CBN had been reluctant to intervene in the banking sector and to let banks fail before 1990s, the government and regulators displayed less willingness to accommodate bank distress through liquidity injections from 1990 onwards and stepped up regulation (Brownbridge, 1998). For instance, between 1991 and 1996 alone, the CBN and NDIC took over the management and control of twenty-four distressed banks (NDIC, 2017). That said, a major criticism in the FSAPs of 2002 and 2012 was regulatory forbearance and the limited willingness of regulators to resolve distressed banks. The 2012 FSAP for instance concludes: 'Notwithstanding the important and substantial progress since 2009, the concern remains that, though the legal and regulatory framework relating to corrective, enforcement and sanctioning actions has improved substantially, the willingness to act may still be weak' (IMF, 2013b, p. 140).

There are some parallels between the process of Basel I adoption and enforcement and Basel II adoption and enforcement in Nigeria. The CBN's Governor Joseph Sanusi announced the adoption of Basel II already in the early 2000s. An important year was 2001, when the BCBS issued a proposal for the new accord and Nigerian regulators, following the discussions in Basel, responded by setting up a CBN-NDIC committee to prepare a roadmap for the implementation of Basel standards in Nigeria (CBN, 2002a). While Nigerian regulators broadly supported the implementation of Basel, they were also aware of the challenges to transplant the standard to Nigeria's environment. As a former CBN regulator who sat on the committee during its inception recalls: 'We pointed it out from day 1 [when the new accord was announced] that Basel should be adopted...We did not set out to reinvent the wheel...but you have to adapt it to the depth of the financial sector, the skillset of the regulator, the capacity, the public policy environment'.[7] In line with this, the 2001 annual report of the CBN's banking supervision department made clear that advanced approaches would not be considered initially (CBN, 2002a, p. 88).

It would, however, take another decade until Basel II implementation began. While work in the CBN-NDIC Basel II committee continued throughout the 2000s, the focus shifted under the next governor, Charles Soludo, towards the consolidation of the banking sector and dealing with its repercussions. Only in the wake of Nigeria's banking crisis, which began in 2009, did Basel II move again to the top of the regulatory agenda. Under CBN governor Sanusi Lamido Sanusi, Basel II implementation was formally announced in a circular in 2013. The new rules, which delineated the basic approaches for the calculation of credit, market, and operational risks in Pillar I, as well as guidelines for the implementation of

---

[7] Interview, former CBN official, Lagos, 20 September 2017.

Pillar II and III, came into effect in 2014. While the 2013 circular also announced the future implementation of Basel III, a draft regulation has not yet been issued. Yet the CBN did, in line with Basel III, specify some rules for domestic systemically important banks (D-SIBs), notably an increase of the minimum CAR to 15 per cent.

Despite the formal commitment to Basel II, its enforcement seems to be challenging. In 2016 and 2017, for instance, there were officially three undercapitalized banks and the CBN exercised regulatory forbearance (IMF, 2017a). Both regulators and industry experts think the number of undercapitalized banks is even higher.[8] In addition, the CBN is not enforcing the higher loss absorbency requirement it had set for the seven identified D-SIBs because some of them are struggling to meet more stringent regulatory requirements.[9] Mock compliance has thus become a feature of the regulatory process. What is more, while some banks seem to lack the capacity to provide adequate data to the supervisors, others seem to make every effort to hide their dismal state.

This is not to say that the CBN has not made significant efforts to address weaknesses in regulation and supervision over the past two decades. While Nigeria was judged to be compliant or largely compliant with fourteen out of twenty-five Basel Core Principles in the 2002 FSAP, it was judged compliant or largely compliant with eighteen out of twenty-five core principles in the 2012 FSAP. Moreover, some of the deficiencies highlighted in the 2012 FSAP such as weaknesses in the Framework for AML/CFT, the lack of a framework for consolidated supervision, and the lack of consideration of market risk have been addressed in recent years.[10] That said, the 2012 FSAP also highlighted deficiencies with respect to enforcement and the regulation of related party lending, large exposure rules, and the definition of Tier 1 and 2 capital. What emerges is thus a picture of early adoption of Basel standards but slow implementation and enforcement.

The political economy of Nigeria's engagement with Basel standards

This section deals with the five major phases of Nigeria's engagement with Basel standards. The international orientation of regulators and conflicted preferences are critical factors in explaining the gap between the declared commitment to Basel standards and the translation of these standards into concrete policies.

---

[8] Several interviews, regulators, and financial industry experts, Abuja and Lagos, September 2017. See also CBN (2017b).

[9] Several interviews and regulators, Abuja and Lagos, September 2017.

[10] Nigeria was blacklisted by the FATF in 2012 because of weaknesses in its AML/CFT framework. In 2013, however, Nigeria was removed from the list because Nigeria's Presidential Committee on the Financial Action Task Force managed to reform the framework quickly. The risk of losing correspondent banking relationships seems to have been an important reason for the quick action and high-level political commitment.

The explanation for Nigeria's path of early adoption and slow implementation and enforcement presented in this section centres on the tension between regulators' incentives to employ best-practice prudential regulation and to enhance the banking sector's contribution to economic development in the short term.

Basel I adoption in an inward-looking, fragile environment, 1990–2000

When the BIS issued Basel I in the late 1980s, Nigeria's banking sector was in a state of chaos. As a result of the financial liberalization and privatization process, a core element of Nigeria's SAP, the number of banks exploded, increasing from forty in 1985 to 107 in 1990 (World Bank, 1994). By 1990, the banking sector was very distressed because of a combination of banks' fraudulent activities, loose regulation, and weak supervisory capacity (Brownbridge, 1998).

When the CBN implemented a minimum CAR in 1990 it did so mainly with an eye to the domestic sphere. The aim was to stabilize the banking sector through a reform package which included a rise in minimum CARs besides other measures such as requiring banks to classify loans according to performance and higher requirements for minimum paid-up share. The policy preferences of regulators were shaped by domestic rather than international debates because the CBN's senior staff, including the governors, were only weakly embedded in international regulatory debates, as also Table 11.3 shows. While there was some exchange between Nigerian regulators and the staff of the IMF and the World Bank in the early 1990s, the role and influence of the IFIs were limited because they provided only little financing and technical assistance as part of Nigeria's SAP (Herbst and Soludo, 2001).[11] If anything, the domestic orientation of Nigerian technocrats increased during the 1990s as Sani Abacha's military regime became internationally increasingly isolated because of human rights abuses and the reversal of structural adjustment reforms.

Enforcing minimum CARs and other regulations proved difficult for three main reasons. One reason was political interference. Politicians limited the autonomy of regulators and protected banks from regulatory intervention because they played an important role in enhancing regime stability. Nigerian banks were largely owned by military officials or individuals that were connected to members of the military regimes of Ibrahim Babangida (1985 until 1993) and of Sani Abacha (1993 until 1998). Politicians benefited from cheap loans from these 'political' banks. Bank owners, in turn, were able to earn exorbitant rents from arbitrage opportunities in parallel foreign exchange markets and fraudulent activities like

---

[11] Nigeria embarked on the SAP mainly because international creditors had made an SAP a precondition for debt negotiations, and less to gain access to foreign aid.

Table 11.4 Nigeria: central bank governors, 1980s to the present

Name	Term in office	Embeddedness in international networks
Alhaji Abdulkadir Ahmed	1982–93	Limited; career in Nigerian civil service before becoming CBN governor
Paul Agbai Ogwuma	1993–9	Limited; career in Nigerian domestically oriented bank before becoming CBN governor
Joseph Odele Sanusi	1999–2004	High; CEO of internationally active bank before becoming CBN governor
Chukwuma Charles Soludo	2004–9	High; Visiting scholar in European and US universities and in the IMF as well as consultant for international organizations before becoming CBN governor
Sanusi Lamido Sanusi	2009–14	High; CEO of internationally active bank before becoming CBN governor
Godwin Emefiele	2014–present	High; CEO of internationally active bank before becoming CBN governor

money laundering, and in exchange supported the regime (Boone, 2005; Lewis and Stein, 1997).

A second reason for weak enforcement was that banks made every effort to evade and circumvent supervision (Lewis and Stein, 1997). Most banks were set up to exploit arbitrage opportunities in Nigeria's foreign exchange and money market and were thus firmly domestically oriented. Given the fragile states of their finances and banks' limited interest in attracting foreign investors or expanding internationally, the banks had limited incentives to support engagement with international standards.

A final and, for Nigeria's story, important factor is that regulators had conflicting preferences. On the one hand, they considered stricter regulations, including a high minimum CAR, important to enhance banking sector stability. On the other, regulators were keen to avoid a collapse of confidence in banks and hesitant to disclose the full extent of problems in the banking sector (Lewis and Stein, 1997). Regulatory interventions risked causing a breakdown of the system that the CBN sought to develop as part of its developmental mandate.

Looking outward: Basel II adoption, 2001–4

When Abacha died in 1998 and Olusegun Obasanjo won elections in 1999, the environment for the engagement with Basel standards changed markedly in Nigeria.

Like his predecessors, Obasanjo's government had a development strategy that emphasized state-led and oil-financed development and was thus broadly domestically oriented. However, Obasanjo also made significant efforts to reform economic governance. In particular, he reformed the public sector by replacing key personnel. In addition, Obasanjo was more internationally oriented than his predecessors, seeking to achieve Paris Club debt relief and to attract foreign investment by improving Nigeria's international reputation and the business environment (Apati, 2012; Reuters, 2000).

The reform orientation of Obasanjo's government shaped financial sector governance in two ways. First, regulators kept more abreast of international policy debates because Nigeria's efforts to secure debt relief required them to engage more with IFIs. Second, Olusegun Obasanjo replaced the leadership of the CBN and appointed, as Table 11.4 also shows, Joseph Oladele Sanusi, an internationally oriented career banker, as CBN governor. With a professional background in internationally active African banks, Sanusi was familiar with developments in financial regulation in the international sphere and convinced of the need to improve the capacity of regulators if they were to keep up with developments in domestic and international finance. In line with his professional background in banking, Sanusi placed a major emphasis on two processes. One was the professionalization of the CBN through trainings and hiring well-qualified staff. The second was the reform of the framework for banking regulation, a centrepiece of which was the adoption of Basel II.[12]

It is in this context that the CBN adopted Basel II in the early 2000s. For Sanusi, the adoption of Basel II was not only an attempt to enhance the stability of the domestic and international banking system but also a way to benchmark Nigeria's performance (CBN, 2002b). Moreover, in his view Basel II should 'be embraced if we are not to be excluded from the international financial system. Since our banks are competing in a global market, we cannot continue to operate on rules that fail to meet international standards' (CBN, 2002b, p. 4). CBN and NDIC staff on the operational level also supported the move towards Basel II but more because of domestic concerns. As a former CBN official recalls: 'We saw it [Basel II] as an opportunity to upscale our regulation... Basel is at the frontiers of knowledge; we wanted to take advantage of it'.[13] Thus, for Nigerian regulators, developments at the international level offered an opportunity to advance their domestic concerns, namely to stabilize a fragile banking sector.

Other actors did not oppose the adoption of Basel standards. The regulators had sensitivized the government and the adoption of Basel II was in line with the government's broader strategy of reintegrating into the international community following the relative isolation under Abacha's regime and of improving regulatory oversight over the banking sector (NNPC, 2004). In fact, in the early 2000s there emerged a consensus in the presidency that significant financial sector reforms would be needed because criminal investigations, in Nigeria and the

---

[12] Interview, former bank CEO, Lagos, 8 September 2017.
[13] Interview, former CBN official, Lagos, 20 September 2017.

United States, repeatedly showed the extent of malpractice, including money laundering and other financial crimes, in Nigerian banks (Apati, 2012). Bankers were only informed after the regulators had already decided to adopt Basel but were invited to consultations on the implementation of the framework. Largely excluded from the discussions were politicians outside the government and representatives from the IFIs. Politicians paid little attention to Basel II because it did not have enough political salience, especially compared to other regulatory issues such as the level of interest rates and bank closures. Nor did the IMF and World Bank shape discussions about the adoption of Basel II. While both institutions criticized weaknesses in Nigeria's system of banking regulation, notably the limited enforcement of existing rules, there is little evidence that the institutions pushed for or discouraged the adoption of Basel II or that regulators listened to their views on Basel II adoption.

Having been preoccupied with closing and resolving banks in the previous years, regulators' focus shifted in 2002 towards Basel implementation. Regulators were aware that implementation would take time. The 2001 annual report of the CBN's banking supervision department highlights a number of challenges that stood in the way of implementation such as the infancy of the credit rating agency sector, data availability, and supervisory capacity (CBN, 2002a). Another factor that turned out to be a crucial impediment in the following years was the lack of prioritization of implementing Basel II.

Standstill of Basel II implementation in the context of banking sector fragility, 2004–12

Even though financial reform and supporting the international expansion of Nigeria's banking sector remained at the top of the agenda of the CBN, efforts to implement Basel II slowed down when Obasanjo appointed Charles Soludo as CBN governor in 2004. The reason was not a lack of regulatory autonomy or interest in international debates. Soludo had been Obasanjo's chief economic advisor and enjoyed presidential backing for financial reform initiatives. Moreover, as Table 11.3 shows, Soludo was well integrated in international policy and academic circles because he had been a visiting scholar at the IMF and various universities in the UK and US and had worked as a consultant for donors like the World Bank. However, when Obasanjo was re-elected for a second term in 2003 his priority was to appoint a central bank governor who was focused on promoting economic growth, diversification, and development (Apati, 2012) and Soludo, who shared these developmental aspirations, oriented financial reform towards achieving these goals.

For Soludo, Nigeria's banking sector exposed major deficiencies, notably: a significant portion of weak banks with persistent illiquidity, poor asset quality, and unprofitable operations; a weak capital base; reliance on public sector deposits rather than making efforts to mobilize savings from the public; and the preference of lending to the government rather than to the productive sectors (Soludo, 2004). In his view, addressing these weaknesses required a major financial reform, the centrepiece of which was the consolidation of the banking sector through an increase of the minimum capital requirement for banks from about US$15 million to US$190 million. The rationale for the increase in capital requirements was that banks with a large capital base would be internationally competitive because of their size, be stronger because of the ability to absorb losses, and face greater incentives to lend to the real economy (Soludo, 2004). In other words, the reform sought to overcome the fragility and marginality of Nigeria's banking sector and to position Nigerian banks better for financial intermediation. Banks were given eighteen months to comply with the requirement, which was envisaged to be achieved through mergers and acquisitions by 2005.

It is difficult to say precisely why Soludo focused on the banking sector consolidation to address the fragility and marginality of the banking sector rather than on Basel II implementation. One factor seems to have been learning from emerging economies considered as peers. Soludo looked in particular to Malaysia and Indonesia, where regulators first sought to consolidate the banking sector before implementing Basel II.[14] In addition, the focus on consolidation was encouraged by advice from international management consultants, with whom the CBN works intensively. Another important factor seems to be that Soludo did not want to prioritize the goal of financial stability as would have been implied by a focus on Basel II implementation but sought to promote simultaneously financial and economic development. Large, well-capitalized banks would, in Soludo's opinion, meet the two goals of banking stability and creating a financial sector that served the real economy. A final factor is that neither the banking sector, which was still largely domestically oriented, nor politicians championed Basel II implementation.

Once the process of the banking consolidation began, there was little prospect for moving forward with the implementation of Basel II. At first, banks were preoccupied with meeting the significant increase in capital and the banking supervisors were preoccupied with overseeing the consolidation. When the consolidation was achieved and the number of banks declined from eighty-nine to twenty-five, supervisory capacity was still bound. One reason was that highly capitalized banks had expanded their operations significantly. Specifically, the consolidation had encouraged universal banking, retail lending, and expansion of banks in the African region, each of which demanded significant supervision. Second, even after the banking consolidation, many banks remained fragile, demanding the attention of the supervisors. While some banks had found it relatively easy to meet the new capital requirement, others had struggled and merged

---

[14] Interview, former IFI official, Lagos, 8 September 2017.

with other struggling banks. Moreover, many banks sought to meet the capital requirements through margin lending and engaged in insider-lending and other fraudulent activities to invest the large amount of capital they had. As stated above, the drop in the oil prices magnified the risks in Nigeria's large but fragile banking system and in 2009 bank examinations revealed that ten out of twenty-five banks, accounting for about a third of banking system assets, were either insolvent or undercapitalized.[15]

The CBN-NDIC committee on Basel II continued to exist in the years following the consolidation. However, all regulatory capacity was focused on overseeing the consolidation. Moreover, the committee lacked the support of the CBN's management to drive forward additional reforms since the primary concern of the management was to ensure that the consolidation was a success and to avoid measures that threatened it. Indeed, the evidence suggests that there was some regulatory forbearance with respect to Basel I and other prudential regulations in an effort to mask increasing banking sector fragility (Sanusi, 2010). It was not until Sanusi Lamido Sanusi, who became CBN governor in 2009, resolved the banking crisis that Basel II implementation in Nigeria moved forward.

Implementing Basel in the context of a stabilized banking sector, 2013–15

Two factors combined to support the implementation of Basel II and the introduction of a framework for D-SIBs from 2013 onwards. One factor was that the banking sector had gained some stability following Sanusi's resolution of the banking crisis through a combination of liquidity injections and regulatory reforms. Banking sector stability was a precondition for the implementation of Basel II because the CBN wanted to ensure that Basel II would not result in widespread intervention, loss of confidence, and a decline in credit to the private sector, which had just recovered from the crisis. Negative effects on credit were not only a general concern for the CBN, which sought to increase bank lending to the real economy, but also for politicians (Apati, 2012).[16]

The second important factor supporting the implementation of Basel II was the commitment of the CBN, notably of its new leadership, to implement international best practice. Sanusi's commitment to Basel II was rooted in his career in two large, internationally active Nigerian banks, first as risk manager and later in their top management. In fact, he had been nominated by President Umaru Musa Yar'Adua as CBN governor because of his insider knowledge of the banking sector which provided Sanusi with strong credentials to spearhead reforms to strengthen

---

[15] For an overview of the causes of the banking crisis see Sanusi (2010) and World Bank (2010).
[16] Interview, consultant, London, 3 October 2017.

banking sector stability. For Sanusi, Basel II was the best available standard for risk management since it required banks to understand and monitor different types of risks but had to be adapted to the Nigerian context.[17] This view was shaped not only through the debates prevailing in the banking community but also through his experience in guiding the transition of two Nigerian banks towards the voluntary operation of Basel II in the late 2000s. The post as governor provided Sanusi, who had taken pride in upgrading the banks 'to the highest standard', with the opportunity to implement this standard at the industry level.

The international orientation of CBN and NDIC staff at the operational level also helps to explain why regulators drove Basel II implementation. In particular, senior staff learned about Basel II through regular attendance at training in the US and continuous exchange with foreign advisors, some of which were funded by donors and IFIs. These regulators considered the need to focus on risk management as a major lesson of Nigeria's banking crisis of 2009 and Basel as the best practice.[18] In addition, CBN staff supported Basel II out of a logic of appropriateness. They considered Basel II the most appropriate framework for a country with a large and internationalized banking sector like Nigeria.[19] Moreover, Nigerian regulators pride themselves on adopting international best practices. As one regulator explains, Basel II 'allows us to benchmark us with other emerging economies. We do not compare ourselves to Sub-Saharan Africa except South Africa; rather we look to Malaysia, India and the Philippines'.[20]

While banks were not driving the Basel II implementation, it was probably of no small importance that they welcomed it. Large, internationally active Nigerian banks supported the move to Basel II and a handful of them had even begun to operate voluntarily according to Basel II in the late 2000s, when regulatory reporting still had to meet Basel I standards. Large banks' support was primarily based on the view that Basel II helped to signal investors, regulators, and their competitors that they were 'up to the highest standards' and financially sound. A reputation of soundness would, these banks believed, also enhance their competitiveness vis-à-vis other banks operating in African markets, for instance South African banks (Layegue, 2013).[21] Moreover, when Basel was implemented in 2013, large banks hoped that the CBN would soon move to more advanced models as these allowed, from their perspective, a more 'efficient'—that is, cost-effective—use of capital.[22] While smaller banks were more concerned about implementation costs, they also supported a gradual implementation of Basel II because they did not want to be seen as non-compliant. In addition, the simpler

---

[17] Interview, CBN official, Abuja, 11 September 2017.
[18] Interview, CBN official, Abuja, 18 September 2017.
[19] Interview, consultant, London, 3 October 2017.
[20] Interview, former CBN official, Lagos, 20 September 2017.
[21] Several interviews, bankers, Lagos, 9 and 21 September 2017.
[22] Interview, financial industry expert, Lagos, 8 September 2017.

financial market structure (for instance, the lack of derivatives and the lack of historical data) implied that the use of complex models would not be required initially, lowering the costs of adoption.

Gradual implementation and consideration of the domestic environment were also principles guiding the CBN's implementation of Basel II. The CBN, for instance, excluded development banks from the operation of Basel II. In addition, the CBN required the use of a risk weight of 100 per cent for all corporate credit given the limited reach of international and domestic credit rating agencies. The CBN has also used some national discretion in defining risk weights, for instance assigning a higher risk weighting to exposures to the oil sector in 2014. Most importantly, the CBN did not permit the use of advanced approaches, even though some banks lobbied to move towards them. The reason was that the CBN believed that both regulators and most of the banks lacked the capacity for these approaches.[23] In addition, the CBN had a deep distrust of the data provided by Nigerian banks. Moreover, by 2013 there were major debates in international policy circles about the misuse of advanced approaches, confirming the CBN's distrust of internal ratings-based approaches.

The consideration of the domestic environment does not mean that external actors did not shape the design of the Basel II guidelines. The CBN studied the approaches of countries considered as peers like Malaysia. International accounting firms and management consultants were hired to contribute to selected elements of Nigeria's Basel II framework or offered their services pro bono. In addition, donors and the IMF have provided technical assistance. The influence of IFIs on implementation was, however, limited. The FSAP of 2012 did criticize the absence of some elements of Basel II like the lack of a consideration of operational and market risk by Nigerian regulators. Yet as a senior IFI official points out, 'FSAPs are pushing on many things. Governments then choose to implement some and remain lagging on others; it is up to the authorities what to push and they tend to and implement what is least politically costly'.[24]

Tied hands: Basel standard engagement in times of crisis, 2015 to the present

The benign economic and political environment for the push for Basel standards came to an end in 2015. Banking supervisors remain committed to Basel II and the CBN's new governor, Godwin Emefiele, has been exposed to debates about global banking standards because he worked in the management of an internationally active bank before he succeeded Sanusi as CBN governor in 2014. However, in the

---

[23] Interview, regulator, Abuja, 18 September 2017.
[24] Interview, IFI official, Abuja, 13 September 2017.

second half of 2014, oil prices declined sharply and in 2016 Nigeria experienced a recession with growth collapsing to −1.5 per cent. One important consequence of the drop in oil revenues and thus of foreign exchange availability was that the newly elected government of Muhammadu Buhari exerted significant pressure on the CBN to focus on exchange rate management and financing government expenditure (CBN, 2017b). As a result, the autonomy of the CBN declined and domestic policy priorities have shaped central bank policy.

The decline in oil revenues has also increased banking sector fragility because of banks' exposure to the oil sector and the devaluation of the Naira. In 2017, four out of twenty-two commercial banks are officially undercapitalized, one of which is an internationally active bank (CBN, 2017b). Industry stakeholders consider the number of banks which fail to meet their minimum CARs even higher.[25] D-SIBs have also struggled to meet their higher CARs and HLA requirements. The real extent of banking sector fragility is, however, difficult to know since regulators face challenges in validating banks' data, partly because of stretched supervisory capacities, and partly because some banks conceal their true status.

The CBN has responded to the environment of banking sector fragility and limited autonomy as it did in earlier periods, namely by slowing down the implementation and enforcement of Basel standards. In particular, the CBN has been slow to publish documents that specify banks' requirements with regard to Pillar II and Basel III guidelines. Moreover, the CBN exercises regulatory forbearance with regard to the four undercapitalized banks and to a breach of single obligor limits. The banking sector, in turn, does not push for implementation and enforcement because it has been hit hard by the decline of the oil price and thus struggles to meet the costs of Basel II compliance, which became more evident over the course of implementation.

The reasons for slow implementation and regulatory forbearance are twofold. On the one hand, regulators are keen to avoid a collapse of confidence in the sector. On the other, there seems to be a concern that enforcing regulation and resolving banks will have adverse consequences on economic development through effects on employment and access to finance.[26] In 2015, for instance, the CBN revoked a rule specifying a risk weight of 125 per cent for loans to the oil and gas sector, which it had issued in 2014. The reason was that oil and gas is considered a development priority sector, not least because of its links with other sectors in the economy and the CBN wanted to avoid negative effects on lending to the oil sector. 'This', a regulator explained, 'is one example for the trade-offs between Basel II and economic development'.[27]

---

[25] Several interviews, former CBN official and bankers, Lagos, September 2017.
[26] Several interviews, regulators and financial industry experts, Lagos, September 2017.
[27] Interview, regulator, Abuja, 18 September 2017.

The CBN has taken significant steps to discipline banks in recent years.[28] However, the catch-22 situation remains where, on the one hand, the CBN seeks to promote Basel II because it is considered the best available set of rules to govern Nigeria's large, internationalized banking sector. On the other hand, regulators are reluctant to move faster on implementation and enforcement because this may require intervention in distressed banks which, they fear, has negative implications for economic development. Widespread bank intervention clashes with the developmental mandate of the CBN and mobilizes resistance by politicians, who are often lobbied by the banks themselves. Both banks and politicians argue that bank interventions must be avoided because of their effects on employment and access to finance.[29]

Conclusion

This chapter has addressed the puzzle of early adoption and slow implementation and enforcement of Basel standards in Nigeria. The case study has three main findings. First, Nigeria's story suggests that an internationalized banking sector provides strong incentives for the adoption of Basel II and III. Banking regulators drove the adoption of these standards because they believed this would enhance the competitiveness of Nigerian banks abroad and because they considered these standards to be more appropriate for a large, internationally oriented banking sector than Basel I. This belief stemmed from learning from the experiences of countries considered as peers and from the experiences the central bank governors Joseph Sanusi and Sanusi Sanusi had as CEOs of internationally active banks.

The IMF and the World Bank have had, despite the international orientation of regulators and in contrast to findings of other studies on Basel standard adoption in developing countries, little influence on regulatory preferences because oil revenues have limited the susceptibility of the Nigerian state to advice from the IFIs.[30] It was, however, important that regulators had political backing for the adoption of these standards because it seemed that there were no evident contradictions between their adoption and the larger developmental strategy. Banks, in turn, welcomed the fact that regulators drove Basel II adoption because they believed that embracing these standards would improve their international

---

[28] For instance, the CBN removed the management of a bank which breached regulatory thresholds in 2016.

[29] Both banks and politicians have made similar claims during previous episodes on banking sector fragility. Politicians, for instance, requested that Sanusi give greater consideration to the effects of his actions to resolve the banking crisis of 2009 on growth and employment (Apati, 2012). It is difficult to say whether the objections by politicians merely reflect concerns about economic development or whether such objections also serve to protect politically connected bankers.

[30] See for instance Wilf (2016) or the case studies of Kenya and WAEMU.

reputation and competitiveness. An important parallel to Pakistan's case is that a financial reform that resulted in the internationalization of the business model prevailing in the banking sector generated incentives to implement Basel standards.

The second major finding is that conflicting preferences may lead to mock compliance. Nigeria is, as one financial industry expert explains, 'a country of rules in books that are not really implemented'.[31] While Nigerian regulators have had strong incentives to engage with Basel II and III because of their international orientation, they have had equally strong incentives for slow implementation and enforcement in a context of oil-induced banking sector fragility because bank interventions involve high developmental and thus political costs. Conflicting preferences also help to explain weak enforcement of Basel I, notably in the run-up to Nigeria's banking crisis which began in 2009. This is an important parallel to Angola's case where mock compliance also results from a clash between domestic political realities and imperatives to adopt international standards arising from an internationally oriented banking sector. With reference to our analytical framework, as mock compliance is driven by the conflicted preferences of regulators, this is a case of regulator-driven mock compliance.

The final, broader point is that Basel standards are not neutral from a developmental perspective. Enforcing these standards may, at least in the short term, involve costs, by affecting lending to development priority sectors and requiring bank interventions, which has effects on employment and access to finance. Considerable work lies ahead not only in examining the developmental consequences for Basel II and III implementation and enforcement but also in determining what strategies could be adopted to reduce the developmental costs of Basel standard adoption in the context of fragile, extraverted financial systems.

References

Apati, S., 2012. *The Nigerian Banking Sector Reforms: Power and Politics.* Springer, New York.

Beck, T., Maimbo, S., Faye, I., Triki, T., 2011. *Financing Africa: Through the Crisis and Beyond.* World Bank, Washington, DC.

Bhattacharyya, S., Hodler, R., 2014. Do natural resource revenues hinder financial development? The role of political institutions. *World Development* 57, 101–13. https://doi.org/10.1016/j.worlddev.2013.12.003.

Boone, C., 2005. State, capital, and the politics of banking reform in Sub-Saharan Africa. *Comparative Politics* 37, 401–20.

---

[31] Interview, academic and former banker, Lagos, 22 September 2017.

Brownbridge, M., 1998. The impact of public policy on the banking system in Nigeria, in: Brownbridge, M., Harvey, C., Fritz Gockel, A. (Eds.), *Banking in Africa: The Impact of Financial Sector Reform Since Independence*. James Currey and Africa World Press, Oxford; Trenton, NJ.

CBN, 2002a. *Banking Supervision Annual Report 2001*. Central Bank of Nigeria, Abuja.

CBN, 2002b. *Keynote address by Chief J.O. Sanusi at the opening ceremony of the CBN/ NDIC workshop on the new capital accord*. Central Bank of Nigeria, Abuja.

CBN, 2003. *Circular BSD/11/2003. Review of the Capital adequacy measurement*. Central Bank of Nigeria, Abuja.

CBN, 2017a. *Financial Stability Report 2016*. Central Bank of Nigeria, Abuja.

CBN, 2017b. *Communiqué No. 114 of the Monetary Policy Committee of 24th and 25th July*. Central Bank of Nigeria, Abuja.

Emefiele, G., 2014. *Entrenching Macroeconomic Stability and Engendering Economic Development in Nigeria*. Central Bank of Nigeria, Abuja.

EY, 2015. *Sub-Saharan Africa banking review: A review of the 2014 calendar year*. Johannesburg, Ernst & Young Africa.

Herbst, J., Soludo, C.C., 2001. Nigeria, in: Shantayanan, D., Dollar, David R. Holmgren, Torgny (Eds.), *Aid and Reform in Africa: Lessons from Ten Case Studies*. World Bank, Washington, DC.

IMF, 2011. *Nigeria: 2010—Article IV consultation* (IMF Country Report 11/57). IMF, Washington, DC.

IMF, 2013a. *Nigeria: Financial sector stability assessment* (IMF Country Report No. 13/140). IMF, Washington, DC.

IMF, 2013b. *Nigeria: Publication of financial sector assessment program documentation. Detailed assessment of compliance of the Basel Core Principles for effective banking supervision* (IMF Country Report No. 13/146). IMF, Washington, DC.

IMF, 2017a. *2017 Article IV consultation* (IMF Country Report No. 17/80). IMF, Washington, DC.

IMF, 2017b. *Nigeria: Selected issues* (IMF Country Report No. 17/81). IMF, Washington, DC.

IMF, 2018. *Financial Soundness Indicators Database*. IMF, Washington, DC.

Layegue, I., 2013. *Risk and regulations: Financial focus*. PwC.

Lewis, P., Stein, H., 1997. Shifting fortunes: The political economy of financial liberalization in Nigeria. *World Development* 25, 5–22. https://doi.org/10.1016/ S0305-750X(96)00085-X.

NDIC, 2017. *History* [Data set] [WWW Document]. URL http://ndic.gov.ng/about-ndic-3/ndic-history (accessed 17.12.18).

NNPC, 2004. *Meeting Everyone's Needs: National Economic Empowerment and Development Strategy*. Nigerian National Planning Commission, Abuja.

Polity IV, 2014. *PolityProject*. Center for Systemic Peace.

Reuters, 2000. Obasanjo wants 'democratic dividend' from Nigerian creditors. *CNN*.

Sanusi, S.L., 2010. *The Nigerian banking industry: What went wrong and the way forward*. Text of Convocation Lecture delivered at Bayero University, Kano. Bayero University, Kano.

Soludo, C.C., 2004. *Consolidating the Nigerian banking industry to meet the development challenges of the 21st century*. Special Meeting of the Bankers' Committee. Central Bank of Nigeria, Abuja.

Wilf, M., 2016. *Financial globalization and domestic regulatory adoption of Basel I*: Paper prepared for the 2016 annual meeting of the American Political Science Association.

World Bank, 1994. *Nigeria: Structural Adjustment Program. Policies, Implementation, and Impact*. World Bank, Washington, DC.

World Bank, 2010. *Achieving Nigeria's Financial System Strategy 2020: Making Finance Work for Nigeria*. World Bank, Washington, DC.

World Bank, 2017a. *World Development Indicators*. World Bank, Washington, DC.

World Bank, 2017b. *World Development Indicators*. 15 September 2017 ed. World Bank, Washington DC.

12

Angola

'For the English to see—the politics of mock compliance'

Rebecca Engebretsen and Ricardo Soares de Oliveira

Introduction

Convergence on international banking standards is expected in countries with internationalized financial sectors (Jones and Zeitz, 2017).[1] The case of Angola challenges this expectation. A high degree of financial sector internalization in the country has only been weakly matched by adherence to banking standards. Rather than acting as advocates, foreign partners and internationally active domestic banks remain apathetic to banking standards. Yet in the aftermath of the 2008–9 global financial crisis (GFC), the above pattern started to change. In 2014, Angola authorities moved ahead with Basel II, although implementation remains highly varied across the sector. In this chapter we ask what prompted Angola to belatedly commit to regulatory reform in the banking sector in line with international best standards after having avoided it for so many years.

We argue that engagement with international banking standards (Basel I and II) is a result of Angola's particular form of financial sector extraversion coupled with the fact that the domestic banking sector remains deeply politicized. In Angola, like in other resource-rich countries, the financial sector plays a key role in facilitating outgoing financial flows. At the same time, the extending of loans, often without collateral, and handing out of bank licences to political insiders remains an important avenue for securing political support for the regime. Before the GFC, the particular constellation of extraversion and politicization of the financial sector meant that Angola's drivers of convergence were much weaker than its drivers of divergence. Strengthening bank regulation threatened to upset the role banks had come to play in Angola's clientelistic system. However, in the wake of the GFC, changes in the international regulatory environment meant that non-implementation of standards was no longer an option. For Angolan banks to

---

[1] 'For the English to see': This phrase dates back to a treaty signed in 1826 between Great Britain and Brazil supposedly ending the slave trade. The notion of 'for the English to see' suggests that the signing of the law was purely Brazil's measure to placate Great Britain, whilst in reality there was no intention of ending the trade.

Rebecca Engebretsen and Ricardo Soares de Oliveira, *Angola: 'For the English to see—the politics of mock compliance'*
In: *The Political Economy of Bank Regulation in Developing Countries: Risk and Reputation.* Edited by: Emily Jones, Oxford University Press (2020). © Oxford University Press. DOI: 10.1093/oso/9780198841999.003.0012

maintain their link to the global financial market, the country needed to signal its readiness to regulate the sector in line with international standards.[2] The result has been an upsurge in regulatory efforts after 2009, and especially since 2014. Yet because the nature of the banking sector has not changed, only some aspects of the standards implemented, and they are not enforced, leading to a situation of 'mock compliance'. As mock compliance is driven by the conflicting preferences of politicians, it is a case of politically driven mock compliance.

This chapter is amongst the first scholarly works to focus on the political economy of banking regulation in Angola.[3] Our analysis builds on fieldwork undertaken in Angola, Portugal, and Washington, DC between 2009 and 2017. Thirty interviews were conducted with current and former government officials including regulators, public and private bankers, and representatives of International Financial Institutions (IFIs) and accounting firms. All interviews were conducted off the record.

Following the introduction, the chapter starts by situating Angola's regulatory trajectory in the broader context of financial sector development in the country. A description of the country's engagement with the Basel standards and other international banking standards to date follows. The chapter then turns to the main analysis to answer the question of what drove regulatory reform in Angola and what characterizes the implementation of international banking standards. We divide the analysis into before and after the GFC in order to highlight the differences and continuity between the two periods. Finally, we conclude.

Political economy context

In order to better understand Angola's engagement with banking standards it is useful to first put the trajectory of banking regulation in the country in a broader perspective.[4] Following the end of the civil war in 2002, Angola's economy grew rapidly to become the third largest in Sub-Saharan Africa (see Table 12.1). The process of reconstruction that ensued was managed by the victorious MPLA regime under the tight control of President José Eduardo dos Santos (Oliveira, 2015), in power from 1979 until September 2017. The impressive growth is inherently linked to the extraction of oil, the dominant force in the economy. Whilst substantial for decades, oil production took off in the late 1990s, from below one million barrels a day in 2002 to reach almost two million by 2008. During the same period, oil prices increased from just over US$20 per barrel to US$147.

---

[2] 'Managing Angola's financial sector', Event at the Blavatnik School of Government, University of Oxford, 24 January 2017.

[3] See also Ferreira and Soares de Oliveira (2018) and Engebretsen (2018).

[4] For a more general background of the Angolan banking sector see Ferreira and Soares de Oliveira (2018).

Table 12.1 Angola: key indicators

Angola	
GDP per capita (current US$, 2017)	4,170
Bank assets (current US$)	39.4 bn
Bank assets (% of GDP)	41.3
Stock market capitalization (% of GDP)	N/A
Credit allocation to private sector (% of GDP)	21.1
Credit allocation to government (% of GDP)	21.2
Polity IV score (2017)	−2

Note: All data is from 2016 unless otherwise indicated.

Source: FSI Database, IMF (2018); GDI Database, World Bank (2017); Polity IV (2014)

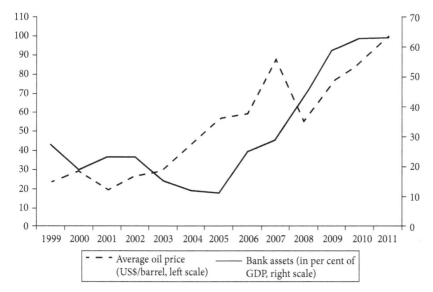

Figure 12.1 Angola: oil price and bank assets.

Source: IMF (2012)

The role of oil in the Angolan economy cannot be overstated and it is within this context that the country's financial sector has emerged. The Angolan financial system grew exponentially from a small and tightly controlled base aided by market liberalization and the end of forty years of conflict in 2002 (Ferreira and Soares de Oliveira, 2018). From only US$3 billion in assets in 2003, by 2013 the sector held an estimated US$60 billion in assets.[5] Sector growth was particularly fast between 2007 and 2009, with yearly average asset growth exceeding 66 per cent (IMF, 2012) (Figure 12.1).

---

[5] Edward George, 'Angola's financial sector: An overview', Presentation, Oxford, 18 June 2015.

Despite the impressive growth of the Angolan financial sector, the sector's development impact is limited, adding weight to the theory that there is a resource curse in financial development (Beck et al., 2011; Bhattacharyya and Hodler, 2014). Like in other resource-rich economies, the sector remains concentrated, with the five largest banks accounting for almost 70 per cent of total assets (Wise, 2015). Banking operations in the country have long been rudimentary, characterized by high fees and a restricted number of services. Angolan banks made 'the bulk of their earnings from government bonds rather than growing their loan books' with a marked preference for short-term operations (Wallace, 2015). Financial inclusion is limited as access to services is low: only 29 per cent of those aged fifteen or older reported having a bank account in 2014, compared to a Sub-Saharan Africa average of 34.2 per cent (World Bank, 2014). Credit to the private sector (as a percentage of GDP) stood at 27 per cent in 2015, below the Sub-Saharan average of 46 per cent (see Figure 12.2) (World Bank, 2018). Loan opportunities are largely limited to politically connected individuals or firms.

The rapid growth of the financial sector, described here, has posed particular challenges for the financial regulator, the Banco Nacional de Angola (BNA). Together with other state institutions, the BNA was deliberately undercut for much of the 1990s to allow the then president maximum discretionary power over oil revenues (Hodges, 2004). The institution has gained strength since then, but ultimately the policy space in which the BNA has to manoeuvre remains at the discretion of the executive who, for much of Angola's modern history, has carried considerable stakes in the financial sector.

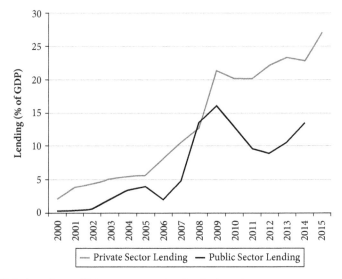

Figure 12.2 Angola: credit to government and private sector.
Source: World Bank (2017)

Commercial banks dominate the Angolan financial system with 99 per cent of financial assets, whilst non-bank financial institutions, including the insurance and pension sectors, are still at an infant stage (IMF, 2012). Another defining feature of the Angolan financial sector is the heavy presence of the state. As is the case in other resource-rich countries, public ownership of oil and gas reserves and equity stakes in the oil and gas industry renders vast revenues to the Angolan state at the expense of the private sector (Beblawi and Luciani, 1987). Angolan banks, both private and public, are extremely dependent on the state for their operations. Public sector entities have equity interests (including minority stakes) in around 90 per cent of the banking system (in terms of assets) (IMF, 2012). Eight banks (including two of the top five) are directly owned by the state or by public enterprises, including the National Oil Company, Sonangol.

The public banks have historically been erratically managed, steered by political purposes rather than on a commercial basis. Angola's major public bank, Banco de Poupança e Crédito (BPC), lends predominantly to public sector institutions and employees.[6] Public banks lend with explicit state guarantees, including as part of the government's programme to support micro, small, and medium enterprises, Angola Investe (Agência Angola Press, 2012), or with an implicit guarantee. In addition to an increasing percentage of non-performing loans (NPLs) arising from the large number of loss-making state-owned enterprises, there is a large quantity of fraudulent or NPLs originating from credit being extended to senior political and military figures. These 'loans' are granted 'recurrently without any collateral or even risk-assessment', with prominent members of the ruling Movimento Popular de Libertação de Angola (MPLA) not expected to repay (Africa Confidential, 2017a). The extent of the problem is amply shown by revelations regarding BPC's extensive NPL burden. According to the BNA, impaired loans reached 30 per cent of BPC's total loans in 2017 (Fitch Ratings, 2017).

Emerging from the shadow of Angola's poorly managed state-owned banks, the rise of Angolan private banks signifies the dual purpose of the country's modern banking sector. Angola's private banks are amongst the most profitable on the continent (see Figure 12.3) (Wallace, 2012). Some are partly owned by public sector entities, including national oil company Sonangol, or are associated with large Angolan private companies (Expansão, 2016). All, however, have so-called Politically Exposed Persons (PEPs) amongst their shareholders, including leading MPLA politicians, ruling party officials, current and former members of the security forces, or close family members of the above. Elite members possess shareholdings in their own names or through front men and/or companies, which have subsequently been revealed to represent their interests.

---

[6] Interview, former banker, Luanda, September 2015.

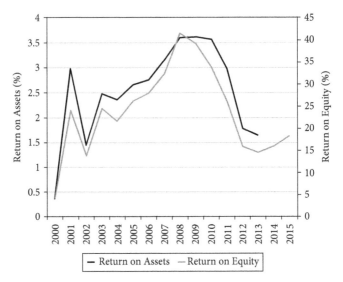

Figure 12.3 Angola: rates of return on assets (RoA) and equity (RoE).
Source: Bankscope and Orbis Bank Focus, Bureau van Dijk (2018)

The category of Angolan private banks is broad, encompassing sizeable (and partly Sonangol-owned) Banco Angolano de Investimentos (BAI), which by now has operations in Portugal, São Tomé and Príncipe, and Cape Verde, as well as a significant number of smaller banks. So far, the smaller 'political banks' have had limited operations.[7]

Angola's private banks also encompass foreign-owned banks, dominating the country's banking sector in terms of total assets and capital. Contrary to the vast majority of African banking systems but similarly to that of Nigeria, Angola has not been reliant on foreign investments to secure capital flows as sizeable foreign exchange is generated by the oil sector. Instead, foreign investors are needed in Angola for their sectorial expertise, introducing modern financial tools in the country. Foreign partners are also important on account of their (and their home jurisdictions') credibility (Ferreira and Soares de Oliveira, 2018).

Meanwhile, these partnerships are formally (through Angolan majority ownership) or informally (a bank's dependence on the Angolan market) calibrated in ways that guarantee Luanda's prominence. Although the legal framework allows foreign banks to have 100 per cent equity stakes, in the course of the boom period of 2004–9, foreign banks generally followed Angolan authorities' advice (and in some cases, such as Banco de Fomento Angola (BFA), were practically pushed) to seek local partners and divest their shareholdings to 51 per cent stakes (IMF, 2012). Foreign banks often sold the remaining stakes to Angolan private

---

[7] Interview, private bank, Luanda, October 2016.

interests. This was the case with Angola's major Portuguese banks, as well as South Africa's Standard Bank (attained by Sonangol before being acquired by the former president's son, José Filomeno dos Santos) (Semanário Angolense, 2008). The result was that, between 2005 and 2015, the percentage of total banking assets in Angolan private ownership rose from 28 per cent to 49.3 per cent.[8]

In light of the above analysis, it appears more fruitful to distinguish the Angolan banks by the purpose they serve rather than their proprietors, a point stressed by Engebretsen (2018). As we have seen, in the majority of cases the proprietor is the Angolan state, and its influence is extensive even in cases in which it doesn't have ownership. As the next section will further elaborate, the heavy presence of the state in finance and the prominence of politically connected persons leave the BNA in a particularly delicate situation.

Basel adoption, implementation, and enforcement

Angola's engagement with international banking standards appears relatively recent and is particularly noticeable following the GFC. Yet, on closer inspection it is clear that Angolan authorities' engagement with standards such as the Basel standards is not new but dates back to 1991. As in other countries covered in this volume, the early introduction of banking standards in Angola followed engagement by the authorities with the IFIs in the late 1980s. The initial law governing Angola's financial sector (Law 5/91) after sector liberalization incorporated capital requirements based on Basel I, requiring banks to maintain a minimum capital ratio of 10 per cent (Deloitte, 2012). Additionally, the 1991 Law outlined rules for prudential regulation, supervision, and compulsory external auditing (World Bank, 1992).

Whilst in line with Basel I, banking standards were at best erratically enforced throughout the 1990s (IMF, 2000). Further liberalization of the financial sector from 1997 saw the enforcement of a new Central Bank Law (Law 6/97) and the new law for Financial Institutions (Law 1/99), both with the stated aim of bringing banking regulation in line with Basel Core Principles (BCPs). To what extent the authorities achieved this is difficult to say, however. Assessments from that time, evaluating Angola's banking regulation against international standards, were not made public.[9]

Angola continued to express its commitment to strengthen bank supervision and fully implement the BCPs throughout the 2000s (IMF, 2011a, 2010, 2009, 2000). In 2009, the IMF reported that the BNA had taken necessary measures to strengthen regulations in line with the BCPs, including adopting a revised loan

---

[8] Authors' estimates based on KPMG (2016) and bank reports.
[9] World Bank and IMF reports indicate that such an assessment took place.

classification and provisioning standard. Banks would now be required to classify loans by their risk as well as make provision for expected losses (IMF, 2010). As of spring 2018, the BNA was still working to 'update the regulatory framework and create the conditions for a risk-based approach supervision' (Agência Angola Press, 2017; Santos and Santos, 2018).

Implementation of new prudential regulation, aiming to bring domestic regulation closer to Basel II, was due in January 2008 but was postponed (African Development Bank, 2008). The BNA reconfirmed its intentions to implement Basel II on several occasions over the next few years but little tangible progress was made (IMF, 2011b). A Financial Sector Assessment Programme (FSAP), a joint programme of the IMF and the World Bank, was conducted for the first time in 2011. The report highlighted the limitations of Angola's regulatory and supervisory framework, noting that the country was compliant or largely compliant with only eight out of twenty-five BCPs. Significant gaps were identified especially when it came to risk assessment, consolidated supervision, and enforcement (IMF, 2012).

It would take until 2015 for Angolan authorities to officially implement Basel II. In one year, draft regulation was published covering all different types of risk under Pillar 1 of the standard (FSI, 2015). Speaking to the *Financial Times* in February of that year, then BNA Governor José Pedro de Morais confirmed that Angola had drafted forty-one new regulations since 2014, with twenty-three issued and the remainder to be published later that year (England, 2016).

Angola went ahead with standardized approaches for calculating risk, discarding more advanced requirements that would require each bank to account for all risk categories.[10] Neither the banks nor the regulators were judged to have the capacity to apply such advanced models. As the IMF noted in 2012, the BNA lacks 'clear understanding concerning banks business models and risks' (IMF, 2012).

With regards to prudential supervision (Pillar 2), Angola has advanced since 2012 when the IMF wrote that 'neither the BNA nor the banks conduct sensitivity or stress tests to assess vulnerabilities and key data are not readily available' (IMF, 2012). The same year, a Financial Stability Committee was established to act as an advisory body to the latter, monitoring evolving conditions and risks in the financial system. BNA also started conducting regular stress tests on banks under different scenarios from 2012 onwards (IMF, 2015). BNA is obliged to conduct inspections of banks (Law No. 16/10) and does this through regular on-site inspections and external audits.[11] Whilst all banks in Angola are subject to external audits on an annual basis, none are publicly listed, thus limiting the effectiveness of market discipline (Pillar 3). That said, the introduction of disclosure requirements for Angolan banks based on Basel standards as well as International Financial Reporting Standards (gradually introduced since 2014) means that there is greater

---

[10] Interview, private bank, Luanda, October 2016.
[11] Interview, private bank, Luanda, September 2016.

Table 12.2 Angola: adoption of Basel standards

Basel component	Adoption	Implementation
Basel I	Financial Institutions Law 5/91	1991
Basel II	Pillar 1 (credit, market, and operational risk, standardized approaches) in force since 2016[12] Elements of Pillar 2 in force since 2013 Elements of Pillar 3 market discipline in force since 2015	Credit risk SA—2016 Market risk SA—2016 Operational risk SA—2016 Pillar 2—2013 Pillar 3—2015 (Financial Institutions Law 12/15)
Basel III	N/A	N/A

disclosure on the evolution of various financial risks in the financial sector (KPMG, 2016a) (Table 12.2).

As part of the larger modernization of the financial sector, Angolan authorities also passed corrective legislation in 2014 aimed at removing the country from the Financial Action Task Force's (FATF) 'grey list' (IMF, 2014). Angola was placed under the surveillance of the Financial Action Task Force in 2010 and again in 2012 before being removed in in 2016, signifying the country's successful efforts in bringing the domestic legal framework in line with AML/CFT standards.

Whereas Angola's recent embrace of international banking standards appears impressive, significant challenges remain. From late 2014, banks have grappled with 'a dollar liquidity crunch amid regulatory concerns, bad loans and low oil prices', leading industry magazine *The Banker* to note in 2016 that 'more work needs to be done to enhance system-wide regulation and compliance' (King, 2016). Whilst oil prices have improved since then, more work is needed to ensure that the Angolan banking sector complies with international standards (Santos and Santos, 2018). In particular, a significant performance gap exists between the banks. Many of the larger institutions, often with international shareholders, have established good governance structures and meet international compliance norms, whilst larger public banks and smaller private banks have fallen behind. As we will argue in the next section, this duality characterizing Angola's banking sector is key to understanding the country's engagement, and lack thereof, with banking standards to date.

[12] Notice No. 09/2016 of 22 June 2016; Notice No. 08/2016 of 22 June 2016; Notice No. 07/2016 of 22 June 2016; Notice No. 06/2016 of 22 June 2016; Notice No. 05/2016 of 22 June 2016; Notice No. 04/2016 of 22 June 2016; Notice No. 03/2016 of 16 June 2016; Notice No. 02/2016 of 15 June 2016; Instruction No. 12/2016 of 8 August 2016; Instruction No. 13/2016 of 8 August 2016; Instruction No. 12/2016 of 8 August 2016; Instruction No. 14/2016 of 8 August 2016; Instruction No. 15/2016 of 8 August 2016; Instruction No. 16/2016 of 8 August 2016; Instruction No. 17/2016 of 8 August 2016; Instruction No. 18/2016 of 8 August 2016; Instruction No. 19/2016 of 30 August 2016 (KPMG, 2016b).

The political economy of Basel adoption, implementation, and compliance

The foundations for Angola's financial sector and the state of regulation pre-2009

How to explain Angola's shift from minimal engagement with banking standards to the active involvement we have witnessed over recent years? And how can we make sense of the implementation pattern that has ensued? To address these questions, we divide the subsequent analysis in two: the first part deals with the period preceding the onset of reforms (pre-2009) and the second deals with the period after 2009. In this way, we are able to identify the differences between the two periods and the drivers of regulatory reform witnessed in recent years, which were absent in the early years.

The Angolan financial sector plays a key role in facilitating the connection between the domestic economy and international markets. The bulk of the country's banking sector activity continues to be trade financing. The salience of trade in the country is due to Angola importing the majority of consumption goods and capital goods, alongside services required for local production.[13] Cross-border banking business is additionally kept high by foreign companies that need to access foreign exchange to repatriate their Kwanza-denominated earnings or to pay for imports. Adding to this, Angolans are large consumers of foreign exchange, using it to hedge against an unstable local currency, for travelling and consumption (Peralta, 2017). It is commission on these kinds of cross-border transactions that has made Angolan banks amongst the most profitable on the continent (Wallace, 2012). Yet to execute these transactions, domestic banks rely on correspondent relationships (BIS, 2017). Because Angolan banks have limited branches overseas,[14] they are only able to access financial services in overseas jurisdictions and provide cross-border payment services to their customers through correspondent banks.

Based on the high degree of internationalization of Angola's financial sector, incumbent politicians, regulatory authorities, and banks pursue a strategy focused on maximizing through-flow of international financial transactions. In order to facilitate these flows, high levels of adoption, implementation, and enforcement of bank standards could be expected (Jones and Zeitz, 2017). Yet this has not been the case.

We argue that the lack of alignment with international banking standards despite high levels of banking sector extraversion is primarily due to financial sector

---

[13] During the last five years the imports increased at an annualized rate of 1.7 per cent, from $15.4B in 2010 to $16.9B in 2015. 'Angola Profile', The Observatory of Economic Complexity (n.d.) (accessed 9 May 2017).

[14] Because of the dominance of the oil industry in Angola, transactions are mainly in US dollars.

extraversion working differently in Angola. The activities of Angolan banks, as described earlier, centre mainly on facilitating outflows of capital. This differs from other cases of financial sector extraversion discussed in this book, Kenya and to a lesser extent Ghana and Rwanda, where the goal is to attract capital. In these cases, politicians and regulators use the adoption and implementation of international standards to reassure foreign investors of their country's regulatory set-up. As the second largest oil producer in Africa, attracting foreign capital is less of a concern for Angola. This is reflected in the way the country has historically interacted with banking standards. Contrary to most African cases, the influence of the IMF and of western donors was always limited (Oliveira, 2015). The same is true of so-called 'regulatory networks' of reformist central bankers and technocrats. As the IMF noted in 2012, there have been traditionally low levels of cooperation with foreign supervisors despite the importance of foreign banks in Angola.[15] Patterns of regional banking reform likewise have little influence on the country's regulatory response. Angola remains poorly integrated in the broader region and does not seek to emulate the policies of neighbouring states.[16]

Simultaneously, foreign banks have been unassertive in Angola and adapted to local terms. Whilst in line with the analytical framework, this finding challenges a common assumption that foreign banks advocate for the implementation of international banking standards such as the Basel standards so as to minimize their transaction costs and/or to gain a competitive edge over domestic banks (Gottschalk, 2010).[17] Rather, in the words of an IFI official, foreign banks in Angola 'mind their own business and do not push anything'.[18] Internationally active Angolan banks are not pushing for greater adherence with banking standards but are concentrating on tapping the domestic market. In sum, the submissive behaviour of private banks in Angola resembles that of Ethiopia, where an environment of steady profits discourages bankers from 'rocking the boat'.

In the pre-GFC time period, the pattern described above landed Angola in the domestic-oriented typology. At the time, Angolan politicians, bankers, and the regulator had few incentives to incur the substantial costs associated with adhering to international standards. Several bank insiders confirmed this to be the case.[19] The disinterest in banking standards held true even for banks that were forced to comply with international standards anyway because of their operations abroad. Private banks' lack of interest in pushing for international standards appears to have little to do with the individual bank's interests, however. Rather, it came down to the fact that more rigid regulatory oversight and increased transparency in banking sector operations would hurt other parts of the financial

<hr>

[15] A long-delayed Memorandum of Understanding with Portuguese authorities was signed in November 2011 (IMF, 2012).
[16] Interview, public bank, Luanda, September 2015.
[17] Interview, private bank, Luanda, October 2016.   [18] Interview, IFI, Luanda, October 2016.
[19] Interview, private bank, Luanda, October 2016; interview, private bank, Luanda, September 2016.

sector in which the owners of private banks also had an interest. Angolan public sector entities hold equity interests in around 90 per cent of the banking system (in terms of assets) (IMF, 2012). Eight banks (including two of the top five) are directly owned by the state, one through national oil company Sonangol.

Specifically, stricter regulation and compliance with international standards was expected to hurt the public banks disproportionally. Public banks continue to be central to the MPLA regime's distribution of patronage through the use of bank credit. The widespread use of the banking sector for political purposes is evident from the public banks' historically poor performance.[20] As an IMF report from 2015 cautioned, 'financial indicators in these [public] banks show relatively high non-performing loans (NPLs) in per cent of total loans, declining or negative return on average assets (ROA), and low capital adequacy ratios' (IMF, 2015, p. 15). Angola's biggest public lender, BPC, extended loans to senior political and military figures, 'recurrently without any collateral or even risk-assessment', with prominent elite members not expected to repay their loans (Africa Confidential, 2017a). In addition to the BPC, other public lenders including national development bank Banco de Desenvolvimento de Angola (BDA) also required bailout after having been granted irrecoverable credit (Africa Confidential, 2017b).

Politicians thus had strong incentives to oppose implementation of bank standards seen to jeopardize the abovementioned arrangements. Public banks were expected to struggle particularly with complying with minimum capital requirements and greater financial disclosure (as required under Pillar 3) as well as stricter enforcement of national guidelines for classification of non-performing loans. Angola's smaller banks would moreover struggle under higher compliance costs as a consequence of bringing the national regulatory framework in line with international standards. Owners of these banks, which include members of the most powerful families in the country, offered especially strong resistance to any rules seen as jeopardizing the viability of their private interests.

In such a context, Angolan politicians had an interest in keeping regulators politically and technically weak, so as to avoid any genuine regulatory interference in the banking sector. Whilst the BNA officially gained greater policy autonomy from the early 1990s (Law 6/97)—having previously been used mainly as a money press for the state—the central bank remained subordinate to the political agenda throughout the first decade of the 2000s. This meant that regulators, like politicians, were domestically oriented. Whereas in other countries, including Ghana, technical assistance from IFIs was an important factor influencing Basel implementation in the country, Angola's engagement with IFIs was ad hoc.[21] To the extent that Angola engaged internationally, this was mainly

---

[20] For further discussion about the public banks' historic performance see (Engebretsen, 2018).
[21] Angola's first stand-by agreement with the IMF was in 2009.

with former colonial master Portugal, also known for its relatively domestically oriented regulators.[22]

The lack of incentive to push for improved regulation meant that before 2009 Angola's engagement with international banking standards was lacking and negligible commitment to Basel standards was made. For the banking sector, implementation of international standards was unnecessary and even seen as counterproductive. This changed after the GFC. As the next section will show, changed external circumstances meant that non-compliance was increasingly difficult given the banking sector's important role in facilitating trade and outgoing financial flows. Yet implementation of international banking standards continued to conflict with the other important role of the banking sector: allocating resources to favoured constituencies. The result has been mock compliance.

Change and continuity post-2009

Following the GFC, it became clear that the equilibrium in Angola's banking sector—characterized by negligible compliance—was no longer viable. This was mainly due to three factors. First, a drastic, if relatively short-lived, fall in global oil prices resulting from the GFC took the nascent banking sector by surprise, undermining its stability. The prices of oil collapsed from $147 in August 2008 to $28 later that year (Ferreira and Soares de Oliveira, 2018). Second and alongside the economic downturn, accusations surfacing that senior BNA personnel had stolen considerable amounts of money degraded the credibility of the BNA leadership (US Senate, 2010). BNA managers were replaced in April 2009 by a new team with a reformist mandate.[23] Third, already prior to the GFC and the BNA scandal, the president and his economic team acknowledged that the rules of engagement in international finance were changing. To maintain their connection with the global markets, Angolan banks needed to adjust or at least signal their inclination to do so.[24] Accordingly, a heightened emphasis on strengthening Angola's regulatory and supervisory framework along the lines of international best practice advanced from 2009. The goal was to 'bring the banking sector up to international standards quickly' (Wallace, 2014).

The political mandate provided by the president, and his economic team, to the regulators was pivotal in transforming the BNA from a passive bystander to an active leader of the reform agenda. The new BNA leadership differed from their predecessors with their international orientation and background in the private

---

[22] Interview, IFI, Washington, DC, December 2016.
[23] Months later, investigation showed that $137 million was siphoned off to offshore accounts. Eighteen BNA and Finance Ministry officials were arrested. Interview, private bank, Portugal, September 2016.
[24] Interview, private bank, Luanda, September 2016.

sector, bolstering their standing with Angolan and foreign banks. Between 2009 and 2012, José de Lima Massano as BNA governor and Ricardo Viegas de Abreu as vice-governor successfully manoeuvred a stand-by arrangement with the IMF, the first in the country's history. The regulators were careful, however, in aligning the IFI reform agenda with regime priorities. Even when a Financial System Assessment Program was carried out in 2012, a prominent Angolan official commented that this was primarily 'a [diagnostic], not a roadmap for reform'.[25]

Yet it would be a few years from this initial reform drive before adaptation of Basel standards was implemented. We argue that this is because, before 2014, Angola's regulatory deficiencies did not jeopardize the country's cross-border transactions. The costs of going ahead with regulatory reform were still too high for politicians to accept in 2009–10. On the one hand, the banking sector still played an important redistributive role, which would likely be jeopardized by stricter regulations. On the other hand, the effects of the GFC proved brief and the Angolan economy rebounded quickly, lessening the financial pressure on the government. After an initial setback, banks had quickly resumed the expansion of services and operations (KPMG, 2016a). The period between 2010 and 2014 was therefore characterized by a degree of reformism, but lacked the sense of urgency that had been brought about by the oil price fall in 2009. In 2014 the situation changed again as the country faced an even worse, and far more durable, downturn. This time, externally driven pressure for change would prove more consequential.

In December 2016, the last supplier of US dollar bank notes to Angola discontinued its service (Almeida et al., 2016). Deutsche Bank followed in the footsteps of several banks that had cut correspondent banking relations with the country since 2014, rendering it increasingly difficult for the country to manage payments for imports and remittances. The worldwide phenomenon of de-risking, which led to a withdrawal of correspondent relationships, was not unique to Angola but because of the country's heavy reliance on imports described earlier, the withdrawal hit it particularly hard (Adriano, 2017). With oil prices falling from 2014, banks in Angola were not generating sufficient returns for correspondent banks to cover rising compliance costs (IMF, 2017). Whilst the pressure started to mount after 2014, it was clear that some foreign banks were dissatisfied with Angola's regulatory compliance before the price fall.[26] In 2003, Citibank relinquished its profitable business and pulled out of Angola because of concerns about money laundering (Almeida, 2010). The more stringent AML/CFT enforcement measures taken by the US Department of Justice from 2010 culminated in an investigation by the US Senate Permanent Sub-Committee into how politically powerful officials in Angola, their relatives, and close associates used US financial institutions to conceal, transfer, and spend funds suspected to be the proceeds of corruption

---

[25] Email correspondence, March 2016.   [26] Interview, private bank, Luanda, November 2015.

(Viswanatha and Wolf, 2012).[27] The report uncovered amongst other things how HSBC staff had facilitated suspicious wire transfers into the US on behalf of BAI. HSBC closed all US dollar accounts and ended fund transfers with Angolan banks that year (Almeida, 2010). As the misconduct of banks received greater attention in the US and subsequently in the European Union, international banks were increasingly wary of the threat of sizeable settlements and fines (Erbenova et al., 2016).[28] Attempts by Angolan authorities to leverage its relationship with China for the purpose of alternative corresponding bank links proved unfruitful, with Chinese banks cautious of falling foul of US and EU restrictions.

It was not only compliance concerns that forced foreign banks to rethink their business strategy in Angola. Both Angolan and Portuguese financial sectors were taken aback in 2014 when BESA, Angola's leading lender and subsidiary of Portuguese Banco Espírito Santo,[29] collapsed with US$5.7 billion in bad loans (Africa Confidential, 2014).[30] BESA could not identify many of its customers, although it emerged subsequently that several were politically influential individuals and groups (Africa Confidential, 2014). The political contours of the case, including direct presidential involvement, meant that regulators were reluctant to intervene earlier, even though 'it was obvious to everyone that something bad was going on'.[31] The BNA was perceived as afraid of 'ruffling the feathers of the elite' (Africa Confidential, 2014). With BESA, Angola's supervisory deficiencies and regulatory forbearance came to the attention of the European Central Bank. In 2015, it ruled that Portuguese banks must reduce their exposure to the Angolan market.[32] Following the incident, Banco BPI, Portugal's third largest private financial group, unwillingly sold its controlling share in Angola's top private bank, BFA.[33]

A common feature of the two abovementioned incidents is that they occurred in a milieu of decreasing bank returns caused by the 2014 oil price fall. This meant that foreign banks were finding it harder to maintain business as usual in Angola as it became increasingly obvious that the risks of operating in the country were outweighing the rewards. The result was the closing of correspondent bank relationships and the disinvestment by Portuguese banks, described above, jeopardizing financial sector operations in the country.

Striving to maintain the status quo in the banking sector by signalling their intention to clean up the banking sector became urgent to Angolan actors.

---

[27] Including former BNA governor, Aguinaldo Jaime. See US Senate (2010).
[28] Especially after Standard Chartered was required to pay over $300 to US authorities in 2012 for breaking sanctions on Iran (BBC News, 2012).
[29] Parent bank BES held a 55.71 per cent stake in the Angolan affiliate.
[30] In late 2013, BESA was the leading lender in Angola with a market share of 27 per cent.
[31] Interview, IFI, Washington, DC, December 2016.
[32] Angola was until then not included by the European Commission in the restricted list of states or territories recognized as having financial institution supervision not on a par with the EU.
[33] The president's daughter Isabel dos Santos holds a controlling share in BFA through telecom company UNITEL.

Forty-one new regulations were drafted between 2014 and 2016, 'covering issues ranging from bank licensing, external auditing, banks' ownership structure and anti-money laundering' as well as the implementation of Basel II (England, 2016). The Basel standards were to apply to all thirty banks in operation,[34] including the state-owned banks and, perhaps more remarkably, the country's state-owned (and poorly managed) development bank, BDA.[35]

In lieu of the significant discrepancies in the mandates and resources of the country's different banks, the implementation of Basel II was planned to happen in stages, with Angola's bigger banks implementing the new minimum capital requirements first, followed by the smaller banks who were due to do so by the end of 2017. Angola's leading private sector banks spearheaded the process,[36] whilst the state-owned banks were on the other end of the spectrum, needing additional capital to comply with the minimal requirements (Fitch Ratings, 2017).[37] As of October 2018, some banks were still due to raise their capital requirements, having been given a new deadline of December 2018 (Pilling, 2018).

It is important to note that Angola's efforts to adopt the Basel standards are part of a larger clean-up of the financial sector as the country works to restore the confidence of the international financial community in its domestic banks (KPMG, 2016a). As the partner of a leading international accounting firm noted, 'The BNA's intention is to be close to international rules'.[38] Alongside Basel adaptation, Angola gradually implemented the International Financial Reporting Standards (IFRS) for all financial institutions from 2014.[39] Currently, IFRS are required for banks and other financial institutions in the country (IFRS, n.d.).[40] Another issue that was subject to increasing concern from foreign partners was Angola's weak framework on Anti-Money Laundering and Combating Financing of Terrorism (ATM/CFT). Although current laws on ATMF/CFT date from 2011,[41] the Financial Action Task Force (FATF) has exposed strategic deficiencies in Angola's legal framework on several occasions since. Following Angola's blacklisting by the organization in 2010, several directives, presidential decrees, instructions,

---

[34] Interview with banker in international bank, Luanda, September 2016.

[35] Because the Basel standards were originally meant for internationally active banks (Sobreira and Zendron, 2011), the requirements of Basel II are not necessarily compatible with the strategic long-term objective of development banks like BDA, whose mandate is to take excessive risk. See http://bda.ao/pt-pt (accessed 12 May 2017).

[36] In a 2008 interview, BAI chief executive José de Lima Massano confirmed that the 'BAI has to adopt procedures that still have not been established by the central bank. International banks don't want to see you as bringing risk if you are dealing with them. The more our banks are exposed to international rules, the more the central bank will have to adapt' (Corbett, 2008).

[37] In 2015 the IMF noted that public banks suffered from low capital adequacy ratios and since then the position of state-owned banks has deteriorated further (Africa Confidential, 2017a).

[38] Interview with partner in international accounting firm, Luanda, October 2016.

[39] IFRS are a single set of accounting standards recognized globally (KPMG, 2016a).

[40] Interview with partner in international accounting firm, Luanda, October 2016.

[41] Law No. 34/11 of 12 December 2011.

and notices have been issued covering ATMF/CFT (FinMark Trust, 2015). Corrective legislation was passed in January 2014 criminalizing money laundering and terrorist financing, helping to remove Angola from the FATF 'grey list' in 2016 (IMF, 2014).

The speed of Angola's regulatory upgrading after many years of inaction is noteworthy. As one senior official explained, 'regulatory reform in Angola has started to converge with international standards but we are so late in the game that we have to run'.[42] Yet despite notable reformist measures and progressive legislation, Angola's efforts have so far fallen short. 'The challenge has been implementation', remarked an Angolan senior official in 2016. 'At this stage, we should concentrate on applying all the reforms we passed in recent years, rather than commit ourselves to more reforms'.[43] The 'significant disconnect between adaptation and implementation' in Angola's financial sector was confirmed by another IFI representative. Whilst resource constraints at the BNA and in the banks may explain some of this lag, over the last decade an increasing number of foreign consultants have been brought in to compensate for the lack of appropriate skills in the sector.[44] Rather than resource constraints, implementation seems mainly hampered by the lack of political will to change the status quo in the financial sector.

In the aftermath of the GFC, regulators could, and to a certain extent were encouraged to, improve sector governance. This was especially true for areas of banking sector regulation that were the focus of negative external attention. Still, we observe that regulators have refrained from exercising their right to intervene in the financial sector. 'The big political decisions are taken higher up', remarked one IFI official when talking about the BNA's mandate to rein in individual banks or to impose costs on bank shareholders. 'Even when the BNA knew that there was something bad going on, they do not have the autonomy to intervene'.[45] Because the banking standards studied here are considerably more rigorous than Angola's pre-existing domestic financial regulatory and supervisory framework, adjustment costs have been high for the domestic banks although with considerable variation between banks (Fitch Ratings, 2017). On the one hand, most of Angola's private banks (the major exception being BESA) were conservative to begin with—extending fewer loans and holding most assets in government bonds or abroad—meaning that adjustment was less of an issue for them.[46] The problem was primarily with Angola's public banks. As one foreign bank executive

---

[42] 'Managing Angola's financial sector', Event at the Blavatnik School of Government, University of Oxford, 24 January 2017.

[43] Email correspondence, March 2016.

[44] 'Managing Angola's financial sector', Event at the Blavatnik School of Government, University of Oxford, 24 January 2017.

[45] Interview with representative of international financial institution, Washington, DC, December 2016.

[46] Private banks were expected to be fully compliant with rules on capital adequacy ratios in line with Basel II by late 2017 (Fitch Ratings, 2017).

complained, 'While we are saddled with paperwork [from the regulators]', Angolan public banks 'have serious lacunae but get away with it for political reasons'.[47] The BNA's willingness and ability to impose costs of compliance on domestic interests—some of which are politically influential—is consequently weak.

In a position like this, where regulators, politicians, and bankers face contradictory pressures of international standards and domestic politics, it is predicted that actors 'often opt for a strategy of mock compliance' (Walter, 2008, p. 5). According to Walter (2008), mock compliance occurs when official legislation and regulatory guidelines are not reflected in the behaviour of either regulators or banks. This strategy 'combines the rhetoric and outward appearance of compliance with international standards together with relatively hidden behavioural divergence from such standards' (Walter, 2008, p. 5). In Angola, mock compliance has been driven by the need to signal to foreign partners that domestic counterparts are doing something to address their concerns. At the same time, the BNA has intentionally refrained from strict enforcement of international standards or chosen to enforce such rules only selectively in order to accommodate political interests that prefer to have significant parts of the banking sector, namely the public banks, remain non-compliant.

Conclusion

In this chapter we argue that Angolan actors find themselves in a difficult situation, having to balance mounting external pressures with domestic political interests. More specifically, over recent years it has become increasingly obvious that Angola needs to align its domestic regulatory framework with international standards in order to salvage the role that domestic banks have played in facilitating trade and outgoing financial flows. The problem is that another vital part of the banking sector, which concerns itself with securing political support for the regime through the granting of bank loans and licences, will struggle if faced with such strict regulation. Consequently, we have shown in this chapter that Angola's engagement with the Basel standards—as with other international banking standards—has historically been characterized by weak compliance. Until 2009, this functioned well but following the GFC, non-compliance was no longer an option. With greater external pressure banking standard alignment, Angola has resorted to mock compliance which has left great variation between the country's banks.

The combination of financial sector extraversion with deep politicization of the banking sector makes the Angolan case an intriguing one. On the one hand, it

---

[47] Interview, foreign bank, Luanda, November 2013.

challenges a common assumption in the international political economy literature that internationally oriented banking sectors will converge towards international banking standards. On the other hand, in line with the analytical framework, the Angolan trajectory demonstrates that even in the case of a highly politicized banking sector, we might see efforts to align domestic regulation with international standards. Thus, the outcome we observe in Angola and the interaction between politicians, regulators, and bankers can be described as conflicting. One thing all actors in the financial sector seem to have in common, however, is that none are there to 'rock the boat'. The financial sector has proved beneficial for all major actors involved and as long as it continues to be important for the survival of the political regime, mock compliance will likely be the way forward. The extent to which this is sustainable will depend on external factors, especially the price of oil, which Angolan actors have little power over. In relation to the analytical framework, as mock compliance is driven by the conflicting preferences of politicians, this is a case of politically driven mock compliance.

This chapter is amongst the first to offer a detailed overview of the political economy of banking regulation in Angola alongside an analysis of the country's adaptation and implementation of Basel to date.[48] We emphasize the uneven pattern of compliance that has emerged in the banking sector but further research is needed to evaluate the efforts of particular banks and whether they will keep to their assigned schedules. As the banking sector and banking regulation in particular are policy areas undergoing significant change—not only in Angola but internationally—it will be crucial for researchers to keep a close eye on future developments. As the example of Angola shows, understanding domestic and global dynamics and how the two interrelate is crucial if one wants to understand local responses to international banking standards.

References

Adriano, A., 2017. When money can no longer travel. *Finance & Development* 54.

Africa Confidential, 2014. Good banks from bad 55.

Africa Confidential, 2017a. The bad loans bite back. *Africa Confidential* 58.

Africa Confidential, 2017b. Bank scandals hit MPLA hard. *Africa Confidential* 58.

African Development Bank, 2008. *African Economic Outlook 2008*. Tunis.

Agência Angola Press, 2012. BPC tem disponível mais de um bilião de kwanzas para Angola Investe. URL http://www.angop.ao.

Agência Angola Press, 2017. Angolan banking with assets of AKZ 10.66 trillion. URL http://www.angop.ao.

---

[48] See also Engebretsen (2018).

Almeida, H., 2010. HSBC shuns Angola banks on corruption fears: source. *Reuters*.

Almeida, H., Mendes, C., Arons, S., 2016. Deutsche Bank said last lender to stop Angola dollar clearing. *Bloomberg*.

BBC News, 2012. Bank hit by $300m in Iran fines. *BBC*.

Beblawi, H., Luciani, G. (Eds.), 1987. The rentier state in the Arab world, in: *The Rentier State: Nation, State and the Integration of the Arab World*. Croom Helm, London.

Beck, T., Maimbo, S., Faye, I., Triki, T., 2011. *Financing Africa: Through the Crisis and Beyond*. World Bank, Washington, DC.

Bhattacharyya, S., Hodler, R., 2014. Do natural resource revenues hinder financial development? The role of political institutions. *World Development* 57, 101–13. https://doi.org/10.1016/j.worlddev.2013.12.003.

BIS, 2017. *Consolidated banking statistics*. BIS.

Bureau van Dijk, 2018. *Bankscope and Orbis Bank Focus*. London, Bureau van Dijk.

Corbett, C., 2008. Banks play catch-up as Angola blossoms. *The Banker*.

Deloitte, 2012. *Deloitte on Africa Banking regulatory environment and supervision in Africa*. Deloitte.

Engebretsen, R., 2018. *Financial sector change in the context of oil-abundance: Angola, 1991–2014*. (PhD). University of Oxford.

England, A., 2016. Angola pledges tighter bank regulation in face of dollar drought. *Financial Times*.

Erbenova, M., Liu, Y., Kyriakos-Saad, N., Mejia, A.L., Gasha, J.G., Mathias, E., Norat, M., Fernando, F., Almeida, Y., 2016. *The withdrawal of correspondent banking relationships: A case for policy action*. Staff Discussion Note No. 16/06. IMF, Washington, DC.

Expansão, 2016. *Banca Especial*. Luanda.

Ferreira, M.E., Soares de Oliveira, R., 2018. Political economy of banking in Angola. *African Affairs*.

FinMark Trust, 2015. *Angola report on AML/CFT and Financial Inclusion in SADC*. FinMark Trust.

Fitch Ratings, 2017. Divergence widens between Angola's BANKS. *Reuters*.

FSI, 2015. *FSI Survey: Basel II, 2.5 and III implementation*. Financial Stability Institute.

Gottschalk, R., 2010. *The Basel Capital Accords in Developing Countries: Challenges for Development Finance*. Palgrave Macmillan, Basingstoke.

Hodges, T., 2004. *Angola: Anatomy of an Oil State*. Fridtjof Nansen Institute.

IFRS, n.d. *IFRS—Angola* [WWW Document]. URL https://www.ifrs.org/use-around-the-world/use-of-ifrs-standards-by-jurisdiction/angola (accessed 29.1.19).

IMF, 2000. *Angola: Letter of Intent—Memorandum of Economic and Financial Policies*. IMF, Washington, DC.

IMF, 2009. *IMF Country Report* No. 09/320. IMF, Washington, DC.

IMF, 2010. *Statement by Mr. Moeketsi Majoro, Alternate Executive Director for Angola*, September 24, IMF Country Report No. 10/302. IMF, Washington, DC.

IMF, 2011a. *Angola: Letter of Intent, Memorandum of Economic and Financial Policies*, and Technical Memorandum of Understanding. IMF, Washington, DC.

IMF, 2011b. *IMF Country Report* No. 11/5. IMF, Washington, DC.

IMF, 2012. *Angola: Financial System Stability Assessment*. IMF, Washington, DC.

IMF, 2014. *IMF Country Report* No. 14/274. IMF, Washington, DC.

IMF, 2015. *Angola: Selected Issues*. IMF, Washington, DC.

IMF, 2017. *Recent Trends in Correspondent Banking Relationships—Further Considerations*. IMF, Washington, DC.

IMF, 2018. *Financial Soundness Indicators Database*. IMF, Washington, DC.

Jones, E., Zeitz, A.O., 2017. The limits of globalizing Basel banking standards. *Journal of Financial Regulation* 3, 89–124.

King, J., 2016. Angola's banks will sink or swim over wave of consolidation and regulation. *The Banker*, 1 July. https://www.thebanker.com/World/Africa/Angola/Angola-s-banks-will-sink-or-swim-over-wave-of-consolidation-and-regulation?ct=true.

KPMG, 2016a. *Angola Banking Survey*. Luanda, KPMG.

KPMG, 2016b. *Novo quadro de Avisos e Instructivos Regulamentares do Banco Nacional de Angola*. Breve Enquadramento e Análise. Luanda, KPMG.

Oliveira, R.S. de, 2015. *Magnificent and Beggar Land: Angola Since the Civil War*. Oxford University Press, Oxford.

Peralta, E., 2017. Foreign currency crisis tells the story of Angola's economic peril. *NPR.org*.

Pilling, D., 2018. Angolan central bank chief warns lenders to boost capital. *Financial Times*.

Polity IV, 2014. *PolityProject*. Center for Systemic Peace.

Santos, H., Santos, F., 2018. *Angola: Banking regulation 2018*. African Law & Business Banking Regulation 2018.

Semanário Angolense, 2008. *Sonangol entra no BFA* [WWW Document]. Angonotícias. URL http://www.angonoticias.com/Artigos/item/18021/sonangol-entra-no-bfa (accessed 11.6.18).

Sobreira, R., Zendron, P., 2011. Implications of Basel II for national development banks, in: Gnos, C., Rochon, L.-P. (Eds.), *Credit, Money and Macroeconomic Policy: A Post-Keynesian Approach*. Edward Elgar Publishing, Cheltenham. https://doi.org/10.4337/9781849808729.00018.

The Observatory of Economic Complexity, n.d. *Angola Profile* [WWW Document]. The Observatory of Economic Complexity. URL https://atlas.media.mit.edu/en/profile/country/ago (accessed 11.6.18).

US Senate, 2010. *Keeping Foreign Corruption out of the United States: Four Case Histories*, Permanent Sub-Committee on Investigations, United States Senate. Washington, DC.

Viswanatha, A., Wolf, B., 2012. DOJ targets banks, others in new money laundering offensive. *Reuters*.

Wallace, P., 2012. Game changers loom for Angolan banks. *The Banker*.

Wallace, P., 2014. Angola's CBG reforms his way to stability. *The Banker*.

Wallace, P., 2015. A new landscape for Angola's fast-growing banks. *The Banker*.

Walter, A., 2008. *Governing finance: East Asia's adoption of international standards*. Cornell University Press, Ithaca, NY.

Wise, P., 2015. The spark amid a slump: Will Angola's banks emerge from oil price dip stronger? *The Banker*.

World Bank, 1992. *Staff Appraisal Report People's Republic of Angola Financial Institutions Modernization Project*. World Bank, Washington, DC.

World Bank, 2014. *Angola—Global Financial Inclusion* (Global Findex) Database 2014. World Bank, Washington, DC.

World Bank, 2017. *World Development Indicators*. World Bank, Washington, DC.

World Bank, 2018. Domestic credit to private sector (% of GDP): Data [WWW Document]. URL https://data.worldbank.org/indicator/FS.AST.PRVT.GD.ZS (accessed 5.12.17).

13

Vietnam

The Dilemma of Bringing Global Financial Standards to a Socialist Market Economy

Que-Giang Tran-Thi and Tu-Anh Vu-Thanh

Introduction

The implementation of international banking standards in Vietnam has been the subject of contestation between reformist and conservative factions within the banking regulatory system. In any given period, the speed of implementation has been affected by which of these factions dominates regulatory decision-making, as well as the health of the banking sector. The existence of two political factions with conflicting preferences regarding Basel standards generates dynamics that lead to mock compliance. With regards to the analytical framework, the dynamics are those of politically driven mock compliance.

The adoption and implementation of Basel standards in Vietnam has gone through three distinctive periods. In the first period (1999–2006), Vietnam actively adopted economic integration as a development strategy. Vietnam signed a bilateral trade agreement with the US in 2001, and concluded its World Trade Organization (WTO) negotiations in 2006. The economy enjoyed a high growth rate of 7.4 per cent in the first half of the 2000s, and everyone seemed to be very optimistic about future economic prospects. In this context, the internationally oriented reformist faction within the government, which pursued international regulations to discipline state-owned banks and improve the functioning of the financial sector, won the tug of war with the conservative faction, at least temporarily. The central bank, the State Bank of Vietnam (SBV), which is always subservient to the prevailing political agenda, informally adopted Basel I and laid out the roadmap for its implementation. Banks—both private and state-owned—did not have a voice in setting Basel-related policies, and were indifferent to plans for its implementation since they thought it was premature and unfeasible.

At the beginning of the second period (2006–13), Vietnam formally adopted Basel II standards. However, the country experienced a banking crisis between 2008 and 2012, when nearly a dozen banks were on the verge of collapse and some actually became technically bankrupt. Facing this crisis, even reformists factions

Que-Giang Tran-Thi and Tu-Anh Vu-Thanh, *Vietnam: The Dilemma of Bringing Global Financial Standards to a Socialist Market Economy* In: *The Political Economy of Bank Regulation in Developing Countries: Risk and Reputation.* Edited by: Emily Jones, Oxford University Press (2020). © Oxford University Press.
DOI: 10.1093/oso/9780198841999.003.0013

hesitated to move forward with Basel, because implementing the standards properly would have exposed the significant weaknesses in both private and state-owned banks, exacerbating the crisis situation. The shift in the preferences of the reformists and the SBV during this period effectively halted the implementation of Basel standards. Meanwhile, the reluctance of banks, many of which were in a difficult situation, made Basel implementation even less feasible than in the previous period.

The third period (2014 onward) has been characterized by a return to pro-Basel preferences. Once the crisis had passed, and the economic integration process had regained its strong momentum, the reformist faction could again push forwards with the implementation of international standards. The SBV wants to use Basel standards to discipline and clean up weak banks. Moreover, many private banks and even state-owned banks now perceive Basel standards as being important for managing their liquidity, improving supervision and risk, signalling their health, and enduring competitive pressures. Thanks to more genuine interests from the politicians, regulators, and banks, the implementation of Basel II has been accelerated, and some elements of Basel III such as liquidity coverage ratio (LCR) and net stable funding ratio (NSFR) are reflected in the banking regulations issued by the SBV.

Through an analysis of aggregate data and thirty interviews with regulators, bankers, financial experts, and politicians in Vietnam, in this chapter we show that Vietnam's case is an example of conflicting preferences for Basel adoption and implementation, particularly in the second period. The reformists rely on Vietnam's international commitments and opt for international standards (Basel in particular) to reform the domestic banking sector. At the same time, interventionist financial policies, costly implementation, the low internationalization level of the banking sector, and the lack of competent technocrats inside both the SBV and domestic private banks have all contributed to a high level of forbearance in Basel implementation.

Table 13.1 Vietnam: key indicators

Vietnam	
GDP per capita (current US$, 2017)	2343
Bank assets (current US$)	267.7 bn
Bank assets (% of GDP)	130.4
Stock market capitalization (% of GDP)	28.6
Credit allocation to private sector (% of GDP)	123.8
Credit allocation to government (% of GDP)	18.1
Polity IV score (2017)	−7

Note: All data is from 2016 unless otherwise indicated.

Source: FSI Database, IMF (2018); GDI Database, World Bank (2017); Polity IV (2014)

The rest of this chapter is organized as follows. The next section provides a brief description of Vietnam's political economic context for the adoption and implementation of Basel standards. The third section traces the three periods of Basel adoption and implementation in Vietnam since 1999. The fourth section provides a political economic explanation of Basel adoption and implementation in Vietnam. The final section concludes and provides some reflections on the analytical framework.

Political economic context of Basel adoption and implementation in Vietnam

Vietnam began Doi Moi—the transformation from a centrally planned economy to a socialist-oriented market economy—in 1986. Since then, international economic integration has been a major driver of economic growth, which has become an increasingly key factor in determining the performance legitimacy of the Vietnamese party-state. A growing list of economic integration commitments, including membership in the WTO, the Trans-Pacific Partnership (TPP), and the Regional Comprehensive Economic Partnership (RCEP), has created an interesting 'dualism' (Vu-Thanh, 2017). On the one hand, in order to continue economic integration, the Vietnamese party-state wishes to express itself as being internationally oriented, by complying with international norms and practices. On the other hand, as a 'socialist-oriented economy', the party-state always wants to maintain firm control over the economy, both directly through state-owned enterprises (including state-owned banks) playing the leading role, and indirectly by means of interventionist regulations.

As of 2017, Vietnam's financial sector relies heavily on banks in which four big state-owned banks account for 45.7 per cent of total assets and 48.3 per cent of the credit market share. Private banks are much smaller and rather concentrated, with the ten biggest private banks making up 33 per cent of total assets and 31 per cent of the credit market share. Foreign-owned banks are of modest size, only accounting for 9.5 per cent of total assets, even though they represent 21.4 per cent of charter capital (State Bank of Vietnam, 2017). Nevertheless, this group of banks has enjoyed quite rapid growth in the last several years, as commitments to open up the financial market come into effect.

Vietnam still has a Leninist state in which the party rules over the government. The government, in turn, rules over the SBV, and the SBV exercises discretionary power over commercial banks. This hierarchical relationship is reflected in the policy cycle in Vietnam. Major strategic orientations (e.g. restructuring the banking system) originate from the Politburo (the highest organ of the Communist Party of Vietnam) through its resolutions and conclusions. When it comes to technical matters (e.g. banking supervision and safety regulations), the SBV will recommend policies to the government for approval. An approved policy will then come back to the SBV for implementation. If these policies are to be legalized, draft legal documents will be passed to the National Assembly for deliberation and approval. After these policies are enacted, commercial banks, which have virtually no voice during the policy process, are forced to comply.

The Party Central Committee exerts direct and indirect influence over the appointment of personnel to key positions, including Central Bank Governor and the chairmen of state-owned banks. This situation creates an ambiguity in the positions of politicians, regulators, and bankers. On the one hand, a number of politicians are in a position to supervise the banking and financial sector, but do not have a professional background in the industry. On the other hand, there are many key regulators who are just temporarily rotated through these positions before becoming political appointees somewhere else. Moreover, the leadership of the SBV plays a 'triple role' as politicians, banking regulators, and representatives of state ownership in state-owned banks. These overlapping and ambiguous roles give rise to many serious regulatory conflicts, as discussed below, where we explain how aspects of Vietnam's implementation of Basel standards are instances of mock compliance (Walter, 2008). In sum, the current institutions, whether in the guise of politicians or personnel, show widespread outright forbearance by the SBV, particularly during the time of the banking crisis between 2008 and 2012.

Since the mid-2000s, Vietnam's economy underwent many changes with long-lasting implications for the financial system. Inheriting a high growth and stable economy, the ambitious new prime minister wanted to accelerate GDP growth even further by loosening both fiscal and monetary policy (Kazmin and Mallet, 2008). As a result, inflation reached 28 per cent in 2008, while abundant credit inflated stock and real estate bubbles in the 2007–8 period. When the bubble burst, a series of banks held huge amounts of bad debt, mostly guaranteed by real estate, the market value of which was now much lower, threatening the collapse of the banking system.

To make matters worse, also during this period, the SBV decided to upgrade rural commercial banks to urban commercial banks, forcing their charter capital to increase rapidly in a very short period of time. As a result, the domestic private banks quickly became the largest sector (Figure 13.1). However, in order to meet charter capital requirements, many smaller banks borrowed from each other or partnered with state conglomerates, thereby leading to cross- and pyramidal-ownership structures. In addition, the rapid GDP growth over this time was accompanied by a myriad of unscrupulous credits, which further exacerbated the rise in bad loans in the banking sector, especially for those that had recently become urban commercial banks.

In 2009, the real estate bubble burst, the stock market plummeted, and state economic groups suffered heavy losses. As a result, the banking system went

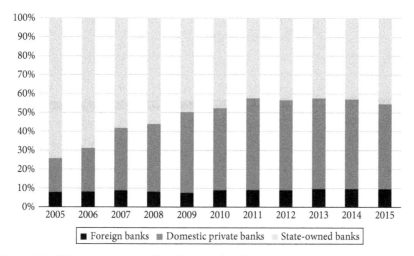

Figure 13.1 Vietnam: patterns of bank ownership (% of total deposits).
Source: Authors' calculations based on the State Bank of Vietnam's Annual Reports, State Bank of Vietnam (2017)

through a serious crisis. At the end of 2011, non-performing loans (NPLs) in the banking system were up to 13 per cent according to Fitch Ratings (National Assembly's Economic Committee and UNDP, 2012). Many banks suffered from liquidity shortages, and some banks were in principle bankrupt.

In the wake of the financial crisis, the SBV took steps to address financial instability, focusing on the banking sector. In 2011, the SBV classified Vietnam's credit institutions into four groups, and imposed a credit growth ceiling on each group (State Bank of Vietnam, 2012a). However, in order to preserve 'system stability', the SBV did not publish the list of institutions in each group. Banks in Group 1 and Group 2 are considered 'healthy' and therefore given a ceiling credit growth of 17 per cent and 15 per cent, respectively. Banks in Group 3 are 'medium risk' and given credit growth of up to 8 per cent. Finally, those in Group 4 are 'high risk' and are not allowed to extend any credit. Facing the risk of a banking crisis, the highest priority of the SBV in this period was not to implement modern financial standards such as Basel, but rather to ensure the safety of the banking system, control interest rates, and ensure its leadership role of state-owned commercial banks through various financial repression measures.

Since 2014, the economy has been recovering, although the NPL ratio is still high at around 10 per cent. The economic recovery has facilitated the resumption in implementation of Basel standards. Moreover, the SBV is now keen to implement Basel standards in order to improve the risk management of banks and avert future bankruptcies.

The adoption and implementation of Basel standards in Vietnam

As described above, there have been three distinct periods in the adoption and implementation of Basel standards in Vietnam. In the first period (1999–2006), Basel I was informally adopted—at this stage, the SBV never announced the adoption of Basel standards explicitly, but incorporated some elements of Basel I into its banking regulations. In the second period (2006–13), the SBV strongly endorsed the adoption and implementation of Basel I, and outlined a roadmap to achieving Basel II compliance by 2010. However, the banking crisis during 2008–12 and the resulting shift in politicians' preferences turned Basel implementation into nothing more than mock compliance in this period. Since 2014, as the economic situation has improved and economic integration has regained momentum, the preferences of politicians, regulators, and banks have shifted again, and this time they are conducive to a more genuine implementation of Basel II, and even some elements of Basel III. The adoption and implementation of Basel standards in Vietnam are summarized in Table 13.2.

1999–2006: The informal adoption of Basel I

Both the Law on the State Bank of Vietnam and the Law on Credit Institutions were first issued in 1997. Two years later, the SBV promulgated Decisions 296 and 297 to introduce Basel-like standards for Vietnam such as customer credit limits, minimum capital requirements, and asset classification in four risk categories. Under Basel I, banks are required to hold a minimum of 8 per cent of risk-weighted capital, including both Tier 1 and Tier 2 capital. However, as revealed in our interviews, because of a misunderstanding of the definition of Tier 1 capital in the Basel I standards, Decision 297 required banks to hold a minimum of 8 per cent of Tier 1 capital. As a result, commercial banks faced fundamental difficulties in dealing with the aftermath of the Asian Financial Crisis, and were unable to meet the minimum capital requirement.

There are two particularly interesting points regarding the implementation of Basel-like regulations in this period. First, the lead time between the issuance of implementation regulations and the effective date was very short—less than a month for both Decisions 297 and 457 (see Table 13.2). This raises the question of whether the SBV really understood the difficulties banks faced when they had to implement these standards, or whether the SBV issued regulations just to be able to say it had without much thought about their enforcement. Secondly, with Decision 457, state-owned banks were granted a grace period of three years. While this means that the SBV understood that these banks could not meet these standards immediately, it also reveals the preferential treatment state-owned banks enjoyed relative to their privately owned peers.

Table 13.2 Vietnam: adoption of Basel standards

Basel component	Adoption	Implementation	Date in force
Basel I	**Informal adoption** *(There was no public commitment to Basel I, but banking regulations were in line with Basel I standards)*	Decisions 297 (25 August 1999) *Simple rules on prudential ratios require Tier 1 at 8%*	9 September 1999 (+ 3 years of grace period)
		Decision 457 (19 April 2005) *Rules on prudential ratios—define CAR (including Tier 1 and Tier 2) at 8%*	4 May 2005 (+ 3 years of grace period for state-owned banks)
	Formal adoption Prime minister's Decision 112 (24 May 2006) *Basel 1 as the supervision standards by 2010* *Implement Basel II guidelines and standards after 2010*	Established Banking Inspection and Supervision Agency under the SBV in 2009 Revised Law on the State Bank of Vietnam and the Law on Credit Institutions (16 June 2010)	January 2011
Basel II	*(Decision 112/2006-PM)*	Circular 13/2010 (20 May 2010) *CAR separate and consolidated at 9%; total liquidity reserves (15%) and 7 days (100%); requirement on stress-testing and scenario analysis* SBV's Official Correspondence No. 1601 (17 March 2014)	October 2010
	Prime minister's Decision No. 254 dated 1 March 2012 *Pillar I: Issue Basel II compliance standards* *Pillar II: Develop risk management systems consistent with the principles and standards of Basel Committee* *Pillar III: Disclose information according to Basel Committee principles*	*Standard approach (credit, operational, and market risks)* *10 pilot banks* *Other banks* Circular 41/2016/TT-NHNN dated 30 December 2016 *Regulating capital adequacy ratio (CAR)* *Credit risk and market risk: SA* *Operational risk: BIA* Pillar II: ICAAP *(Circular 13/2018-TT-NHNN dated 18 May 2018)*	By 2015 By 2018 January 2020 January 2019
	Prime minister's Decision No. 1058 (19 July 2017) *Basel II, pillars I and II by 2020* *Roadmap*	SBV decision No. 1533 dated 20 July 2017 *Action plan in detail*	2017–20
Basel III	**Informal adoption** *(No public commitment to Basel III, but banking regulations were in line with Basel III standards)*	Prime minister's Decision No. 986 (8 August 2018) *Banking development strategy—BCP and Basel II SA*	2020–5
		Circular 36/2014 dated 20 November 2014 *CAR at 9% and liquidity ratio:* *(proxy) LCR 30 days: 50% for VND, 10% for other currencies;* *(proxy) NSFR: 10%*	2 February 2015

2006–13: The formal adoption of Basel I and Basel II

It was not until 2006 that Vietnamese regulators officially referred to Basel I and II in Decision 112 of the prime minister. This decision stipulated a plan for the 2006–10 period to improve regulations on banking security, supervision, and management in accordance with Basel I, and to implement Basel II guidelines and standards after 2010. The project, which was implemented in the context of Vietnam's preparations for joining the WTO, aimed to develop the banking industry by deepening its integration and strengthening its competitiveness. However, no legal document existed that specified a roadmap to ensure the implementation of Basel II.

The Banking Inspection and Supervision Agency under the SBV was established in 2009, marking an important step towards the implementation of Basel standards. The revised Law on the State Bank of Vietnam and the Law on Credit Institutions of 2010 made important changes to the definition of the status and functions of state-owned banks, including clear definitions of important concepts such as banking operations, principles of bank governance, internal control, and information transparency.

When Circular 13 on the safety ratios was issued in May 2010, developed countries had been on their way to adopt Basel III. This Circular is more ambitious than Basel II, since it sets the minimum capital adequacy ratio (CAR) at 9 per cent. However, it does not consider operational risk, or market risk, or Basel III standards for a capital conservation buffer and countercyclical buffer requirements. Circular 13 encountered a lot of opposition from banks because the lead time given to them was only five months. Once again, the SBV appears to have understood that it takes time and a great deal of effort for banks to implement Basel standards, which they could otherwise only comply with using manipulated data.

Although regulatory reforms were made on paper, implementation of Basel standards and compliance with Basel Core Principles were limited, reflecting the regulators' priority of controlling the banking system and preventing its collapse, as well as the lack of competent SBV technocrats. Available evaluations show that by the early 2010s, most Basel Core Principles were complied with either partially or not at all. According to the self-assessment conducted by the SBV (NFSC, 2018), 'the banking supervision system says 4/25 principles are compliant, 9/25 are largely compliant, 11/25 largely non-compliant, and 1/25 not compliant'.

Indeed, SBV's mock compliance with the Basel standards is evident in the fact that it has permitted the use of compromised and falsified data by banks. For instance, during the time of the banking crisis, the SBV largely overlooked the CAR of banks. This results in an ironic paradox: stronger and larger banks often reported a CAR of around 10 per cent, while many weaker and smaller banks,

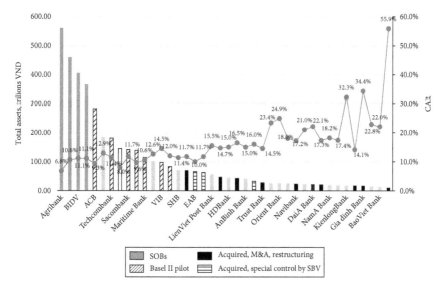

Figure 13.2 Vietnam: bank capital adequacy ratios (2011).

Source: STOXPLUS data (30-Sep-2012). *Vietnam Banks - A Helicopter View* - Issue 4. Asset and Capital Quality

which were later acquired or restructured, reported a CAR above 10 per cent or even up to 30 per cent (Figure 13.2).

The second piece of evidence of the SBV's forbearance towards regulation is that it turns a blind eye to banks' NPLs. On paper, most banks in Vietnam have met the NPL ratio requirements (i.e. less than 3 per cent). However, NPL figures from other sources seem to be at odds with official figures (Figure 13.3). According to the SBV, the official average NPL ratio in June 2011 was 3.2 per cent, while according to Fitch it was about 13 per cent. In 2012, the bad debt shown in bank reports fluctuated around 4.4 per cent, while the supervisory agency reported 8.6 per cent, and other independent institutions estimated it at around 15–17 per cent. Later, the SBV also admitted the bad debt had occasionally been 17.2 per cent in 2012.[1]

Thirdly, in this period, when the banking system was in trouble—liquidity risks and bad debts were high, and some banks were bankrupt at times—the SBV decided to wholeheartedly support these banks in every way it could. This included adjusting the rules to help them hide bad debt, and establishing the Vietnam Asset Management Company (VAMC) to help banks freeze bad debts and clean up their accounting books.

---

[1] Report No. 36/BC-NHNN dated 4 April 2017 of the SBV to review the enforcement of legal regulations to handle weak credit institutions.

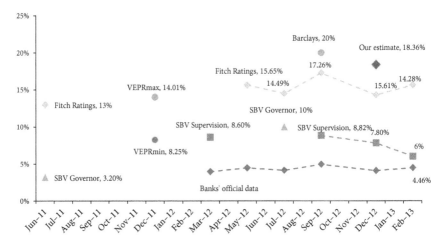

Figure 13.3 Vietnam: non-performing loans (NPLs) in times of crisis (2011–13).
Source: Vu-Thanh et al. (2013)

Interestingly, faced with the banking system's severe liquidity problems and bad debts in the 2008–12 period, the prime minister's Decision No. 254 from March 2012, titled 'Decision on Approving the Scheme of Restructuring the System of Credit Institutions for the period of 2011–2015', referred to Basel II as the solution to the problem. The focus was 'to issue capital adequacy standards in line with Basel II, providing standards for disclosure of information by credit institutions in line with reality in Vietnam and the principles of the Basel Committee'. However, in the context of widespread troubles in banks and capital shortages, Basel implementation was essentially impossible, and perhaps merely cosmetic. Indeed, in this period, the State Bank even promulgated regulations that assisted banks in reclassifying debts (see SBV's Decision No. 780, State Bank of Vietnam, 2012b) in order to improve their operational safety ratios and keep their NPL ratio within limits.

2014 onwards: The acceleration of Basel II

In the third period, the implementation of Basel standards accelerated. Basel II was strongly emphasized in the SBV's Official Correspondence No. 1601 in March 2014, regarding implementing capital adequacy regulations. Specifically, ten domestic banks were selected to carry out the capital and risk management pilot under Basel II standards.[2] It was expected that by 2015, these ten banks would

---

[2] These banks are BIDV, Vietinbank (CTG), Vietcombank (VCB), Techcombank (TCB), Asia Commercial Bank (ACB), VPBank, Military Bank (MBB), Maritime Bank (MSB), Sacombank (STB), and International Bank (VIB).

follow the standardized approaches with respect to evaluating credit risk, market risk, and operational risk under Basel II, and would be fully in line with Basel II standards by 2018. Foreign-invested banks and banks with 100 per cent foreign capital were expected to implement the same Basel standards as those adopted by their parent banks, and from 2015 they were required to implement standards at least as stringent as Basel II. All other domestic private banks were expected to implement basic Basel standards II at a minimum by 2018. In sum, according to the roadmap laid out by the SBV in 2014, all banks in Vietnam were expected to be implementing the basic standards of Basel II by 2018. Circular 36 (November 2014) regulated the safety ratios of credit institutions and was considered a stepping stone for further development of Basel II in the sector. This Circular also adjusted liquidity risk requirements and brought them closer in line with Basel III.

Despite these intentions, by the end of 2015, after the assessment of data gaps[3] and the quantitative impact study (QIS) of ten pilot banks, the original plan was abandoned because the original ten banks did not meet the requirements and there remained a serious lack of enforcement by the SBV. In our interviews, pilot banks pointed out that there was a significant difference between the CAR calculations in the SBV's guidance and international standards.[4] Indeed, the SBV did not truly force the pilot banks to follow the roadmap because its immediate concern at that time was 'crisis management' (i.e. avoiding bank failures) rather than improving banks' governance. At the same time, banks got used to the SBV's 'compromise', in the form of *ad hoc* forbearance or modification of regulations—sometimes right before their effective dates—and did not make serious efforts to comply.

By 2016, the goal of preventing banks from failing was viewed as accomplished, at least according to the government's judgement, and the SBV returned its focus to strengthening banks' governance, in order to prevent future failures. In November 2016, the National Assembly issued Resolution No. 24 on the Economic Restructuring Plan for the period 2016–20. Its aim was to 'generally complete the restructuring of credit institutions, step up settlement of bad debts and gradually apply Basel II to credit institutions. By 2020, it is expected that commercial banks have their own capital satisfactory to Basel II including at least 12–15 commercial banks in which Basel II is successfully applied'.

Following this National Assembly Resolution, in December 2016 the SBV issued Circular 41, which will enter into force by 1 January 2020, and which prescribes the capital adequacy requirements for commercial banks. It is worth

---

[3] According to an SBV leader who is in charge of Basel implementation, banks' current data can only meet about 45 per cent of Basel II requirements. Also, more information is needed to develop internal credit rating models and systems.

[4] According to the National Financial Supervisory Council, applying Basel standards to calculate CAR for ten pilot banks shows a much lower ratio than the current one, mostly due to increased risky assets. For the four State Owned Commercial Banks (SOCBs), the current CAR is about 9 per cent, while it would be lower than 8 per cent if Basel II were used.

noting that this time it is not only the ten pilot banks that are subject to the new regulation, but all commercial banks (including foreign-invested banks and 100 per cent foreign-owned banks) are required to participate. Circular 41 is considered to be very close to Basel II standards, and even refers to elements of Basel III, as well as the most up-to-date Bank for International Settlements (BIS) discussions on incorporating Basel criteria for a standard approach and the internal ratings-based approach. The resolve to implement Basel II seems to be stronger than in previous periods. The prime minister and SBV approved the plan to restructure credit institutions and deal with NPLs—the so-called Project 1058—and Basel II was highlighted as a benchmark for improving the financial and governance capacities of credit institutions. Banks also appear to be taking implementation more seriously. Although progressing at different rates, in the last few years the group of pilot banks have demonstrated considerable efforts to implement Basel II in a more genuine way than just for the sake of meeting the requirements of the SBV.

The acceleration of Basel implementation is part of a wider trend by the SBV to apply international financial standards in Vietnam. The SBV has also begun to introduce international standards on anti-money laundering (AML), credit rating agencies, CAMELS standards, anti-dollarization, and the reduction of cash transactions.

The political economy of Basel adoption and implementation in Vietnam

Although Vietnam has a unitary political system, within the Vietnamese Communist Party there are factions with different views on state-owned banks and financial reform. While reform-minded politicians, who are often more internationally oriented, expect to use international yardsticks such as Basel standards to impose discipline on state-owned banks and reform the banking system, conservative-minded politicians fear that imposing 'capitalist rules' on the state-owned banks not only makes the Party look bad, but also exposes the weaknesses of these 'leading' state-owned banks. These conservatives, therefore, face a dilemma: they are aware that in order to reinforce the legitimacy of the Party-State's performance, economic integration (i.e. opening trade, investment, and finance) is inevitable; at the same time, they fear that economic integration will erode the primacy of the state-owned sector, and, therefore, Vietnam's socialist orientation.

The SBV is a ministerial-level agency under the government, which in this Leninist state makes it subservient to politicians, meaning it has hardly any autonomy (Vu-Thanh, 2011). In addition, the SBV is expected to pursue multiple goals simultaneously: it plays the role of both a central bank and a government bank; it is supposed to stabilize the currency value as well as ensure the safety of the banking system; it is also given the political task of 'contributing to the socio-economic development along the socialist orientation'; and it is the regulatory body that supervises the credit institution system and, at the same time, the representative of state ownership in state-owned banks. These multiple goals and mandates give rise to many conflicts in banking regulation. Moreover, since leaders of the SBV are political appointees, when these conflicts emerge, they are supposed to follow the Party's instructions and safeguard its legitimacy.

Commercial banks in Vietnam can be classified into three groups according to their ownership: state, domestic private, and foreign. In Vietnam state-owned banks, despite their ineffectiveness and lack of transparency, are always considered by the party-state as an important instrument for controlling the monetary market and ensuring macro-economic stability. Meanwhile, domestic private banks have grown very quickly since the early 2000s, to become the biggest actor in the banking sector in Vietnam today. This group can be divided into two sub-groups. The first consists of relatively weak banks (those with small assets and high NPLs), most of which were upgraded from rural banks in the early 2000s. The second subgroup is made up of the relatively strong banks (i.e. large assets, moderate NPLs) that have the ambition to expand by searching for foreign strategic shareholders or advancing into international markets. The third group is made up of foreign banks, and currently accounts for only about 10 per cent of market share. As noted above, private banks, both domestic and foreign, have virtually no voice in the policy process.

The remainder of this section provides a political economy explanation of how and why Basel implementation has changed over time in Vietnam, with a particular focus on the second period (i.e. 2006–13). The summary of our analysis is presented in Table 13.3.

Informal adoption and slow implementation of Basel I

The period from 1999 to 2006 witnessed some of Vietnam's most important and successful market reforms since Doi Moi. As the country recovered from the negative impact of the Asian financial crisis, Vietnam stepped up its domestic reforms and international integration.

The reformist faction of policymakers took advantage of this exuberant domestic reform and international integration to introduce international standards in order to discipline state-owned banks and improve the functioning of the financial sector. The SBV, which is always subservient to the prevailing political will, informally adopted Basel I and laid out the roadmap for its implementation by issuing Decision 297 in 1999, and Decision 457 in 2005, to require banks to satisfy prudential ratios. It could be argued further that since things appeared to be

Table 13.3 Vietnam: preferences of major actors with respect to Basel adoption and implementation

	Economic context	Politicians		Regulator (SBV)	Banks				Basel standards	
		Reformist	Conservative		Weak POBs	Strong POBs	Foreign	SOBs	Adoption	Implementation
Period 1 1999–2006	Active integration (BTA 2001, conclusion of WTO 2006) High growth, bright perspectives	+	+/–	+	~	~	NA	~	+	+
Period 2 2007–13	Not much integration Growth slow down Banking crisis	+/–	–	+/–	–	–	~	–	+	–
Period 3 Since 2014	Active integration (TPP 2015, AEC 2015, EVFTA 2016) Growth recovery Bank consolidation	+	+/–	+	–	+	~	+	+	+

Note: [+] means 'support Basel' [–] means 'not support Basel' [+/–] means 'conflicting preferences' [~] means 'indifferent' SOBs: state-owned banks; POBs: private-owned banks; SBV: State Bank of Vietnam
Source: Authors' evaluation

going well, and no one, including the reformist faction, was asking many questions, even if SBV officers knew at the time that there were a lot of inefficiencies, they had an incentive to keep quiet or otherwise risk harming their own careers as political appointees.

Having little experience with banking reforms of the likes of Basel, the SBV imposed very demanding requirements on commercial banks. As mentioned above, Decision 297 required banks to meet Tier 1 capital requirements of up to 8 per cent, while Basel standards required 8 per cent for both Tier 1 and Tier 2 capital together. When no bank met this ambitious requirement, the SBV issued Decision 457, which was more in line with Basel I standards. However, the SBV gave banks only one month to meet this new regulation, a timeline that was impossible for the banks to meet.

In summary, the excitement of reform and the integration efforts of reformist politicians led the SBV to informally adopt, but prematurely implement, Basel I. It is not surprising to see that the SBV's Basel-implementing regulations merely existed on paper, without effective compliance from banks.

Mock compliance with Basel II

During the period 2006–12, mock compliance with the adoption and implementation of Basel standards was prevalent. Why was this? We argue that this mock compliance resulted from conflicting preferences at various levels.

At the core of Vietnam's political economic system, there has always been an inherent tension between economic openness and political 'closed-ness'. The process of opening up and integration at an international level over the course of Vietnam's joining the WTO in 2007 has had many implications for the financial system. One of these is that Vietnam is seeking to foster international- and market-oriented policies in a bid to improve the country's competitiveness and attract foreign investment. The adoption of international practices in corporate governance, accounting and auditing, and banking and financial systems is perceived to be vital to achieving these aims. From our interviews with a senior SBV officer who is a member of the SBV's Basel Task Force, and with several commercial banks' senior managers who are part of their respective Basel Project Management Offices, it was confirmed repeatedly that the first motivation to implement Basel comes from their need to 'speak the same language' as foreign partners in the process of international integration.

If economic openness is an essential means for enhancing the party-state's legitimacy, then political closed-ness is necessary for preserving its absolute power. This also implies that economic integration, and its accompanying adoption of international norms and best practices, is valued only as long as it does not interfere with the party-state's legitimacy and its control of the economy.

In the mid-2000s when the economy was booming, everybody was optimistic; economic integration was on the rise, and Basel II was formally adopted in the prime minister's Decision 112 in 2006. However, two years later, macro-economic imbalances and the banking crisis took hold, and even the reformists lost their enthusiasm for implementing Basel standards—doing so would suddenly expose all the hitherto unaddressed weaknesses in domestic banks, both private and state-owned, and therefore exacerbate already-difficult banking conditions. As a result, the reformists and conservatives together reached a consensus to hold back further Basel implementation.

It is important to emphasize that weaknesses in the domestic banking sector during this period had a lot to do with the biggest state-owned enterprises—the so-called state economics groups (SEGs) or state general corporations (SGCs). In this period, these state conglomerates were given directed lending and allowed to invest in multiple sectors even outside their core businesses. Their heavy losses during the 2007–8 crisis resulted in a large number of NPLs in the banking system. A proper implementation of Basel standards would inevitably expose these significant and non-transparent NPLs, and for this reason politicians avoided addressing the issue.

The SBV had an even deeper understanding of the detrimental consequences of implementing Basel II during the time of crisis. Indeed, as a ministry under the government, the SBV was supposed to keep politicians informed about the risks of properly implementing Basel standards. Moreover, as the ministry responsible for ensuring financial security, the SBV had the strongest incentive not to create or aggravate any financial instabilities during times of crisis. Predictably, then, during this period the SBV repeatedly reassured the market that it would never let any banks fail.

As mentioned earlier, the SBV's ambiguous and overlapping roles gave rise to conflicting incentives, and these conflicts were intensified over this time. For example, a president or CEO of a state-owned bank who later became an SBV Governor or a high-profile politician would have tended to turn a blind eye to the weaknesses of their own bank at the time, for some of which they might have to take personal responsibility down the line. In other cases, it was difficult to maintain the SBV's objectivity, as it filled the roles of both the regulator and the owner of state-owned banks, especially with regards to costly sanctions and enforcement. These ambiguous and overlapping roles of the SBV therefore resulted in widespread regulatory forbearance on the whole.

During this period, banks were passive players that wanted to adopt a better system of risk management but were constrained from doing so by limited financial and human resources. Coupled with having to take the lead from the SBV, this made them reluctant to implement Basel, particularly during a systemic crisis.

Notably during this period, even if the politicians, regulators, and banks had wished to implement Basel II standards properly, they would have faced major institutional and technical challenges. The SBV has always lacked independence and its technical human resources have been limited. Low institutional and governance quality throughout the banking system continue to pose important barriers to the effective implementation of international standards such as Basel. In addition, fully implementing CAR in accordance with Basel II would have forced the SBV either to recapitalize state-owned banks (at a time when its budget was already in distress), or allow participation by foreign investors (something the political leadership has long been averse to). Moreover, fundamental institutional problems persist: the banking database system is not centralized, credit transactions are not updated, cash transactions are still popular, there are no independent rating agencies, and the accounting system is not up to international standards. These factors together have led to a low level of data credibility, implying that regulators and even bank owners may not know exactly the bank's real financial position, and the data can be easily manipulated in order to comply with the SBV's requirements.

Our interviews reveal that in this period, even banks with strategic foreign shareholders did not have the right incentives to implement Basel II. In Vietnam, because of the fear of losing control and the desire to maintain the dominant role of state-owned banks, the government restricts foreign ownership in Vietnamese banks to less than 30 per cent (no individual can own more than 5 per cent, and foreign owners cannot own more than 20 per cent). This level of ownership does not provide foreign shareholders with sufficient incentives to transfer technology and governance systems in accordance with their international parent bank's practices. Initially, some foreign counterparts suggested that Vietnamese banks adopt international practices, but after calculating the associated costs and benefits, they reconsidered and decided to follow the practice of Vietnamese banks. Moreover, even in cases where the foreign partners are in charge of risk management, they are unlikely to have sufficient and adequate data to do their job in the Vietnamese context, because of the differences in accounting practices and data manipulations commonly found in banks. Thus, in Vietnam, the implementation of Basel and other international practices—such as internal controls and International Financial Reporting Standards (IFRS) accounting—is rarely promoted or initiated by foreign shareholders.

A shift towards accelerated and more genuine implementation of Basel II

In a way, the context from 2014 onwards is somewhat similar to the period between 1999 and 2006: the economy began to recover from the crisis, brighter economic prospects returned, and Vietnam stood on the threshold of its highest level of international integration, joining several trade agreements in 2015/16.

In this context, politicians and regulators decided to complete the unfinished business of Basel adoption and implementation.

The most important difference between periods 1 and 3 probably lies in the preferences of the banks themselves. After struggling with the crisis, strong banks restructured, weak banks had been consolidated or faced bankruptcy, and the others knew that they had to become competitive in order to survive, especially in the context of increasing market pressure from foreign banks as financial integration increased. These shifting incentives continue to have significant implications for the implementation of Basel standards, because ultimately, such standards need to be implemented by banks themselves.

As already mentioned, in 2014 when the SBV announced a roadmap for Basel II implementation, it selected ten domestic banks to participate in a pilot programme.[5] In our interviews with these pilot banks, they all agreed that their participation in the programme was perceived as a credible and positive signalling device to the market.[6] If, during the time of a bank crisis (e.g. 2008–12), being in Group 1 (the 'healthy' group) was considered to be a positive thing, then since the roadmap for Basel II was announced, being a pilot bank selected by the SBV has similarly been interpreted as being one of the best banks in the market. This signalling device proves to be very valuable in creating a good reputation for banks' investments and trading partners, particularly in an environment characterized by pervasive asymmetric information, as is the case in Vietnam.

An interesting question is how these ten banks were selected. Responses from our interviewees reveal that the institutions were not selected on the basis of clearly defined and publicly available criteria. The biggest three state-owned banks were selected for an obvious reason, i.e. their size and leading position in the sector. However, some of the banks that were selected were not at all among the top ten biggest banks, measured either in terms of total assets or charter capital.

Another interesting question is to whom the banks were signalling. Obviously, the signal was not for the SBV's benefit, since it was the SBV itself that hand-picked these pilot banks. Neither was the signal intended for the depositors, because the SBV virtually guarantees that no bank will ever fail in Vietnam. Interview answers suggest that the main targets for this signalling mechanism were foreign stakeholders and future partners. Most of the ten pilot banks have foreign shareholders, and all of them have been rated by Moody's. In addition,

---

[5] In this period, although Basel III has not yet appeared in official regulations, some Basel III elements such as LCR and NSFR have been adopted. However, the exact definition of these concepts is somewhat different from Basel III. For instance, under Basel III, the minimum LCR required is 100 per cent irrespective of the type of assets, while the minimum LCR under Vietnam's regulation is 50 per cent for VND and 10 per cent for foreign currencies.

[6] At the beginning, the initial pilot programme consisted of only eight banks, but two other banks successfully lobbied the SBV to join.

these banks are either listed, or were about to be listed, on the stock exchange in Hanoi (HNX) or Ho Chi Minh City (HOSE).

The SBV's clear roadmap for Basel implementation, including in Correspondence 1601 in 2014, provided important impetus for banks to move forward with the regulations. Interviews with bankers, both inside and outside the Basel pilot programme, show that since 2014, many banks started working with consulting firms to prepare their own roadmaps for Basel II implementation. Thanks to their proven resilience during the banking crisis, the ten pilot banks had a wider leeway to adopt Basel and improve their risk management and banking governance. However, even for these banks, strict application of Basel standards would inevitably have reduced their liquidity coverage ratio, CAR, and return on equity compared to the status quo. As a result, banks had little incentive to implement Basel until the SBV's Basel implementation roadmap became credible and banks believed they would be liable to strict SBV supervision.[7] Once this happened, the leading banks invested efforts in meeting the deadlines more sincerely, thereby creating pressure for other banks to keep up. Our interviews show that non-pilot banks have already prepared for Basel II by evaluating their data gaps. These banks understand that implementing Basel now will send a positive signal to the market, and that once the Basel regulation is officially issued, it will apply to the whole banking system, so it is better to start sooner rather than later.

Big banks, especially the ten pilot banks, need to raise more capital to meet the new CAR requirements. These institutions have found that Basel II offers a way of reducing their cost of capital. They all argue that if a bank adopts Basel II, it will become more transparent and its risk management system will be better, so that their credit rating could be improved, implying a lower cost of debt issuance and making it easier to attract international investors. As the domestic financial market is not big enough, these banks really need to raise capital from international investors, and are seeking strategic shareholders from foreign financial institutions to do this.

Expansion overseas provides further incentive for banks to support Basel II implementation, as is illustrated with the experiences of Vietinbank (one of the ten pilot banks). Vietinbank chose to establish its first representative office in Europe in Frankfurt (Germany) in April 2010. A year later, in July 2011, its first branch office was approved by BaFin, to be opened in Frankfurt (Tuyet, 2011). Its second branch office was opened in May 2012 in Berlin. One of our interviews revealed that the main motivation for Vietinbank to open these branch offices

---

[7] A rational roadmap is necessary for its credibility. Even pilot banks, especially the state-owned banks, experience great difficulties raising capital to meet the CAR requirement of Basel II. This is why Decision 41 (December 2016) on Basel implementation pushes the implementation deadline to January 2020 from 2019, and CAR has been reduced to 8 per cent from 9 per cent as required by Circulation 13 (2010).

was to send a positive signal and help it improve its reputation as the first and only Vietnamese bank to comply with European banking standards. Although the effort to comply with European standards in operating and managing these two branches does not imply that Vietinbank headquarters will necessarily implement Basel standards, this overseas venture has indirectly compelled the bank's Board to educate itself about international standards, and facilitated the discussion of Basel adoption in its strategic planning. Vietinbank is considered to be among the most advanced of Vietnamese banks in implementing Basel II.

Finally, competition has been providing strong incentives for banks to adopt and implement Basel standards. For a few leading banks trying to establish their activities in advanced economies, meeting the host country's standards (including Basel) is not a matter of choice (Nguyen, 2017).[8] For most banks, trying to keep up with increasing competition even in Vietnam is hard enough. Financial liberalization and economic integration create a much more competitive environment for domestic financial institutions. Indeed, ten years after joining the WTO, the number of foreign-invested and foreign-owned banks has increased rapidly (Tran, 2017).

In sum, shifts in the domestic banking sector and increased engagement with international finance have created new incentives for banks, especially the stronger ones, to support the implementation of Basel and other international standards. For weaker POBs, the adoption of Basel II is perceived more as 'compliance'. For stronger POBs, however, it is considered as a means to differentiate themselves from weaker banks and send a positive signal to their partners. The pressure to implement Basel comes not only from the SBV, but also from the intrinsic needs of banks, which view Basel as an opportunity to improve their governance and attract foreign strategic investors.

In 2016, a new political leadership took office and has being trying to signal a wave of reform. Whether it is Politburo direction or National Assembly Resolution or a government decision, virtually all policy messages refer to the priority of restructuring the banking sector. This is indeed an important factor driving the SBV's efforts to implement banking restructuring measures, including the implementation of Basel II. As the banks have somehow managed to bring down the NPL ratio, they are readier to implement Basel standards. Meanwhile, from the SBV's perspective, the implementation of Basel is perceived as a mechanism for preventing further financial crises and has therefore been carried out in a more active and substantive manner. This time, the roadmap is more rational, considering the readiness of banks, and the implementation timeline has been delayed to 2020 and then until 2025.

---

[8] Vietcombank, ACB, and BIDV have also been allowed by the SBV to open a representative office in the US. However, only Vietcombank has been approved recently by the US Federal Reserve. Vietcombank receives a permit to open representative office in the US (2018, 1 November) (Nhan Dan Online, 2018).

Conclusions and reflections on the analytical framework

This chapter argues that regulators, politicians, and banks face conflicting interests and incentives when it comes to Basel adoption and implementation. The country's politics are domestically oriented and closed, but its economy is internationally integrated and open. Economic openness is an essential means for enhancing the legitimacy of the party-state's performance, while political closed-ness is imperative to retaining its absolute power. As for the regulator (the SBV), ambiguous and overlapping roles have given rise to conflicting regulatory policies. Finally, banks have been passive players who want to approach international standards, but are constrained from doing so by limited financial and human resources, and the SBV's discretionary interventions. Politicians are the most powerful actors when it comes to deciding banking regulations, and the approach to Basel standards reflects the preferences of the political faction that won the tug of war. These conflicting interests and incentives have given rise for the longest time to extensive forbearance in the enforcement of banking regulations, and to mock compliance with Basel adoption and implementation. With reference to the analytical framework, this is an instance of politically driven mock compliance.

The existence of conflicting interests and incentives at all levels implies that the context in which Basel standards are adopted and implemented is critically important. In the case of Vietnam, economic difficulties unfolded during the 2008–12 period with the mounting problem of NPLs, and then the adoption of Basel presented an obvious dilemma: implementation would help signal the government's continued reform efforts, but it would expose the substantial inherent weaknesses of most commercial banks, which could plausibly have triggered a series of bank runs.

It is instructive to compare the experiences of Vietnam and Ethiopia, because of their common socialist legacy and shared model of a developmental state. Indeed, the economic system of Ethiopia today is very similar to that of Vietnam before Doi Moi, and the two countries' financial systems were quite similar until the late 1990s. The Ethiopia chapter of this volume essentially argues that the shift from Basel I to Basel II would empower the market and market access in a way that is totally against the power of the regulator, and that Ethiopia decided not to implement Basel II and III because it wanted to retain control over its economy. As discussed earlier, the Vietnamese party-state also wants to exert firm control over not only the financial sector, but also the economy as a whole. The key factor that sets the Vietnamese and Ethiopian experience apart is that while Vietnam's politics remain closed, a political decision has been taken to open up the economy in order to stimulate economic growth. This fundamental political economic principle shadows almost every aspect of the Vietnamese economy, including the adoption and implementation of Basel standards. How this dilemma unfolds will determine not only the divergent paths Vietnam and Ethiopia take, but also the economic futures of both countries entirely.

References

IMF, 2018. *Financial Soundness Indicators Database*. IMF, Washington, DC.

Kazmin, A., Mallet, V., 2008. FT interview: Nguyen Tan Dung. *Financial Times*.

National Assembly's Economic Committee, UNDP, 2012. *From macroeconomic instability to restructuring*. UNDP.

NFSC, 2018. *Giám sát hợp nhất tập đoàn tài chính (Supervision of Consolidated Financial Groups)*. NFSC.

Nguyen, L., 2017. Vietnam is about to have another 100% foreign-owned bank. *The LEADER*.

Nhan Dan Online, 2018. Vietcombank receives permit to open representative office in the US. *Nhan Dan Online*.

Polity IV, 2014. *PolityProject*. Center for Systemic Peace.

State Bank of Vietnam, 2012a. *Directive 01 on Organizing the Implementation of Monetary Policies and Ensuring the Banking Activity to Be Safe and Efficient in 2012*, N.01/CT-NHNN. The State Bank of Vietnam, Hoan Kiem, Hanoi.

State Bank of Vietnam, 2012b. *Decision No. 780 on Classification of Rescheduled Loans*, No. 780/QD-NHNN. The State Bank of Vietnam, Hoan Kiem, Hanoi.

State Bank of Vietnam, 2017. *Annual Report 2017*. The State Bank of Vietnam, Hoan Kiem, Hanoi.

STOXPLUS, 2012. *Vietnam Banks - A Helicopter View - Issue 4*. Asset and Capital Quality.

Tran, T., 2017. First wholly Singapore-owned bank to operate in Vietnam. *Saigon Times*.

Tuyet, N., 2011. First Vietnamese Bank to open in Europe. *Vietinbank*.

Vu-Thanh, T.-A., 2011. *Building a Modern Central Bank for Vietnam*. Fulbright Economics Teaching Program, Mimeo.

Vu-Thanh, T.-A., 2017. Does WTO accession help domestic reform? The political economy of SOE reform backsliding in Vietnam. *World Trade Review* 16, 85–109. https://doi.org/10.1017/S1474745616000409.

Vu-Thanh, T.-A., Tran-Thi, Q.-G., Do-Thien, A.-T., 2013. *The Vietnamese Non-Performing Loan Market and Vietnam Asset Management Company*. Fulbright Economics Teaching Program, Mimeo.

Walter, A., 2008. *Governing Finance: East Asia's Adoption of International Standards*, Cornell studies in money. Cornell University Press, Ithaca, NY.

World Bank, 2017. *World Development Indicators*. World Bank, Washington, DC.

14

Ethiopia

Raising a Vegetarian Tiger?

Toni Weis

> Transforming Ethiopia into an East African tiger is hardly possible
> without adequate financial resources. After all, there is no vegetarian
> tiger.
>
> (Fortune, 2010)

Introduction

The Ethiopian economy, among the fastest-growing in Africa for fifteen years
and counting, defies many of the common ideas about the continent's economic
resurgence. Although Ethiopian politicians embrace the slogan of a 'rising'
Ethiopia, the country's developmental trajectory differs sharply from the modal
patterns of the Africa Rising literature (Mahajan, 2011). The latter is driven to a significant extent by images from the financial sector—the success of pan-African
banks, for example, or the success of fintech innovations like Kenya's M-Pesa.
Ethiopia's financial industry, on the other hand, is among the less impressive aspects
of the country's economic transformation: small and shallow, technologically back-
wards, dominated by public institutions, and closed to foreign competition.

Ethiopia's financial regulators are similarly inward-looking. Despite significant
exposure to international banking standards through donors and the IMF,
banking supervisors at the National Bank of Ethiopia (NBE) have little use for
the Basel framework, at least in its more recent iterations. Neither Basel II nor
Basel III are currently being implemented, and there are no plans to introduce
them in the near future—in fact, an introduction of Basel II was briefly considered
in 2009, but ultimately rejected. The capital adequacy requirements enshrined in
Basel I were adopted during the partial liberalization of Ethiopia's banking sector
during the mid-1990s, and the Basel Core Principles are occasionally referenced
as good regulatory practice. However, even these elementary standards have
been adapted to the realities of the Ethiopian financial sector rather than
adopted wholesale.

Toni Weis, *Ethiopia: Raising a Vegetarian Tiger?* In: *The Political Economy of Bank Regulation in Developing Countries: Risk and Reputation.* Edited by: Emily Jones, Oxford University Press (2020). © Oxford University Press. DOI: 10.1093/oso/9780198841999.003.0014

Ethiopia's reluctant approach to the Basel framework does not just stem from the relative isolation of its banking sector or its regulators, but is the result of a strong preference for political control over the financial industry. The Ethiopian government seeks to emulate the example of East Asian 'tiger' economies for whom financial repression represented a key tool in the pursuit of rapid industrialization. After more than twenty-five years in power, the ruling party's control over the regulatory apparatus, including the central bank, is complete and uncontested. Regulators, in turn, enjoy wide-ranging powers over the financial industry, which remains dominated by state-owned players and off limits to foreign institutions. Ethiopia is therefore a powerful illustration of policy-driven divergence. The domestic orientation of all key actors—politicians, regulators, and banks—has thus far outweighed the preferences of the IMF and foreign investors. As a consequence, Ethiopia is a case of policy-driven divergence from global standards. However, as Ethiopia's domestic banks struggle to sustain transformative growth and the political leadership is relaxing its approach to state-led economic development, pressures for greater financial opening (and, by extension, for increased regulatory convergence) are beginning to mount.

Despite its obvious significance for understanding the economic policies of a 'developmental' state regime, the issue of financial regulation has received little academic attention in the Ethiopian context.[1] The present study, therefore, draws chiefly on primary sources: a systematic review of regulatory texts, central bank publications, and policy documents; newly compiled data on Ethiopian private banks as well as the professional background of financial regulators; and a total of fifteen interviews with central bank regulators, risk and compliance professionals at both private and public banks, and experts from IMF and the World Bank.

Political economy of the Ethiopian banking sector

Ethiopia is a landlocked country in the Horn of Africa which, despite significant economic gains in recent years, remains among the world's poorest. As the only African polity that escaped colonization by European powers, Ethiopia's recent history has been characterized by a relatively inward-looking, nationalist political culture. During the second half of the twentieth century, Ethiopia's political economy underwent a series of transformations as three fundamentally different regimes followed each other in rapid succession. The feudal government of Haile Selassie (1931–74), the socialist military dictatorship of the Derg (1974–91), and the 'revolutionary democrats' of the EPRDF (1991–current) all pursued ambitious visions of national development, but they disagreed radically on the respective roles of government and private sector in bringing about this transformation (Table 14.1).

---

[1] An exception is Alemu Zwedu (2014).

Table 14.1 Ethiopia: key indicators

Ethiopia	
GDP per capita (current US$)	767
Bank assets (current US$)	6.86 bn (2008)
Bank assets (% of GDP)	25.33 (2008)
Stock market capitalization (% of GDP)	N/A
Credit allocation to private sector (% of GDP)	17.71 (2008)
Credit allocation to government (% of GDP)	5.99 (2008)
Polity IV score	−3

Note: All data is from 2017 unless otherwise indicated.

Source: FSI Database, IMF (2018); GDI database, World Bank (2017); Polity IV (2014)

This is particularly true for the financial sector. Control of Ethiopia's banks was a common concern for all three regimes, yet the level of control (and its effect on the nascent banking sector) differed starkly from one set of leaders to the next. In 1963, Haile Selassie established the Commercial Bank of Ethiopia (CBE), the state-owned behemoth which continues to dominate the sector to this day. Private commercial banks, including banks with (minority) foreign ownership, began to operate shortly after. A military coup in 1974 put an end to this experiment, as private banks were nationalized and integrated into the CBE. However, the CBE retained a significant amount of managerial autonomy and escaped relatively unscathed when the Derg government fell to the Ethiopian People's Revolutionary Democratic Front, a coalition of ethnic insurgent movements, in 1991.

Despite being firmly rooted in Marxism-Leninism itself, the EPRDF signed off on a structural adjustment programme which included a partial liberalization of the banking sector. Two landmark pieces of legislation—the Monetary and Banking Proclamation (83/1994) and the Licensing and Supervision of Banking Business Proclamation (84/1994)—reorganized the country's financial industry, and the first private bank of the post-socialist era was established in 1995. However, the EPRDF fought hard to avoid what it considered to be excessive demands for liberalization. It refused to open the Ethiopian banking industry to foreign competition, restricting ownership of financial institutions to Ethiopian citizens. Just as importantly, the EPRDF rejected the IMF's calls to privatize the remaining state-owned banks or break up the CBE (Stiglitz, 2003, p. 31).

The EPRDF's shift towards a 'developmental state' framework since the early 2000s has brought about a final transformation of the Ethiopian banking sector. State banks are increasingly taking on a policy lending role: the CBE was fundamentally restructured and turned into a highly profitable institution whose revenue finances key infrastructure projects and the expansion of state-owned enterprises. A second state-owned bank, the Development Bank of Ethiopia (DBE), was tasked with providing long-term financing to priority industries. Regulators have also been brought in line with the government's new economic vision. Controversial regulation introduced in 2011 is forcing private banks to reduce liquidity by purchasing NBE bills which, in turn, are used to expand the DBE's portfolio. The central bank has also kept interest rates artificially low to encourage investment, yet high levels of government borrowing are pushing the private sector's access to credit well below the regional average (IMF, 2016, p. 106).

At the same time, accelerated growth has resulted in a significant expansion of the financial sector. The combined assets of Ethiopia's commercial banks have almost tripled since 2010, from US$9.3 billion to US$26.5 billion, and are growing at about twice the rate of GDP (see Figure 14.1).[2] Although the number of private banks has risen to 16, the CBE continues to control about two thirds of these assets. Financial intermediation has expanded as a result; in 2016, total bank deposits stood at US$20 billion—up from US$7.6 billion in 2010—while annual loan disbursement doubled during the same time. Nevertheless, the industry remains minuscule by global standards: in 2016, the total assets of the Ethiopian banking system amounted to roughly 1 per cent of the assets managed by HSBC UK.

The Ethiopian banking sector also remains exceptionally shallow. Ethiopia has neither a secondary equity market nor a secondary market for corporate debt, although the creation of these institutions has been discussed occasionally since the early 1990s. A recent NBE directive (SBB/60/2015) clarifies that banks must limit themselves to 'customary' banking activities and that '[n]o bank shall deal in securities'. An interbank money market exists; however, since Ethiopian banks rarely suffer from short-term liquidity problems, it has not seen any transactions

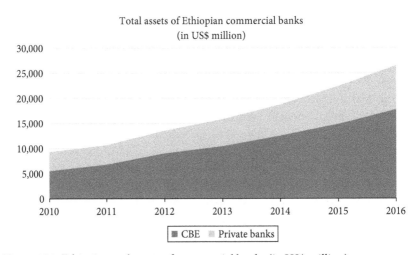

Figure 14.1 Ethiopia: total assets of commercial banks (in US$ million).
Source: Data from Abdulmenan (2017) and IMF (2016)

---

[2] Unless otherwise indicated, all data in the remainder of this section has been compiled from the NBE's annual reports and from Abdulmenan (2017).

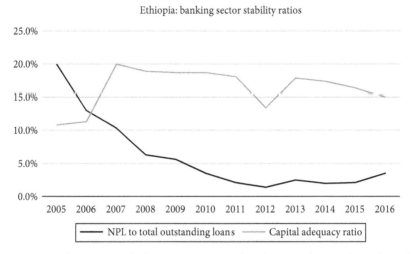

Figure 14.2 Ethiopia: capital adequacy ratios (CAR) and non-performing loans (NPLs).
Source: Data compiled from IMF (2016)

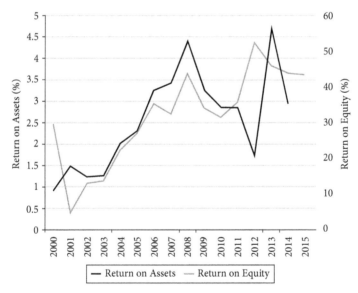

Figure 14.3 Ethiopia: rates of return on assets (RoA) and equity (RoE).
Source: Data from World Bank (2018)

in almost a decade (Alemu Zwedu, 2014, p. 12). The continued isolation of the Ethiopian banking industry also means that the country remains cut off from wider trends and innovations in the banking industry: Ethiopia is one of just two African countries without foreign banks, and one of only four countries where none of the pan-African banks are present (European Investment Bank, 2015, p. 6).

The characteristics outlined above translate into a relatively conservative risk profile, at least among private banks. Market power is relatively dispersed among the latter, interbank lending is negligible, and the law provides strict limits on the extent of cross-ownership and capital concentration. The isolation and lack of depth of Ethiopia's banking sector means that it is sheltered from the vagaries of the global financial markets, and the country has not experienced a major financial crisis. Ethiopia's commercial banks are also highly capitalized and profitable. Their average capital adequacy ratio is hovering between 15 and 20 per cent, well above the 8 per cent stipulated by Basel I, while the ratio of non-performing loans has remained exceptionally low (see Figure 14.2). A substantial interest rate spread, combined with low costs and high non-interest income, also provides domestic banks with a safe business model and a strong return on assets (see Figure 14.3).

The role of the Basel standards

The inward-looking nature of the Ethiopian financial sector is reflected in the regulatory framework that governs the country's banking industry. Unlike some of its African peers, Ethiopia has been highly selective in adopting global standards, and its financial regulators do not consider compliance with international 'best practices' a value in itself. This is particularly evident with regard to the implementation of the Basel framework for banking supervision. Ethiopian regulators are well aware of the Basel standards and have implemented their most basic element—Basel I's minimum capital requirement. At the same time, NBE regulators do not consider the more complex (and costly) supervisory elements of Basel II and III to be a necessary upgrade at this stage, and they have not signalled any intention to adopt all or part of these frameworks (Table 14.2).

The Basel framework represented an important point of reference when Ethiopia began re-licensing private banks in the mid-1990s. The federal proclamation that established the new supervisory framework included the minimum

Table 14.2 Ethiopia: adoption of Basel standards

Basel component	Adoption	Implementation
Basel I	1994 (minimum capital requirement of 8% established in Supervision of Banking Business Proclamation)	1995 (simplified Basel I risk weights introduced in NBE's Computation of Risk-Weighted Asset Directive)
Basel II	n/a	n/a
Basel III	n/a	n/a

capital requirement of 8 per cent stipulated in Basel I (Supervision of Banking Business Proclamation 84/1994). This provision has been reaffirmed by subsequent laws and regulations. However, the rules implemented by the NBE are de facto a simplified version of Basel I, as many of the asset classes included in Basel I do not exist in the Ethiopian financial sector (Computation of Risk-Weighted Asset Directive, SBB/9/95). This includes on-balance sheet assets such as mortgages and municipal bonds, as well as most kinds of off-balance sheet assets. What is more, the NBE's banking supervisors do not distinguish between Tier 1 and Tier 2 capital.[3]

Ethiopia is not currently implementing any elements of Basel II or III, nor are there plans to do so in the near future. An internal study conducted as part of a wider restructuring of the NBE in 2009 considered the introduction of Basel II, but the idea was ultimately rejected.[4] The NBE's Monetary Policy Committee at the time asserted its commitment to 'improve the existing macro-prudential indicators for banks based on [the] Basel Standards' (NBE, 2009, p. 11), but did not further specify any particular element of the framework. A working paper by Getnet, who draws on interviews with NBE staff, asserts that Ethiopian regulators have no interest in adopting Basel II or III 'as a package' but might introduce individual elements that 'fit to the Ethiopian context' (Alemu Zwedu, 2014, p. 33). However, interviews conducted for this study did not indicate that this is happening at present. Instead, an NBE banking supervisor assessed that central bank staff are only following developments around Basel III 'distantly'.[5]

Despite Ethiopia's lack of interest in Basel II and III, the broader work of the Basel Committee has served as an important point of reference for its banking supervisors. When the country's main state-owned bank suffered from an excess of non-performing loans in the early 2000s, the NBE assured IMF staff that it was working on 'bringing prudential regulations in line with Basel standards' (IMF, 2001a) and would base its measures on 'Basel Committee guidelines for the restructuring of troubled debt and credit risk' (IMF, 2001b). Documents published by the Basel Committee also informed the NBE's strategy for gradually moving towards a risk-based supervision system. The NBE's updated risk-management guidelines, issued in 2010, draw heavily on the Basel Core Principles, at times reproducing sections of these documents word for word (Basel Committee, 2004, 2003, 2000a, 2000b; NBE, 2010).

Ethiopia's commercial banks have responded by introducing new risk-management policies of their own. Compliance staff at Wegagen Bank, a large private bank with ties to the EPRDF government, showed familiarity with Basel, but did not draw on Basel Committee documents in the development of their comprehensive 'enterprise risk assessment' system.[6] Staff at the private NIB bank,

---

[3] Interview, NBE banking supervisor, Addis Ababa, 15 February 2017.   [4] Ibid.   [5] Ibid.
[6] Interview, compliance manager at Wegagen Bank, Addis Ababa, 17 January 2017.

on the other hand, specifically looked to Basel when designing their internal risk-management processes, citing their will to be one step ahead of the regulatory requirements of the NBE. For example, NIB's management monitors the bank's net stable funding ratio, an indicator of liquidity borrowed from Basel III.[7]

While Ethiopian officials are showing little inclination to move beyond Basel I in banking supervision, they have advanced the adoption of international financial standards in other areas. Ethiopia recently adopted a law mandating businesses to comply with the International Financial Reporting Standards (IFRS; Financial Reporting Proclamation 847/2014); however, implementation remains patchy. In a similar vein, Ethiopia began working with the Financial Action Task Force (FATF) in 2009 but has struggled to satisfy the group's expectations. Ethiopia introduced anti-money laundering legislation in 2009 and began with the establishment of a Financial Intelligence Centre. Nevertheless, the country was 'greylisted' as a 'jurisdiction with strategic deficiencies' from 2010 until 2014, at which point the FATF considered Ethiopia's commitment to a mutually agreed reform agenda to be satisfactory. Citing 'a lack of effective implementation', the FATF put Ethiopia back on alert in early 2017 (FATF, 2017).

The politics of banking regulation in Ethiopia

As the previous sections have shown, the relatively low level of financial-sector development in Ethiopia limits the relevance and applicability of global financial standards. However, a simple reference to the regulatory fit of Basel II and III is not a satisfactory explanation for why Ethiopia's banking supervisors have shown little enthusiasm for the framework—especially compared to their counterparts in other cases discussed in this volume. Understanding the interests of Ethiopian regulators, and those of other key actors, requires a look at the politics behind the regulation of Ethiopia's banking industry. The remainder of this chapter therefore traces the ways in which the EPRDF's mission to create an Ethiopian 'developmental state' provides these different groups with an inward-looking set of incentives, while Ethiopia's dependence on foreign funding is raising pressures for financial opening.

The primacy of political control

Ethiopia has been following the statist developmental model exemplified by the East Asian 'tiger' economies since the early 2000s, when the leadership of state and ruling party was consolidated under prime minister Meles Zenawi (Abbink

---

[7] Interview, risk manager at NIB Bank, Addis Ababa, 17 January 2017.

and Hagmann, 2016; Vaughan, 2011; Weis, 2016). The EPRDF's avowed ambition is to turn the country into a mid-income manufacturing powerhouse by 2025, following a strategy of 'agricultural development-led industrialization'. Massive investments in public infrastructure—industrial parks, electricity, roads, and railways—have been undertaken to attract companies producing for the export market, while new state-owned enterprises seek to reduce the dependence on the importation of basic commodities such as fertilizer or sugar. The five-year Growth and Transformation Plan (GTP), now in its second phase (2015–20), coordinates the efforts of different ministries, while key operational decisions are taken within the prime minister's office.

Government control of the financial sector plays a crucial role in the developmental state: as Woo-Cumings (1999, p. 10) puts it, '[f]inance is the tie that binds the state to the industrialists'.[8] This is particularly true with regard to the banking sector, as state-led economies have traditionally preferred credit-based—rather than market-based—financial systems (Zysman, 1984). By influencing the process of financial intermediation, governments gain the ability to allocate capital across firms and industries. They are also able to maintain interest rates beneath the market rate, thus lowering the cost for capital investment and government borrowing alike. Whether such a policy of financial repression can ultimately be beneficial to low-income countries has been subject to much debate; however, the fact that the East Asian 'tiger' economies have in fact been built 'over the dead bodies of [...] savers' seems hard to dispute (Woo-Cumings, 1999, p. 17).

In their policy and internal training documents, the EPRDF and its government have been remarkably explicit on how their interventionist approach to financial-sector development fits with the movement's larger political agenda. As the latter changed over time—from orthodox Marxism-Leninism during the guerrilla years to the uneasy liberalism of the 1990s, and on to the current paradigm of the 'developmental state'—the EPRDF's attitude towards the banking sector evolved as well. The EPRDF's first manifesto from 1989 demanded that 'economic institutions must be brought under the control of a genuine people's government'. After coming to power, the EPRDF embraced the idea of (partial) financial liberalization while establishing a foothold in the fledgling private financial sector. An internal position paper from 1993 thus advised the party to 'monopolize rural credit services' while establishing private banks in the urban centres; within three years, the EPRDF had founded Wegagen Bank, as well as microcredit institutions serving its rural heartlands.

The first formulation of the current approach, which looks at financial regulation primarily through the lens of industrial policy, can be found in an internal party document published in 2000 as part of the EPRDF's 'renewal' campaign.

---

[8] For a more recent theorization of the role of finance in the context of 'developmental state' policies, see Heep (2014, p. 26).

The paper argues that the Ethiopian underdeveloped financial market is characterized by pervasive market failures, which inevitably result in a misallocation of capital. Consequently, 'it is mandatory for the state to establish its own banks' and direct credit to those firms that offer the greatest economic promise (EPRDF, 2000, p. 15). Because foreign banks threaten to undermine this policy, the state should 'bar them temporarily until the financial and banking system of the country becomes stable' (ibid., p. 16). In an incomplete draft of his 2006 master's thesis, Meles Zenawi develops these ideas further. He suggests learning from Taiwan and South Korea, whose governments 'largely replaced the financial market and allocated investible resources in accordance with their development plan' (ibid., p. 18), adding that 'financial repression can be a powerful instrument to promote growth and investment' (ibid., p. 27).

If the approaches and arguments have evolved over time, one theme has remained constant: the primacy of the political sphere over the financial market and its interests. From the beginning, the EPRDF government has been acutely aware of the enormous gap in capacity between international banks and local regulators, and it has sought to preserve the autonomy of the latter. This position was most clearly expressed by Meles Zenawi (2012) at a World Economic Forum event in Addis Ababa, shortly before his death, and is worth quoting in full:

> These giants [major international banks] can wreck giant economies such as that of the United Kingdom. Ours is a flimsy one…They come in, they use instruments we cannot control, that in most instances we can't even understand. The best of us can't even understand. How are you going to regulate them? How are you going to regulate these people? It's not possible. We don't have the capacity now.
>
> So what did we do? We allowed the private sector in Ethiopia, which is not infinitely more complex than the public sector, and which therefore could easily be regulated by the public sector, we allowed the private banks to operate here. Is it going to be a permanent feature? No. As we grow, as we develop, and as we become more sophisticated in our regulatory capacity, of course we'll liberalize. But not now. And we have lost nothing because of this policy.

Domestic regulators: professionalism, not autonomy

The centrality of the banking sector to the political vision of the EPRDF government ascribes particular importance to those in charge of regulating it. Staff at the National Bank of Ethiopia consequently resort to 'developmental' vocabulary when talking about their employer: one senior expert in the NBE's banking supervision directorate describes the central bank as the 'engine of economic transformation,[9] while a former colleague characterizes it as 'a key policy agent in the developmental state system'.[10] Interestingly, this 'developmental' ambition has also found its way into the legal framework of the central bank: the federal law which formally re-established the NBE in 2008 tasks the bank with creating conditions 'conducive to the *rapid* economic development of Ethiopia' (Proclamation 591/2008, emphasis added), while the original 1994 banking law instead spoke of 'balanced growth' (Proclamation 83/1994).

Given the high degree of political intervention in the Ethiopian financial system, it comes as no surprise that the Ethiopian central bank is a thoroughly political rather than a politically independent institution. The political nature of the NBE reflects the EPRDF's attitude towards the civil service more broadly, which emphasizes professionalism over autonomy: the government has invested significant resources in building the technical capacity of public servants, but it expects them to implement policy, not to shape or question it (Vaughan and Tronvoll, 2003; Weis, 2016, p. 160). Regulators must maintain their independence from those they regulate, not from those they serve; in Meles Zenawi's terms, 'autonomy must be defined in class terms, not institutional terms' (cited in de Waal [2013, p. 473]). Measures that increase the regulatory independence of private banks, such as the promotion of internal risk models or a general deference to 'market discipline' (introduced under pillars 2 and 3 of Basel II, respectively), thus run counter to the EPRDF's philosophy.

The political role of the Ethiopian central bank is enshrined in its governing documents. Article 4 of the 2008 NBE law stipulates that the bank 'shall be accountable to the Prime Minister', while the seven members of the NBE's board of directors are also appointed by the federal government. The board is dominated by senior members of the administration and ruling party, such as the minister of finance, the head of the national planning commission, and the chief economic adviser to the prime minister (who currently serves as chairman of the board). Teklewold Atnafu, who served as governor of the NBE for almost two decades until June 2018, was a key member of the macro-economic team in the prime minister's office—the command centre of the EPRDF state—as well as a member of the central committee of the SEPDM, one of the four ethno-regional parties that form the EPRDF coalition (Sebsibe, 2015). His successor, Yinager Dessie, is a career politician who most recently served as head of Ethiopia's National Planning Commission and is a senior member in the EPRDF's Amhara party (Addis Standard, 2018; Fortune, 2018).

The EPRDF government is also exerting efforts to ensure that lower-level central bank staff are aware of, and subscribe to, the NBE's political mission. A government directive issued in 2008 which lays out the rights and obligations of NBE

---

[9] Interview, NBE banking supervisor, Addis Ababa, 15 February 2017.
[10] Interview, former NBE banking supervisor, Addis Ababa, 1 March 2017.

staff thus specifies that '[a]ny employee shall...respect and implement government policies' (Council of Ministers Regulation 157/2008). The NBE has certainly succeeded in ensuring that its employees remain on message: one World Bank official describes the bank as 'monolithic', with a highly disciplined staff that 'sings from the same hymn book' when communicating with outside experts.[11] Nevertheless, NBE regulators strongly reject the allegation of private bank employees that the central bank is a political institution—referring to it as 'highly independent' with 'no government influence'—and argue that there is no difference between its relationships with private and state banks.[12]

At the same time, the Ethiopian government has invested heavily in building the technical and supervisory capacity of the central bank. Between 2005 and 2012, the NBE benefited from a World Bank-led capacity-building programme which focused on introducing risk-based supervision methods, establishing new liquidity forecasting and macro modelling tools, and updating the bank's IT infrastructure (World Bank, 2012a). The NBE also continues to increase its technical staff: in 2011, there were twenty-seven experts in the NBE's banking supervision department, of whom only one had a higher academic degree (World Bank, 2012b); by 2017, the number of staff had grown to forty, a dozen of whom held graduate degrees. Despite the progress made in recent years, however, NBE staff still consider the 'brain drain' towards the private banks and the resulting shortage of skilled supervisors to be essential challenges.[13]

IFIs and the importance of 'policy independence'

If Ethiopian financial regulators are conscious of the domestic political context in which they are embedded, they are even more determined to retain their independence from the international financial institutions. Ethiopia's state-led economic model, as well as the highly interventionist financial policies that underpin it, goes against the grain of the reform measures promoted by the World Bank and the IMF, and Ethiopian policymakers regularly find themselves at odds with the representatives of these organizations. Arkebe Oqbay, the head of the Ethiopian Investment Commission and one of the main thinkers behind the country's economic agenda, summarizes the stance of the EPRDF government thus:

> Ethiopia is able to achieve this because it chose its own development path. We have not always been good students of the IMF and other financial institutions. We have always been choosing our way because policy independence is important to us.   (cited in Tamrat, 2015)

[11] Interview, World Bank financial sector expert, Washington, DC., 21 February 2016.
[12] Interview, NBE banking supervisor, Addis Ababa, 15 February 2017.
[13] Interview, former NBE banking supervisor, Addis Ababa, 1 March 2017.

This emphasis on 'policy independence' expresses itself in two ways. On the one hand, it means that the professional culture of Ethiopia's financial regulators is inward-looking, concerned primarily with domestic concerns rather than developments in the global financial centres. In contrast to other African economies, Ethiopia's banking regulators are trained and recruited locally; exposure to the global financial industry is both less prevalent and less relevant than in other countries. Money is certainly an important factor in this context: salaries at the central bank range from US$150/month for entry-level positions to US$900 at the director level,[14] while jobs in the modern private sector, international organizations, or the non-profit sphere are considerably higher and receive greater attention from Ethiopians who received an international education.

A review of the LinkedIn profiles of 126 current and former technical experts at the National Bank—while certainly not a fool-proof methodology—highlights some interesting patterns in this regard: of the 126 NBE staff, only five received an education outside Ethiopia, while the remaining 121 were trained inside the country. Just as importantly, the majority of the latter—seventy-three in total—studied at one of Ethiopia's new regional universities, whose academic credentials have often been disparaged; a large minority of forty-eight employees graduated from Addis Ababa University, the most prestigious—and, until the mid-1990s, the only—university in the country. Central bank staff also tend to join the NBE quite young and inexperienced; out of the total 126 employees, eighty started working for the bank within one year of obtaining their undergraduate degree. Lastly, staff tend to migrate from the NBE to the private banks, rather than vice versa: at least twenty-two out of sixty former NBE employees reported a new position at a private bank, while only one of sixty-six current NBE employees previously worked for a private bank.

On the other hand, Ethiopia's insistence on 'policy independence' has made for a rocky relationship with the Bretton Woods institutions, and particularly the IMF (Gill, 2010, pp. 79–96). Ethiopia's difficulties with the Fund reach back to the 1990s, when government officials and IMF staff clashed over the EPRDF's reform agenda and loan disbursement was suspended twice. Relations improved later on without ever becoming cordial. In 2014, the IMF closed its office in Addis Ababa because of the government's lack of interest in engaging with the Fund beyond the bare minimum of activities: Ethiopia is one of very few countries of its size that has never requested a Financial Sector Assessment Programme (FSAP), and publishing reports or even press releases on the annual Article IV consultations—otherwise a mere formality—has often been a contentious issue in Ethiopia.[15]

This is not to say that there are not areas of mutual collaboration. Today, World Bank and Fund officials largely acknowledge the government's reluctance towards

---

[14] Interview, NBE banking supervisor, Addis Ababa, 15 February 2017.
[15] Interview, IMF official, Washington, DC, 27 April 2017.

greater financial liberalization and try to 'work in the margins'.[16] They also do not push for the adoption of the Basel II or III packages, acknowledging that these do not represent a good fit with Ethiopia's regulatory capacity or requirements.[17] Ethiopian officials regularly request IMF or World Bank assistance on specific technical issues, and foreign consultants from these institutions have been involved in a range of projects at the central bank recently, from the development of a liquidity forecasting model to assisting in the drafting of directives in new issue areas.[18] NBE regulators also attend trainings and experience-sharing meetings at the IMF's Regional Technical Assistance Center (AFRITAC) in Tanzania (Gottschalk, 2015, p. 9); however, these are primarily concerned with macroeconomic rather than regulatory issues, and NBE staff are perceived to be less integrated into regional expert networks 'because they do not have to be'.[19]

The acquiescence of private banks

In debates (if indeed the term is warranted) about financial regulation in Ethiopia, the voice of the commercial banks themselves—and of the private banks in particular—is noticeable mostly by its absence. Somewhat surprisingly, all private bank employees interviewed for this study characterized their communication with the central bank as constructive: they reported that central bank staff regularly consult with private banks—both at the board level and with technical experts—during the development of new laws or regulations. However, they also did not feel that their feedback was ultimately taken into account by the NBE.[20]

As a consequence, controversial or openly punitive measures may provoke initial protest from private bank staff, but are enforced and obeyed nevertheless, and with little attempt to push back. The most striking example is the introduction of a regulation in 2011 that requires all private banks (but not the CBE) to purchase five-year NBE bills equivalent to 27 per cent of new loan disbursements. The 3 per cent interest paid on these bills is well below the rate of inflation, and their maturity far exceeds that of the average bank loan. In the absence of a secondary debt market, this means that a growing part of private bank assets are invested in government debt, which has in turn been used to finance long-term industrial projects. Ethiopia's private banks initially protested vigorously against the new rule (Mesfin, 2011). However, the Ethiopian government remained

---

[16] Interview, World Bank financial sector expert, Washington, DC, 21 February 2016.
[17] Interview, IMF official, Washington, DC, 27 April 2017.
[18] Interview, NBE banking supervisor, Addis Ababa, 15 February 2017.
[19] Interview, IMF official, Washington, DC, 27 April 2017.
[20] Interview, compliance manager at Wegagen Bank, Addis Ababa, 17 January 2017; and interview, risk manager at NIB Bank, Addis Ababa, 17 January 2017.

unimpressed by the objections (including those of the IMF later on), and the rule remains in place today.

The relative lack of power of Ethiopia's private banks vis-à-vis their federal supervisors is partly a reflection of market structure. With two thirds of the country's total banking assets under the control of the CBE, systemic risk is largely concentrated within one state owned institution. Meanwhile, the structural risks emanating from the private banking sector are modest. The largest of the sixteen private banks, Awash International Bank, has a market share of just over 5 per cent. Risk exposure between different private banks is minimal, as interbank lending and cross-ownership are non-existent. What is more, Ethiopian banking law prevents the concentration of ownership structures: the 2008 Revised Banking Business Proclamation stipulates that an individual or family can own no more than 5 per cent of a bank's total shares,[21] while an 'influential shareholder' owning 2 per cent of a bank's shares or more cannot purchase stock in any of the other institutions.

Remarkably, and in contrast to other 'developmental' states, there are also few indications of outright clientelism between banks and political elites which could raise the former's influence with policymakers. The CBE's annual reports, for example, list all of its major non-performing loans, and none of the firms and individuals listed are known to be major political operators (CBE, 2014). A small number of private banks do have ties to the EPRDF—most importantly Wegagen Bank, an institution which was established with funds accumulated by the EPRDF during the war against the Derg, but is now formally part of a charitable endowment. However, they do not seem to benefit from preferential treatment, and there have been few allegations levelled against them recently. At the same time, the central bank has not been involved in any of the high-profile corruption cases which the Ethiopian courts have (very publicly) prosecuted in the past years.

There is, of course, another reason for the relative acquiescence of Ethiopia's private banks: the fact that they are, overall, among the main beneficiaries of the NBE's inward-looking and protectionist policies. According to data compiled by Abdulmenan (2017), Ethiopia's private banks are profitable without exception, and have been so since at least 2010. Operating in a rapidly growing yet significantly under-banked economy, private banks have their pick of relatively safe short-term and highly collateralized loans. Non-interest income from banking fees, forex services, and trade financing represents an additional revenue stream, amounting to a third of total revenues on average. Opening the financial sector to foreign banks would expose domestic institutions to a much more difficult competitive environment; as long as their profits are safe, there is thus little reason for private banks to rock the boat.

---

[21] This number was revised downward from the 20 per cent figure included in the original banking law of 1994.

Pressures for financial liberalization and convergence

Even foreign observers who are generally sympathetic to the EPRDF's vision of state-led economic transformation, however, question the financial arrangement that underpins it (Bienen et al., 2015). The 'developmental' financial policies of the East Asian tigers were premised on high savings rates, a sizeable private banking sector, undervalued currencies, and a large current-account surplus. In Ethiopia, the situation is the exact opposite: the savings rate is low and the banking industry in its infancy; the Ethiopian birr is propped up by strict capital controls, and the rapid increase in imports far outpaces the sluggish export growth (World Bank, 2016a, pp. 20–1).

The result has been a growing financing gap, which has in turn increased the demand for foreign capital. From 2010 to 2015, total investment—disproportionally driven by public spending—increased from 22 to 40 per cent of GDP (NPC, 2015, p. 13), while savings remained at 22 per cent. Since the Ethiopian financial sector is struggling to sustain economic growth by mobilizing the necessary amount of savings at home, the country has to bring in foreign savings. The growing interaction with global financial markets that results from this dependency has increased the linkages between an otherwise isolated Ethiopian financial sector and global capital markets. This, in turn, is slowly introducing new pressures for financial opening and regulatory convergence.

While there is no indication that the Ethiopian banking sector will be opened to foreign competition in the immediate future, it is slowly starting to acquire an international outlook. On the one hand, the state-owned Commercial Bank has become the first Ethiopian bank to venture out of the country.[22] In April 2017, the CBE opened a new branch in Djibouti, the main economic gateway for land-locked Ethiopia (Yewondwossen, 2017). According to a CBE representative, this move is part of a larger expansion plan which will see the bank opening offices primarily serving the growing Ethiopian community in diaspora hubs like Washington, DC, Dubai, and Johannesburg. At the same time, foreign banks have also begun opening representative offices in Ethiopia. These offices act as overseas correspondent banks for their Ethiopian counterparts and underwrite letters of credit for local businesses who trade internationally. In 2007, the German Commerzbank was the first to open such an office in Addis Ababa (Kifle, 2007). Since 2014, several other banks—notably (pan-)African banks such as Ecobank and Standard Bank—have followed (Strydom, 2015).

Outside the banking industry, the gradual internationalization of Ethiopia's financial sector has manifested itself even more strongly. One key event was the

---

[22] The CBE maintained an office in Djibouti which was closed by Djiboutian regulators in 2004, and it also opened several offices in South Sudan after 2009, most of which have since been closed again.

issuing of Ethiopia's first Eurobond in 2014—the country's first foray into the global debt market, and oversubscribed by 260 per cent. In Ethiopia's first credit ratings, obtained just before the issue, the agencies specifically commented on the particularities of the Ethiopian financial sector and their impact on the country's sovereign credit risk. Moody's, for example, noted 'the high concentration in the banking sector and the dominance of state-owned banks' which, in addition to government policies undermining the process of credit allocation, had 'a negative effect on the development of the financial sector' (Moody's, 2014). While these declarations do not create any immediate pressure for reform in the financial sector, they certainly introduce a new set of incentives.

The EPRDF government has made it clear that it does not consider the current level of financial restriction as a goal in itself, but rather as a means to an end, to be phased out over time. As Meles Zenawi (2012) said at the World Economic Forum, '[a]s we grow, as we develop, and as we become more sophisticated in our regulatory capacity, of course we'll liberalize'. The trends outlined above all create pressures in this direction. The long-term objective of Ethiopian regulators is convergence with global regulatory standards, but at their own pace, and without sacrificing control over the process. In the words of one World Bank official, where the Ethiopian government does show an interest in global financial norms, it is primarily interested in 'future compliance': there is no urgent need to be compliant quite yet, but once Ethiopia's financial regulators introduce a new set of reforms, they do not want to be taken by surprise.[23]

In the meantime, the Ethiopian central bank is undertaking a number of measures to strengthen the competitiveness of local commercial banks. In 2017, the NBE announced a likely increase in minimum capital requirements, which had already risen rapidly in recent years: not accounting for inflation, the NBE's minimum capital requirement for the establishment of a new commercial bank rose by a factor of 200 (from 10 million birr to 2 billion birr) between 1995 and 2015. The NBE also raised the prospect of promoting the consolidation of the commercial banking sector through mergers between private banks, something that has not happened since the EPRDF government first started licensing private banks in 1994 (Taye, 2017). Similarly, the second phase of the Growth and Transformation Plan, in a section on capacity building in the financial sector, announces plans to develop 'regulations that meet international standards', although the latter are not further specified (NPC, 2015, p. 110). And the establishment of a working group on financial-sector reform—with the participation of experts from both IMF and World Bank—by the new NBE Governor Yinager similarly indicates a willingness to revise existing institutions and policies (Fick and Maasho, 2018).

However, it would be short-sighted to see these instances of gradual change towards greater compliance with global financial norms as signs of a more radical

---

[23] Interview, World Bank financial sector expert, Washington, DC, 21 February 2016.

shift in the immediate future. To date, every reference by Ethiopian politicians and regulators to the eventual liberalization of the financial sector has been accompanied by a caveat that the time for this measure has not yet come. To complete Meles Zenawi's quote from above: '...of course we'll liberalize. But not now'.

Conclusion

This chapter has argued that Ethiopia's divergence from international standards in banking supervision is not simply a reflection of the bad regulatory 'fit' of Basel II and III, but more fundamentally a consequence of the policy orientation and strong domestic orientation of key actors. The EPRDF government sees itself as a 'developmental' regime in the tradition of the East Asian tigers and therefore considers control of financial markets to be a key component of industrial policy. Central bank regulators, on the other hand, take pride in increasing their technical competence, but their loyalty lies with domestic political leaders rather than with foreign institutions or networks. As key beneficiaries of the ERPDF's protectionist policies, finally, domestic commercial banks have little incentive to go abroad. However, the growing need to attract foreign capital is likely to usher in a gradual internationalization of the Ethiopian financial sector, and with it a greater interest in global financial standards.

As a highly aid-dependent country with significant exposure to the donor community, Ethiopia should be expected to converge on international standards. The analytical framework presented in this volume helps explain why this is not the case. It does so by drawing attention to the preferences of key actors: while Ethiopia's politicians, regulators, and banks are well aware of global norms and the community that promotes them, this awareness alone is not sufficient to sway them from their strong domestic agendas. Ethiopia provides an excellent example of the dynamics behind policy-driven divergence. This straightforward causal story is complicated only by the need to account for likely moves towards greater regulatory convergence in the future. Vietnam, for example, is regularly cited as an example of the kind of economy Ethiopia's state-led industrialization strategy might eventually engender (e.g. World Bank, 2016b). However, whether Ethiopia will mirror Vietnam's approach of gradual financial liberalization—and, consequently, demonstrate a similar willingness to embrace global standards like the Basel framework—remains speculation at this point.

The contrast between Rwanda and Ethiopia, countries that are held up as African 'developmental states', is striking. Like Ethiopia's EPRDF, the government of Paul Kagame has its roots in an armed insurgency movement and has rejected calls for political liberalization in favour of a state-led approach to economic transformation (Matfess, 2015). However, the two countries follow fundamentally different economic strategies. In contrast to Ethiopia's focus on labour-intensive industries with strong backward linkages to agriculture, the Rwandan government pursues the development of a skills-based service economy. As Behuria argues in this volume, the promotion of a competitive financial industry is a key aspect of this endeavour. In comparison to their Ethiopian counterparts, Rwandan politicians and regulators therefore have a more internationalist agenda for the financial sector, and they are more likely to embrace compliance with international standards as a means of boosting the competitiveness of the Rwandan banking sector.

Comparison with the Angolan case highlights the importance of distinguishing conceptually between politically driven and policy-driven lending. As the discussion of the Angolan banking industry in this volume illustrates, both kleptocratic and 'developmental' regimes are driven by domestic concerns which motivate them to control the banking sector—elite enrichment and economic transformation, respectively. Although both regime types can be expected to reject supervisory frameworks that reduce their control over the process, the implications for financial regulators are very different. This highlights the importance of closely examining actor preferences.

Acknowledgements

The author would like to thank all who contributed to this chapter, particularly Abdulmenan Mohammed for generously sharing data and insights and Awet Bahta for facilitating interviews in Addis Ababa.

References

Abbink, J., Hagmann, T., 2016. *Reconfiguring Ethiopia: The Politics of Authoritarian Reform*. Routledge, London.

Abdulmenan, 2017. *Database on financial reports of Ethiopian private banks* (Microsoft Excel file, unpublished, made available to the author).

Addis Standard, 2018. Updated: PM Abiy Ahmed appoints 55 state ministers today. *Addis Standard*. URL https://addisstandard.com/news-pm-abiy-ahmed-appoint-state-ministers-today (accessed 22.11.18).

Alemu Zwedu, G., 2014. *Financial Inclusion, Regulation and Inclusive Growth in Ethiopia*. Overseas Development Institute, London.

Basel Committee, 2000a. *Principles for the Management of Credit Risk*. Basel Committee on Banking Supervision.

Basel Committee, 2000b. *Sound Practices for Managing Liquidity in Banking Organisations*. Basel Committee on Banking Supervision.

Basel Committee, 2003. *Sound Practices for the Management and Supervision of Operational Risk*. Basel Committee on Banking Supervision.

Basel Committee, 2004. *Principles for the Management and Supervision of Interest Rate Risk*. Basel Committee on Banking Supervision.

Bienen, D., Ciuriak, D., Ferede, T., 2015. *Financing Ethiopia's development: Confronting the gap between ambition and means* (SSRN Scholarly Paper No. ID 2477384). Social Science Research Network, Rochester, NY.

CBE, 2014. 2013/14 *Annual Performance Report*. Commercial Bank of Ethiopia.

de Waal, A., 2013. The theory and practice of Meles Zenawi: A reply to René Lefort. *African Affairs* (Lond) 112, 471–5. https://doi.org/10.1093/afraf/adt022.

EPRDF, 2000. *The Development Lines of Revolutionary Democracy*. Partial English translation of an unpublished Amharic original brochure.

European Investment Bank, 2015. *Recent trends in banking in sub-Saharan Africa—From financing to investment* [WWW Document]. URL http://www.eib.org/infocentre/publications/all/economic-report-banking-africa-from-financing-to-investment.htm (accessed 19.11.18).

FATF, 2017. *Improving global AML/CFT compliance: On-going process* [WWW Document]. URL http://www.fatf-gafi.org/countries/a-c/afghanistan/documents/fatf-compliance-february-2017.html (accessed 19.11.18).

Fick, M., Maasho, A., 2018. Exclusive: Ethiopia set on economic reforms, but won't be rushed. *Reuters*.

Fortune, 2010. Limiting financial institutions deprives potential tiger of meat. *Fortune* [Addis Ababa].

Fortune, A., 2018. Yinager, Bekalu top in the list to head the NBE. *Addis Fortune*.

Gill, P., 2010. *Famine and Foreigners: Ethiopia Since Live Aid*. Oxford University Press, Oxford.

Gottschalk, R., 2015. *What financial regulation for stability and financial inclusion in Africa? The views of regulators of Ethiopia, Kenya and Lesotho*. Overseas Development Institute, London.

Heep, S., 2014. *China in Global Finance: Domestic Financial Repression and International Financial Power*. Springer Science & Business Media, New York.

IMF, 2001a. *Ethiopia: Letter of Intent*. International Monetary Fund, Washington, DC.

IMF, 2001b. *Ethiopia: Memorandum of Economic and Financial Policies for the Period October 2001–September 2002*. International Monetary Fund, Washington, DC.

IMF, 2016. *The Federal Democratic Republic of Ethiopia: 2016 Article IV Consultation*. International Monetary Fund, Washington, DC.

IMF, 2018. *Financial Soundness Indicators Database*. International Monetary Fund, Washington, DC.

Kifle, E., 2007. Germany's Commerzbank to open Ethiopia office. *Ethiopian Review—Ethiopian News*. URL https://www.ethiopianreview.com/index/1235 (accessed 19.11.18).

Mahajan, V., 2011. *Africa Rising: How 900 Million African Consumers Offer More Than You Think*. Pearson Prentice Hall, London.

Matfess, H., 2015. Rwanda and Ethiopia: Developmental authoritarianism and the new politics of African strong men. *African Studies Review* 58, 181–204. https://doi.org/ 0.1017/asr.2015.43.

Mesfin, M., 2011. Ethiopia: Bankers' association wants T-bill directive revised. *Addis Fortune* (Addis Ababa).

Moody's, 2011. *Moody's assigns B1 issuer ratings to the Government of Ethiopia; stable outlook* [WWW Document]. URL https://www.moodys.com/research/Moodys-assigns-B1-issuer-ratings-to-the-Government-of-Ethiopia%97PR%5F298848 (accessed 19.11.18).

NBE, 2009. *NBE's Monetary Policy Framework*. National Bank of Ethiopia.

NBE, 2010. *Bank Risk Management Guidelines (Revised)*. National Bank of Ethiopia.

NPC, 2015. *Growth and Transformation Plan II (GTP II) (2015/16–2019/20)*. National Planning Commission of the Federal Democratic Republic of Ethiopia I.

Polity IV, 2014. *PolityProject*. Center for Systemic Peace.

Sebsibe, M., 2015. Handing over the baton. *The Reporter* (Addis Ababa daily, English edition), 1 September.

Stiglitz, J., 2003. *Globalization and Its Discontents*. WW Norton, New York.

Strydom, T., 2015. South Africa's Standard Bank opens office in Ethiopia. *Reuters*.

Tamrat, G., 2015. Interview: The singularly focused man. *Fortune* [Addis Ababa weekly].

Taye, D., 2017. Private banks are united in their integration [translated from Amharic original]. *The Reporter* [Addis Ababa daily].

Vaughan, S., 2011. Revolutionary democratic state-building: party, state and people in the EPRDF's Ethiopia. *Journal of Eastern African Studies* 5, 619–40. https://doi.org/1 0.1080/17531055.2011.642520.

Vaughan, S., Tronvoll, K., 2003. *The culture of power in contemporary Ethiopian political life*. Sida Studies 10.

Weis, T., 2016. *Vanguard capitalism: Party, state, and market in the EPRDF's Ethiopia* (PhD Dissertation). Department of Politics and International Relations, University of Oxford.

Woo-Cumings, M., 1999. Introduction: Chalmers Johnson and the politics of nationalism and development, in: Woo-Cumings, Meredith (Ed.), *The Developmental State*. Cornell University Press, Ithaca, NY, pp. 1–31.

World Bank, 2012a. *Implementation and Completion and Results Report (IDA-H2390) on a Grant in the Amount of SDR 10.3 Million (US$ 15 Million Equivalent) to the Federal Democratic Republic of Ethiopia for a Financial Sector Capacity Building Project*. World Bank, Washington, DC.

World Bank, 2012b. *Bank Regulation and Supervision Survey*. World Bank. URL http:// www.worldbank.org/en/research/brief/BRSS (accessed 24.11.18).

World Bank, 2016a. *Ethiopia's Great Run: The Growth Acceleration and How to Pace It* (Working Paper No. 99399). World Bank, Washington, DC.

World Bank, 2016b. *Ethiopia: Priorities for Ending Extreme Poverty and Promoting Shared Prosperity* (Systematic Country Diagnostic No. 100592). World Bank, Washington, DC.

World Bank, 2017. *World Development Indicators*. World Bank, Washington, DC.

World Bank, 2018. *Global Financial Development Database* [WWW Document]. URL https://datacatalog.worldbank.org/dataset/global-financial-development (accessed 24.11.18).

Yewondwossen, M., 2017. CBE returns to Djibouti. *Capital* [Addis Ababa weekly].

Zenawi, M., 2012. Remarks at World Economic Forum on Africa.

Zysman, J., 1984. *Governments, Markets, and Growth: Financial Systems and the Politics of Industrial Change*. Cornell University Press, Ithaca, NY.

PART III

CONCLUSION

15

Conclusion

Key Findings and Policy Recommendations

Emily Jones

The preceding chapters have provided a wealth of empirical evidence on the political economy dynamics that lead regulators in peripheral developing countries to converge on, and diverge from, international standards. In this chapter we distil key findings, highlight areas for further research, and make a series of policy recommendations, proposing ways to reform international standard-setting processes to better reflect the interests of peripheral developing countries.

Our case studies provide compelling evidence of the powerful reputational, competitive, and functional incentives generated by financial globalization that lead regulators to adopt international standards, even when they are ill suited to their local context. A striking finding from our case studies is that politicians and regulators were the main drivers of convergence. In the countries where implementation was most ambitious, politicians played a vital role, championing the expansion of financial services and integration into global finance as an important component of their country's development strategy. In some cases, regulators advocated convergence on prudential grounds, concerned about the increasing risks posed by internationally active banks. But we also found evidence of strong reputational incentives to implement the latest international standards, which are considered the 'gold standard' in international policy circles.

Where there were pressures to diverge, these usually came from politicians and regulators as well. In several countries, politicians were concerned implementation of international standards would undermine their ability to allocate credit to productive sectors of the economy, as part of a developmental state model, or to channel credit to political allies. In many cases regulators were sceptical about the suitability of international standards for their jurisdiction, particularly the most complex aspects of Basel II and III. Where politicians and regulators faced conflicting preferences, this led to mock compliance. A striking finding is that banks were rarely central players in these dynamics of convergence or divergence.

We explain how our findings speak to wider debates in the literature, including over the agency of actors from peripheral developing countries in the global

Emily Jones, *Conclusion: Key Findings and Policy Recommendations* In: The *Political Economy of Bank Regulation in Developing Countries: Risk and Reputation*. Edited by: Emily Jones, Oxford University Press (2020).
© Oxford University Press. DOI: 10.1093/oso/9780198841999.003.0015

economy; relationships between firms, politicians, and the state in developing countries; the importance of policy ideas, particularly the role of the financial sector in economic development; and the inner workings of bureaucracies in developing countries. We highlight areas for future research, including fine-grained analysis of political dynamics within government institutions in developing countries, and the trade-offs associated with independent regulatory institutions.

Our final contribution is to set out some detailed policy proposals to reform international banking standards so that they are better aligned with the interests of peripheral developing countries. We highlight the different strategies that regulators can use at the national level to modify international standards at the point of implementation. We also propose ways to improve the voice of governments from peripheral developing countries in international standard-setting processes, by improving their representation, consolidating the evidence base from which regulators can develop alternative policy proposals, and strengthening collaboration among regulators from peripheral developing countries.

Insights from case studies: drivers of convergence and divergence

Our case studies provide compelling evidence that regulators in peripheral developing countries face very strong incentives to converge on international banking standards. Moves to implement international standards reflects some prudential concerns, with regulators seeking to regulate internationally active banks. But the most powerful drivers of convergence are political, emanating from politicians and regulators, rather than banks. We also found evidence of strong incentives to diverge from international standards. Again, politicians and regulators tended to oppose implementation the most, with banks playing a relatively minor role. We provide a summary of how each of our case studies maps onto our analytical framework in Table 15.1, and discuss the most salient features below.

Drivers of convergence

In five of our cases (Pakistan, Rwanda, Ghana, Angola, Vietnam), the main impetus to converge on international standards came from politicians. In Pakistan, Rwanda, and Ghana politicians championed the expansion of financial services and integration into global finance as an important component of their country's development strategy, and perceived implementation of the latest international banking standards as vital for signaling the attractiveness of their financial services sectors to prospective investors. In Vietnam, reformist politicians championed the implementation of international standards as part of a wider strategy to integrate their country into the global economy, rather than to attract investment into the financial services sector per se.

Table 15.1 Drivers of convergence and divergence in our case studies

Country	Drivers of convergence				Drivers of divergence				Pathway	Outcome (number of BII and BIII components implemented)
	Politicians seeking international capital	Regulators engaging with peers	Domestic banks expanding into international markets	Sustained engagement with the World Bank and IMF	Politicians pursuing interventionist financial policies	Politicians and business oligarchs using banks to direct credit to allies	Sceptical regulator	Fragile domestic banks		
Pakistan	✓*	✓	✓	(✓)	✕	✕	(✓)	✕	Policy-driven convergence	Ambitious implementation (14)
Rwanda	✓*	✕	✕	✓	✕	✕	✕	✕	Policy-driven convergence	Ambitious implementation (10)
Ghana	✓*	✓	✕	✓	(✓)	(✓)	(✓)	✓	Policy-driven convergence	Ambitious implementation (8)
WAEMU	✕	✓*	✕	✓*	✕	✕	✕	(✓)	IFI-driven convergence	Ambitious implementation (10)

(continued)

Table 15.1 Drivers of convergence and divergence in our case studies (Continued)

Country	Drivers of convergence				Drivers of divergence				Pathway	Outcome (number of BII and BIII components implemented)
	Politicians seeking international capital	Regulators engaging with peers	Domestic banks expanding into international markets	Sustained engagement with the World Bank and IMF	Politicians pursuing interventionist financial policies	Politicians and business oligarchs using banks to direct credit to allies	Sceptical regulator	Fragile domestic banks		
Tanzania	✗	✓*	✓	✓	✓	✓	✗	(✓)	Regulator-driven convergence	Selective implementation (8)
Kenya	✓	✓*	✓	✓	✗	✗	✓	✗	Regulator-driven convergence	Selective implementation (7)
Bolivia	✗	✓*	✗	(✓)	✓*	✗	✗	✗	Regulator-driven convergence	Selective implementation (5)
Nigeria	(✓)	✓*	✓	✗	✗	✗	✓*	✓	Regulator-driven mock compliance	Mock compliance (6)

Angola	✓*	×	✓*	×	✓*	×	×	Politically driven mock compliance	Mock compliance (5)
Vietnam	✓*	✓	✓	×	✓	✓*	✓	Politically driven mock compliance	Mock compliance (3)
Ethiopia	×	×	✓*	×	✓	✓	×	Policy-driven divergence	No implementation (0)

Notes: ✓★ denotes factor that was strongest influence in driving convergence or divergence; ✓ denotes influential factor; (✓) denotes factor that was present but weak (e.g. there are domestically oriented banks in all case study countries, but they did not always mobilize to shape regulatory decisions); ✗ denotes factor was not present in a meaningful way. With regards to outcomes: Ambitious implementation = includes at least one of the more complex components (internal models under Basel II and/or liquidity or macroprudential/liquidity standards under Basel III); Selective implementation = standardized approaches under Basel II and only microprudential capital requirements under Basel III; Mock compliance = on paper, not enforced.

In contrast to the logic of politicians seeking deeper integration into global finance, in Angola, and to some extent Pakistan, there were pressures to implement international standards to stay connected to global finance. These were particularly strong in the wake of blacklisting by the Financial Action Taskforce. In Angola the implementation of international standards was seen by politicians as an unattractive but necessary condition for maintaining linkages to international banks, a vital mechanism for channelling profits from the oil sector out of the country. Implementation was a defensive move made to restore the country's legitimacy in the eyes of international actors and maintain connections to international finance, rather than an offensive move to expand financial services.

In another five cases (West African Economic and Monetary Union (WAEMU), Tanzania, Kenya, Bolivia, Nigeria) the main impetus to converge on international standards came from regulators, although they tended to be more circumspect than politicians. Regulators were aware of the challenges that international standards pose in nascent financial sectors and in the face of acute resource constraints, and were more likely to push for selective rather than wholesale implementation. In some cases, regulators acted out of prudential concerns. This was most notable in Nigeria where the regulator sought to upgrade regulations and improve supervision in order to manage the risks posed by increasingly complex and internationally active banks. In other cases, regulators advocated implementation to improve home-host supervision and coordinate with other regulatory authorities.

Beyond these more functional drivers, we found evidence that regulators face strong reputational incentives to implement the latest international standards, which are considered the 'gold standard' in the international policy circles in which regulators are engaged. This was particularly striking in Bolivia. In other countries extensive engagement with the IMF, and to a lesser extent the World Bank, generated incentives to converge on international standards. In the West African Economic and Monetary Union (WAEMU), there was direct pressure from the IMF to implement Basel II and III standards.

In most other cases, the IMF and World Bank played an important, but indirect, role. They were a major source of training and technical advice on bank regulation and supervision, and a striking number of central bank governors and senior officials in our case studies had spent portions of their career in international financial institutions. While the advice and training rarely advocated implementation of the full suite of international standards, extensive engagement with international financial institutions helped create a culture of receptivity to international standards and 'best practices' within regulatory authorities. For many senior officials, implementing the latest international standards became a source of professional pride, providing kudos and legitimacy in international policy circles and at home. These dynamics were particularly striking in Kenya, Tanzania, Ghana, and Pakistan.

Surprisingly, banks were not a major driver of regulatory outcomes in any of our countries. In Pakistan the role of banks was most pronounced, but they only emerged as a powerful lobby for convergence once the financial services sector had gained a preeminent position in the economy and domestic banks had reoriented their business models to the international market. Thus it was the changes brought by policy and regulatory decisions that created a powerful vested interest group in favour of convergence, which arguably makes the convergence trajectory hard to reverse.

In Nigeria there was also a critical mass of large internationally active domestic banks, but the drive for convergence came largely from the regulator's concerns about the risks international domestic banks posed, rather than advocacy by the banks themselves. A few domestic banks in Vietnam and Kenya had international operations and while they were generally supportive of convergence, they were not strong advocates. Larger banks in Tanzania expected to derive a competitive advantage vis-à-vis their smaller competitors from the implementation of international standards. They acted collectively through a business association and the creation of institutionalized channels gave them substantial purchase over regulatory decisions accelerating convergence.

The local subsidiaries of internationally active banks were not strong advocates of convergence. In Angola, and to some extent Tanzania, foreign and domestic banks perceived compliance as an unattractive yet important move in the face of rising concerns about compliance with anti-money laundering standards. In other countries, notably Kenya, foreign subsidiaries were a source of technical advice and support to domestic banks and regulators but did not actively call for the implementation of international standards.

The relative absence of banks as the main driver of convergence is surprising, as statistical analysis of Basel implementation in countries outside of the Basel Committee shows that banks with international operations are significant drivers of convergence (Jones and Zeitz, 2019). The discrepancy between the findings of the case studies in this volume and this wider statistical analysis is likely explained by our focus on countries with nascent levels of financial sector development, a stage at which there are few internationally active domestic banks. As the Pakistan case study suggests, it is only when domestic banks have a substantial international presence that they become champions of convergence.

Drivers of divergence

Our research also highlights powerful drivers of divergence from international standards. These were most pronounced in Ethiopia, where regulators have opted not to implement any elements of Basel II or III. However, there were strong incentives to diverge from international standards in eight other countries too, with Pakistan and Rwanda as the only exceptions.

In five countries (Ethiopia, Bolivia, Tanzania, Vietnam, Angola), politicians were wary of implementing international standards. In Ethiopia and Bolivia, and to a lesser extent Tanzania and Vietnam, governments are pursuing a developmental state approach and using a variety of policy instruments to direct credit, which sits uneasily with the market-based approach to credit allocation assumed in the Basel framework. In Vietnam, which is transitioning from a socialist economy to a market economy, conservative factions of the political elite were opposed to the implementation of international standards lest this speed up the marketization of the financial sector and wider economy. Political considerations loomed large for politicians in Angola where politicians were concerned that implementing international standards would undermine their extensive control over domestic banks and allocation of credit to political allies.

Regulators in most of our case studies were sceptical about the suitability of some aspects of international standards for their local contexts. While many faced strong reputational incentives to implement international standards, and pressure from politicians, many officials we interviewed questioned the applicability of more complex aspects of Basel II and III for regulating banks in their jurisdiction. While some regulators were able to reconcile these tensions through selective adoption and modifying standards to fit the local context, regulators did not always have the support from governors and politicians to deviate from what is perceived to be international 'best practice' and design more suitable alternatives.

Regulators also opposed implementation where they thought that it would publicly expose the fragility of some banks and, in the worst case, precipitate a financial crisis. These concerns were particularly pronounced in Vietnam and Nigeria.

Pathways to convergence, divergence, and mock compliance

Overall, the balance of incentives and political economy dynamics between politicians and regulators tipped countries towards convergence, with seven of our eleven cases converging on international standards, albeit to varying extents (Pakistan, Rwanda, Ghana, WAEMU, Tanzania, Kenya, Bolivia). As we might expect, convergence was most extensive when politicians, regulators, and banks supported implementation, as the case of Pakistan illustrates. Convergence also tended to be higher when politicians were the main drivers of convergence than when the impetus came from regulators. Where politicians dominated the dynamics of regulatory convergence, the regulator tended to have less autonomy and fewer resources, and was less likely to be a source of sceptical push-back. This led to more ambitious levels of implementation.

Conversely, where regulators drove the convergence process, usually in cases where they had a relatively high level of autonomy from politicians and substantial institutional strength, they tended to be more aware of the challenges and while they drove convergence, they took a more selective approach to implementation. This was the case in Kenya and Tanzania. In Bolivia, there was a high level of contestation between regulators who sought very ambitious levels of implementation, and politicians pursuing interventionist financial policies who opposed implementation. This led to a far lower level of implementation than the regulatory authorities had hoped for.

In three cases (Nigeria, Angola, and Vietnam), conflicting incentives on the part of regulators and politicians led to mock compliance. In Nigeria, the regulator was both eager to implement international standards to better supervise large international banks, and worried that implementation would be detrimental to smaller banks. The result was regulatory forbearance towards the smaller banks. In Angola, politicians were conflicted, feeling under pressure to implement international standards in order to persevere correspondent banking links, and worried that implementation would undercut their ability to distribute credit to their allies. In Vietnam, there was contestation among reformist politicians who sought to implement international standards as part of wider efforts to open the economy, and conservative politicians who opposed further marketization. Meanwhile, regulators were attracted to international standards as a means of communicating with bank supervisors in other countries, yet worried that implementation would cause the collapse of weak banks.

Ethiopia is our one case of divergence. Its regulators have remained with Basel I standards and opted out of Basel II and III. Ethiopia is striking as it is the one country where no actor championed implementation. While it is tempting to attribute this to the fact that there are no foreign banks in Ethiopia, and domestic banks are prohibited from operating internationally, we have seen from our other case studies that the interests of banks have not been a decisive factor in explaining convergence. Instead, Ethiopia's decision to diverge is the result of politicians pursuing a state-led development strategy in which the government retains a high level of discretionary control over the allocation of credit. The regulatory authority is fully aligned with this policy. It is striking that Ethiopia and Rwanda, which are often cited as examples of developmental states in Africa (e.g. Clapham, 2018; Goodfellow, 2017; Mann and Berry, 2016), have responded in such different ways to international banking standards. We reflect on this more below.

Insights for scholarship and areas for further research

Several aspects of our research stand out when we situate our findings in the wider literature on developing countries in the global economy, and on the politics of economic reform within developing countries.

Constrained agency in the global economy

It is striking that our cases defy the stereotype of peripheral countries being pressured by international actors to converge on international standards. Such pressures undoubtedly exist in many areas, including other aspects of international finance (Chwieroth, 2010; Drezner, 2007; Gallagher, 2015; Jawara and Kwa, 2003; Phillips, 2017; Sharman, 2008; Simmons, 2001). Yet coercive pressure played a minor role in our case studies. Only in WAEMU, where the IMF championed implementation, and Angola, where the threat of correspondent banks withdrawing their services catalysed action, were external pressures significant drivers of convergence.

Instead convergence was driven primarily by politicians and regulators, and to a lesser extent internationally oriented domestic banks, actively seeking greater levels of integration in the global economy and international policy circles. It was this dynamic of actively seeking insertion into international processes that led to convergence. This does not mean politicians and regulators in our case study countries did not face external constraints; their policy options and regulatory choices were heavily circumscribed by the international context in which they operated. Crucially, because politicians and regulators had few alternative mechanisms for signalling to international investors and professional peers, their quest for international capital and international recognition led them to support the implementation of international standards that were cumbersome and ill suited in many ways to their local contexts.

More profoundly, the preferences and interests of politicians and regulators have been conditioned by their countries' precarious position in the global economy. Vulnerability led to long-term relationships with the IMF and World Bank which, as we have shown, decisively shaped the types of regulatory institutions that exist in our case study countries, and close ties to these institutions continued to mould the underlying preferences of regulatory authorities. Similarly, profound levels of underdevelopment and a shortage of capital led many politicians to make attracting international investment a policy priority. We have shown how the actions of politicians, regulators and banks, are shaped by their connections to international finance as well as domestic factors, and how they manoeuvre within external and domestic constraints. In doing so we contribute to a growing body of literature that draws attention to the agency of actors from weak states in the global economy (e.g. Brown, 2013; Cooper et al., 2009; Jones, 2013; Jones et al., 2010; Lee and Smith, 2008; Mohan and Lampert, 2013; Whitfield, 2009).

The weak influence of banks in the politics of regulation

We have been struck by the finding that banks played a relatively minor role in the domestic politics of banking regulation in our case study countries. Banks rarely exerted a direct influence over regulatory outcomes. In some countries, banks were subordinate to the state, or politicians. In other countries banks had greater autonomy from the state and politicians, yet they rarely mobilized to try and shape regulatory outcomes.

This finding is striking as banks play an out-sized role in shaping regulatory outcomes in more advanced economies and in larger developing countries (e.g. Johnson and Kwak, 2011; Mattli and Woods, 2009; Maxfield, 1991; Pepinsky, 2013; Stigler, 1971). They also shape international standard-setting processes. Private associations of major firms have played a leading role in setting international standards in areas like accounting and, even when they aren't the principal decision-makers, large financial firms have become adept at shaping international standards (Baker, 2010; Goldbach, 2015; Johnson and Kwak, 2011; Pagliari and Young, 2014; Romano, 2014; Tsingou, 2008; Underhill and Zhang, 2008; Young, 2012).

The difference appears to lie in the nascent nature of the financial sector in many low and lower-middle income countries, where banks have yet to develop the economic and political clout to decisively shape regulations. As we have shown, this leads a distinctive set of political economy logics around banking regulation in low and lower-middle income countries, in which the preferences of politicians and regulators are decisive, and the anticipated reactions of international market actors loom large.

Given how important finance is in processes of development, we have been surprised at how thin the literature is on the politics of credit allocation in low and lower-middle income countries. The relationship between banks, businesses, politicians, and regulators in low-income countries deserves greater scrutiny by scholars, as we have seen how influential these relationships have been in other emerging economies on the trajectory of economic development (e.g. Hutchcroft, 1998; Maxfield, 1991; Pepinsky, 2013). There is a literature on the role of business associations in developing countries, including in African countries, which identifies a series of conditions under which business associations facilitate or impede economic growth (e.g. Bräutigam et al., 2002; Doner and Schneider, 2000). So far scant attention has been paid to the role of banks and other financial institutions in economic development trajectories in low- and lower-middle-income countries, particularly in Africa, and this would be a fascinating area for further research.

The role of policy ideas

While the narrow material, party-political, and reputational interests of politicians and regulators played a role in shaping regulatory outcomes, it is hard to overlook the powerful impact of ideas. Ideas about the financial sector's role in the wider economy, and the role banks should play, decisively shaped regulatory outcomes. This was most striking in Ethiopia where a very strong set of policy ideas focused on state-led industrialization in which the state retains control over credit allocation. These policy ideas help explain Ethiopia's divergence from international standards.

Equally strong yet very different sets of ideas explain why Pakistan, Rwanda, and Ghana were ambitious adopters of international standards. In these cases, and to some extent Kenya, convergence was driven by policy agendas focused on becoming a financial services hub, as politicians looked to emulate countries like Mauritius, Hong Kong, and Singapore. Implementing the very latest international banking standards is seen as imperative for establishing a financial services hub, just as keeping up with these standards is a priority for many existing financial services hubs (Brummer, 2012; Sharman, 2009). A similar vision has propelled other developing countries to look to expand their financial services sectors (Ghosh, 2007; Patnaik, 2007). In India, a commission was appointed to develop Mumbai as a regional financial centre, on the understanding that the financial centre would generate real sector development throughout the country (Reddy, 2010).

These policy agendas are linked to the fast growth of the global financial sector since the 1980s, and the expansion of pan-regional banks in many developing countries in the past decade. As McKinsey notes in a recent report, 'Africa's banking markets are among the most exciting in the world. The continent's overall banking market is the second-fastest-growing and second-most profitable of any global region, and a hotbed of innovation... Africa's retail banking markets are ripe with potential and present huge opportunities for innovation and further growth' (Chironga et al., 2018, pp. 3–4).

Among academics there is a growing literature on industrial policy and the insertion of African countries into global value chains (e.g. Oqubay, 2016; UNECA, 2016; Whitfield et al., 2015). Scholars are, so far, paying much less attention to policies focused on the expansion of financial services and the re-orientation of economies to serve regional markets. In today's age of financial globalization, the strategies of governments in peripheral developing countries towards global finance deserve greater scrutiny.

The accountability of independent government institutions

Our research shows the value of opening up the black box of 'the state' in peripheral developing countries, unpacking the rules, the motives and motivations, and the tensions, capacity, and interests inside bureaucratic institutions. All too often the state is treated as a black box, with little attention paid to the politics within and among government institutions. Our work highlights the importance of central banks as economic and political actors and contributes to the literature on the trade-offs associated with delegating important policies to independent regulatory institutions.

The creation of independent institutions for regulating banks has long been hailed as an important move to insulate policy decisions from predatory inclinations of politicians, particularly in developing countries (Barth et al., 2006). Having an independent central bank can act as an important commitment device for reassuring international and domestic actors of policy continuity (Ghosh, 2007; Gilardi, 2007; Maxfield, 1997).

But the role of independent institutions is also highly political, and has substantial trade-offs. The global financial crisis and its aftermath have stimulated a very live debate about the merits of central bank independence in countries at the core of the global financial system (e.g. Restoy, 2018; Tucker, 2018). Central to this debate is the observation that central banks have become powerful actors, yet operate with very little oversight. This has led to calls for greater transparency in decision-making and structural reforms to improve political accountability (e.g. Balls et al., 2018).

Scholars have asked similar questions about the merits of independent regulatory institutions in developing countries. While praised by some for being islands of efficiency in a sea of unprofessional corrupt states, such institutions have also been criticized for removing policymaking from the democratic arena (Dargent, 2015). Boylan (2001) argues that central bank independence is often used by right-leaning authoritarian governments to tie the hands of unwilling successors during transitions to democracy, to ensure continuity of economic policies that favour powerful business interests. Teodoro and Pitcher (2017) raise important normative questions about the desirability of creating independent regulatory institutions, particularly in fragile democracies. Rather than insulate technocrats from politics, engagement between bureaucrats and interest groups is important for fostering long-term, politically sustainable policies.

Our research contributes to this debate by revealing the ways in which independent regulatory institutions are not only *dis-embedded* from local politics, but are also more likely to be *embedded* in international processes that make them receptive to international policy ideas, pressures, and incentives. Such embeddedness may lead to learning and an improvement of the quality of decision-making. But we have also have shown how it can also lead to the adoption of international standards that fail to reflect local realities, a phenomenon of 'dysfunctional policy transfer' (Sharman, 2010). Scholars have found a similar trend in other areas, including in intellectual property rights (Deere-Birkbeck, 2009). Dysfunctional policy transfer is particularly likely when regulatory institutions have independence but few resources, making them receptive to international policy solutions without the ability to critically appraise and push-back against them. The WAEMU case shows how the supranational nature of regional institutions renders them particularly vulnerable to detachment from local politics and contexts.

More generally, there is the need for more fine-grained research on the role of bureaucrats and inner workings of government institutions in developing countries. This is particularly true for African countries where the literature on bureaucratic politics is thin and scholars are too quick to dismiss formal bureaucratic institutions as ineffectual (Pitcher and Teodoro, 2018; Teodoro and Pitcher, 2017). Our case studies illustrate the substantial variation in the autonomy and power that regulatory institutions have over banking regulation, and we started to explore some of the reasons for this. Given how important government institutions are and yet how little we really know about their inner workings in African countries, this is an important area for further research. From where do bureaucrats derive power? How insulated are technocrats from political considerations, and with what implications? How can we account for variation in the politics of bureaucracy across institutions within the same government, and across governments?

Policy implications

Our research generates a series of insights for policymakers that contribute to a wider policy discussion on how to reform international banking standards so they better reflect the interests of developing countries.

Given the problems that implementing international standards poses for peripheral developing countries, many experts advocate greater reliance on sui generis national regulations and strengthened roles for host regulators (Eichengreen et al., 2018; Persaud, 2013). For instance, national authorities could insist that foreign banks can only operate as subsidiaries, not branches, in their jurisdictions, thereby enabling peripheral governments to have greater control over their operations (Persaud, 2013; The Warwick Commission, 2009). They could also make greater use of capital controls and macroprudential measures to help temper destabilizing inflows and outflows of capital (Rey, 2015; Gallagher, 2015; Griffith-Jones et al., 2012; Gallagher, 2015; Akyuz, 2010).

Yet we have shown how the uneven distribution of structural power in the global financial system limits the extent to which national authorities in peripheral countries can act unilaterally, as it can be costly to diverge from international standards. Politicians and regulators in small developing countries, particularly those with nascent financial sectors, are often looking to attract international capital, maintain (or attain) investment grade ratings from international ratings agencies, and stay on good terms with international financial institutions like the IMF. Our research highlights the powerful reputational, competitive, and functional incentives generated by financial globalization that lead regulators to adopt international standards even when they are ill suited to their local context.

Given these strong incentives, regulators can modify international standards to suit their local context, in order harness their reputational benefits while avoiding the costs of an off-the-shelf implementation. But modifying international standards is costly—sitting through the full suite of international standards and adapting them to fit the local context is a painstaking and resource-intensive task. Such an approach also shifts the burden of retrofitting international standards onto the world's most acutely resource-constrained regulators. An alternative option is to redesign international standards so that they can be more readily used in a wider range of contexts, including low- and lower-middle-income countries.

In the wake of the global financial crisis, there were calls for international standards to be simplified and to build proportionality into their design. But little has changed. The Basel Committee set up a Task Force on Simplicity and Comparability in 2012 but the Task Force paid no attention to the implementation challenges faced by developing countries (BCBS, 2013). Despite concerns raised by regulators from developing countries about the complexity of specific elements of Basel III, the Basel Committee has not addressed them (World Bank, 2015; BCBS, 2017).

Redesigning international standards to better reflect the interests of peripheral developing countries requires providing peripheral developing countries with greater influence over decision-making processes. This in turn requires greater representation of peripheral developing countries at the tables where decisions are made, a stronger evidence base from which to make alternative proposals, and greater institutionalized cooperation among peripheral developing countries, so that they can better champion reforms.

Below we discuss the steps that national regulators in peripheral developing countries can take to modify international standards, and then discuss the reforms needed in international standard-setting.

Modifying international standards before implementing them

Regulators in peripheral developing countries have substantial room for manoeuvre when they implement international standards. International standards are soft-law (Brummer, 2012) and countries outside of the Basel Committee are not subject to peer-review assessments. In previous chapters we have highlighted the manifold incentives and pressures that regulators in developing countries face to implement international 'best practice' standards. While this means it is extremely difficult for regulators to develop their own sui generis regulations and abandon international standards altogether, they still have room to substantially modify international standards before implementing them.

A first option, common among the regulators in our case studies, is to implement international standards selectively. As we have seen, Basel II and III are in practice compendia of different standards so regulators can select those components that are most desirable and feasible to implement. In many peripheral countries, regulators are choosing not to adopt the controversial internal model approaches for assessing risk. They are also cautious in implementing the macroprudential components of Basel III, which pose significant technical and data challenges for regulators.

Regulators can also modify the elements of the standards that they opt to implement, rather than copying and pasting form the Basel II and III rulebook. They can use their intimate knowledge of the domestic financial system to write rules that match local circumstances better than the Basel template. In the Philippines, for example, regulators have adjusted the risk weights for small and medium enterprises to reduce the incentive of banks to move away from lending to these firms.[1] In a more dramatic move, regulators can adjust the perimeter of banking regulation, so that regulations that are aligned with international standards only apply to large internationally active banks, and simpler (although not necessarily less stringent) rules apply to small commercial banks. This approach is common in countries belonging to the Basel Committee (Castro Carvalho et al., 2017). Although regulators in our case study countries are making some minor modifications to international standards, our over-riding impression is that they are nowhere near as bold as many Basel member countries in tailoring the standards to suit their local circumstances.

Greater representation of peripheral developing countries in global standards-setting

A more optimal approach would be to modify international standards to better reflect the interests of developing countries. As discussed in Chapter 1, the vast majority of developing countries do not have a seat at the table where international standards are negotiated. The prevailing system imposes a rigid divide between the countries at the core of global financial governance which set the standards, and countries on the periphery, which have no voice in the process.

In the wake of the global financial crisis, the G20 asked standard-setting institutions to assess the implications of international financial standards for developing countries, and to further open up decision-making processes. In response, the Financial Stability Board (FSB) created an internal workstream on the effects of regulatory reform on emerging market and developing economies (FSB et al. 2011). It also established six Regional Consultative Groups where members and non-members exchange views on financial stability issues and the global regulatory

---

[1] Discussion with regulator, via videoconference, September 2018.

reform agenda. Little is known about the nature of participation and quality of dialogue because public summaries of the meetings carry very little information, but our interviews with regulators suggest that these fora do not provide meaningful input into or influence over the design of international standards. Instead they function as fora for regulators to trouble-shoot implementation.

There have been calls for a more radical overhaul of global financial governance since the global financial crisis, and many proposals would provide peripheral developing countries with greater representation. Proposals include the creation of an entirely new inter-governmental organization featuring wide or even universal membership in a constituency system akin to that of the IMF or the World Bank, where members of the governing board represent several member countries (Claessens, 2008; Eichengreen, 2009; Stiglitz, 2010).

Yet there is little appetite at the level of the FSB for radical reforms. The FSB members considered, and dismissed, the proposal of conversion into a classic inter-governmental organization as undesirable. They also rejected the proposal of adopting a constituency-based membership system because it would be inconsistent with its institutional model (individual financial agencies are members of the FSB, not states) and because it 'would make FSB discussions more rigid' (FSB, 2014, p. 1). In 2014 the FSB rearranged the Plenary to give more seats to officials from emerging market member jurisdictions (FSB, 2014). At the same time, it reduced the seats of international organizations such as the IMF and the World Bank, who could in principle represent developing country voices, but in practice have done so with negligible effectiveness.

While there is little political appetite for a radical overhaul of global financial governance, more moderate reforms could be pursued. The Basel Committee could amend its charter to explicitly recognize the need for differentiated standards and commit to build proportionality into their design, so that Basel standards can be readily adapted for use in a wide range of jurisdictions. It could also broaden its mandate beyond an exclusive focus on financial stability to recognize the importance of other objectives such as financial sector development and financial inclusion. Even bringing these in as secondary considerations would incentivize more careful analysis in international standard-setting. It would also better align the Basel Committee's mandate with the domestic mandates of regulators from most developing countries, and a sizable minority of high-income countries, which include objectives beyond financial stability (Jones and Knaack, 2019). Rather than waiting to see whether standards generate adverse impacts on developing countries, the Basel Committee could undertake ex ante assessments.

An interesting proposal is the creation of a small multilateral organization to audit international standard-setting bodies, akin to auditor-generals in national jurisdictions, or the Independent Evaluation Office of the IMF and Independent Evaluation Group of the World Bank (Helleiner and Porter, 2010). Outside of the Basel Committee, the Basel Consultative Group could review its membership to ensure it is broadly representative, inviting new members from low- and lower-middle-income countries. The Basel Consultative Group and the Regional Consultative Groups could move away from the current top-down *modus operandi* of focusing on the implementation of global standards towards facilitating bottom-up proposals to influence their design (Jones and Knaack, 2019).

Creating influential clubs of regulators from peripheral developing countries

Strengthening professional networks among regulators from peripheral developing countries could strengthen their voice in international standard-setting. Informal clubs among the regulators from the world's largest financial centres, often including senior executives from the world's largest financial firms, have had an outsized impact on the design of international financial standards. Yet there are few fora in which regulators from peripheral developing countries meet to develop strong ties and alternative policy proposals.

Regulators from advanced countries, and senior officials from the world's largest financial firms, have used informal clubs to shape international financial institutions. The G30 brings together, on an invite-only basis, very senior representatives from the public and private sectors and academia to work on international economic and financial issues, with international banking a core focus area.[2] Such clubs are together by elite peer recognition, common and mutually reinforcing interests, and pursuit of a common goal. There is competition for ideas and influence but discussions are highly protected from outside pressures, and clubs tend to converge around specific sets of policy ideas (Tsingou, 2015). The fostering of close relations between members of elite clubs can have a powerful effect on decision-making in other fora, including standard-setting bodies in international finance, which are often dominated by members of these informal clubs (Baker, 2009).

Regulators from peripheral developing countries are at a disadvantage because they do not have the equivalent clubs in which to meet and forge a strong sense of identify and cohesion. Thus, even when regulators from developing countries gain a seat at the decision-making table, they encounter a level of cohesion among their counterparts from advanced countries which they do not match. Regulators from peripheral developing countries do meet, particularly through regional professional networks, but the level of engagement and cooperation varies from region to region, and there are very few fora for regulators from different regions to meet each other and strategize.[3] Moreover, these networks rarely publish proposals for the reform of international financial standards. Investing in the creation of an informal club to generate a stronger sense of common identity and formulate

---

[2] http://group30.org.
[3] A notable exception is the Alliance for Financial Inclusion, which brings together regulators from developing countries to promote financial inclusion: https://www.afi-global.org.

alternative policy proposals, is a mechanism through which regulators from peripheral developing countries could strengthen their influence over international financial regulation.

Strengthening the evidence base for regulators in peripheral developing countries

Our research highlights the paucity of information and evidence available for developing country regulators seeking to diverge from international standards, and develop alternative policy proposals.

The Bank for International Settlements is the primary international institution for supporting central banks to ensure monetary and financial stability, and is renowned for its high-quality research. However it focuses almost exclusively on the regulatory priorities of developed countries. The Financial Stability Institute (FSI), which is a small organization housed within the Bank for International Settlements, does conduct research on countries outside of the Basel Committee, but its core mandate is to support worldwide implementation of global standards, rather than shaping their design.[4]

The IMF and World Bank are the other high-profile international organizations with a focus on financial regulation and, as we have shown in this book, they engage extensively with regulators in low- and lower-middle-income countries Yet, so far they have focused on providing technical advice on how to *implement* international standards, rather than supporting developing countries to shape these standards during the design phase. Despite experts closely affiliated with the IMF and World Bank challenging the relevance of Basel standards for peripheral developing countries (e.g. Barth and Caprio, 2018; Demirgüç-Kunt and Detragiache, 2010) and strong connections to standard-setting bodies, the IMF and World Bank have invested little effort in shaping international standards to better reflect the needs of developing countries. In the context of Financial Sector Assessment Programmes, the IMF and World Bank have warned against hasty Basel II or III implementation in some low- and lower-middle-income countries, but to date they have provided little systematic analysis of how regulators can modify international standards to their needs.

The Bank for International Settlements, IMF, and World Bank could invest greater resources in analysing international financial standards from the perspective of regulators from low- and lower-middle-income countries, increasing their dialogue with regulators from these jurisdictions, and making recommendations to the Basel Committee. Rather than focusing on ways to minimize the harm

---

[4] For details on the Financial Stability Institute, see here: https://www.bis.org/fsi/index.htm?m=1%7C17%7C629.

and challenges that international standards pose for developing countries, this research agenda should start from the question of what regulations are most needed in peripheral developing countries. This will help to address the fact that there are glaring gaps in the current international regulations, including on regulatory measures to mitigate volatility in international capital flows and address commodity price shocks, two of the biggest sources of financial instability in low- and lower-middle-income countries (Gottschalk, 2016, p. 61; Kasekende et al., 2012; Repullo and Saurina, 2011).

Recognizing the inherent conservatism of these institutions, a challenge associated with the continued dominance of advanced economies in their governance structures, it is equally important that resources are channelled to strengthen policy institutions led by experts from low- and lower-middle-income countries. As we have seen from the international trade sphere, international experts from the global South have been instrumental in supporting the governments of developing countries in their efforts to shape international rules (Scott, 2015). Strengthening such research and policy institutions would help to generate the policy alternatives that are badly needed in order to ensure that financial regulations support sustainable development in countries at the periphery of the global economy.

References

Abdel-Baki, M., 2012. *Forecasting the costs and benefits of implementing Basel III for North African emerging economies: An application to Egypt and Tunisia*, AfDB Economic Brief. African Development Bank.

Akyuz, Y., 2010. The management of capital flows and financial vulnerability in Asia, in: Griffith-Jones, S., Ocampo, J.A., Stiglitz, J.E. (Eds.), *Time for a Visible Hand: Lessons from the 2008 World Financial Crisis*. Oxford University Press, New York, pp. 219–41.

Bailey, A., 2014. *The capital adequacy of banks: Today's issues and what we have learned from the past*. Speech given by Andrew Bailey, Deputy Governor, Prudential Regulation and Chief Executive Officer, Prudential Regulation Authority at Bloomberg, London, 10 July. https://www.bankofengland.co.uk/-/media/boe/files/speech/2014/the-capital-adequacy-of-banks-todays-issues-and-what-we-have-learned-from-the-past.

Baker, A., 2009. Deliberative equality and the transgovernmental politics of the global financial architecture. *Global Governance: A Review of Multilateralism and International Organizations* 15, 195–218.

Baker, A., 2010. Restraining regulatory capture? Anglo-America, crisis politics and trajectories of change in global financial governance. *International Affairs* 86, 647–63. https://doi.org/10.1111/j.1468-2346.2010.00903.x.

Balls, E., Howat, J., Stansbury, A., 2018. *Central bank independence revisited: After the financial crisis, what should a model central bank look like?* (M-RCBG Associate Working Paper Series No. 87). Harvard Kennedy School.

Barth, J.R., Caprio, G., 2018. Regulation and supervision in financial development, in: Beck, T., Levine, R. (Eds.), *Handbook of Finance and Development*. Edward Elgar Publishing, Cheltenham, pp. 393–418. https://doi.org/10.4337/9781785360510.

Barth, J.R., Caprio, G., Levine, R., 2006. *Rethinking Bank Regulation: Till Angels Govern*. Cambridge University Press, Cambridge; New York.

Basel Consultative Group, 2014. *Impact and implementation challenges of the Basel framework for emerging market, developing and small economies* (Working Paper No. 27).

BCBS, 2013. *The regulatory framework: balancing risk sensitivity, simplicity and comparability—discussion paper*. Basel.

BCBS, 2017. *Simplified alternative to the standardised approach to market risk capital requirements*. Basel.

Boylan, D.M., 2001. *Defusing Democracy: Central Bank Autonomy and the Transition from Authoritarian Rule*. University of Michigan Press, Ann Arbor, MI.

Bräutigam, D., Rakner, L., Taylor, S., 2002. Business associations and growth coalitions in Sub-Saharan Africa. *The Journal of Modern African Studies* 40. https://doi.org/10.1017/S0022278X02004056.

Brown, W., 2013. *African Agency in International Politics*, 1st ed. Routledge, London. https://doi.org/10.4324/9780203526071.

Brummer, C., 2012. *Soft Law and the Global Financial System: Rule Making in the 21st Century*. Cambridge University Press, New York.

Castro Carvalho, A.P., Hohl, S., Raskopf, R., Ruhnau, S., 2017. *Proportionality in banking regulation: a cross-country comparison* (FSI Insights No. 1). Financial Stability Institute.

Chey, H., 2016. International financial standards and emerging economies since the global financial crisis, in: Henning, C.R., Walter, A. (Eds.), *Global Financial Governance Confronts the Rising Powers*. CIGI, Waterloo, pp. 211–36.

Chironga, M., Cunha, L., De Grandis, H., Kuyoro, M., 2018. *Roaring to life: Growth and innovation in African retail banking* (Global Banking). McKinsey & Company, New York.

Chwieroth, J.M., 2010. *Capital Ideas: The IMF and the Rise of Financial Liberalization*. Princeton University Press, Princeton, NJ.

Claessens, S., 2008. The new international financial architecture requires better governance, in: Eichengreen, B., Baldwin, R. (Eds.), *What G20 Leaders Must Do to Stabilise Our Economy and Fix the Financial System*. Centre for Economic Policy Research, London, pp. 29–33.

Clapham, C., 2018. The Ethiopian developmental state. *Third World Quarterly* 39, 1151–65. https://doi.org/10.1080/01436597.2017.1328982.

Cooper, A.F., Shaw, T.M., Centre for International Governance Innovation, 2009. *The Diplomacies of Small States between Vulnerability and Resilience*. Palgrave Macmillan, Basingstoke.

Dargent, E., 2015. *Technocracy and Democracy in Latin America: The Experts Running Government*. Cambridge University Press, New York.

Deere-Birkbeck, C., 2009. *The Implementation Game: The TRIPS Agreement and the Global Politics of Intellectual Property Reform in Developing Countries.* Oxford University Press, Oxford; New York.

Demirgüç-Kunt, A., Detragiache, M.E., 2010. *Basel Core Principles and Bank Risk: Does Compliance Matter?* International Monetary Fund, Washington, DC.

Doner, R., Schneider, B.R., 2000. Business associations and economic development: Why some associations contribute more than others. *Business and Politics* 2.

Drezner, D.W., 2007. *All Politics Is Global: Explaining International Regulatory Regimes.* Princeton University Press, Princeton, NJ; Oxford.

Eichengreen, B., 2009. *Out of the box: Thoughts about the international financial architecture* (Working Paper No. WP/09/116). International Monetary Fund, Washington, DC.

Eichengreen, B., Lombardi, D., Malkin, A., 2018. Multilayered governance and the international financial architecture: The erosion of multilateralism in international liquidity provision. *Global Policy* 9, 7–20. https://doi.org/10.1111/1758-5899.12561.

FCA, PRA, 2015. *The failure of HBOS plc.* Financial Conduct Authority and Prudential Regulatory Authority, London.

FSB, 2014. *Report to the G20 Brisbane Summit on the FSB's Review of the Structure of its Representation.* Basel.

FSB, IMF, WB, 2011. *Financial Stability Issues in Emerging Market and Developing Economies: Report to the G20 Finance Ministers and Central Bank Governors.* Financial Stability Board, International Monetary Fund, World Bank, Basel.

Fuchs, M., Losse-Mueller, T., Witte, M., 2013. The reform agenda for financial regulation and supervision in Africa, in: Beck, T., Maimbo, S.M. (Eds.), *Financial Sector Development in Africa: Opportunities and Challenges.* The World Bank, Washington, DC.

Gallagher, K., 2015. *Ruling capital: Emerging markets and the reregulation of cross-border finance.* Cornell University Press, Ithaca, NY.

Ghosh, J., 2007. Central bank 'autonomy' in the age of finance, in: Bagchi, A.K., Dymski, G. (Eds.), *Capture and Exclude: Developing Economies and the Poor in Global Finance.* Tulika Books, New Delhi, pp. 39–51.

Gilardi, F., 2007. The same, but different: Central banks, regulatory agencies, and the politics of delegation to independent authorities. *Comparative European Politics* 5, 303–27. https://doi.org/10.1057/palgrave.cep.6110098.

Goldbach, R., 2015. Asymmetric influence in global banking regulation: Transnational harmonization, the competition state, and the roots of regulatory failure. *Review of International Political Economy* 22, 1087–127. https://doi.org/10.1080/09692290.2015.1050440.

Goodfellow, T., 2017. Taxing property in a neo-developmental state: The politics of urban land value capture in Rwanda and Ethiopia. *African Affairs* 116, 549–72. https://doi.org/10.1093/afraf/adx020.

Gottschalk, R. (Ed.), 2010. *The Basel Capital Accords in Developing Countries: Challenges for Development Finance.* Palgrave Macmillan, Basingstoke; New York.

Gottschalk, R., 2016. Assessing capacity constraints for effective financial regulation in Sub-Saharan Africa, in: Griffith-Jones, S., Gottschalk, R. (Eds.), *Achieving Financial Stability and Growth in Africa*. Routledge, London, pp. 61–82.

Gottschalk, R., Griffith-Jones, S., 2006. *Review of Basel II Implementation in low-income countries* (Report prepared for the UK Department for International Development) Institute of Development Studies.

Griffith-Jones, S., Ocampo, J.A., Gallagher, K.P., 2012. *Regulating global capital flows for long-run development*, Task Force Report. Pardee Center.

Held, D., Young, K.L., 2009. *Global financial governance: Principles of reform*. Report, LSE Research Online. London. http://eprints.lse.ac.uk/43602/1/The%20world%20crisis_%20global%20financial%20governance(lsero).pdf.

Helleiner, E., Porter, T., 2010. Making transnational networks more accountable. *Economics, Management, and Financial Markets* 5, 158–73.

Hohl, S., Sison, M.C., Sastny, T., Zamil, R., 2018. *The Basel framework in 100 jurisdictions: Implementation status and proportionality practices*. (No. 11), FSI Insights on policy implementation. Bank for International Settlements.

Hutchcroft, P.D., 1998. *Booty Capitalism: The Politics of Banking in the Philippines*. Cornell University Press, Ithaca, NY.

Jawara, F., Kwa, A., 2003. *Behind the Scenes at the WTO: The Real World of International Trade Negotiations*. Zed, London.

Johnson, S., Kwak, J., 2011. *13 Bankers: The Wall Street Takeover and the Next Financial Meltdown*, 1st Vintage Books ed. Vintage Books, New York.

Jones, E., 2013. *Negotiating Against the Odds: A Guide for Trade Negotiators from Developing Countries*. Palgrave Macmillan, UK.

Jones, E., Knaack, P., 2019. Global financial regulation: Shortcomings and reform options. *Global Policy*. https://doi.org/10.1111/1758-5899.12656.

Jones, E. and A. O. Zeitz 2019. Regulatory Convergence in the Financial Periphery: How Interdependence Shapes Regulators' Decisions *International Studies Quarterly*, https://doi.org/10.1093/isq/sqz068.

Jones, E., Deere-Birkbeck, C., Woods, N., 2010. *Manoeuvring at the Margins Constraints Faced by Small States in International Trade Negotiations*. Commonwealth Secretariat, London.

Kasekende, L.A., Bagyenda, J., Brownbridge, M., 2012. *Basel III and the global reform of financial regulation: How should Africa respond? A bank regulator's perspective*. Bank of Uganda mimeo.

Lee, D., Smith, N.J., 2008. The political economy of small African states in the WTO. *The Round Table* 97, 259–71. https://doi.org/10.1080/00358530801962071.

Mann, L., Berry, M., 2016. Understanding the political motivations that shape Rwanda's emergent developmental state. *New Political Economy* 21, 119–44. https://doi.org/10.1080/13563467.2015.1041484.

Mattli, W., Woods, N., 2009. *The Politics of Global Regulation*. Princeton University Press, Princeton, NJ.

Maxfield, S., 1991. Bankers' alliances and economic policy patterns: Evidence from Mexico and Brazil. *Comparative Political Studies* 23, 419–58. https://doi.org/10.1177/0010414091023004001.

Maxfield, S., 1997. *Gatekeepers of Growth: The International Political Economy of Central Banking in Developing Countries*. Princeton University Press, Princeton, NJ.

Mohan, G., Lampert, B., 2013. Negotiating China: Reinserting African agency into China–Africa relations. *African Affairs* 112, 92–110. https://doi.org/10.1093/afraf/ads065.

Oqubay, A., 2016. *Made in Africa: Industrial Policy in Ethiopia*, First paperback edition. Oxford University Press, Oxford.

Pagliari, S., Young, K.L., 2014. Leveraged interests: Financial industry power and the role of private sector coalitions. *Review of International Political Economy* 21, 575–610. https://doi.org/10.1080/09692290.2013.819811.

Patnaik, P., 2007. The illusionism of finance, in: Bagchi, A.K., Dymski, G. (Eds.), *Capture and Exclude: Developing Economies and the Poor in Global Finance*. Tulika Books, New Delhi, pp. 52–64.

Pepinsky, T.B., 2013. The domestic politics of financial internationalization in the developing world. *Review of International Political Economy* 20, 848–80. https://doi.org/10.1080/09692290.2012.727361.

Persaud, A., 2013. *Reinventing Financial Regulation: A Blueprint for Overcoming Systemic Risk*. Apress, New York.

Phillips, N., 2017. Power and inequality in the global political economy. *International Affairs* 93, 429–44. https://doi.org/10.1093/ia/iix019.

Pistor, K., 2013. A legal theory of finance. *Journal of Comparative Economics* 41, 315–30.

Pitcher, M.A., Teodoro, M.P., 2018. The bureaucracy: Policy implementation and reform, in: Cheeseman, N. (Ed.), *Institutions and Democracy in Africa*. Cambridge University Press, Cambridge, pp. 160–88. https://doi.org/10.1017/9781316562888.007.

Posner, E., 2010. Sequence as explanation: The international politics of accounting standards. *Review of International Political Economy* 17, 639–64.

Powell, A., 2004. *Basel II and Developing Countries: Sailing through the Sea of Standards*, Policy Research Working Paper. World Bank.

Reddy, Y.V., 2010. Regulation of the financial sector in developing countries, in: Griffith-Jones, S., Ocampo, J.A., Stiglitz, J.E. (Eds.), *Time for a Visible Hand: Lessons from the 2008 World Financial Crisis*. Oxford University Press, Oxford, pp. 242–52.

Repullo, R., Saurina, J., 2011. *The countercyclical capital buffer of Basel III: A critical assessment* (No. wp2011_1102), Working Papers. CEMFI.

Restoy, F., 2018. *Central banks and financial oversight*. Presented at the Fundación Ramón Areces, Bank for International Settlements, Madrid, Spain.

Rey, H., 2015. *Dilemma not trilemma: The global financial cycle and monetary policy independence* (No. w21162). National Bureau of Economic Research, Cambridge, MA. https://doi.org/10.3386/w21162.

Romano, R., 2014. For diversity in the international regulation of financial institutions: Critiquing and recalibrating the Basel architecture. *Yale Journal on Regulation* 31.

Scott, J., 2015. The role of southern intellectuals in contemporary trade governance. *New Political Economy* 20, 633–52. https://doi.org/10.1080/13563467.2014.951615.

Seabrooke, L., Tsingou, E., 2009. Power elites and everyday politics in international financial reform. *International Political Sociology* 3, 457–61.

Sharman, J.C., 2008. Power and discourse in policy diffusion: Anti-money laundering in developing states. *International Studies Quarterly* 52, 635–56.

Sharman, J.C., 2009. The bark is the bite: International organizations and blacklisting. *Review of International Political Economy* 16, 573–96. https://doi.org/10.1080/09692290802403502.

Sharman, J.C., 2010. Dysfunctional policy transfer in national tax blacklists. *Governance* 23, 623–39. https://doi.org/10.1111/j.1468-0491.2010.01501.x.

Simmons, B., 2001. The international politics of harmonization: The case of capital market regulation. *International Organization* 55, 589–620.

Slaughter, A.-M., 2004. *A New World Order*. Princeton University Press, Princeton, NJ.

Stigler, G.J., 1971. The theory of economic regulation. *The Bell Journal of Economics and Management Science* 2, 3. https://doi.org/10.2307/3003160.

Stiglitz, J.E., 2010. *The Stiglitz report: Reforming the international monetary and financial systems in the wake of the global crisis*. The New Press, New York.

Teodoro, M.P., Pitcher, M.A., 2017. Contingent technocracy: Bureaucratic independence in developing countries. *Journal of Public Policy* 37, 401–29. https://doi.org/10.1017/S0143814X16000258.

Tett, G., 2017. How we all became addicted to cheap debt. *Financial Times*.

The Warwick Commission, 2009. *In praise of unlevel playing fields*. University of Warwick, Warwick.

Tsingou, E., 2008. Transnational private governance and the Basel process: Banking regulation, private interests and Basel II, in: Nolke, A., Graz, J.-C. (Eds.), *Transnational Private Governance and Its Limits*. Routledge, London, pp. 58–68.

Tsingou, E., 2015. Club governance and the making of global financial rules. *Review of International Political Economy* 22, 225–56. https://doi.org/10.1080/09692290.2014.890952.

Tucker, P.M.W., 2018. *Unelected Power: The Quest for Legitimacy in Central Banking and the Regulatory State*. Princeton University Press, Princeton, NJ.

Underhill, G.R.D., Zhang, X., 2008. Setting the rules: Private power, political underpinning and legitimacy in global monetary and financial governance. *International Affairs* 84, 535–54.

UNECA (Ed.), 2016. *Transformative Industrial Policy for Africa.* UNECA, Addis Ababa.

Walter, A., 2016. Emerging countries and Basel III: Why is engagement still low?, in: Henning, C.R., Walter, A. (Eds.), *Global Financial Governance Confronts the Rising Powers.* CIGI, Waterloo, pp. 179–210.

Whitfield, L., 2009. *The Politics of Aid: African Strategies for Dealing with Donors.* Oxford University Press, Oxford; New York.

Whitfield, L., Therkildsen, O., Buur, L., Kjar, A.M., 2015. *The Politics of African Industrial Policy: A Comparative Perspective.* Cambridge University Press, Cambridge. https://doi.org/10.1017/CBO9781316225509.

World Bank, 2015. *World Bank survey on the proposed revisions to the Basel II standardised approach for credit risk: Analysis of survey responses.* World Bank.

Young, K.L., 2012. Transnational regulatory capture? An empirical examination of the transnational lobbying of the Basel Committee on Banking Supervision. *Review of International Political Economy* 19, 663–88. https://doi.org/10.1080/09692290.2011.624976.

Index

For the benefit of digital users, indexed terms that span two pages (e.g., 52–53) may, on occasion, appear on only one of those pages.